RENAISSANCE THOUGHT

Renaissance Thought: A Reader is a rich collection of key essays on the Renaissance, focusing on humanism, scholarship and philosophy. The Renaissance and humanism have always been difficult to define, and this book provides a greater understanding of their essential features. These fundamental concepts in turn illuminate other essential aspects of Renaissance culture such as philology, political thought and scholastic and Platonic philosophy. *Renaissance Thought: A Reader* explores major themes and leading figures including:

- the Greek revival
- printing
- "civic humanism"
- Petrarch, Poliziano and Ficino
- rhetoric and logic
- magic and the occult sciences
- the spread of humanism in Italy and Germany.

This collection of seminal articles is essential reading for students of the Renaissance. *Renaissance Thought: A Reader* allows readers to join the debate on the Renaissance, a theme which has stimulated intellectual interest since the earliest days of the Renaissance itself.

Robert Black is Reader in Renaissance History at the University of Leeds. His books include *Benedetto Accolti and the Florentine Renaissance* and *Humanism and Education in Medieval and Renaissance Italy*.

Renaissance Thought

Edited by

Robert Black

London and New York

First published 2001
by Routledge
11 New Fetter Lane, London EC4P 4EE

Simultaneously published in the USA and Canada
by Routledge
29 West 35th Street, New York, NY 10001

Routledge is an imprint of the Taylor & Francis Group

© 2001 Robert Black for selection and editorial matter

Typeset in Perpetua by
Florence Production Ltd, Stoodleigh, Devon
Printed and bound in Great Britain by
TJ International, Padstow, Cornwall

British Library Cataloguing in Publication Data
A catalogue record for this book is available from the British Library

Library of Congress Cataloging in Publication Data
Renaissance thought: a reader/edited by Robert Black.
    p. cm.
  Includes bibliographical references and index.
  1. Renaissance – Italy.   2. Italy – Civilization – 1268–1559.
  I. Black, Robert, 1946–
  DG533.R454 2001
  945′.05–dc21   2001019235

ISBN 0–415–20592–1 (hbk)
ISBN 0–415–20593-X (pbk)

Contents

List of illustrations

Preface

Definition is a particularly irksome problem for readers and students wishing to come to terms with the Renaissance and with humanism, its most characteristic feature. The idea of the Renaissance has become heavily overladen with anachronistic connotations for so many years that even many non-specialist scholars and teachers can hardly cope with the layers of inappropriate and misguided accretion and distortion. It is essential, in approaching the Renaissance and humanism, to return to original, contemporary concepts and contexts, but this fundamental task has not always been well served by textbooks and general surveys. In attempting to cover a broad range of topics from social and political history to art and architecture, such literature has at times failed to focus on key definitions and concepts, without which it is impossible to progress in the study of the intellectual and cultural context of learning and thought in Italy and the rest of Europe from the fourteenth to the sixteenth century. My experience as a university teacher and an active researcher in the field of the Italian Renaissance has led me to the view that there are a number of seminal articles which will enable students and non-specialist readers readily to grasp the essential features of what the Renaissance and humanism were, and perhaps even of greater importance, what they were not. Once workable definitions for the Renaissance and humanism have been reached, I have found that other key aspects of Renaissance culture, such as philology, political thought and even scholastic and Platonic philosophy, are more easily and naturally understood.

The series of key studies collected here are those from which my students have particularly profited in coming to terms with humanism and the wider Renaissance. They have helped me to develop my own approach to the Renaissance, and I offer them as a source of understanding and stimulation to others. I do not pretend that they are comprehensive or definitive; instead, I hope that by coming to terms with these fundamental studies, students and other readers will be able to join in the unending debate on the Renaissance, a theme which has never ceased to stimulate intellectual interest since the earliest days of the Renaissance itself.

I regret that it has been impossible to publish the articles comprising this anthology in full, with their complete scholarly apparatus of footnotes and appendices. Unabridged publication would have doubled the length of the volume and therefore reduced drastically the number of studies included; it has seemed best to me to present the essence of these important articles, whose original and full versions can be found in most university libraries.

I am extremely grateful to Christopher Celenza, Martin Davies, Ernst Gombrich, John Najemy, Paolo Rossi and Louis Waldman for their suggestions about this anthology. As always, I have greatly profited from discussions with my wife, Jane Black. My warm thanks go to the authors and other copyright holders for their permission to republish the studies which make up this collection.

I should like to dedicate this book to the memory of the greatest Renaissance scholar of the twentieth century, Paul Oskar Kristeller, who was, for me personally as well as for Renaissance scholarship in general, a profound source of enlightenment and encouragement.

Translations of Latin, Italian, Greek and Old French passages included in the articles are my own; they are published here as notes to be found at the end of the relevant chapters.

Further information on proper names mentioned in this book can be found in the index, compiled by the editor.

Robert Black
School of History, University of Leeds

Acknowledgements

The editor and publishers wish to thank the following for their permission to reproduce copyright material:

E. H. Gombrich for permission to reproduce "The Renaissance – period or movement?"; H. Gray, "Renaissance Humanism: The Pursuit of Eloquence", *Journal of the History of Ideas*, 24 (1963), pp. 497–514, © 1963 Journal of the History of Ideas, Inc, reprinted by permission of The Johns Hopkins University Press; Robert Black, "Humanism", pp. 243–77 from C. Allmand (ed.), *The New Cambridge Medieval History*, Vol. VII, c.1415–c.1500, 1998, reprinted by permission of Cambridge University Press; Ian Thomson, "Manuel Chrysoloras and the early Italian Renaissance", *Greek, Roman and Byzantine Studies*, 7 (1966), reprinted by permission of Duke University Press; Anthony Grafton for permission to reproduce "On the scholarship of Politian and its context" from the *Journal of the Warburg and Courtauld Institutes*, 40 (1977); Dennis E. Rhodes for permission to reproduce Victor Scholderer, "Printers and readers in Italy in the fifteenth century" from *Fifty Essays in Fifteenth- and Sixteenth-Century Bibliography*, edited by D. E. Rhodes (Amsterdam, 1966); The American Philosophical Society for permission to reproduce from C. T. Davis, "Ptolemy of Lucca and the Roman Republic" from the *Proceedings of the American Philosophical Society*, 118 (1974); La Società Editrice Dante Alighieri for permission to reproduce from R. Witt, "The *De Tyranno* and Coluccio Salutati's view of politics and Roman history", *Nuova rivista storica*, 53 (1969); *Renaissance Quarterly* for permission to reproduce from David Quint, "Humanism and modernity: a reconsideration of Bruni's *Dialogues*", *Renaissance Quarterly*, 38 (1985); Edizioni di Storia e Letteratura for permission to reproduce N. Rubinstein, "Florentine constitutionalism and the Medici ascendancy in the fifteenth century" from *Florentine Studies: Politics and Society in Renaissance Florence*, edited by Nicolai Rubinstein (1968), and shortly to be reproduced in three volumes of N. Rubinstein's writings, *Studies in Italian History of the Middle Ages and the Renaissance: vol. I, Political thought and the language of politics. Art and politics; vol. II, Politics, diplomacy, and the constitution in Florence and Italy; vol. III, Humanists, Machiavelli, and Guicciardini. Miscellanea* (2000–3); Alison Brown for permission to reproduce "The humanist portrait of Cosimo de' Medici, pater patriae" from the *Journal of the*

Warburg and Courtauld Institutes, 24 (1961) and from Alison Brown, *The Medici in Florence. The Language and Exercise of Power*, Florence, 1992, pp. 3–52; The American Society of Church History for permission to reproduce P. O. Kristeller's essay, "Florentine Platonism and its relations with humanism and scholasticism" from *Church History*, 8 (1989); Associated University Presses for permission to reproduce from B. P. Copenhaver, "Hermes Trismegistus, Proclus and the question of a philosophy of magic in the Renaissance", in *Hermeticism and the Renaissance: Intellectual History and the Occult in Early Modern Europe*, edited by Ingrid Merkel and Allen Debus (1988); Science History Publications for permission to reproduce from C. B. Schmitt, "Towards a reassessment of Renaissance Aristotelianism", *History of Science*, 11 (1973); the *Journal of the History of Philosophy* for permission to reproduce J. Monfasani, "Lorenzo Valla and Rudolph Agricola", *Journal of the History of Philosophy*, 28 (1990); Editions Rodopi BV (Netherlands) for permission to reproduce pp. 277–306 from C. G. Nauert Jr., "The humanist challenge to medieval German culture", *Daphnis: Zeitschrift für mittlere deutsche Literatur*, 15 (1986); The Medieval Academy of America for permission to reproduce excerpts from C. C. Bayley, "Petrarch, Charles IV, and the 'Renovatio imperii'", *Speculum*, 17 (1942), pp. 323–41.

Every effort has been made to contact copyright holders. Any omissions or errors will be rectified in any subsequent printings if notice is given to the Publishers.

Introduction

■ Robert Black

I N 1860 THE SWISS SCHOLAR Jacob Burckhardt published what has since become the most influential work ever written on the Renaissance: *The Civilization of the Renaissance in Italy: An Essay*.[1] Burckhardt did not invent the Renaissance, but he welded many previous interpretations into a coherent and powerful synthesis; indeed, the simplicity of his vision goes far to explaining the potent effect exerted by his book.

Burckhardt's fundamental assumption in *The Civilization* was that the Renaissance constituted a new and distinct age or period in the history of culture. His aim was to portray this age not in terms of detailed narrative but rather topically. He set himself apart from political historians whose concern was to establish facts and the sequence of events; the job of the historian of civilization was, for Burckhardt, to portray the mentality of the people in a given period, or, in other words, to delineate the spirit of the age. Burckhardt assumed that there was a distinctive character or spirit common to a whole nation in a particular epoch. Burckhardt's aim was to discover the common features of the Renaissance, what was typical of its culture. *The Civilization* was intended as an investigation of the inner character of Italy during the Renaissance.

The spirit of the age in Renaissance Italy was easy for Burckhardt to identify. Its distinguishing stamp was individualism, a quality which he proceeded to relate to the various aspects of Italian culture from the thirteenth to the sixteenth century. The peculiar political conditions of Italy, lacking as it did an overall legal and political structure, created a new type of individuality, first noticeable among the illegitimate despots of North and Central Italy and then permeating throughout society at large; these new individuals were wholly dependent on themselves and entirely egotistical, completely without the inhibitions imposed by traditional moral and religious standards. According to Burckhardt, man as an individual – modern, secular man – emerged first in Renaissance Italy; during the middle ages, in contrast, man had received his identity not through his own individuality but by

association with some corporate body. Because individualism was the hallmark of
the Renaissance, it followed that the revival of classical antiquity was not an essential element of its development. Nevertheless, Buckhardt conceded that the
influence of the ancients was a fundamental support to Renaissance civilization.
Burckhardt devoted the rest of his book to an analysis of how this new individualism determined the cultural, social and moral life of the epoch. In the chapter
with a title borrowed from Jules Michelet's famous motto, "The discovery of
the world and of man," Burckhardt developed his view of the objective and subjective emergence of the individual: man not only became aware of the outside world through geographical exploration, aesthetic discovery of natural beauty
and scientific progress, but also found his own inner self and personality, as
expressed particularly in literary forms such as poetry and biography. In the chapter
on "Society and festivals," Burckhardt argued that individualism was at a prem-
ium in a society based on wealth and culture rather than birth. In his treatment
of "Morality and religion" Burckhardt turned to what he saw as the "grave moral
crisis" of Renaissance society. In an age of unbridled egotism, free rein was given
to profligacy. Individualism made Renaissance Italians in all respects the first
modern men.

Burckhardt's attempt to portray the Renaissance in Italy as a homogenous
historical period has been powerfully compelling[2] but it is inherently flawed; it is
impossible to demonstrate that political, social and cultural history moved in
marvellous coordination from the thirteenth to the sixteenth century in Italy (see
Chapter 1 below). The force of logic compelled Burckhardt to suggest the "equality
of classes":

> Social intercourse in its highest and most perfect form now ignored all
> distinctions of caste, and was based simply on the existence of an
> educated class . . . the main current of the time went steadily towards
> the fusion of classes.[3]

Radical individualism had to mean that people in the Renaissance were valued not
as members of privileged social groups but simply for their own talents, and so
he was even led to suggest "that women stood on a footing of perfect equality
with men."[4] Few sociologists would argue that, even in an era of mass democracy
such as the second half of the twentieth century, social class had disappeared, and
the perfect equality of men and women is still a distant aspiration. Burckhardt's
unfounded claims about women are even contradicted by his own book, where a
glance at the index will reveal just a handful of women mentioned and hardly any
(apart from the poetess Vittoria Colonna) more than once, in contrast to hundreds
of "dead white European males."

Burckhardt's thesis encouraged him not only to see an untenable chronological and geographical uniformity in Renaissance Italy, but also to distort the middle
ages. Of course, there were egregious instances of Renaissance immorality, but it
would be hard to find examples in the Renaissance to exceed the ruthlessness and
egotism, for instance, of some of the Latin princes during the First Crusade or of
French kings such as Philip Augustus or Philip the Fair. Individualism too was
hardly lacking in famous medieval characters such as Peter Damian, Gregory VII,

Abelard, Abbot Suger of St Denis, Innocent III or St Francis, some of whom even left autobiographies.[5]

It is futile to try to see, in the Burckhardtian manner, the Renaissance as a chronological block informed by a unifying ethos such as individualism. Social, political and cultural developments were far too diffuse and complex to admit of such simplistic harmonization as suggested by Burckhardt. The Renaissance cannot be reduced to a hallmarked period of history (see Chapter 1 below). Even the view, current among some historians today, that the Renaissance somehow represented a new spirit of secularism, is untenable. It would be hard, for example, to find a more secularized group of literary intellectuals than the practitioners (known as *dictatores*) of medieval rhetoric (the so-called *ars dictaminis*) who flourished in Italy during the twelfth and especially the thirteenth century: not only were they nearly all laymen, but their writings are almost entirely secular in subject matter, lacking virtually any reference to religious authorities. This could not be said of their successors, the Renaissance humanists, many of whom were clerics; moreover, a significant proportion of the latter's writings were on religious themes and cited Christian texts. Another obvious point is that, for example, the city of Florence – the hub of the Renaissance – witnessed a burst of church and chapel building and decoration during the fifteenth century, besides a large-scale growth in religious confraternities among the laity, not to mention a major burst of Christian fundamentalism from Savonarola and his followers at the end of the 1400s. Indeed, Giovanni Rucellai, writing in mid-fifteenth-century Florence, declared that "men and women attend mass and divine offices with more devotion than had been customary in the past."[6]

If the Italian Renaissance was not a period of history in the Burckhardtian sense, then perhaps (as Gombrich suggests in Chapter 1 below), it was a movement.

> Movements, as distinct from periods, are started by people. Some of them are abortive, others catch on. Each movement in its turn has a core of dedicated souls, a crowd of hangers-on, not to forget a lunatic fringe. There is a whole spectrum of attitudes and degrees of conversion. Even within the individual there may be various levels of conviction, various conscious and unconscious fluctuations in loyalty. What seemed acceptable during the mass rally or revivalist meeting may look pretty crazy on the way home. But movements would not be movements if they did not have their badges, their outward signs, their style of behaviour, style of speech and of dress . . . The Renaissance, for instance, certainly had all the characteristics of a movement. It gradually captured the most articulate sections of society and influenced their attitude in various but uneven ways.[7]

There is much to recommend this view of the Renaissance. *The Shorter Oxford English Dictionary* defines a movement as "a series of actions and endeavours by a body of persons, tending more or less continuously towards some special end." It could be argued that the "special end" of the Renaissance was the revival of classical learning which was thought to have been eclipsed during the barbarous middle ages. Movements work "continuously" towards their ends; in other words one follower converts his contemporaries and so on. Again, it could be suggested that Petrarch, the first great Renaissance man, communicated to contemporaries such as Boccaccio his enthusiasm for the classical revival and together they handed on the torch to the next generation in the person of Coluccio Salutati, who in turn inspired younger men such as Niccolò Niccoli, Leonardo Bruni and Poggio Bracciolini. Most important, movements are the work of a "body of persons," and the protagonists of the Renaissance soon acquired a special name: humanists, who were, in their own terms, not lovers of humanity or devotees of man rather than God but rather simply teachers or students of the humanities (known from the fourteenth century as the *studia humanitatis*) or, in modern parlance, the classics.

There is little question that Renaissance humanism was a movement: Gombrich's insight into the character of humanism (see Chapter 1 below) is borne out by many texts in which leading figures such as Bruni and Poggio speak of the *studia humanitatis* as their particular specialism, so confirming Renaissance humanism as a self-conscious movement, with a genuine *esprit de corps*[8] (see Chapter 3 below). It is sometimes said that the Renaissance is the work of the humanists, and yet the equation of the Renaissance with humanism cannot be quite the whole story. If the Renaissance were only or overwhelmingly the work of humanists attempting to substitute the civilization of antiquity for the culture of the barbarous middle ages, then it must be wondered why various Renaissance achievements were so deeply indebted to sources other than classical antiquity.

The diverse roots of the Renaissance are clear, for example, in the case of fifteenth-century Italy's two greatest philosophers, Marsilio Ficino and Giovanni Pico della Mirandola. Both Ficino and Pico were trained as humanists, with an up-to-date knowledge not only of classical Latin but also of Greek; Ficino undertook the first complete Latin translations of Plato, while Pico added a knowledge of ancient Hebrew to his linguistic armoury. Both laid the foundations for the most innovatory contribution of Renaissance philosophy: the revival of Platonism. But their passion for Plato did not have its sole origins in the humanist enthusiasm for all things ancient. Ficino came from a thoroughly traditional non-humanist back-ground: he emerged from a scholastic medical family, and, through his teachers and his own early study, he was deeply influenced by the medieval Aristotelian tradition (see Chapter 14 below); moreover, his Platonism did not build simply on a fresh reading of the genuine texts of Plato but was based more directly on the medieval Byzantine Platonic tradition, which itself had diverged significantly from pure early ancient Platonism. Pico was even more indebted to traditions ranging beyond ancient Greece and Rome. He attempted a synthesis of already hybrid Ficinian Platonism with medieval Arabic and Latin scholasticism (see Chapter 14 below) as well as with the medieval mystical tradition of Jewish scholarship (the so-called Cabbala). In his later works, he rejected humanist in favour of scholastic Latin (see Chapter 14 below), considered by him to be more suitable for technical philosophical discourse; moreover, he even affiliated himself shortly before his death with the arch-enemy of avant-garde humanism, the Dominican fundamentalist preacher Savonarola.

Another example of the diverse roots of Renaissance culture comes from the history of Renaissance political thought. It was once argued by Hans Baron that the Renaissance represented a pure revival of classical republicanism. In Baron's view, the middle ages had favoured monarchical government, whose most famous champion was, of course, Dante in his treatise *De monarchia*. Early Renaissance figures such as Petrarch and Salutati, who had dabbled with the classical republicanism advocated by Roman authors such as Cicero, had in the end, according to Baron, reverted to medieval monarchism at the close of their lives. It was only in the fifteenth century, with the complete burgeoning of Renaissance humanism and the full-scale revival of Cicero accomplished by mature humanists such as Leonardo Bruni, that, so Baron argued, genuine classical republicanism was definitively relaunched.[9] However, few scholars today would agree with Baron's stark analysis.[10] It is now clear that republicanism had itself enjoyed a significant tradition in the middle ages. Bruni was not the first to sustain unequivocally that republics were superior to monarchies. The medieval Italian communes produced a series of pro-republican and anti-monarchical apologists, from Brunetto Latini to Ptolemy of Lucca and Marsilius of Padua (see Chapter 8 below). In fact, medieval scholastic thought, on both sides of the Alps, could be richly republican, anti-monarchical and favourable to active political participation, with notable figures in this context including non-Italians such as Nicole Oresme, John of Paris, Engelbert of Admont and William of Ockham.[11] There can be no doubt that the republicanism of Leonardo Bruni and his successors was built on a long and powerful medieval republican tradition.

Gombrich, of course, recognizes the medieval roots of pre-eminent Renaissance figures such as Brunelleschi and Michelozzo:

> What strikes us, in the vocabulary of quattrocento architecture, is less its classical character than its link with the medieval past.[12]

Indeed, much Italian architecture in the fifteenth century is now acknowledged to owe more to Romanesque prototypes than to the direct influence of antique models.[13] Nevertheless, it is one thing to acknowledge that the Renaissance was not identical with Renaissance humanism, and to recognize that the sources of the Renaissance extended beyond classical Greek and Roman antiquity; it is another to deny the entire existence of the Renaissance as a meaningful historical phenomenon. The fact is that contemporaries, beginning in the early fourteenth century, constantly referred to a rebirth of culture. To cite just a few examples, an early fourteenth-century commentator, Fra Guido of Pisa, declared that through Dante, "dead poetry was resuscitated . . . he revived poetic knowledge and made the ancient poets live again in our minds."[14] Writing a little later in 1338, Petrarch declared, "better ages are in store. The sleep of forgetfulness will not continue in all the years to come. Once the darkness has been broken, our descendants will perhaps be able to return to the pure, pristine radiance."[15] In a letter from about 1370, Boccaccio said,

> In our age . . . more illustrious men have come from heaven, generous spirits who wish to raise up again with all their strength the oppressed art of poetry, and to recall it from exile into its former abode; and not in vain.[16]

In his life of Petrarch, written in 1435, Leonardo Bruni declared that "Francesco Petrarca was the first who had such grace of talent, and who recognized and restored to light the ancient elegance of style which was lost and dead."[17] In his renowned study of the Latin language,[18] Lorenzo Valla wrote in the mid-fifteenth century that

> those arts which are most closely related to the liberal arts, the arts of painting, sculpture, modelling, and architecture, had degenerated for so long and so greatly and had almost died with letters themselves, and that in this age they have been aroused and come to life again, so greatly increased is the number of good artists and men of letters who now flourish.[19]

Giovanni Rucellai, writing in the 1450s, declared that in the fifteenth century

> there have been more men learned in Greek, Latin and Hebrew than in past times; Latin style has been more ennobled, purified and ornamented than at any time since Cicero's day; these learned men have brought back to light ancient stylistic elegance previously lost and extinguished.[20]

And at the end of the fifteenth century, Marsilio Ficino observed,

> A golden age is doubtless a period which is distinguished by golden talents, and this is certainly true of our own age, in which learning has been brought back from darkness to light. This age has equalled what had been achieved by the ancients but almost forgotten since their day.[21]

These contemporary commentators obviously erred if they intended to suggest that this revival of the arts to which they constantly referred represented a pure revival of antiquity; we now know that the Renaissance's sources were wide-ranging chronologically and geographically, extending not only to Greek and Roman pagan antiquity, but to early Christianity, to medieval culture and scholasticism, to Arabic, Jewish and Byzantine learning. But to realize that the Renaissance was not an unadulterated revival of antiquity is not tantamount to saying that there was no Renaissance. Indeed, a number of interpretative problems recede if the focus shifts from looking at the Renaissance as a revival of antiquity to investigating it as a reinvigoration of the arts, or disciplines of learning, drawing on a variety of chronological and geographical sources. This is the approach adopted by the pre-eminent scholar of Renaissance learning in the twentieth century, Paul Oskar Kristeller. He extended his investigation of the Renaissance beyond humanism to concentrate on the study of the various traditions and disciplines which made up Renaissance culture. Here he highlighted the diverse roots of humanism, showing that it was an amalgam of ancient and medieval grammatical and rhetorical learning, as well as of the Byzantine tradition, once Greek was added to Latin as a principal scholarly concern. He also established that, in the history of Renaissance philosophy, humanism was only a peripheral element; more important here were the Platonic and

Aristotelian traditions, both of which had independent sources and directions not fundamentally connected with humanism (see Chapters 2 and 14 below). Kristeller's Renaissance was a hybrid phenomenon, with ancient as well as medieval, Arabic and Byzantine as well as Greek and Roman, Christian as well as pagan, roots.

It is this wider-ranging perspective on Renaisssance culture, its sources and its development, that forms the approach taken in this present collection of articles. The scope of the Renaissance has been limited here to the disciplines of learning, or arts, which were explicitly thought by contemporaries in the fourteenth, fifteenth and sixteenth centuries to have been undergoing a process of reinvigoration; among these particular attention has been concentrated on the areas of classical learning, political thought and philosophy. Little attempt has been made to link this revival, in the Burckhardtian manner, to social history: although this renewal of the arts may have been encouraged in certain specific ways and at particular times by changing social attitudes (see, for example, Chapters 4, 7 and 18 below), nevertheless the overall evolution of Renaissance society is a complex story of its own, distinct from the subject of this collection, the history of thought and learning. Many recent preoccupations with diverse aspects of social life in Italy from the fourteenth to the sixteenth century (marriage, birth, child-rearing, social and religious rituals, sexuality and so on) may be interesting in themselves and may be legitimate topics for historical research but they have no intrinsic connection with the Renaissance.

Part One focuses on the definition of the Renaissance and of humanism. Chapter 1 presents Gombrich's summary of his thesis that the Renaissance was a historical movement, not a period. Gombrich illustrates how the idea of the Renaissance itself was developed by contemporaries such as Petrarch and Bruni to substantiate their claim to have revived the culture of antiquity, in contrast to preceding times, which they called the dark or middle ages, when, in their view, this ancient heritage had been neglected. Beginning in the eighteenth century, philosophers and historians connected this threefold scheme of history (antiquity–middle ages–Renaissance) with the notion of progress, suggesting that the Renaissance formed a phase of the general progress of man towards modernity, variously identified with qualities such as humanity, liberty or individualism. Rejecting these progressive schemes of historical development and the very idea of "Ages" in the sense of "a uniform spirit or mentality shared by everyone in a society," Gombrich suggests that, instead of a period in history, the Renaissance should be seen as a movement whose followers achieved a sense of superiority through their greater knowledge of antiquity and in particular through their better Latin style; in the fine arts, this feeling of one-upmanship was often identified with Renaissance artists' mastery of the science of perspective and the drawing of the nude.

Chapter 2 is Kristeller's article "Humanism and scholasticism in the Italian Renaissance." Like Gombrich, Kristeller refers to a movement, but he limits this term to humanism, rather than associating it with the Renaissance as a whole. Moreover, he emphasizes the medieval background to the Italian Renaissance: without rejecting the Renaissance as a revival of antiquity, he also points out that Renaissance humanism represented a development of important medieval traditions, especially medieval rhetoric (known as the *ars dictaminis*) and medieval grammatical studies focusing on classical authors. He rejects the theory that Renaissance humanism constituted a new philosophy, replacing Aristotelian scholasticism, the philosophy characteristic of the middle ages: not only were the Renaissance humanists "no philosophers at all," but scholasticism continued to flourish in Italy into the sixteenth century and beyond. Renaissance humanism was a movement whose core subjects consisted of the so-called *studia humanitatis*, normally identified with the disciplines of grammar, rhetoric, poetry, history and moral philosophy; the humanists were the successors of the medieval Italian *dictatores*, but were distinguished from these predecessors by a new interest in the direct study of ancient sources, as well as by a first-hand knowledge of Greek language and texts, almost unprecedented in the Western middle ages.

Chapter 3 presents Hanna Gray's study entitled "Renaissance humanism: the pursuit of eloquence." Gray accepts Kristeller's stress on the rhetorical aspects of Renaissance humanism, but questions whether there is too much emphasis in his approach on continuity with medieval rhetoric. She points out that, although there may be objective continuity in terms of the same professions and literary genres, the transition to Renaissance humanism was marked by a different subjective attitude to eloquence and rhetoric. For Renaissance humanists, eloquence was the path to moral and civic improvement; the humanists' criticism of the scholastics did not simply represent a departmental rivalry within or among various educational institutions such as schools or universities, but actually put forward a different set of goals for rhetoric than had existed in the middle ages. Gray implies that rhetoric and humanism, in the Renaissance, represented an abandonment of the narrow technical and professional context of medieval rhetoric; eloquence in the Renaissance constituted a broad teacher of life, and thereby the humanists were able fully to revive the wide culture of the rhetoric, originally embodied in the oratorical works of Cicero and Quintilian.

The fourth article is my own treatment of "Humanism." Rejecting Burckhardt's anthropological interpretation of humanism as extreme individualism, I follow Kristeller's view that humanism must be defined in contemporary fourteenth- and fifteenth-century terms as the *studia humanitatis*; on the basis of evidence that many humanists rejected the notion of the dignity of man, I suggest that it is impossible to associate human or secular qualities with humanism in general. Like Kristeller, I also argue that the roots of humanism are often to be found in medieval traditions, and that in their core disciplines of grammar (embracing elementary and secondary education as well as poetry), rhetoric, moral or political philosophy and history, the achievements of humanists did not represent an entirely radical break with the past. In many fields, such as Greek studies and classical philology, humanists did make enormous and profound innovations, but, during the fifteenth century, these achievements were limited to relatively few original geniuses such as Valla and Poliziano; humanism as a widespread phenomenon offered comparatively few such radical innovators. The question then arises of why humanism received such a powerful backing in Italian and then in European society. I suggest that this "question is never asked much less answered by Kristeller" because of his focus on humanism's roots; the issue of humanists' novel appeal does not arise if the emphasis is on continuity with the past. Here, Gray's stress on subjective factors is important, but I suggest that these cannot hold out the whole reason for humanism's undoubted long-term and Europe-wide success; there must have been objective benefits offered by humanism. I conclude by arguing that much of humanism's appeal was due to the emergence of humanist education as a distinguishing badge for the leaders of Italian and European society, a means of differentiating, through education, society's leaders from its followers; the objective advantage of humanism was access to the ruling élite, with all its consequent economic, social and political rewards.

Part Two of this collection offers three contributions to the history of learning during the Renaissance. The importance of the Greek revival is exemplified by Ian Thomson's study, "Manuel Chrysoloras and the early Italian Renaissance." Direct knowledge of Greek language and writings was rare in the Western middle ages; as a result, most of Greek philosophy (apart from Aristotle), science (apart from Galen and Euclid) and literature was unknown to the medieval Latin West. Early humanists such as Petrarch and Boccaccio wanted to learn Greek, but had little or no success; the Renaissance Greek revival was launched by the great teacher from Constantinople, Manuel Chrysoloras, who first arrived in Italy to lecture during 1397. Thomson points to the essential role in the rebirth of Greek studies exercised by Chrysoloras, whom he shows to have been a charismatic teacher and to have had a profound influence on the first generation of Italian humanist Greek scholars, including Bruni, Roberto Rossi, Pier Paolo Vergerio the elder, Jacopo di Agnolo da Scarperia and Guarino Veronese; moreover, Thomson suggests the powerful effect that Chrysoloras must have had in the genesis of humanist educational ideology.

The innovative philological methods developed by Italian humanists are illustrated in Anthony Grafton's article, "On the scholarship of Politian and its context." According to Grafton, Poliziano was responsible for a "revolution in philological method": breaking away from the methods of his immediate humanist predecessors and contemporaries such as Domizio Calderini, Poliziano not only explicitly favoured miscellaneous notes over traditional line-by-line commentaries, but also emphasized "the quality and quantity of his sources," the importance of precise citation, and the identification of intermediate sources; moreover, he "was the first to compare and evaluate sources in a historical way," a method still employed by modern classical scholars. Following Kenney,[22] Grafton illustrates how Poliziano turned textual criticism into an "historical study"; avoiding conjectural emendation, he returned to the oldest manuscripts, believing that "they were the closest extant approximations" to the original ancient texts. Most important, Poliziano began to examine texts genealogically, attempting to discover how they were related to one another and thus for the first time articulating the principles which form the basis of modern stemmatic editing of texts. Indeed, his historical perspective made him appreciate the importance of identifying Greek sources of Latin works; for Poliziano, "only a critic who had mastered Greek literature could hope to deal competently with Latin."

Victor Scholderer's essay, "Printers and readers in Italy in the fifteenth century," deserves to be better known, offering as it does a comprehensive panorama of Italian incunabular printing history in remarkably few pages. Scholderer shows how Italian printing began near and in Rome in the mid-1460s: the early presses were entirely manned by North Europeans, under ecclesiastical or papal patronage – a fact which, in Scholderer's view, accounts for the limited success of Roman printing: there was no significant mercantile class in Rome to exploit the commercial possibilites of the new industry. The same was not true of Venice, which soon became the greatest centre of Italian publishing, followed by Milan, Florence and Bologna; southern Italy produced hardly any presses of significance, substantiating Scholderer's hypothesis of the link between printing and commercial economic development – far weaker in southern than in northern Italy. After an initial burst of humanist and classical activity, Venice became the great centre for the printing of legal texts, while Florence specialized in Greek editions, vernacular literature and short devotional tracts; particularly notable was the outburst of Savonarolan literature there in the 1490s: "This is, in fact, the first occasion in the history of printing when the art was pressed into the service of a propaganda campaign appealing to the public at large." Testimony to the diffusion of humanism throughout Italy at the end of the century is the publication there of more than 900 editions of the Latin classics, with Cicero and Vergil leading the field. Religious literature did not constitute as high a percentage of output as in France or Germany, but it did run second to humanist production; particularly significant were Italian editions of the Vulgate Bible. Reflecting the important status of traditional university study in Italy is the fact that, like law, the other great subject of Italian higher education – medicine – was dominated by Italian printing. Particularly significant is the importance of vernacular literature among the Italian presses: in contrast to Northern Europe, where printing in the vernacular was (apart from England) relatively rare, numerous editions of the great vernacular classics by Dante, Petrarch and Boccaccio as well as of lesser works by Pulci, Boiardo and Andrea da Barberino, not to mention a large diffusion of devotional vernacular poetry, suggest that the northern half of Italy by the later fifteenth century had emerged as the first mass literate society of Europe.[23]

The third section of this collection is devoted to Renaissance political thought. Here the figure of Hans Baron emerges as a significant stimulus to historical debate. Few scholars now accept his view that the Florentine wars against the Duke of Milan, Giangaleazzo Visconti, represented a decisive turning point in the history of political consciousness.[24] "Civic humanism" is a label invented by Baron in 1925 to describe what he believed to have been a decisive moment of change in Western thought: from the contemplative, monarchical emphasis of the middle ages to the active, republican ideals of the Renaissance and beyond. However, it is now commonly accepted that Bruni, like Salutati[25] before him, was an apologist for the oligarchic regime in Florence instituted after 1382; Bruni and many of his compatriots were not the idealistic and patriotic republicans portrayed by Baron.[26] Eliminating Baron's claim to have found the moment of transition from medieval to modern thought reduces "civic humanism" to a more or less fleeting ideology, fashioned from pre-existing traditions of political ideas. It is misleading to call these apologetics "civic humanism": it is well known from Kristeller's work that humanism did not constitute a philosophy, and so any civic variety of humanism could not involve a new direction for humanist thought (see Chapter 2 below). It is a misunderstanding of the nature of humanism to see it as an evolving series of philosophical outlooks: humanism was not a developing philosophy but rather a rhetorical/philological approach and method. The quantity of pro-monarchical works (for example "mirror of princes" tracts) far outweighs genuinely pro-republican productions during the Renaissance, a fact hardly surprising in a period which saw the withering and virtual demise of the Italian communal tradition. "Civic humanism" is a misnomer: most Renaissance political thought was not civic, and much medieval and Renaissance civic thought was not humanist.

Charles Davis's study, "Ptolemy of Lucca and the Roman Republic," refutes Baron's view that Petrarch and his humanist successors were the first to rediscover the merits of the Roman republic. Many medieval writers (for example John of Salisbury) extolled the virtues of republican Roman heroes, and the negative portrait of pre-imperial Rome given by Augustine and Orosius was forcefully contradicted in the political thought of the earlier Italian communes. Petrarch ultimately gave a negative judgement on Cicero as an active statesman, but Brunetto Latini, writing a century before and drawing on a still earlier French compendium, the *Fet des Romains* (soon translated into Italian), presented Cicero as one of the greatest Roman patriots, "a virtuous rhetorician who was the teacher and civilizer of his fellow citizens." The "significant wave of enthusiasm for the Roman republic in late thirteenth- and early fourteenth-century Tuscany" extended to Remigio de' Girolami, Dante and Ptolemy of Lucca, the last of whom actually produced a reasoned defence of a republic "as, under optimal conditions, the best form of government . . . In terms both of historical and political theory, we can say that Ptolemy was the first self-conscious medieval republican."

Baron not only tended to overlook the medieval republican tradition but also sometimes misunderstood the humanist attitude to Rome. For Baron, monarchism was characteristic of the middle ages, whereas the republicanism of pre-imperial Rome was revived only gradually by the Renaissance humanists. In his youth, according to Baron, Petrarch had preferred the Roman Republic to the Empire, but in old age he reverted to a more typically medieval imperialism.[27] This scheme, however, involved an egregious misreading of Petrarch's early epic poem, *Africa*, which Baron interpreted as a pro-republican, anti-imperial manifesto: "The *Imperium* that Caesar founded emerges in the *Africa* almost exclusively in its darker aspects."[28] The problem is that Baron passed over in silence a long passage of unqualified praise in *Africa* for Augustus, the founder of the Roman Empire. In fact, Petrarch's attitude in *Africa* was neither pro-republican nor pro-imperial but rather pro-Roman. For Petrarch, what counted was Rome's greatness: Scipio made Rome glorious with his conquest of Carthage, just as Caesar did with his victories over the Gauls and the Germans. Caesar was criticized by Petrarch only when he turned his sword on Rome itself during the civil wars, but Rome for Petrarch was restored to greatness once again by Caesar's nephew, Augustus, who brought foreign triumphs and domestic peace to the city. For Baron, Petrarch's political thought showed a chronological regression from republicanism to monarchism, but, in his article "Petrarch, Charles IV, and the 'Renovatio Imperii'," C. C. Bayley shows that Petrarch's political attitudes remained notably consistent throughout his life. Bayley argues that what mattered to Petrarch was Roman renewal itself; the means were less important than this all-important end. For Petrarch the renewal of Rome might be set in motion by an efficient tyrant like Robert II of Naples; or by an unexpected revival of the antique *virtù* of the Roman people, inspired by the tribune Cola di Rienzo; or by an emperor-messiah such as Charles IV, transformed into a Roman by the ceremony of coronation; or even by a union of the *grandi*, combining to thrust the barbarian from Italian soil.

Indeed, Petrarch's sympathies in *Africa* with great Roman heroes – whether republican or imperial – were consistent with the various political affinities that he developed over the years. Petrarch was less concerned with constitutional forms than with his ultimate goal of achieving a genuine Roman revival.

Ronald Witt's article, "The *De Tyranno* and Coluccio Salutati's view of politics and Roman history," illustrates the problems involved in trying to extract a coherent political philosophy from humanist texts. Baron's view was that the patriotic republicanism of Salutati's maturity was replaced by conservatism, medievalism and political quietism in the last ten years of his life.[29] In his study, however, Witt concludes that there was no real development in Salutati's political thought: "his political ideas seem to have had no real history." In substantiation of this thesis, Witt describes the various assessments of Julius Caesar made during the thirteenth and fourteenth centuries, besides portraying Salutati's own vacillating attitude to Caesar throughout his life. While Caesar had numerous champions in the middle ages, he also had many critics and detractors, and so Salutati's defence of Caesar in *De Tyranno* was hardly more medieval than his previous criticisms had been. Moreover, Witt shows that Salutati's vindication of Caesar there did not represent a new attitude in contrast to his former unchanging hostility to Caesar, as Baron would have it. The only apparently consistent view of Caesar maintained by Salutati was confined to the years 1398–1401; earlier and afterwards there seems to have been no pattern in Salutati's attitude. The view of Caesar is one of the cornerstones of Baron's scheme for the regression of Salutati's thought from humanist to medieval in the last years of his life; Witt's comprehensive analysis must undermine the theory that Salutati underwent a fundamental change of political outlook in old age.

Baron's approach tends to minimize the importance of rhetoric in analysing humanist texts. The political ideas of a humanist such as Salutati can never be fully understood or reconciled as a coherent political philosophy, like that of Aristotle, Aquinas, Dante or Marsilius; humanists may have been political thinkers but they were not political philosophers. They did not construct comprehensive political theories through Aristotelian dialectic and terminology but rather put forward political ideas on the basis of rhetorical methods. As rhetoricians they constructed and developed arguments; what mattered was not consistency but flexibility. As a humanist rhetorician Salutati did not feel it necessary to resolve the contradictions inherent in his thought; rhetoric allowed him to appreciate the arguments in favour of both monarchy and republic. Rhetoric enabled humanists to see the complexity of issues raised in political thought but did not compel them to come up with simple-minded, black-and-white solutions. Eventually the humanists found in the Ciceronian dialogue a medium ideally suited to discussing complex issues.

In his article, "Humanism and modernity: a reconsideration of Bruni's *Dialogues*," David Quint illustrates the subtlety of this first Ciceronian dialogue of the Renaissance. Rejecting Baron's interpretation of Bruni's seminal *Dialogues for Pier Paolo Vergerio*, Quint emphasizes the rhetorical and literary dimensions of this key work. Bruni's *Dialogues* are modelled on Cicero's *De oratore*, a work which turned on a recantation by the principal speaker; in Bruni's case, the attack on the Florentine heritage of Dante, Petrarch and Boccaccio in favour of radical classicism is apparently reversed. In Baron's view, this represented two different stages in the work's evolution: an earlier phase, in which Bruni was still a radical humanist intolerant of the patriotic Florentine cultural inheritance represented by these three literary crowns; and a later phase, where Bruni, stirred by Florence's miraculous survival from the onslaught of Giangaleazzo Visconti's armies in 1402, was suddenly roused to appreciate the achievement of this trio of indigenous literary giants. Quint, however, shows that the principal speaker, Niccoli, does not genuinely recant his earlier attacks on Dante, Petrarch and Boccaccio, emphasizing the irony omnipresent in the second dialogue. Indeed, "scholars now generally consider the two dialogues to have been conceived as an integrated work from the beginning."[30]

If Baron failed to appreciate the rhetorical dimensions of much humanist literature, he also often mistook its actual ideological implications. Bruni's political thought was not so much a reflection of patriotic Florentine republican idealism inspired by a struggle against encroaching Milanese tyranny as an expression of the ideological needs of an increasingly oligarchic and manipulative regime, as is suggested in Nicolai Rubinstein's article, "Florentine constitutionalism and Medici ascendancy in the fifteenth century." In his description of the Florentine constitution (1439), Bruni paid court to the oligarchic tendencies of Florentine regimes over the past half century, by pointing out that "the Florentine constitution has an aristocratic or oligarchical rather than a democratic slant." In the same treatise, moreover, he omitted to mention "safeguards against autocratic power" which had been found in Bruni's earlier political writing: "By 1439, Cosimo de' Medici's ascendancy had been established for over four years, and . . . there was clearly a case . . . not to harp too much on the suppression of autocratic tendencies."

In her article, "The humanist portrait of Cosimo de' Medici, pater patriae," Alison Brown too emphasizes the ideological dimensions of humanist political writings. As Medici influence and authority in Florence grew in the course of the fifteenth century, so the image of Cosimo in humanist panegyrics was gradually transformed. In the earliest texts, dating from the first half of the century, he was praised only as a leading republican statesman and patriot; after 1450 he began to be seen as philosopher-ruler; towards the end of the century, in the period of his grandson Lorenzo's predominance, Cosimo emerged in Vergilian imperial garb as Florence's Maecenas and Augustus. These images did not come from the Medici themselves and obviously humanists in search of employment and patronage did not restrain their hyperbolic inclinations; nevertheless, it is clear that the increasingly extravagant praise of Cosimo served the ideological needs of the Medici regime, as its grip on power in Florence became ever stronger towards the end of the fifteenth century.

The fourth part of this anthology is devoted to Renaissance philosophy. The rich and diverse sources of the Renaissance philosophical revival are indicated in Kristeller's essay, "Florentine Platonism and its relations with humanism and scholasticism." For Kristeller, the early humanism of Petrarch and Bruni was a literary movement; repelled by the barbarous Latin of the medieval scholastics, they focused on philology, morals, political thought and education, without developing "metaphysical ideas or speculative systems." It was in the second half of the fifteenth century that a genuine Renaissance contribution to philosophy emerged with the Florentine Academy of Ficino and Pico. On the one hand, they were undeniably humanists: their Latin style, translations, commentaries and literary interests linked Ficino and Pico to the mainstream of Italian humanism; Ficino explicitly saw his recovery of Plato as part of the general humanist revival of antiquity. On the other hand, both Pico and Ficino were also connected with scholasticism. Pico not only studied in Padua and Paris, the leading centres of contemporary scholasticism, and composed scholastic works, but also defended scholasticism in his famous letter to Ermolao Barbaro. Ficino too was immersed in the scholastic tradition, constantly adopting Aristotelian and medieval philosophical terminology, genres and sources. Earlier humanism's philosophical poverty obliged both Ficino and Pico, the greatest Italian philosophers of the earlier Renaissance, to look positively upon the medieval philosophical heritage.

The rich sources of Renaissance philosophy and science also come to the fore in Brian Copenhaver's article, "Hermes Trismegistus, Proclus, and the question of a philosophy of magic in the Renaissance." The central importance of magic and the occult for Renaissance thought was highlighted in the work of D. P. Walker and Frances Yates.[31] According to Yates, the "view of the cosmos as a network of magical forces with which man can operate" was "the chief stimulus of that new turning toward the world and operating on the world which . . . was to turn into seventeenth-century science." Yates believed that "the core of [this] . . . movement was Hermetic," that is, founded on a group of texts spuriously associated with a legendary ancient Egyptian priest, Hermes Trismegistus, collected and mainly translated into Latin by Ficino in the early 1460s. Copenhaver accepts the potential importance of magical theory in the genesis of modern science and possibly even on Newton himself, but he disputes Yates's emphasis on the role of the Hermetic texts themselves. The central figure for both Yates and Copenhaver here is Ficino, but Copenhaver points to the theoretical poverty of the Hermetica, particularly in terms of magical doctrine; far more important for Ficino's magic, in his view, were the philosophical writings of the ancient Neoplatonists, Plotinus, Porphyry, Iamblichus and particularly Proclus. The importance of the Hermetica in the genesis of Ficino's philosophy and theology are beyond dispute: these were texts which Ficino interrupted his early work on Plato's dialogues to translate. Copenhaver's contribution here is to broaden the scope of Ficino's inspiration in the fields of magic and science beyond the narrower genealogical and historical potentialities held out by the Hermetica to the wider theoretical possibilites offered by the late-ancient Neoplatonists themselves.

The potency of the scholastic and Aristotelian traditions, demonstrated by Kristeller for Ficino and Pico, is traced during the later Renaissance and well into the seventeenth century by Charles Schmitt, in his article, "Towards a reassessment of Renaissance Aristotelianism." Schmitt suggests that Aristotelianism "thrived throughout the sixteenth century, as it never had before, and was still in full bloom for most of the seventeenth century," maintaining its place "as the dominant university philosophy." Moreover, Aristotelianism offered a flexible approach, transformed, for example, under humanism's influence, with the rejection of spurious texts and the increasing use of original Greek versions as a basis for teaching. Aristotelian logic, scientific method and core conceptions remained powerfully in force: Copernicus accepted the Aristotelian "closed universe," Galileo the Aristotelian idea of the eternity of circular motion and Ramus the Aristotelian "basic logical unit, the syllogism." It was only after the mid-seventeenth century that the rise of new mathematical, quantitative and experimental methods undermined Aristotelian physics: "The fully-demonstrated power of the New Science in matters of physics seems to have occasioned the dropping of Aristotle as a basis for scientific and philosophical education in general."

Radical innovators – because of their very radicalism – can have a limited effect on their more conventional contemporaries and immediate successors, and this was arguably the case for two of fifteenth-century Italy's most original figures, Valla and Poliziano. As seen above, Grafton argues for Poliziano as a philological revolutionary, but he also concludes that "Politian's principles did not triumph at once . . . Even Politian's disciple, Pietro Crinito, seems to have learned relatively little from his master." One of Valla's most original contributions was his philological study of the New Testament – a revolutionary step, since the Vulgate had been revered as divinely inspired and authoritative during the middle ages; but in his own century Valla's biblical criticism remained an aberration, unpublished until Erasmus's edition of 1505. As James Hankins has observed,

> no Italian humanist has been more studied in modern times than Lorenzo Valla, and he is often presented in modern studies as a gigantic figure on the stage of Renaissance letters. In a recent three-volume survey of Renaissance humanism, for instance, he is given a chapter to himself (entitled "Italy's Leading Humanist"), and made generally into a paradigmatic figure for the humanist movement as a whole. Yet Valla's writings, apart from the *Elegantiae*, which enjoyed moderate popularity, survive in fewer than a hundred manuscripts and a handful of printed editions. It is clear that his audience was confined to a small circle of professional humanists, and that he had been largely forgotten until rescued from oblivion by Erasmus in the early sixteenth century.[32]

Indeed, Mirko Tavoni has emphasized the overall lack of influence of Valla's *Elegantiae* at the school level in Italy:

> Presumably its innovative stucture, the difficulties of its subject matter and an unmanageable text prevented a wide-spread diffusion in schools.[33]

In his article "Lorenzo Valla and Rudolph Agricola," John Monfasani, too, shows the limits of Valla's direct impact. In this case, the focus is Valla's logic. It has been suggested that Valla laid the foundations for the humanist revolution in logic by rejecting scholasticism's emphasis on certainty in favour of probability; in this sense, so it has been argued, he exercised a decisive effect on the most influential humanist logician, Rudolf Agricola, whose work would revolutionize the teaching of logic in Northern Europe during the sixteenth century.[34] Monfasani shows, however, that Valla in fact had only a negative impact on Agricola, who actually seems to have been refuting Valla: Valla subordinated logic to rhetoric, whereas Agricola did exactly the opposite, transferring the normal scope of rhetoric to logic and devaluing rhetoric as "mere verbal ornament." Indeed, in Northern European schools the companion piece to Agricola's humanist logic was not Valla's work, nor textbooks from the humanist mould by educators such as Melanchthon, but George of Trebizond's traditional Aristotelian "compendium of scholastic logic."

The final section of this anthology is devoted to the spread of humanism. The humanist movement began in the late thirteenth and early fourteenth century with figures such as Lovato Lovati, Albertino Mussato and Geri d'Arezzo (now conventionally but not altogether logically known as pre-humanists). In these early days of the Renaissance, as well as at the time of Petrarch and Boccaccio during the mid-fourteenth century, humanism had no strong association with any partic-ular Italian centre: both Petrarch and Boccaccio were itinerant personalities, and it was not until the end of the fifteenth century that humanism's benefits were appreciated by a wider social following. Humanism first took root in Florence during and after the long and prestigious career enjoyed in the chancery there by Salutati from 1375 to 1406. The Florentine élite came to value the ideological potentialities of humanist rhetoric in furtherance of their political ascendancy within the city of Florence itself as well as outside in their growing Tuscan territorial empire; moreover, it was in Florence that the social advantages of a humanist education were first realized: in Florence's fluid society, where there were no fixed legal definitions of rank or nobility, the status conferred by a classical educa-tion came to be prized with remarkable rapidity and zeal by the city's élite.[35]

It was only in the course of the fifteenth century that humanism and the Renaissance began to win a firm place in other Italian centres such as Venice. This is not entirely surprising, in view of Venice's legally defined patrician class, who, unlike the Florentines, evidently did not feel such an acute need to secure their social status. The penetration of humanism into Venice is discussed by Felix Gilbert in his paper, "Humanism in Venice," adopting in part "a sociological approach." Gilbert points to many famous humanists who remained only briefly in Venice; figures such as Guarino were unable to develop their careers there beyond the insecure world of private tutoring. The problem was the Venetian bureaucracy: in Florence from the time of Salutati the chancery became the hub of humanist activity and patronage, but Venice failed to build on the heritage of two early humanist chancellors from the later fourteenth century, Benintendi dei Ravagnani and Lorenzo de Monacis; the office of Venetian Grand Chancellor in the fifteenth century became bogged down in bureaucracy and made almost no positive contri-bution to humanism. Venetian educational institutions were hardly more propitious: the School at the Rialto taught scholastic logic and philosophy, while the School of San Marco, which opened in 1450 to teach Latin to the Venetian bureaucrat class, failed to attract leading humanists because of excessive teaching demands, exclusion from public affairs and bad pay. Humanism began to take root in Venice only when it attracted the attention of the patrician class in the course of the fifteenth century: here, Gilbert suggests, it was Venice's new expansionist policy on the Italian mainland that may have drawn potential humanists into the main-stream of peninsular intellectual life; even more important were Venice's traditionally close links with the Greek world: as humanist interest in the Greek revival developed, it was inevitable that Venetians would favour a movement of such immediate relevance to their own cultural sphere and interests.

The spread of humanism beyond Italy is exemplified in Charles Nauert's review article, "The humanist challenge to medieval German culture." Although humanism penetrated all German universities by 1500 and by 1535 had deprived medieval scholasticism of its educational predominance, its success was not built on indig-enous foundations: the supposed basis provided by the native lay pious movement known as the Devotio moderna has been shown to be non-existent; German human-ism was an Italianate import, introduced by scholars and patrons who had themselves studied in Italy. The decisive forces in establishing humanism in German universities were the Reformation and secular authorities: because of Lutheranism's indissoluble link to humanism, wherever the Reformation triumphed so did humanism; moreover, keen and convinced secular authorities provided the backing and financial support which universities themselves were incapable of mustering. In the end, humanism became such a powerful force in Germany that even Catholic universities such as Ingolstadt "underwent successful humanist reform"; conserva-tive centres such as Cologne sank into insignificance in the course of the sixteenth century. All German universities "offered a liberal arts education . . . broadened by the abolition of many scholastic practices and the incorporation of the linguistic-literary-philological method of humanism into the heart of their curriculum."

This discussion of humanism's spread to Northern Europe should act as a caution against too uniform an approach to humanism and the Renaissance in general. The Renaissance cannot be seen as a monolithic challenge to medieval traditions, institu-tions, practices and texts, as a basically homogenous movement which first spread through Italy and then was imported to ultramontane Europe. It is necessary to give adequate attention to the diverse and varied contexts in which this phenomenon took place. In Italy, for example, Renaissance humanism represented a development of long-standing educational movements, primarily in the disciplines of grammar and rhetoric. It had an established place in the educational hierarchy, mainly at the secondary-school level and largely outside the universities.[36] This meant that humanism in Italy did not represent a fundamental challenge to the educational establishment, powerfully ensconced in the university faculties of law and medicine. Because of humanism's deep roots in the medieval traditions of grammar and rhetoric, it was slow to achieve a reform of secondary teaching in Italy; in the field of Latin language and literature, humanist education had a considerable impact only in the closing decades of the fifteenth century,[37] whereas even in the area of rhetoric there was never a complete discarding of medieval practices.[38] The acceptance of the traditional hierarchy of learning is generally evident throughout Italian humanism: as has been seen above, humanists such as Pico and Ficino embraced outright scholastic philosophy and theology, while others turned to medicine and law. It is no accident that sixteenth-century Italy saw Early Modern Europe's most intense study of Aristotelian philosophy and science, in many ways the culmination of medieval scholasticism (see Chapter 16 below).

Humanism had a different face in Northern Europe. In Germany, for example, grammatical and rhetorical education were traditionally associated with the universities: indeed, in Germany "university students normally began their studies at an early age, about thirteen or fourteen."[39] Italian-style specialized curriculum development, whereby the teaching of Latin was relegated to specialist secondary schools and teachers, was less prevalent. As a result, when humanism was imported to Germany in the later fifteenth century, it assumed a garb more challenging than any previously worn in Italy. Unlike Italy, the context of German humanism was the universities. Because of Germany's more homogeneous, non-specialized educational traditions, curricula and structures, it was natural for German humanists to become university reformers. In Germany, humanism offered the kind of basic challenge to scholasticism which it could never have represented in Italy.

The Renaissance was a complex, hybrid phenomenon: not only were its roots diverse and varied chronologically and geographically, but its later development in Europe was far from uniform. Recent research has shown and will continue to show that there can be no simplistic approach to this heterogeneous series of historical developments: the clock can never again be turned back to Burckhardt.

Notes

1   London, 1990 (Penguin edition), tr. by S. G. C. Middlemore, intro. by Peter Burke, notes by Peter Murray.
2   The best treatment of Burckhardt's influence in the first century after publication is W. K. Ferguson, *The Renaissance in Historical Thought: five centuries of interpretation*, Cambridge, Mass., 1948. See also the bibliography published by Burke in Burckhardt, *The Civilization*, pp. 15–16.
3   Burckhardt, *The Civilization*, p. 230.
4   Ibid., p. 250.
5   See, for example, C. Morris, *The Discovery of the Individual, 1050–1200*, London, 1972.
6   *Giovanni Rucellai ed il suo zibaldone. I: "Il zibaldone quaresimale,"* ed. A. Perosa, London, 1960, p. 62, my translation. NB: all translations in this introduction will be my own unless otherwise indicated.
7   E. H. Gombrich, "In search of cultural history," in his *Ideals and Idols. Essays on values in history and in art*, Oxford, 1979, pp. 50–51 (first published separately, Oxford, 1969).
8   See the anthology of citations published by B. G. Kohl, "The changing concept of the *studia humanitatis* in the early Renaissance," *Renaissance Studies*, 6 (1992), pp. 185–209, esp. 192, 193, 200.
9   H. Baron, *The Crisis of the Early Italian Renaissance. Civic humanism and republican liberty in an age of classicism and tyranny*, Princeton, 1966 (rev. edn in one vol.; first published 1955 in two vols).
10   See J. Hankins, ed., *Renaissance Civic Humanism. Reappraisals and reflections*, Cambridge, 2000.

11 See most recently J. Blythe, "'Civic humanism' and medieval political thought," in Hankins, *Renaissance Civic Humanism*, Cambridge, 2000, pp. 30–74.

12 E. H. Gombrich, "From the revival of letters to the reform of the arts: Niccolò Niccoli and Filippo Brunelleschi," in his *The Heritage of Apelles: studies in the art of the Renaissance*, London, 1976, pp. 93–110, cited at p. 106 (first published in D. Fraser *et al.*, eds, *Essays in the History of Art presented to Rudolf Wittkower*, London, 1967, pp. 71–82).

13 H. Burns, "Quattrocento architecture and the antique: some problems," in *Classical Influences on European Culture, A.D. 500–1500*, ed. R. R. Bolgar, Cambridge, 1971, pp. 269–287.

14 Cited in R. Black, "The Donation of Constantine: a new source for the concept of the Renaissance?," in *Language and Images of Renaissance Italy*, ed. A. Brown, Oxford, 1995, p. 83.

15 Cited in Chapter 1 below, p. 24.

16 J. B. Ross and M. M. McLaughlin, eds, *The Portable Renaissance Reader*, New York, 1953, p. 123.

17 Ibid., p. 128.

18 *Elegantiarum libri sex*, in his *Opera omnia*, Turin, 1962.

19 Ross and McLaughlin, *Renaissance Reader*, p. 134.

20 *Zibaldone*, p. 60.

21 Ross and McLaughlin, *Renaissance Reader*, p. 79.

22 E. J. Kenney, *The Classical Text: aspects of editing in the age of the printed book*, Berkeley, Los Angeles and London, 1974.

23 See my chapter "Education and the emergence of a literate society," in *Italy in the Renaissance (1300–1550)*, ed. J. Najemy, Oxford, forthcoming.

24 See Hankins, *Renaissance Civic Humanism*.

25 See R. Black, "The political thought of the Florentine chancellors," *The Historical Journal*, 29 (1986), pp. 991–1003.

26 See Hankins, *Renaissance Civic Humanism*, esp. the articles by J. Najemy and M. Hörnqvist; A. Field, "Leonardo Bruni, Florentine traitor? Bruni, the Medici and an Aretine conspiracy of 1437," *Renaissance Quarterly*, 51 (1998), pp. 1109–1150.

27 Baron, *Crisis*, pp. 55–57, 102, 119–120.

28 Ibid., p. 56.

29 Ibid., esp. pp. 100ff, 123ff, 146ff.

30 R. Witt, "The *Crisis* after forty years," *American Historical Review*, 101 (1996), p. 112.

31 D. P. Walker, *Spiritual and Demonic Magic from Ficino to Campanella*, London, 1958; F. Yates, *Giordano Bruno and the Hermetic Tradition*, London, 1964.

32 J. Hankins, *Repetorium Brunianum. A critical guide to the writings of Leonardo Bruni*, I: *Handlist of Manuscripts*, Rome, 1997, p. xx.

33 M. Tavoni, "La linguistica rinascimentale. 2. L'Europa occidentale," in *Storia della linguistica*, ed. G. Lepschy, Bologna, 1990, pp. 170–245, at p. 174.

34 For example, R. Waswo, *Language and Meaning in the Renaissance*, Princeton, 1987, pp. 109–110; L. Jardine, "Humanism and the teaching of logic," in *The Cambridge History of Later Medieval Philosophy*, ed. N. Kretzmann *et al.*, Cambridge, 1982, p. 800 and "Humanistic logic," in *The Cambridge History of Renaissance Philosophy*, Cambridge, 1988, p. 182.

35 See R. Black, "Florence," in *The Renaissance in National Context*, ed. R. Porter and M. Teich, Cambridge, 1992, pp. 21–41.

36 See R. Black, *Humanism and Education in Medieval and Renaissance Italy. Tradition and innovation in Latin schools from the twelfth to the fifteenth century*, Cambridge, 2001, Chapter 1.

37 Ibid., Chapters 3 and 4.

38 See J. Monfasani, "Humanism and Rhetoric," in *Renaissance Humanism. Foundations, forms and legacy*, ed. A. Rabil Jr., Philadelphia, 1988, III, pp. 171–235.

39 See Chapter 19 below, pp. 282.

PART ONE

Renaissance and Humanism: Definition

E. H. Gombrich

■   from **THE RENAISSANCE – PERIOD OR MOVEMENT?**, in A. G. Dickens *et al.*, *Background to the English Renaissance. Introductory Lectures*, London, 1974, pp. 9–30[1]

IT IS QUITE A TALL ORDER to talk about the Renaissance as such, or to introduce a course on the Renaissance by discussing the concept, or the idea of the Renaissance, or revival, or rebirth, or whatever equivalent you may choose for this loaded term. The first thing to ask is really whether we should look at the Renaissance – as is conventionally done – as a particular period in Western history, or whether there may be an alternative to this conventional view, one which simply looks at our periodization of history in a way (as it will soon turn out) connected with the term "Renaissance." Connected, and I may anticipate here, because if the term Renaissance, or rebirth or revival, is understood to mean the revival of classical antiquity, or classical values, or ancient civilization, then the period between antiquity and the revival will be the middle period, the "medium aevum," the Middle Ages, and this, of course, is what the period between these two ages has been called. The term "Middle Ages" was therefore an invention of the Renaissance, because in the Renaissance, whatever it may be, the people who proclaimed the importance of rebirth, postulated that something had been dead, and had to be re-born, and the period that had been responsible for this death was the Middle Ages. We cannot understand the way in which Western history was viewed without seeing very clearly that the term "Renaissance" was charged with a particular system of values. But what these values are is a matter we have to interpret because, in some respects, the interpretation of what the Renaissance stood for, or stands for, even now, has shifted, and shifted often, almost kaleido-scopically, particularly during the last one hundred years. It is important, after all this debate, to go back and ask what the Renaissance thought of the Renaissance. This problem of what the Renaissance thought of itself is the topic of the first chapter of Erwin Panofsky's *Renaissance and Renascences in Western Art*, which is significantly called "Renaissance, self-description or self-deception?" In other words, it raises the question whether those who proclaimed the rebirth were in fact deceiving themselves, or whether there was something in it.

The question is typical of the unease, the *malaise*, with which the claims of the Renaissance have been met in the last few decades, although it seems to me that more recently again other problems have moved into the centre of interest.

Renaissance as recovery

It is generally agreed that the man who was mainly responsible for the proclamation of the rebirth, or the need for a rebirth, was Francesco Petrarca. His dates are 1304–1374. He was, as you know, an Italian who lived a good deal of his life in France. He had to live in Avignon because of the Babylonian captivity of the Roman Church, and surely the feeling of dissatisfaction, the longing for a renewal of Italy, had a good deal to do, among many other things, with this blow to the pride of Rome – that the Roman Church was no longer centered on Rome. For Petrarch (as we call him) considered history, all history, a praise of Rome. An heir to the great Imperial tradition, the heir to the praise of the conquerors of the world, he had to see the seat of power transferred to France, and this was certainly one of the motives in his life which made him long for a return in every sense of the term. But, most of all, Petrarch was a poet. He was a poet with a wonderful ear for language – for the beauty of language, beautiful Latin as well as beautiful Italian – and for articulateness. He disliked and despised the crabbed technical terminology used at the Universities. He longed for a revival not only of the power and glory of Rome, but of the beautiful language of Virgil, of Horace and of Cicero. He, himself, began a poem, in 1338, in Latin hexameters, on Scipio Africanus, called *Africa*, and it is in the preliminary lines of this epic that he addresses his poem and uses the terms to which I shall have to refer:

> But if you [meaning the poem], as is the hope and desire of my mind, will long live after me, better ages are in store. The sleep of forgetfulness will not continue in all the years to come. Once the darkness has been broken, our descendants will perhaps be able to return to the pure, pristine radiance.

This "return to the pure, pristine radiance," for which Petrarch longed, could be interpreted in religious as well as in secular terms. The world had become corrupted, soiled by bad tradition, and the need was to recover what had been lost in the *tenebrae*, in the darkness, in the *medium aevum*, the Middle Ages.

There were solid reasons for Petrarch's complaint and longing. He knew perfectly well that many of the classical authors he much admired were not easily, if at all, accessible in manuscript. His friends hunted them out and he himself discovered new letters by Cicero and new Decades of Livy. He started the fashion for the recovery of ancient authors whose works had been lost or mislaid in the monastic libraries. Together with the study of the beautiful style of these ancient authors he so much admired, there was an awareness that certain of their values and much of their knowledge had also been lost. Not least, of course, the knowledge of Greek. The ancient authors constantly refer to Homer, to Plato and to other authors. Petrarch, who tried to learn Greek and made contact with Byzantine scholars, never managed to learn it, but he was very much aware of the need to recover something which was demonstrably lost in the West – that is to say the ability to read Greek. I do not want to give the impression that no one in the Latin West ever read Greek in what we now still call the Middle Ages, but there were very few opportunities to learn it.

Now this new emphasis on the beautiful style of the ancients, on the knowledge that had been lost and that had to be recovered, was from the beginning linked with the idea of "ages." The idea that there are various "ages," periods, in history can be traced back to a mythical idea – the Golden Age, the Silver Age, the Iron Age and so forth – and the hope for the return of the Golden Age which was enshrined in one of the most famous of ancient poems, the Fourth *Eclogue* by Virgil, who had prophesied that the reign of Saturn would return again – "*redeunt Saturnia regna*" – and who had hoped that with this return of a golden age civilization would be reborn. Now here you had a new faith in something coming, something that would cleanse away the adulteration of the past and begin afresh, and the main target of criticism here – and this is interesting in connection with our present-day situation – was the educational system and the universities. What on earth had they been doing, and what were they doing if they allowed these great treasures of antiquity to be so badly neglected?

I shall concentrate for a moment on the relation between the university situation and this idea that something had to be recovered, that the old corrupt routine had to be swept aside, because those who were particularly intent on a good style, learning proper Latin and Greek, felt that there was not really a very good niche for them in the university system. The medieval system of learning, as you may know, was divided into the so-called "liberal" arts. There were seven of them. Three were preliminary; they were Grammar, Dialectic, Rhetoric. They had to do with words because before you learnt anything you had to learn to express yourself, to be articulate. And that is why you learnt Grammar, Latin grammar of course; Dialectic, logical argument; and Rhetoric, speech. This was the Trivium – the three ways – and our term "trivial" is still an echo of the fact that these were the elementary subjects. You may say "this is what one learns at primary school, this is trivial." The Quadrivium was the next phase, the higher disciplines, based on real knowledge as distinct from mere words, and this was the knowledge of numbers – Arithmetic, Geometry, Astronomy and Music. When we speak today of the Arts subjects and of the Science subjects, and of the alleged conflict between the two, we still echo, in a way, this great division between those who are interested in elegant forms of expression and those who are interested in knowledge rather than opinion. That is how the mathematical sciences were seen at that time. It has been said, and well said, that in the universities the Renaissance was a rebellion of the Trivium against the Quadrivium; a rebellion of those concerned with language, who did not want to take the second role any more because the Faculties of the universities were divided according to quite different principles. According to the career somebody wanted to take up, there was Law, there was Medicine, there was Theology, and each of these was enshrined in very technical language and technical textbooks. Those who wished to teach Rhetoric and the others were asking, "Where do we come in?" It was these people who became known as the "*umanisti*" – we speak of the "humanists." They were men who emphasized the importance of language. In real life many of them were diplomats, secretaries, scholars, people in whose careers the facility in writing a good letter or making an impressive speech was very important. Very often they were not theologians, but laymen. And yet it is totally misleading to think of "humanism" as a movement which reacted against the Roman Church. The term "humanism," as distinct from "*umanista*," is a nineteenth-century invention and we shall see that the nineteenth century tended altogether to exaggerate the opposition between the Renaissance and the so-called Christian centuries.

What the humanists also claimed was that the past had had a very bad tradition of learning and so they concentrated first of all on cultivating the ancient authors and their own style. There is a dialogue by Leonardo Bruni from the early fifteenth century, where one of these humanists, a merchant and amateur called Niccolò Niccoli, is asked by a friend why he does not conduct any of those disputations which had been dear to the Middle Ages. He rejoins:

> If only we had the books that contained the wisdom. If only our ances-
> tors had not been so ignorant. Even the few books that do exist are so
> corrupted in their texts that they cannot teach us anything. What a
> time we live in, where people promise to teach what they evidently
> don't know themselves! When they open their mouths they utter more
> solecisms than words. If you ask them what their authority is they'll
> invoke Aristotle, but the books they refer to are so harsh, inept and
> dissonant in style that one cannot listen to them, and this cannot be
> the true Aristotle. He would not recognise himself in such a guise.[2]

So here you have the attitude of the young generation towards the traditional university teachers. In 1397, at the turn of the century, we hear a complaint about this *brigata*, the young men who considered themselves superior.

> In order to appear erudite to the man in the street, they cry out in the
> public square, arguing about how many diphthongs exist in the language
> of the ancients, and why today the anapaest with four short metrical
> feet is no longer used. And with such fantastic speculations they waste
> all their time.

But the claim that they wasted their time was soon no longer tenable. At least the students of these men gradually acknowledged that something had been redis-covered. Bruni himself was praised for having found again "the ancient ease of style." It is this ease of style that these men treasured and really did recover. Very few people, too few, I believe, nowadays spend their time reading humanist Latin. But those who do will know that in fact there is a fine flow of language. Sometimes it becomes more elegant than substantial but the need, or the feeling that some-thing has to be recovered there, travels from Italy to the North across the Alps, and this is what I want to show you here since you are particularly interested in how the Renaissance hit England.

It first came across the Alps as a movement in the Universities for the reform of teaching. In 1492, the German humanist Conrad Celtis wrote a letter to

Ingolstadt University which is worth quoting in this context. He writes how grieved he is when he hears those who expound the law from the university chair lacking all sweetness and art, offending the ear rather like cackling geese or lowing cattle, using abject vulgar and corrupt words, whatever comes into their mouths, barbarously and harshly mistreating the sweet Roman tongue. He greatly wondered how it was possible

> that in all these centuries, in all the many schools of Germany, with their scholastic clamour, all of which pretend to learning, nobody had been found who could write letters or speeches, poems or histories in a civilized and polished way – as it is the custom in Italy where there are fewer but much more learned universities. Thus [he continues] I was sorry for my Germany because in all its schools I have seen no one to expound Cicero.

Out of love for "the republic of learning" he offered to remedy these ills by becoming a professor himself. Here you find a much more obvious clash in the North between the traditions of the Middle Ages and the university courses and those who had learnt their new ideas in Italy after the movement started by Petrarch gathered momentum. In 1515, these brash young men, who called themselves "*poetae*" – the poets – as distinct from the learned men, launched a wonderful hoax. They published a book called *Epistolae Obscurorum Virorum*, the Letters of Obscure Men. These letters pretend, or purport, to be letters by conservative university teachers who complain to each other about the dreadful movement that has deprived them of their prestige. I can only read to you the translation of one of these letters, or an extract from it, to give you the flavour of the satire which must have had a good deal of truth and probably echoes the accent of those who deplore the *poetae* very well indeed. Needless to say, they are deliberately written in atrocious Latin style, but that I cannot imitate:

> I believe the devil is in these poets. They destroy all the universities and I've heard it of an old Magister of Leipzig, who taught there for thirty-six years, who said to me that when he was young the University was in good shape, for among twenty thousand students there was not one poet, and it was considered a scandal for any student to go to the market square without Petrus Hispanus or the *Parva Logicalia* under his arm. And when they saw a Magister they were as frightened as if they saw the devil . . . At that time the University truly flourished and if any of them confessed that they secretly heard a lecture on Virgil the priest imposed a heavy penalty . . . If only things were still like that in the University! Now when there are twenty students, hardly one of them wants to proceed to a degree, but all the others want is to study the humanities. And if the Magister lectures he has no audience, but the poets in their lectures have such an audience that it seems a miracle. And we must pray to God that all poets should die, for is it not better that a few poets should die than that all the universities should perish?

This feeling of superiority over the traditionalist teachers was shared by the great Northern humanists, most of all by Erasmus of Rotterdam, who exulted in 1517, "Polite letters, which were almost extinct, are now cultivated by Scots, Danes and Irishmen." The humanists had taught their pupils something which the others did not know – the ancient beauty of style.

It might be useful to put this in diagrammatic form:

Classical antiquity +   Dark Ages –   Recovery +

                                                         1300–1400

The first thing to note about this diagram is that the problem of *when* this recovery happened wasn't very important, but the event was placed between 1300 and 1400. Secondly, and more importantly, the recovery was seen as something static. The Arts had simply revived again, just as plants revive. The organic metaphor which is connected with the idea of rebirth had a strong hold. The Arts – and we shall see that it applies to painting and sculpture as well – had been lost and they had been reborn. There are absolute standards of goodness and beauty – certainly in the Latin style the absolute standard is set by Cicero and the great classics; the term "classic," after all, means that these are the authors one should take as models. Classical antiquity is the canon of perfection, and one can recover this perfection.

Renaissance as progress

The reason why I stress this quality of *stasis* in this idea of the Renaissance is that gradually, but in a very important way, the notion of the Renaissance got involved with a very different idea, which is not static, but, if you like, dynamic – the idea of progress.[3] There is no necessary implication in the idea of the Renaissance of progress as such, but during the Renaissance, when the aim had been to recover the beauty of the ancient style and of ancient art, the debate began or, if you like, the discovery was made, after a time, that in fact one wasn't living in a reborn classical antiquity.

Why not? Because meanwhile a number of shattering inventions had been made. Shattering in the true sense of the term, because one of them is, of course, gunpowder, which had changed the nature of warfare. There was also printing, which had changed the nature of communication; and there was the marine compass, which had changed the possibilities of navigation. All this raised the question whether one was simply recovering antiquity, or whether an entirely new age was coming, or had dawned. One can express this by adding an extra + on the diagram towards the end of the century:

                 +   –   +   ++

It is interesting, by the way, that all these discoveries which distinguish the later ages, or the modern age, from antiquity, are inventions which had come to the West somehow from the East – from China mainly. This is certainly true of the marine compass, and almost certainly of gunpowder, and even printing was certainly practised in China before it was known in the West. So that, in a sense, what distinguishes the new from the old age, and what creates an incipient hope, at least, not in the recovery of lost values but of a future which will be better and better – the idea of progress in other words – comes partly through a culture clash; through the new ideas or inventions which percolated across the world and reached the West. It was this that created the hopes of Francis Bacon in the development of science, the domination of nature and, in fact, what made him devalue purely humanistic knowledge.

All these great changes – and I must be very summary in this matter – made for reflection on the course of history. The first systematic reflection on human history as such is *The New Science*, by the Neapolitan philosopher Giambattista Vico, in the early eighteenth century.[4] Vico took up the idea of "Ages," but he thought they came back in cycles very much like the seasons. Every civilization must pass through certain phases, as human beings do. The first, which interested him most, he called the Age of the Gods; it is the harsh, primitive phase that gave rise to myth; the second, the Age of Heroes, is the epic age of wars and chivalry, which is followed by the Age of Man, the rational age in which we find ourselves.

This interest in primitivism combined with faith in man is characteristic of many philosophies of the period we call the Enlightenment. To the German critic and historian J. G. Herder, who may have been influenced by Vico, all history aimed at making man more human, an ideal he called *Humanität*. However much these thinkers differed – and we must not forget that Rousseau challenged the very faith in progress at the time – they were all concerned with the conditions that made for a good society.

In this respect the first cultural historian was certainly Voltaire, with his book *Essai sur les moeurs et l'esprit des nations* of 1756.[5] In his *Age of Louis XIV* he had written of our periods of happiness in the past. Three were those of powerful rulers, of Alexander the Great, of Augustus, and of Louis XIV. But the fourth was the Renaissance for which he gave credit to a family of middle-class bankers, the Medici, who had done their duty by civilization which had been neglected by the Nobility and by the Church. The Age of Man, to refer to Vico's division, was a middle-class age where bankers favoured artists and scholars. It was a new interpretation that was consolidated in England in the late eighteenth century when William Roscoe published the first full biography of Lorenzo de' Medici in 1795. Roscoe's book expresses what has been called by Herbert Butterfield "the Whig conception of history." He was a Liverpool banker and a member of the Wilberforce movement for the abolition of slavery, and his interpretation of the Renaissance is coloured by his enthusiasm for liberty. Let me quote the opening lines of his first chapter:

> Florence has been remarkable in modern history for the frequency and violence of its internal dissension, and for the predilection of its inhabitants for every species of science and every production of art.

However discordant these characteristics may appear, they are not difficult to reconcile. The same active spirit that calls forth the talents of
individuals for the preservation of their liberty, and resists with uncon-
querable resolution whatever is supposed to infringe them, in the
moments of domestic peace and security seeks with avidity other objects
of employment.

So the Renaissance was such a period of domestic peace when the active
middle-class Italian turned to other objects of employment and created a new
civilization. There was a link connecting the contradictory aspects of the period,
its violence and its culture – even the individualism of the period, even the disso-
lution of the Church, as Macaulay stressed in his famous essay on Machiavelli of
1827.

But while the Renaissance was thus married, as it were, to the idea of political progress, the new age, the march of progress, the very events of the period
when Roscoe wrote caused a reaction in the true sense of the term. This was the
time of the French Revolution and also the time when these values of progres-
sivism were thoroughly questioned by those who were disillusioned by the
Revolution – the Romantics. The Romantics, who longed to go back to what had
become known as the Age of Faith, denied the conventional valuation of the
Renaissance because they saw destruction where the Renaissance and later periods
had seen an upward movement. In diagrammatic form:

Classical antiquity –   Middle Ages +   Renaissance –

For the Romantics the Age of Faith was the unitary age, when the individual
still knew his place, and everybody joined in the building of cathedrals and when,
generally speaking, there was no rift in the mind of men. The great upholder of
this reading of the Middle Ages in England was John Ruskin, who hated the
Renaissance and wrote – typically – in 1853 that the Renaissance scholars "discovered suddenly that the world for ten centuries had been living in an ungrammatical
manner, and they made it forthwith the end of human existence to be grammatical." He was being satirical, but there is something more in this quip than
some interpreters of the Renaissance may be ready to concede. In any case, for
Ruskin the Renaissance was pernicious, and it was pagan. It was part of death
rather than of life because its art was created for the sake of enjoyment rather
than for the sake of service.

What is important, and what I can only touch upon relatively briefly, is that
these two opposing views could be reconciled by a sleight of hand in a larger,
embracing system of historical philosophy, and this is what Hegel did by his
dialectic. I am admittedly biased here for I have been convinced by Karl Popper's
logical arguments that the pretensions of this method which have survived in
Marxism are quite untenable.[6] Be that as it may, Hegel wanted to show that
history could be seen as a vast syllogism, a logical progression which was there-

fore demonstrably inevitable. This is the meaning of his famous dictum that the real is the rational and the rational is the real.

For Hegel, the whole course of history, the whole development of the human mind, is a continuation of a cosmic process. It starts with the creation of the world and goes along the great chain of being, the ladder of creation; from stones we go to plants and from plants to animals, and from animals to man. So the various ages represent ever higher stages of awareness of the spirit or the Godhead in reflecting about itself. Therefore, one cannot, in history, speak of good or evil. The process of unfolding that goes on all the time embraces the ancient world, the Middle Ages, and the coming of the Renaissance.

But the course of progress is not straight. From antiquity we could not have entered the Renaissance and importantly, the Reformation, right away. There had to be the stage of feudalism in the Christian countries, and every such stage is valuable in its own way, as a necessary step forward, for forward it goes. What led to the Renaissance, in Hegel's view, was that certain "internal contradictions" (as Marxists would say) made for the disintegration of the Middle Ages and created a new Age. Among these dissolving agents identified by Hegel was Art which turned man towards the sensual, the study of Antiquity which turned him away from heaven, and the geographical discoveries which turned the spirit outwards towards this Earth. To quote his own words at least in extract:

> The term *humaniora* is very significant, for those works of antiquity celebrate what is essentially human and what makes us human. These three facts, the so-called Revival of Learning, the flourishing of the Fine Arts and the Discoveries of America and of the sea-route to the East Indies may be compared to the blush of dawn which for the first time after protracted storms announces a beautiful day. This day is the day of the Common Man, which breaks at last after the long, fateful and terrible night of the Middle Ages, a day that is marked by Science, Art and the urge to discovery, in other words by the most noble and exalted manifestations of the human spirit after it had been made free by Christianity and emancipated by the Church.

It is a movement which culminates for Hegel in the "all-transfiguring sunrise of the Reformation." Thus the idea of progress is saved, while the Romantic valuation of the Middle Ages is conceded through the notion of "historical necessity."[7]

Hegel's interpretation of the Renaissance had a tremendous influence, because he really consolidated the idea that any chronological period was marked by a distinctive "Spirit of the Age." Thus the Renaissance was not to be seen simply as a movement for the revival of certain values, but as an entirely new age, a new ring in the growth of humanity.

The most influential French historian – Michelet – says so quite explicitly in the volume he dedicated to the French Renaissance in 1855. He says in the Preface that he has devoted ten years of his life to writing the history of France in the Middle Ages, and ten years to the French Revolution. What remains, he says, is to bridge the gap by writing the history of the Renaissance and the Modern Age. And he adds:

To the lover of beauty, the attractive word Renaissance implies no more than the arrival of new art; to the scholar it means a renewal of the studies of antiquity; to the lawyer, the end of the chaos of ancient customs. But is that all? If so, this colossal effort, a revolution of such scale and complexity and strength, had given birth to nothing. Could anything be more discouraging to the human mind?

But Michelet continues

These specialists had forgotten two things, small matters, it is true, which belong to that Age to a larger extent than to all the ages that came before: the discovery of the world and the discovery of man.

He lists Columbus, Copernicus, Galileo, Vesalius, Servetus, Luther, Calvin, Montaigne, Shakespeare, Cervantes, as typical of this new discovery of the world and of the new discovery of man. This preface became immensely important in the history of our study because five years later, in 1860, the great Swiss scholar, Jacob Burckhardt, published his book *The Civilization of the Renaissance in Italy*, in which he used this remark (which was an incidental or polemical aside by Michelet, who was himself very anti-clerical). He used it as a scaffolding for his book in which the civilization of the Renaissance became the discovery of the world, and the discovery of man. Henceforward we find very few books on the period where the discovery of man is not mentioned. Personally, I think it is time to put the catchword to rest. It was for this reason that I tried to show you how the word "man" got mixed up with the Renaissance, largely through the accident of the term *umanista* and its fusion with philosophies of progress which contrasted the Age of Man or of *Humanität* with early stages. As an historian I find it hard to picture any group of men and women who have not yet "discovered man," and harder still so to describe people whose religion, after all, centred on the belief that God himself had become Man. If the truth is to be told, I have come to regard the word Man with a capital M in any new book on the Renaissance as a kind of warning signal. It makes me suspect that I shall be subjected once more to a string of tired clichés, rather than being allowed to learn something new about the period.

We must not blame this on Burckhardt, who simply used Michelet's remark as a peg on which to hang his avowedly personal selection of facts. But I have attempted to demonstrate elsewhere[8] that in doing so he also imposed a Hegelian interpretation on the period. He valued the Renaissance as the harbinger of the Modern Age, and he saw the Italians as the first-born of the moderns. But he achieved this interpretation by pushing back the frontiers of the Renaissance, so that anything he liked in the Middle Ages was promoted to the Renaissance. The songs of the wandering scholars of the twelfth century were made to herald the Renaissance, and Dante was made one of its principal witnesses, though few people would call Dante a Renaissance figure nowadays. Although the Renaissance remained the age of the discovery of man and the world, the border with the Middle Ages was partly dissolved.

I would hate to leave you with the impression that such criticism will dispose of Burckhardt. If one can call an historian a great man, he certainly is a candidate for this title. He knew, and he said, that his vision of the period was a subjective one and that other readers of the identical sources he had used might form a very different picture. But he had such artistic gifts that it was his vision which was generally accepted. But even when the time came for doubters to raise their voices it was from a criticism of his book that the debate invariably started.[9]

At first *The Civilization of the Renaissance* was a slow seller but a generation later it became immensely famous and popular, not only among historians but also with the general reading public. It touched a chord, because in the Victorian age the Renaissance had acquired a curious air of topicality. Its evaluation had an obvious bearing on some of the central issues of the nineteenth century, the issue of emancipation, of liberation from dogma, of social mobility. Individualism and liberalism were projected on to the Renaissance while Ruskin and the medievalizers drew their analogies of social virtue from the closed society of the Middle Ages.

If you walk through our cities you may notice that this allegiance to the two contrasting "ages" influenced the adoption of Gothic or Renaissance forms for building in the nineteenth century. Gothic was felt to be the essentially Christian style and thus churches, but also schools and colleges, were generally built in imitation of medieval buildings. The Houses of Parliament in London were also rebuilt in the Gothic style to recall the medieval roots of English liberties. Characteristically, such buildings as the Reform Club in London (1837) were designed on a Renaissance pattern. Indeed, when Palmerston had the Foreign Office designed by a famous architect, Gilbert Scott, in 1857, he rejected the first project, which was Gothic and insisted on a Renaissance building. Apparently he sensed that on the Continent of Europe the medievalizers were identified with political reaction. It was in this charged atmosphere that there arose an almost hysterical cult of the Renaissance among the "progressives." Browsing in any old library you will find many, many books, historical novels, plays and travelogues crowded with colourful visions of Renaissance "supermen," highly artistic and highly unprincipled. Even serious histories such as J. A. Symonds's panoramic views of the period are coloured by this bias. In France, Hippolyte Taine and Count Gobineau represent this trend, and in Germany the philosopher Nietzsche fostered it. The great essayist Walter Pater, the now forgotten authoress "Vernon Lee" (Violet Paget), both saw in the Renaissance mainly a reaction to the Christian Middle Ages and therefore, in the words of *1066 and All That*, it was "a Good Thing." Certain standard quotations such as Lorenzo de' Medici's Carnival Song in Praise of Youth were always wheeled out, often out of context, to colour this picture of a reaction against the medieval Church, a reaction, indeed, against Christianity – "the glorification of the body"; "the glorification of man" – and it was against these exaggerations that the reaction came.

Reinterpreting the Renaissance

Quite naturally it started largely in the Roman Catholic camp. The devaluation of the Age of Faith, of the Catholic period, when the world was united under one faith, naturally irked these scholars and they asked a number of connected questions.

One of these questions was whether the Middle Ages had been as dark as all that; and the second one was whether the Renaissance had been as bright as all that. Each of these questions could be answered according to the selection of your material. But the first thing to note is perhaps the claim that, far from being in opposition to the rebirth of civilization, for which the Church had been pilloried, it was the Church, Christianity, which was responsible for the new turning, for the rediscovery of the world, and of man. Unlikely as it may sound, perhaps, the very man who brought about this great turning was not Petrarch, but St. Francis of Assisi. *He* praised the beauty of the creation, *he*, with his emphasis on individual conscience, first understood the individual, and therefore it is in the Franciscan movement (so the French scholar Sabatier and his German contemporary, Thode, claimed) that we must see the true beginning of the Renaissance. Moreover, far from being pagan, or anti-religious, the great humanists themselves were very religious people, as were the great artists. Now there is certainly a lot in that claim. If you go to the National Gallery, or any other collection, and look at Renaissance paintings it is not very hard to see that most of them represent the Virgin Mary. In other words, far from concentrating on pagan subjects, the Renaissance artists concentrated very much on traditional religious subjects. And if you then read the lives of the humanists and their patrons you will soon see that they were also very much concerned with their own salvation; that they dedicated chapels and altars and were greatly worried about what would happen to them if they led a sinful life. So that the reaction against the cult of the Renaissance as something totally pagan was just as down to earth, as it were, in stressing the role of popular piety in this period. One of the people who had a share in this revision was Aby Warburg, the founder of the Warburg Institute. There are a number of names, Zabughin, and Toffanin, and others, Roman Catholic writers, who stressed the importance of the religious ingredient in the Renaissance – sometimes even over-stressed it.

But another attack, and a more exact one, came against the schematic idea of a new age in which everything progressive had been discovered. This attack came from the history of science. You remember that the Renaissance was a devaluation, in some respects, of the Quadrivium, of the knowledge of numbers and of mathematics, and in fact it could be claimed that the Renaissance was not very fertile in scientific thought. The great break, as was particularly stressed by Lynn Thorndike,[10] comes only at the end of the sixteenth century. If we are interested in the history of science, we are not so much interested in what Petrarch recovered of the letters of Cicero as we are interested in one man, and that is Galileo Galilei, and his principal work falls after 1600.[11] Moreover, the despised scholastics, who were ridiculed by the humanists, were much better scientists than the Renaissance humanists had ever been. In fact in the Franciscan movement in Oxford, Robert Grosseteste and Roger Bacon and others, we have the dawn of Western science,[12] which continues in the universities in the discussions of certain problems such as the problem of impetus and the nature of movement, while the humanists remained in the past. True, there are outsiders like Leonardo, but the situation of Leonardo, who called himself a man without letters – *uomo sanza lettere* – is very ambiguous, and how much he owed to the scholastic books is again a matter for debate.[13] Now I believe that this view that all scientific progress is really medieval, and that the Renaissance was cultivating the arts at the expense of everything else is also a travesty of the truth. After all, what has become known as the Copernican Revolution is very intimately connected with the Renaissance. Copernicus was, among other things, a humanist who translated a minor Greek author into Latin and his search for an alternative world picture began with a scrutiny of such classical authorities as Cicero and Plutarch.

The question is now rather what it was that made Copernicus search these ancient texts. It is here that the interpretation of Renaissance science has taken an unexpected turn, of late, largely through the brilliant researches of Frances Yates[14] and D. P. Walker.[15] They have shown that the lost knowledge some tried to retrieve was not so much what we today would call scientific knowledge as mystical insights which were believed to give something like magical power. There is ample evidence for this irrational longing in the Renaissance, evidence which was largely played down by those who were committed to either the "progressive" or the "medieval" interpretation of the period. How much of Copernicus can be explained in this light is a different matter. Generalizations can easily become a trap and a snare unless they are controlled by a thorough reading of the sources.

This is really the point to which I wanted to come. What can any generalization about an "Age" ever tell us? There are no "Ages," in the sense that there's a uniform spirit or mentality shared by everyone in a society. People differ in the degree of their education, in their partisanship, in their taste, in their intelligence and, as we know, in their opportunities. The question of who in the Renaissance was actually a Renaissance man would really be ludicrous if you asked it in those terms – certainly not the "hewers of wood and drawers of water," or the ordinary merchant, or the ordinary churchgoer. The number of people who talk about their age, who are articulate in that sense, is always small – particularly before the invention of the mass media. Moreover they also are, each of them, individuals in quite a different sense. Human beings are complex; they may pay lip service to one thing because an element of prestige is involved, while they may at the back of their mind, or in the hour of their death, suddenly remember their old pieties. Every person belongs in many layers to many aspects of civilization. What I think we can say, what I wanted to clarify a little, is that the Renaissance was not so much an "Age" as it was a movement. A "movement" is something that is proclaimed. It attracts fanatics, on the one hand, who can't tolerate anything that doesn't belong to it and hangers-on who come and go; there is a spectrum of intensity in any movement just as there are usually various factions or "wings." There are also opponents and plenty of neutral outsiders who have other worries. I think we can most effortlessly describe the Renaissance as a movement of this kind, but, needless to say, a description is not an explanation. What the historian would like to find out is rather what it was that made the Renaissance such a successful movement that it spread throughout Europe. Of course economics, the social position of the laity, the new role of the cities would have to come into any such analysis, but the question that should never be omitted is still why certain innovations are taken up and imitated by an ever increasing number of individual people. With technical inventions the answer is simple. They spread because they are useful. Take spectacles: we know when and where they were invented; in Pisa round about 1300. Two generations later spectacles were found in China because people who didn't see well found it immensely useful to have this thing made for them. In other words, we hardly have to ask in the case of inventions why they were adopted. Sometimes we might ask why something that has an obvious advantage doesn't catch on; there may be religious taboos in the way of their adoption. But very often the provable superiority of inventions serves as a vanguard, as a path-maker, for other things, which then connect with the prestige that movement has acquired. Certainly Italian culture in the sixteenth century had a tremendous prestige in Europe; this also led to suspicion of Italy in England in the sixteenth century: "an Englishman Italianate is the devil incarnate." But the two things belong together: superiority creates envy, opposition and an insistence on traditional values, as we have seen it satirized in the *Epistolae obscurorum virorum*. Any change provides criticism and some of the criticism may be quite justified.

I have concentrated on the solid achievement of the Renaissance movement which, alas, I cannot here demonstrate – I mean the recovery of an elegant and supple Latin style. I have not so far touched at all on another such achievement which filled the leaders of the movement with pride – I mean the so-called "rebirth" of art. Lovers of medieval art, not to speak of the champions of primitive styles or of the twentieth-century revolutions, naturally do not much care for these claims. Nobody, after all, thinks nowadays as Vasari had done in the sixteenth century that the arts had been "dead" till the Florentines revived them around the year 1300. But this change in our taste should not and need not obscure the fact that certain inventions had been made in the period which gave Renaissance art an edge over earlier traditions. When Albrecht Dürer (1471–1528), the German master, wanted to sum up what he meant by the "rebirth" or "renewed growth" of art, he spoke of two skills that the Italians had conquered – the science of perspective and that of drawing the nude.[16] Let me sum up in a few illustrations what this implied.

Perspective allows the artist to put his figures upon a convincing stage. This picture by Masaccio (Fig. 1) shows how he could handle perspective, whereas in the fresco (Fig. 2) by Masolino, painted not much earlier, the perspective is not correct and the buildings do not seem to cohere properly. This was what later artists and writers particularly objected to in paintings of the period before perspective was developed. It was demonstrable that certain mistakes had been made by earlier artists. Dürer admired Martin Schongauer, a master of the previous generation, but he appears deliberately to have corrected Schongauer's version of the Death of the Virgin (Fig. 3–4) by making the perspective more coherent and consistent. There was a solid achievement here which drew artists to Italy to learn what had been discovered. Or take the nude of which Dürer spoke. I believe that if we describe Giorgione's Venus (Fig. 5) or Michelangelo's Adam (Fig. 6) – both painted around 1510 – as "beautiful" we are not simply expressing our subjective preference. I realise that ideals of physical beauty have varied from culture to culture and will continue to vary, but I am not sure that this observation warrants a complete relativism in these matters any more than in the case of perspective. We are not surprised, after all, that artists and laymen were deeply impressed, almost intoxicated, by the new mastery in creating beautiful images which had been achieved in Italy.

Not that this mastery could be achieved overnight. The creations of the great Renaissance artists remained in demand by princely collectors all over Europe because they were rightly felt to be unique. But the Renaissance style itself could be imitated and carried with it a certain glamour and prestige.

We have seen indeed that even in the nineteenth century, style could be used as something like a badge of allegiance. (It is still so used in our own time, regardless of whether we are modernists or traditionalists.) It is not too far-fetched to think that building styles could function in the same way in earlier centuries. When a fifteenth-century lord or merchant insisted on his palace or villa being built in the style known as *all'antica* (in the manner of the ancients), he, too, wanted to proclaim his allegiance to the Renaissance movement, to show that he was a man of culture and taste.

Like the pure style of Renaissance painting, the pure style of Renaissance architecture could not easily be mastered – it did not reach England before Inigo Jones in the seventeenth century. But it was always possible to pay tribute to the Italians by introducing some elements of the new repertory of forms, columns, pilasters, terms into one's design and it is in this way that Renaissance features first reached England, frequently via Flemish pattern books.[17] Like other Italianate forms in literature or in life, we may interpret them as tokens of respect for the Renaissance achievement.

The success or failure of movements such as the Renaissance depends on many factors, on fashion, on prestige, on the search for novelty. But unless we also take into account the possibility of real achievements, real conquests, history is really no more than "one damned thing after another." I have been critical of the various philosophies of progress and most of all of the metaphysical belief that the course of history is predetermined by some Hegelian spirit. But I think, with Karl Popper,[18] that a rejection of these determinist interpretations of history does not commit us to an acceptance of complete scepticism. Limited explanations are possible for limited problems. The detailed analysis of a given situation can sometimes enable us to ask sensibly what it was that secured the triumph of a particular movement in a given society. The success of the Renaissance was not simply an accident.

Question: One matter on which students might find it helpful to hear your opinion is that once the historiographical concept of the Renaissance is established, people tend to push it about. You mentioned how Burckhardt pushed it back, but we have gone further back than that since, have we not? Would you like to say something about this?

G: Certainly. An American scholar, C. H. Haskins, wrote a book called *The Renaissance of the Twelfth Century*,[19] and a very good book it is. There is, earlier, the "Carolingian Renaissance," meaning the attempt of Alcuin and others to recover or preserve the classics.[20] This is really the theme of Erwin Panofsky's *Renaissance and Renascences in Western Art* which I quoted in my lecture and which has an excellent bibliography. There are many individual attempts, sometimes in relatively small circles – such as the School of Chartres, and others – to get back to these texts and to learn what they teach, but they differ in emphasis, and Panofsky wants to distinguish these "Renascences" from the great upsurge because he very much believed in a unitary age, which is the Renaissance.

Figure 1 Masaccio, *St Peter healing the sick with his shadow*, fresco in Sa Maria del Carmine, Florence. Source: Photo Scala, Florence.

Figure 2 Masolino, *St Peter healing a cripple*, fresco in Sa Maria del Carmine, Florence. Source: Photo Scala, Florence.

Figure 3 Albrecht Dürer, *Death of the Virgin*, woodcut. Source: The Warburg Institute, London.

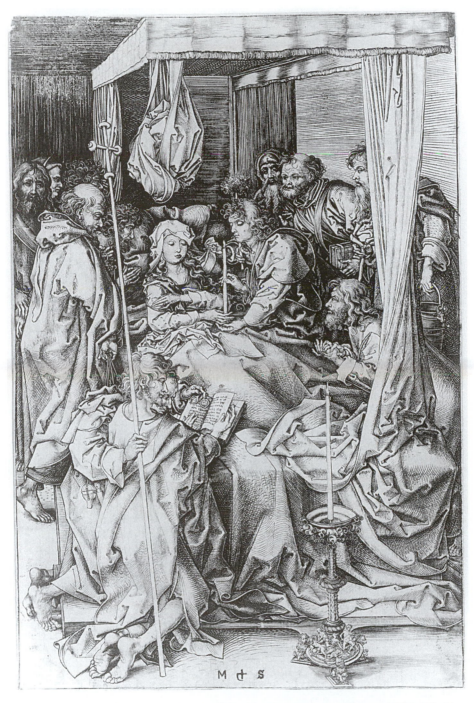

Figure 4 Martin Schongauer, *Death of the Virgin*, engraving. Source: The Warburg Institute, London.

Figure 5 Giorgione, *Reclining Venus*, Dresden, Gemäldegalerie. Source: Photo Scala, Florence.

Question: Was one of the reasons why he disallowed Chartres as a full-scale Renaissance and just called it a "Renascence" its local character?

G: It is local character, but Panofsky also has an interesting idea, which I am not quite sure is totally tenable though it is very fertile as he uses it. For him those processes of recovery in the Middle Ages did not really involve a conscious sense of distance – they thought that the ancients were still "our people," they still used "their texts." For Petrarch there is an intervening gulf. He looks at antiquity with a sense of distance, as some lost paradise which he wants to recover. A different age, in fact. Panofsky argues that it is this sense of distance that makes all the difference between local attempts to learn something about ancient authors and the systematic recovery of a lost age.

Question: You said that Petrarch went to a great deal of trouble to learn Greek and started to do so. When was Greece "rediscovered," opened up?

G: Actually, William of Moerbeke did go to Greece in the thirteenth century and translated Aristotle, but the real systematic study of Greek started when Florentine followers of Petrarch, Coluccio Salutati and others, seized on the opportunity that a Byzantine scholar – Manuel Chrysoloras – was coming to Italy and asked him to teach Greek in Florence. True, they paid him so little that after a very short time he left again but, even so, they had learned enough to go on on their own. The second element in the situation was South Italy. In Sicily, Greek *was* known and a Sicilian called Aurispa travelled to Byzantium when the craze for manuscripts had properly started and collected Greek manuscripts. For in Byzantium, of course, the works of Greek literature had never been forgotten and existed in the libraries. We owe it to Aurispa, largely, who was not a very attractive individual, that we have the Greek authors, for, as you know, Constantinople fell under the onslaught of the Turks, in 1453, and that was the end. Whether one would still have recovered many of these manuscripts later is an open question. So that if you look down a list of Greek authors, Sophocles, Euripides, Aristophanes, or whatever, you are very likely to find that the manuscripts came to the West through Aurispa [. . .] There was a famous book by a Cambridge don – Sandys, *A History of Classical Scholarship*,[21] where you'll find a good deal of information about this, to which more recent research, of course, is always adding fresh information.

Bibliographical note

The best brief introduction to the general problem is Denys Hay, *The Italian Renaissance in its Historical Background*, Cambridge, 1961. Apart from the titles listed in the notes to this lecture, the student is advised to turn soon to original texts dating from the period, some of which are available in English translation. In this way a good first-hand idea of the Humanists can be obtained from their biographies written by the Florentine fifteenth-century bookseller Vespasiano da Bisticci, translated as *The Vespasiano Memoirs* by W. George and E. Waters. The autobiography of the humanist Pope Pius II has been translated in a shortened version of *Memoirs of a Renaissance Pope*, by F. A. Gragg and L. C. Gable, New York, 1959.

For first-hand accounts of Renaissance artists we turn, of course, to G. Vasari, *The Lives of the Painters, Sculptors and Architects*, first published in 1550 (second edn. 1568), and existing in many translations. Vasari may not be a reliable historian, but he is a splendid eye witness of contemporary events and so his biographies of sixteenth-century artists are especially recommended. An equally immediate picture is conveyed by the famous *Autobiography* of Benvenuto Cellini, the Florentine goldsmith and sculptor (1500–1571), which also exists in many translations. The life of a small court is vividly evoked in one of the most famous and influential books of the period, Baldassare Castiglione, *The Courtier* (1528), which became a popular handbook of manners in Elizabethan England in the translation by Sir Thomas Hoby, 1561.

Author's Notes

1   [This text is based on a tape-recorded lecture, which the author subsequently revised for publication.]
2   For this and the following see my article "From the Revival of Letters to the Reform of the Arts: Niccolò Niccoli and Filippo Brunelleschi" in D. Fraser *et al.* (editors), *Essays in the History of Art presented to Rudolf Wittkower*, London, 1967.
3   J. B. Bury, *The Idea of Progress*, 1920 (Dover paperback, 1955).
4   Giambattista Vico, *Scienza Nuova*, revised ed. Naples, 1744. English translation by T. G. Bergin and M. H. Fisch, 1948; Cornell paperback, 1970. For Vico's later influence see also Edmund Wilson, *To The Finland Station*, 1940.
5   There is an excellent chapter on Voltaire's influence in W. K. Ferguson, *The Renaissance in Historical Thought*, Cambridge, Mass. 1948.
6   K. R. Popper, *The Open Society and its Enemies*, London, 1945 (Routledge paperbacks, 1967).
7   There is an English translation of this work by T. Sibree, 1899, but the translation in the text is my own. See also my book *In Search of Cultural History*, Oxford, 1969.
8   *In Search of Cultural History*, as quoted above.
9   See W. K. Ferguson, *The Renaissance in Historical Thought*, as quoted above.
10 L. Thorndike, *A History of Magic and Experimental Science*, 7 vols., New York, 1923–41.
11 H. Butterfield, *The Origins of Modern Science*, London, 1949.
12 A. C. Crombie, *Augustine to Galileo: Science in the Middle Ages*, London (1952, Mercury paperback, 1961).
13 For a balanced view see V. P. Zubov, *Leonardo da Vinci*, Cambridge, Mass., 1968.
14 F. A. Yates, *Giordano Bruno and the Hermetic Tradition*, London, 1964.
15 D. P. Walker, *The Ancient Theology*, London, 1972.
16 For the following see my article "The Leaven of Criticism in Renaissance Art" in C. Singleton (ed.) *Art, Science and History in the Renaissance*, Baltimore, 1967.
17 John Summerson, *Architecture in Britain 1530–1830* (The Pelican History of Art), 1953.

18   K. R. Popper, *The Poverty of Historicism*, London, 1957.
19   Cambridge (Mass.), 1927 (Meridian paperbacks, 1957).
20   Roger Hinks, *Carolingian Art*, London, 1935.
21   J. E. Sandys, *A History of Classical Scholarship*, Cambridge, 1908, esp. Vol. II, "From the Revival of Learning to the End of the Eighteenth Century."

Chapter 2

P. O. Kristeller

■ from **HUMANISM AND SCHOLASTICISM IN THE ITALIAN RENAISSANCE**, in his *Renaissance Thought and its Sources*, New York, 1979, pp. 85–105

[. . .]

THE CHIEF CAUSE OF THE ENTIRE Renaissance controversy, at least in its more recent phases, has been the considerable progress made during the last few decades in the field of medieval studies. The Middle Ages are no longer considered as a period of darkness, and consequently many scholars do not see the need for such new light and revival as the very name of the Renaissance would seem to suggest. Thus certain medievalists have questioned the very existence of the Renaissance and would like to banish the term entirely from the vocabulary of historians.

In the face of this powerful attack, Renaissance scholars have assumed a new line of defense. They have shown that the notion embodied in the term "Renaissance" was not an invention of enthusiastic historians of the last century, but was commonly expressed in the literature of the period of the Renaissance itself. The humanists themselves speak continually of the revival or rebirth of the arts and of learning that was accomplished in their own time after a long period of decay [. . .] Even if we were convinced that it was an empty claim and that the humanists did not bring about a real Renaissance, we would still be forced to admit that the illusion itself was characteristic of that period and that the term Renaissance thus had at least a subjective meaning.

Without questioning the validity of this argument, I think that there are also some more objective reasons for defending the existence and the importance of the Renaissance. The concept of style as it has been so successfully applied by historians of art might be more widely applied in other fields of intellectual history and might thus enable us to recognize the significant changes brought about by the Renaissance, without obliging us to despise the Middle Ages or to minimize the debt of the Renaissance to the medieval tradition.

Moreover, I should like to reexamine the relation between the Middle Ages and the Renaissance in the light of the following consideration. Scholars have become so accustomed to stress the universalism of the medieval church and of medieval culture and also to consider the Italian Renaissance as a European phenomenon that they are apt to forget that profound regional differences existed even during the Middle Ages. The center of medieval civilization was undoubtedly France, and all other countries of Western Europe followed the leadership of that country, from Carolingian times down to the beginning of the fourteenth century. Italy certainly was no exception to that rule; but whereas the other countries, especially England, Germany, and the Low Countries, took an active part in the major cultural pursuits of the period and followed the same general development, Italy occupied a somewhat peculiar position. Prior to the thirteenth century, her active participation in many important aspects of medieval culture lagged far behind that of the other countries. This may be observed in architecture and music, in the religious drama as well as in Latin and vernacular poetry in general, in scholastic philosophy and theology, and even, contrary to common opinion, in classical studies.

On the other hand, Italy had a narrow but persistent tradition of her own which went back to ancient Roman times and which found its expression in certain branches of the arts and of poetry, in lay education and in legal customs, and in the study of grammar and of rhetoric. Italy was more directly and more continually exposed to Byzantine influences than any other Western European country. Finally, after the eleventh century, Italy developed a new life of her own which found expression in her trade and economy, in the political institutions of her cities, in the study of civil and canon law and of medicine, and in the techniques of letter-writing and of secular eloquence. Influences from France became more powerful only with the thirteenth century, when their traces appeared in architecture and music, in Latin and vernacular poetry, in philosophy and theology, and in the field of classical studies. Many typical products of the Italian Renaissance may thus be understood as a result of belated medieval influences received from France, but grafted upon, and assimilated by, a more narrow, but stubborn and different native tradition. This may be said of Dante's *Divine Comedy*, of the religious drama which flourished in fifteenth-century Florence, and of the chivalric poetry of Ariosto and of Tasso.

A similar development may be noticed in the history of learning. The Italian Renaissance thus should be viewed not only in its contrast with the French Middle Ages, but also in its relation to the Italian Middle Ages. The rich civilization of Renaissance Italy did not spring directly from the equally rich civilization of medieval France, but from the much more modest traditions of medieval Italy. It is only about the beginning of the fourteenth century that Italy witnessed a tremendous increase in all her cultural activities, and this enabled her, for a certain period, to wrest from France her cultural leadership in Western Europe. Consequently, there can be no doubt that there was an Italian Renaissance, that is, a cultural Renaissance of Italy, not so much in contrast with the Middle Ages in general or with the French Middle Ages, but very definitely in contrast with the Italian Middle Ages [. . .]

The most characteristic and most pervasive aspect of the Italian Renaissance in the field of learning is the humanist movement. I need hardly say that the term "humanism," when applied to the Italian Renaissance, does not imply all the vague and confused notions that are now commonly associated with it. Only a few traces of these may be found in the Renaissance. By humanism we mean merely the general tendency of the age to attach the greatest importance to classical studies, and to consider classical antiquity as the common standard and model by which to guide all cultural activities. It will be our task to understand the meaning and origin of this humanist movement which is commonly associated with the name of Petrarch.

Among modern historians we encounter mainly two interpretations of Italian humanism. The first interpretation considers the humanist movement merely as the rise of classical scholarship accomplished during the period of the Renaissance. This view which has been held by most historians of classical scholarship is not very popular at present. The revival of classical studies certainly does not impress an age such as ours which has practically abandoned classical education, and it is easy to praise the classical learning of the Middle Ages in a time which, except for a tiny number of specialists, knows much less of classical antiquity than did the Middle Ages. Moreover, in a period such as the present, which has much less regard for learning than for practical achievements and for "creative" writing and "original" thinking, a mere change of orientation, or even an increase of knowledge, in the field of learning does not seem to possess any historical significance. However, the situation in the Renaissance was quite different, and the increase in, and emphasis on, classical learning had a tremendous importance.

There are indeed several historical facts which support the interpretation of the humanist movement as a rise in classical scholarship. The humanists were classical scholars and contributed to the rise of classical studies. In the field of Latin studies, they rediscovered a number of important texts that had been hardly read during the Middle Ages. Also in the case of Latin authors commonly known during the Middle Ages, the humanists made them better known, through their numerous manuscript copies and printed editions, through their grammatical and antiquarian studies, through their commentaries, and through the development and application of philological and historical criticism.

Even more striking was the impulse given by the humanists to the study of Greek. In spite of the political, commercial, and ecclesiastic relations with the Byzantine Empire, during the Middle Ages the number of persons in Western Europe who knew the Greek language was comparatively small, and practically none of them was interested in, or familiar with, Greek classical literature. There was almost no teaching of Greek in Western schools and universities, and almost no Greek manuscripts in Western libraries. In the twelfth and thirteenth centuries, a great number of Greek texts were translated into Latin, either directly or through intermediary Arabic translations, but this activity was almost entirely confined to the fields of mathematics, astronomy, astrology, medicine, and Aristotelian philosophy.

During the Renaissance, this situation rapidly changed. The study of Greek classical literature, which had been cultivated in the Byzantine Empire throughout the latter Middle Ages, after the middle of the fourteenth century began to spread in the West, both through Byzantine scholars who went to Western Europe for a temporary or permanent stay, and through Italian scholars who went to

Constantinople in quest of Greek classical learning. As a result, Greek language and literature acquired a recognized place in the curriculum of Western schools and universities, a place which they did not lose until the present century. A large number of Greek manuscripts was brought from the East to Western libraries, and these manuscripts have formed the basis of most of our editions of the Greek classics. At a later stage, the humanists published printed editions of Greek authors, wrote commentaries on them, and extended their antiquarian and grammatical studies as well as their methods of philological and historical criticism to Greek literature.

No less important, although now less appreciated, were the numerous Latin translations from the Greek due to the humanists of the Renaissance. Almost the whole of Greek poetry, oratory, historiography, theology, and non-Aristotelian philosophy was thus translated for the first time, whereas the medieval translations of Aristotle and of Greek scientific writers were replaced by new humanist translations. These Latin translations of the Renaissance were the basis for most of the vernacular translations of the Greek classics, and they were much more widely read than were the original Greek texts. For in spite of its remarkable increase, the study of Greek even in the Renaissance never attained the same general importance as did the study of Latin which was rooted in the medieval tradition of the West. Nevertheless, it remains a remarkable fact that the study of the Greek classics was taken over by the humanists of Western Europe at the very time when it was affected in the East by the decline and fall of the Byzantine Empire.

If we care to remember these impressive facts, we certainly cannot deny that the Italian humanists were the ancestors of modern philologists and historians. Even a historian of science can afford to despise them only if he chooses to remember that science is the subject of his study, but to forget that the method he is applying to this subject is that of history.

However, the activity of the Italian humanists was not limited to classical scholarship, and hence the theory which interprets the humanist movement merely as a rise in classical scholarship is not altogether satisfactory. This theory fails to explain the ideal of eloquence persistently set forth in the writings of the humanists, and it fails to account for the enormous literature of treatises, of letters, of speeches, and of poems produced by the humanists. These writings are far more numerous than the contributions of the humanists to classical scholarship, and they cannot be explained as a necessary consequence of their classical studies. A modern classical scholar is not supposed to write a Latin poem in praise of his city, to welcome a distinguished foreign visitor with a Latin speech, or to write a political manifesto for his government. This aspect of the activity of the humanists is often dismissed with a slighting remark about their vanity or their fancy for speech-making. I do not deny that they were vain and loved to make speeches, but I am inclined to offer a different explanation for this side of their activity. The humanists were not classical scholars who for personal reasons had a craving for eloquence, but, vice versa, they were professional rhetoricians, heirs and successors of the medieval rhetoricians, who developed the belief, then new and modern, that the best way to achieve eloquence was to imitate classical models, and who thus were driven to study the classics and to found classical philology. Their rhetorical ideals and achievements may not correspond to our taste, but they were the starting point and moving force of their activity, and their classical learning was incidental to it.

The other current interpretation of Italian humanism, which is prevalent among historians of philosophy and also accepted by many other scholars, is more ambitious, but in my opinion less sound. This interpretation considers humanism as the new philosophy of the Renaissance, which arose in opposition to scholasticism, the old philosophy of the Middle Ages.

Of course, there is the well-known fact that several famous humanists, such as Petrarch, Valla, Erasmus, and Vives, were violent critics of medieval learning and tended to replace it by classical learning. Moreover, the humanists certainly had ideals of learning, education, and life that differed from medieval modes of thinking. They wrote treatises on moral, educational, political, and religious questions which in tone and content differ from the average medieval treatises on similar subjects.

Yet this interpretation of humanism as a new philosophy fails to account for a number of obvious facts. On one hand, we notice a stubborn survival of scholastic philosophy throughout the Italian Renaissance, an inconvenient fact that is usually explained by the intellectual inertia of the respective philosophers whom almost nobody has read for centuries and whose number, problems and literary production are entirely unknown to most historians. On the other, most of the works of the humanists have nothing to do with philosophy even in the vaguest possible sense of the term. Even their treatises on philosophical subjects, if we care to read them, appear in most cases rather superficial and inconclusive if compared with the works of ancient or medieval philosophers, a fact that may be indifferent to a general historian, but which cannot be overlooked by a historian of philosophy.

I think there has been a tendency, in the light of later developments, and under the influence of a modern aversion to scholasticism, to exaggerate the opposition of the humanists to scholasticism, and to assign to them an importance in the history of scientific and philosophical thought which they neither could nor did attain. The reaction against this tendency has been inevitable, but it has been equally wrong. Those scholars who read the treatises of the humanists and noticed their comparative emptiness of scientific and philosophical thought came to the conclusion that the humanists were bad scientists and philosophers who did not live up to their own claims or to those of their modern advocates. I should like to suggest that the Italian humanists on the whole were neither good nor bad philosophers, but no philosophers at all.

The humanist movement did not originate in the field of philosophical or scientific studies, but it arose in that of grammatical and rhetorical studies. The humanists continued the medieval tradition in these fields, as represented, for example, by the *ars dictaminis* and the *ars arengandi*, but they gave it a new direction toward classical standards and classical studies, possibly under the impact of influences received from France after the middle of the thirteenth century. This new development of the field was followed by an enormous growth, both in quantity and in quality, of its teaching and literary production. As a result of this growth, the claims of the humanists for their field of study also increased considerably. They claimed, and temporarily attained, a decided predominance of their field in elementary and secondary education, and a much larger share for it in professional and university education. This development in the field of grammatical and rhetorical studies finally affected the other branches of learning, but it did not displace them. After the middle of the fifteenth century, we find an increasing number of professional jurists, physicians, mathematicians, philosophers, and theologians who cultivated humanist studies along with their own particular fields of study. Consequently, a humanist influence began to appear in all these other sciences. It appears in the studied elegance of literary expression, in the increasing use made of classical source materials, in the greater knowledge of history and of critical methods, and also sometimes in an emphasis on new problems. This influence of humanism on the other sciences certainly was important, but it did not affect the content or substance of the medieval traditions in those sciences. For the humanists, being amateurs in those other fields, had nothing to offer that could replace their traditional content and subject matter.

The humanist criticism of medieval science is often sweeping, but it does not touch its specific problems and subject matter. Their main charges are against the bad Latin style of the medieval authors, against their ignorance of ancient history and literature, and against their concern for supposedly useless questions. On the other hand, even those professional scientists who were most profoundly influenced by humanism did not sacrifice the medieval tradition of their field. It is highly significant that Pico, a representative of humanist philosophy, and Alciato, a representative of humanist jurisprudence, found it necessary to defend their medieval predecessors against the criticism of humanist rhetoricians.

Yet if the humanists were amateurs in jurisprudence, theology, medicine, and also in philosophy, they were themselves professionals in a number of other fields. Their domains were the fields of grammar, rhetoric, poetry, history, and the study of the Greek and Latin authors. They also expanded into the field of moral philosophy, and they made some attempts to invade the field of logic, which were chiefly attempts to reduce logic to rhetoric.

Yet they did not make any direct contributions to the other branches of philosophy or of science. Moreover, much of the humanist polemic against medieval science was not even intended as a criticism of the contents or methods of that science, but merely represents a phase in the "battle of the arts," that is, a noisy advertisement for the field of learning advocated by the humanists, in order to neutralize and to overcome the claims of other, rivaling sciences. Hence I am inclined to consider the humanists not as philosophers with a curious lack of philosophical ideas and a curious fancy for eloquence and for classical studies, but rather as professional rhetoricians with a new, classicist idea of culture, who tried to assert the importance of their field of learning and to impose their standards upon the other fields of learning and of science, including philosophy.

Let us try to illustrate this outline with a few more specific facts. When we inquire of the humanists, it is often asserted that they were freelance writers who came to form an entirely new class in Renaissance society. This statement is valid, although with some qualification, for a very small number of outstanding humanists like Petrarch, Boccaccio, and Erasmus. However, these are exceptions, and the vast majority of humanists exercised either of two professions, and sometimes both of them. They were either secretaries of princes or cities, or they were teachers of grammar and rhetoric at universities or secondary schools. The opinion so often repeated by historians that the humanist movement originated outside the schools and universities is a myth which cannot be supported by factual evidence. Moreover, as chancellors and as teachers, the humanists, far from representing a new class, were the professional heirs and successors of the medieval rhetoricians, the so-called *dictatores*, who also made their career exactly in these same two professions. The humanist Coluccio Salutati occupied exactly the same place in the society and culture of his time as did the *dictator* Petrus de Vineis one hundred and fifty years before. Nevertheless there was a significant difference between them. The style of writing used by Salutati is quite different from that of Petrus de Vineis or of Rolandinus Passagerii. Moreover, the study and imitation of the classics which was of little or no importance to the medieval *dictatores* has become the major concern for Salutati. Finally, whereas the medieval *dictatores* attained considerable importance in politics and in administration, the humanists, through their classical learning, acquired for their class a much greater cultural and social prestige. Thus the humanists did not invent a new field of learning or a new professional activity, but they introduced a new, classicist style into the traditions of medieval Italian rhetoric. To blame them for not having invented rhetorical studies would be like blaming Giotto for not having been the inventor of painting.

The same result is confirmed by an examination of the literary production of the humanists if we try to trace the medieval antecedents of the types of litera-ture cultivated by the humanists. If we leave aside the editions and translations of the humanists, their classical interests are chiefly represented by their numerous commentaries on ancient authors and by a number of antiquarian and miscella-neous treatises. Theoretical works on grammar and rhetoric, mostly composed for the school, are quite frequent, and even more numerous is the literature of humanist historiography. Dialogues and treatises on questions of moral philosophy, educa-tion, politics, and religion have attracted most of the attention of modern historians, but represent a comparatively small proportion of humanist literature. By far the largest part of that literature, although relatively neglected and partly unpublished, consists of the poems, the speeches, and the letters of the humanists.

If we look for the medieval antecedents of these various types of humanist literature, we are led back in many cases to the Italian grammarians and rhetori-cians of the later Middle Ages. This is most obvious for the theoretical treatises on grammar and rhetoric. Less generally recognized, but almost equally obvious is the link between humanist epistolography and medieval *ars dictaminis*. The style of writing is different, to be sure, and the medieval term *dictamen* was no longer used during the Renaissance, yet the literary and political function of the letter was basically the same, and the ability to write a correct and elegant Latin letter was still a major aim of school instruction in the Renaissance as it had been in the Middle Ages.

The same link between humanists and medieval Italian rhetoricians which we notice in the field of epistolography may be found also in the field of oratory. Most historians of rhetoric give the impression that medieval rhetoric was exclu-sively concerned with letter-writing and preaching, represented by the *ars dictaminis* and the somewhat younger *ars praedicandi*, and that there was no secular eloquence in the Middle Ages. On the other hand, most historians of Renaissance humanism believe that the large output of humanist oratory, although of a somewhat dubious value, was an innovation of the Renaissance due to the effort of the humanists to revive ancient oratory and also to their vain fancy for speech-making. Only in recent years have a few scholars begun to realize that there was a considerable amount of secular eloquence in the Middle Ages, especially in Italy. I do not hesitate to conclude that the eloquence of the humanists was the continuation of the medieval *ars arengandi* just as their epistolography continued the tradition of the *ars dictaminis*. It is true, in taking up a type of literary production developed by their medieval predecessors, the humanists modified its style according to their own taste and classicist standards. Yet the practice of speech-making was no invention of the humanists, of course, since it is hardly absent from any human society, and since in medieval Italy it can be traced back at least to the eleventh century.

Even the theory of secular speech, represented by rules and instructions as well as by model speeches, appears in Italy at least as early as the thirteenth century. Indeed practically all types of humanist oratory have their antecedents in this medieval literature: wedding and funeral speeches, academic speeches, political speeches by officials or ambassadors, decorative speeches on solemn occasions, and finally judicial speeches. Some of these types, to be sure, had their classical models, but others, for example, academic speeches delivered at the beginning of the year or of a particular course or upon conferring or receiving a degree, had no classical antecedents whatsoever, and all these types of oratory were rooted in very specific customs and institutions of medieval Italy. The humanists invented hardly any of these types of speech, but merely applied their standards of style and elegance to a previously existing form of literary expression and thus satisfied a demand, both practical and artistic, of the society of their time. Modern scholars are apt to speak contemptuously of this humanist oratory, denouncing its empty rhetoric and its lack of "deep thoughts." Yet the humanists merely intended to speak well, according to their taste and to the occasion, and it still remains to be seen whether they were less successful in that respect than their medieval predecessors or their modern successors. Being pieces of "empty rhetoric," their speeches provide us with an amazing amount of information about the personal and intellectual life of their time.

[. . .]

The same [continuity between humanism and the Middle Ages] may be said with more confidence of the literature of commentaries on the Latin classics, which are the direct result of school teaching. It is often asserted that Italy throughout the Middle Ages was closer to the classical tradition than any other European country. Yet if we try to trace the type of the humanist commentary back into the Middle Ages, we find hardly any commentary on a Latin poet or prose writer composed in Italy prior to the second half of the thirteenth century, whereas we find many such commentaries, from the ninth century on, written in France and the other Western countries that followed the French development. Only after 1300, that is, after the earliest phase of humanism, did Italy produce an increasing number of such commentaries. Also, there is very little evidence of antiquarian studies in Italy prior to the latter part of the thirteenth century.

Whereas we have abundant information about the reading of the Latin poets and prose writers in the medieval schools of France and other Western countries, and whereas such centers as Chartres and Orléans in the twelfth and early thir-teenth centuries owed much of their fame to the study of the Latin classics, the sources for Italy are silent during the same period and begin to speak only after the middle of the thirteenth century. It was only after the beginning of the four-teenth century that the teaching of poetry and the classical authors became firmly established in the Italian schools and universities, to continue without interruption throughout the Renaissance. Italian libraries, with the one exception of Monte Cassino, were not so well furnished with Latin classical poets as were some French and German libraries, and it has been noticed that the humanists of the fifteenth century made most of their manuscript discoveries not in Italy but in other coun-tries. The conclusion seems inevitable that the study of classical Latin authors was comparatively neglected in Italy during the earlier Middle Ages and was intro-duced from France after the middle of the thirteenth century. The Italian humanists thus took up the work of their medieval French predecessors just about the time when classical studies began to decline in France, and whereas the classical schol-arship of the earliest humanists in its range and method was still close to the medieval tradition, that of the later Renaissance developed far beyond anything attained during the Middle Ages. Consequently, if we consider the entire literary production of the Italian humanists we are led to the conclusion that the humanist movement seems to have originated from a fusion between the novel interest in classical studies imported from France toward the end of the thirteenth century and the much earlier traditions of medieval Italian rhetoric.

We have seen that the humanists did not live outside the schools and univer-sities, but were closely connected with them. The chairs commonly held by the humanists were those of grammar and rhetoric, that is, the same that had been occupied by their medieval predecessors, the *dictatores*. Thus it is in the history of the universities and schools and of their chairs that the connection of the human-ists with medieval rhetoric becomes most apparent. However, under the influence of humanism, these chairs underwent a change which affected their name as well as their content and pretenses. About the beginning of the fourteenth century poetry appears as a special teaching subject at Italian universities. After that time, the teaching of grammar was considered primarily as the task of elementary instruc-tors, whereas the humanists proper held the more advanced chairs of poetry and of eloquence. For eloquence was the equivalent of prose writing as well as of speech. The teaching of poetry and of eloquence was theoretical and practical at the same time, for the humanist professor instructed his pupils in verse-making and speech-making both through rules and through models. Since classical Latin authors were considered as the chief models for imitation, the reading of these authors was inseparably connected with the theoretical and practical teaching of poetry and of eloquence.

[. . .]

Later on, the fields of study cultivated by the humanists were given a new and more ambitious name. Taking up certain expressions found in Cicero and Gellius, the humanists as early as the fourteenth century began to call their field of learning the humane studies or the studies befitting a human being (*studia human-itatis, studia humaniora*). The new name certainly implies a new claim and program, but it covered a content that had existed long before and that had been designated by the more modest names of grammar, rhetoric, and poetry. Although some modern scholars were not aware of this fact, the humanists certainly were, and we have several contemporary testimonies showing that the *studia humanitatis* were considered as the equivalent of grammar, rhetoric, poetry, history, and moral philosophy.

These statements also prove another point that has been confused by most modern historians: the humanists, at least in Italy or before the sixteenth century, did not claim that they were substituting a new encyclopaedia of learning for the medieval one, and they were aware of the fact that their field of study occupied a well defined and limited place within the system of contemporary learning. To be sure, they intended to emphasize the importance of their field in comparison with the other sciences and to encroach upon the latter's territory, but on the whole they did not deny the existence or validity of these other sciences.

This well defined place of the *studia humanitatis* is reflected in the new term *humanista* which apparently was coined during the latter half of the fifteenth century and became increasingly popular during the sixteenth. The term seems to have originated in the slang of university students and gradually penetrated into official usage. It was coined after the model of such medieval terms as *legista, jurista, canonista*, and *artista*, and it designated the professional teacher of the *studia humanitatis*. Thus the term *humanista* in this limited sense was coined during the Renaissance, whereas the term *humanism* was first used by nineteenth-century historians. If I am not mistaken, the new term *humanism* reflects the modern and false conception that Renaissance humanism was a basically new philosophical movement, and under the influence of this notion the old term humanist has also been misunderstood as designating the representative of a new *Weltanschauung*. The old term *humanista*, on the other hand, reflects the more modest, but correct, contemporary view that the humanists were the teachers and representatives of a certain branch of learning which at that time was expanding and in vogue, but well limited in its subject matter. Humanism thus did not represent the sum total of learning in the Italian Renaissance.

If we are to look beyond the field of the humanities into the other fields of learning as they were cultivated during the Italian Renaissance, that is, into jurisprudence, medicine, theology, mathematics, and natural philosophy, what we find is evidently a continuation of medieval learning and may hence very well be called scholasticism. Since the term has been subject to controversy, I should like to say that I do not attach any unfavorable connotation to the term scholasticism. As its characteristic, I do not consider any particular doctrine, but rather a specific method, that is, the type of logical argument represented by the form of the *Questio*.

It is well known that the content of scholastic philosophy, since the thirteenth century, was largely based on the writings of Aristotle, and that the development of this philosophy, since the twelfth century, was closely connected with the schools and universities of France and England, especially with the universities of Paris and Oxford. The place of Italy, however, is less known in the history and development of scholastic philosophy. Several Italians are found among the most famous philosophers and theologians of the twelfth and thirteenth centuries, but practically all of them did their studying and teaching in France. Whereas Italy had flourishing schools of rhetoric, jurisprudence, and medicine during the twelfth and early thirteenth century, she had no native center of philosophical studies during the same period. After 1220 the new mendicant orders established schools of theology and philosophy in many Italian cities, but unlike those in France and England, these schools of the friars for a long time had no links with the Italian universities. Regular chairs of theology were not established at the Italian universities before the middle of the fourteenth century, and even after that period, the university teaching of theology continued to be spotty and irregular.

Aristotelian philosophy, although not entirely unknown at Salerno toward the end of the twelfth century, made its regular appearance at the Italian universities after the middle of the thirteenth century and in close connection with the teaching of medicine. I think it is safe to assume that Aristotelian philosophy was imported at that time from France as were the study of classical authors and many other forms of intellectual activity. After the beginning of the fourteenth century, this Italian Aristotelianism assumed a more definite shape. The teaching of logic and natural philosophy became a well-established part of the university curriculum and even spread to some of the secondary schools. An increasing number of commentaries and questions on the works of Aristotle reflect this teaching tradition, and numerous systematic treatises on philosophical subjects show the same general trend and background. During the fourteenth and fifteenth centuries, further influences were received from Paris in the field of natural philosophy and from Oxford in the field of logic; and from the latter part of the fourteenth century on we can trace an unbroken tradition of Italian Aristotelianism which continued through the fifteenth and sixteenth century and far into the seventeenth century.

The common notion that scholasticism as an old philosophy was superseded by the new philosophy of humanism is thus again disproved by plain facts. For Italian scholasticism originated toward the end of the thirteenth century, that is, about the same time as did Italian humanism, and both traditions developed side by side throughout the period of the Renaissance and even thereafter.

However, the two traditions had their locus and center in two different sectors of learning: humanism in the field of grammar, rhetoric, and poetry and to some extent in moral philosophy, scholasticism in the fields of logic and natural philosophy. Everybody knows the eloquent attacks launched by Petrarch and Bruni against the logicians of their time, and it is generally believed that these attacks represent a vigorous new movement rebelling against an old entrenched habit of thought. Yet actually the English method of dialectic was quite as novel at the Italian schools of that time as were the humanist studies advocated by Petrarch and Bruni, and the humanist attack was as much a matter of departmental rivalry as it was a clash of opposite ideas or philosophies. Bruni even hints at one point that he is not speaking quite in earnest.

Such controversies, interesting as they are, were mere episodes in a long period of peaceful coexistence between humanism and scholasticism. Actually the humanists quarreled as much among each other as they did with the scholastics. Moreover, it would be quite wrong to consider these controversies as serious battles over basic principles whereas many of them were meant to be merely personal feuds, intellectual tournaments, or rhetorical exercises. Finally, any attempt to reduce these controversies to one issue must fail since the discussions were concerned with many diverse and overlapping issues. Therefore, we should no longer be surprised that Italian Aristotelianism quietly and forcefully survived the attacks of Petrarch and his humanist successors.

But the Aristotelianism of the Renaissance did not remain untouched by the new influence of humanism. Philosophers began to make abundant use of the Greek text and the new Latin translations of Aristotle, his ancient commentators, and other Greek thinkers. The revival of ancient philosophies that came in the wake of the humanist movement, especially the revival of Platonism and of Stoicism, left a strong impact upon the Aristotelian philosophers of the Renaissance. Yet in spite of these significant modifications, Renaissance Aristotelianism continued the medieval scholastic tradition without any visible break. It preserved a firm hold on the university chairs of logic, natural philosophy, and metaphysics, whereas even the humanist professors of moral philosophy continued to base their lectures on Aristotle. The literary activity of these Aristotelian philosophers is embodied in a large number of commentaries, questions, and treatises. This literature is difficult of access and arduous to read, but rich in philosophical problems and doctrines. It represents the bulk and kernel of the philosophical thought of the period, but it has been badly neglected by modern historians. Scholars hostile to the Middle Ages considered this literature an unfortunate survival of medieval traditions that may be safely disregarded, whereas the true modern spirit of the Renaissance is expressed in the literature of the humanists. Medievalists, on the other hand, have largely concentrated on the earlier phases of scholastic philosophy and gladly sacrificed the later scholastics to the criticism of the humanists and their modern followers, a tendency that has been further accentuated by the recent habit of identifying scholasticism with Thomism.

Consequently, most modern scholars have condemned the Aristotelian philosophers of the Renaissance without a hearing, labeling them as empty quibblers and as followers of a dead past who failed to understand the living problems of their new times. Recent works on the civilization of the Renaissance thus often repeat the charges made against the Aristotelian philosophers by the humanists of their time, and even give those attacks a much more extreme meaning than they were originally intended to have. Other scholars who are equally unfavorable to the humanists include both scholastics and humanists in a summary sentence that reflects the judgments of seventeenth-century scientists and philosophers. Only a few famous figures such as Pietro Pomponazzi seem to resist the general verdict.

There has been a tendency to present Pomponazzi and a few other thinkers as basically different from the other Aristotelians of their time and as closely related with the humanists or with the later scientists. This is merely an attempt to reconcile the respect for Pomponazzi with modern preconceptions against the Aristotelians of the Renaissance. Actually Pomponazzi does not belong to the humanists or to the later scientists, but to the tradition of medieval and Renaissance Aristotelianism. The number of modern scholars who have actually read some of the works of the Italian Aristotelians is comparatively small [. . .]

Thus we may conclude that the humanism and the scholasticism of the Renaissance arose in medieval Italy about the same time, that is, about the end of the thirteenth century, and that they coexisted and developed all the way through and beyond the Renaissance period as different branches of learning. Their controversy, much less persistent and violent than usually represented, is merely a phase in the battle of the arts, not a struggle for existence. We may compare it to the debates of the arts in medieval literature, to the rivaling claims of medicine and law at the universities, or to the claims advanced by Leonardo in his *Paragone* for the superiority of painting over the other arts. Humanism certainly had a tendency to influence the other sciences and to expand at their expense, but all kinds of adjustments and combinations between humanism and scholasticism were possible and were successfully accomplished. It is only after the Renaissance, through the rise of modern science and modern philosophy, that Aristotelianism was gradually displaced, whereas humanism became gradually detached from its rhetorical background and evolved into modern philology and history.

[. . .]

Chapter 3

Hanna Gray

■   from **RENAISSANCE HUMANISM: THE PURSUIT OF ELOQUENCE**, *Journal of the History of Ideas*, 24 (1963), pp. 497–514

T HE DIFFICULTIES AND DANGERS of reducing Renaissance humanism to some single formula have become increasingly apparent. Renaissance humanism contained many schools of thought, and it is clear that the differences and changes within humanism must be examined both in themselves and in their relation to particular historical situations in order to gain a true appreciation of the humanist movement. But even while stressing the essential elements of diversity, it is possible to discern some constant features in the tradition of Renaissance humanism, certain basic presuppositions and attitudes which identify the movement as a whole. To suggest such a common denominator is not to maintain that one may thereby explain humanism – for this cannot be done by treating the history of ideas in isolation – nor to claim that one may thus assess the full significance of any individual humanist. Nonetheless, some understanding of what makes humanists alike may provide a meaningful background to the analysis of humanist texts and can throw into sharper focus the manner in which various schools of humanism do differ.

Modern commentators have too often distinguished between "form" and "substance" in their consideration of humanist literature. In their anxiety to penetrate to the significant ideas of humanism, they have regarded these as separable from the formal structures within which those ideas were expressed. So, paradoxically, the conventions which, to the humanists, created an intelligible and constant frame of reference through which they could communicate clearly with their audience have been cast aside by a later age as irrelevant to the exposition and comprehension of their mode of thought. As a result, the particular assumptions underlying the humanists' own stress on form have not always been treated sufficiently as an integral dimension of their thought. It is curious that many interpreters who have pointed out the humanists' insistence on reading classical works as a whole and in context should not have drawn from such assertions the conclusion that the humanists intended their works to be approached in the same spirit; that their writings were, perhaps, designed with that specific expectation in mind.

It may be objected that much humanist writing is wordy, tedious, repetitive, so that the historian of ideas can justifiably abstract what is really interesting. Or it may be objected that much humanist writing cannot be taken seriously as literature. But in the analysis of the humanists' thought and work, their pretensions must be considered, their stated purposes kept in mind. To that end, it is essential to understand the humanists' reiterated claim, that theirs was the pursuit of eloquence. That claim, indeed, reveals the identifying characteristic of Renaissance humanism. The bond which united humanists, no matter how far separated in outlook or in time, was a conception of eloquence and its uses. Through it, they shared a common intellectual method and a broad agreement on the value of that method. Classical rhetoric – or classical rhetoric as interpreted and adapted in the Renaissance – constituted the main source for both. It provided the humanists with a body of precepts for the effective communication of ideas and, equally important, with a set of principles which asserted the central role of rhetorical skill and achievement in human affairs.

In pointing to the rhetorical concerns of Renaissance humanism, it is not necessary to conclude, as has sometimes been done, that humanist writing was "merely rhetorical" or that humanism was a "merely literary" movement. The term "rhetoric" must be divorced from its pejorative associations. By "rhetoric" the humanists did not intend an empty pomposity, a willful mendacity, a love of display for its own sake, an extravagant artificiality, a singular lack of originality, or a necessary subordination of substance to form and ornament. Nor did the humanists identify rhetoric with "sophistry" in the popular sense, as the specious manipulation of language and argument for purposes of deception. They distinguished carefully between "true eloquence" and "sophistry," perceiving in the latter a perversion, not a consequence, of the former. True eloquence, according to the humanists, could arise only out of a harmonious union between wisdom and style; its aim was to guide men toward virtue and worthwhile goals, not to mislead them for vicious or trivial purposes. It was this conception of eloquence which the humanists placed in opposition to scholastic philosophy. Scholasticism they criticized both on aesthetic grounds and for its failure to concentrate on "wisdom," on really essential matters. In this controversy, the humanists were not contrasting one finished philosophical system with another, but neither were they simply opposing literary form to philosophical substance.

Professor Kristeller has demonstrated conclusively that the interpretation of humanism as a new system of thought locked in mortal combat with scholasticism cannot be maintained. Systematic philosophy, as he points out, was precisely what the earlier humanists did not profess; their interest lay rather in the realm of the *studia humanitatis*, or of the liberal arts, understood generally as comprising the studies of grammar, rhetoric, poetry, history, and moral philosophy. Hence the term "humanist" originally had reference to this preoccupation with the "humanities" and was first used to describe the professional teacher of the *studia humanitatis*. Professor Kristeller has argued also – and here his emphasis seems to me somewhat misleading – that in their capacity as teachers and practitioners of this largely literary culture, the humanists belonged to and continued an older profession, that of the medieval *dictatores;* that their concerns can be understood to a considerable extent as an outgrowth of their calling as rhetoricians; and that their contribution lay not in the creation of a new field of activity, but rather in their insistence on the cultivation of a more classical style, on the imitation of classical models, within the forms already prescribed and followed by their medieval predecessors. Thus the humanists emerge as a professional group whose activities and ideas can be explained as a function of their calling, and their conflicts with scholastics may be seen as typical academic disputes between disciplines which were always struggling to achieve a larger jurisdiction without questioning one another's existence.

That Renaissance humanism falls into the larger rhetorical tradition of the West, a tradition which persisted in the Middle Ages, is beyond doubt. The humanists did not invent rhetoric, and many of their ideas, including their stress on classicism, had been anticipated in the thirteenth-century *ars dictaminis*. It is true, too, that the rhetorical tradition carried with it certain kinds of writing, certain types of educational activities, a tendency toward certain beliefs. But with internal variations accompanying that tradition there may come important shifts in the specific convictions which define the intellectual outlook of its adherents. Those variations may not be so great objectively as they appeared subjectively to those who developed them, but the subjective consciousness of novelty is of some historical significance. To say that the humanists merely introduced a more classical tone into a fixed series of activities does not indicate why it appeared so essential to them to return to the classical models of the *studia humanitatis*, or why they failed to recognize, indeed disclaimed, continuity with medieval practice. To suggest that their attitudes are explicable in terms of their professional concerns, which are naturally in competition with those of other professions, does not explain how they articulated those concerns, how and why in a particular age men should have turned to rhetoric and claimed for it a special educational and cultural role.

A given Renaissance humanist might be in the technical sense a professional rhetorician; the humanist as such need not be. Certainly the term "humanist," as first applied in the later fifteenth and earlier sixteenth centuries, referred specifically to the professional teachers of the humanities, and these teachers often occupied chairs of rhetoric. Yet many who participated in the humanist movement would not come under this description. Before the word "humanist" gained general currency, the humanists were referring to themselves and to their colleagues by other names – sometimes "philosophers," often "poets." Most frequently, however, they called themselves "orators." By this, they meant not that they made a living by the teaching or practice of oratory, but that they wished to be known as men of eloquence. An "orator" could have made his career in government, in the Church, in leisured study and collecting, in teaching or writing or scholarship. He might have written poetry or history or commentaries on classical texts; he might have composed treatises on moral or political philosophy; he might have devoted himself to translation or editing. Usually, of course, his work included a variety of these activities. The orator was, by definition and inclination, a non-specialist. Further, the humanist's attack on scholasticism and his defense of the studies of the humanities represented more than a struggle for academic precedence, even though it was not all-out war of displacement. While the humanists did not oppose a new systematic philosophy to the systems of the scholastics, they did oppose to the method of the scholastics another method, and to the values which they believed implied in scholastic method, a different ideal of the aims of knowledge and debate.

The Renaissance humanists believed that education should equip a man to lead a good life, and that therefore the function of knowledge was not merely to demonstrate the truth of given precepts, but to impel people toward their acceptance and application. They believed also that men could be moulded most effectively, and perhaps only, through the art of eloquence, which endowed the precept with life, immediacy, persuasive effect, and which stimulated a man's will as well as informing his reason. In attacking scholastic logic and scholastic Latin, the humanists were condemning at once an attitude toward knowledge which appeared to stress the abstract and intellectual, to have no true utility or direct relevance for human life, and criticizing what they regarded as the failure of the scholastics to communicate important truths with persuasive effect. The humanists had a horror of abstract speculation carried on for its own sake, of specialization which led to absorption in purely "theoretical" questions or in the elaboration of exclusively "technical" concerns. Their orientation was toward rhetoric rather than logic, ethics rather than metaphysics; their interest lay in questions of education rather than of epistemology, in the subject-matter of literature rather than of natural philosophy. The humanists were contrasting a general and practical culture to the professional and academic activities and attitudes which, in their interpretation, were symbolized by scholasticism. Whether their understanding of scholasticism was correct is, for the moment, immaterial. What matters is the image of scholasticism which they built up and the ideal of eloquence which they proposed to substitute. The central point of this contrast was formulated in terms of the "merely intellectual" on the one side, the "actively persuasive" on the other.

Always, in comparing and preferring the classical author of eloquence to the scholastic philosopher, the humanist states that the first not only makes one see what virtue is, but makes one feel and will to practice it. "The object of the will," Petrarch maintained, "is to be good; that of the intellect is truth. It is better to will the good than to know the truth." Against the Aristotle of the scholastics, from whom one may gain a greater learning, but not a more intense desire for virtue, Petrarch asserts the claims of the great Roman authors, Cicero, Seneca, and Horace in particular:

> . . . they stamp and drive deep into the heart the sharpest and most ardent stings of speech, by which the lazy are startled, the ailing are kindled, and the sleepy aroused, the sick healed, and the prostrate raised, and those who stick to the ground lifted up to the highest thoughts and to honest desire. Then earthly things become vile; the aspect of vice stirs up an enormous hatred of vicious life; virtue and "the shape, and as it were, the face of honesty," are beheld by the inmost eye "and inspire miraculous love" of wisdom and of themselves, "as Plato says."

[. . .] For the humanists, it was of course the studies of the liberal arts which affected will as well as intellect in the appropriate way. These studies had been given eloquent expression in classical literature; they were concretely embodied in a series of texts. The ancient texts as they stood proved, to the humanist, that knowledge and eloquence were necessarily related. The *studia humanitatis* could be pursued through the masterpieces of the past. Their relevance to human experience needed no demonstration. Their capacity to teach men, to spur them to achievement, had been tested. While individually the *studia humanitatis* possessed different subject-matters and aims, together they represented an interconnected whole, sharing the common purposes and methods of eloquence. What was needed was a return to those sources which exemplified the humanists' ideals. The liberal arts were to be re-endowed with eloquence through the imitation of the classical models. They would become again the basis of a general education and of an integrated culture, replacing the arid specialization of contemporary learning. The modern orator, reviving ancient tradition, would become a teacher of life as well as of letters.

The humanists' stand on eloquence implied an almost incredible faith in the power of the word. The sweeping claims which ancient writers on rhetoric had made for the impact of oratory were reiterated by the humanists for the written as for the spoken word. The classical precepts governing the art of oratory were now applied to all forms of literature. The process of merging rhetoric and literature within a generalized view of eloquence had been initiated already in later antiquity, and the humanists continued and extended this development. For them, after all, the existing models of eloquence were precisely the surviving texts. The written word of the past still possessed vital authority, still enclosed the essential material of useful knowledge and right action, still enabled men to visualize and benefit from the heroes, institutions, and ideas of the ancient world. Antiquity had life and force because of its perpetuation in literature.

For Petrarch and his successors, Cicero's oration *Pro Archia* was a sacred text. They often cited or adopted the passage which celebrated the role of letters as bestowing glory upon subject and author alike, maintaining that letters provide the best, even the exclusive vehicle of immortality for men, deeds, and ideas. The speech might be invoked in its original sense to apply to poetry, as by Petrarch in his coronation oration, but it was also used to expound the claims of eloquence as a whole. And a favorite commonplace of the fifteenth century was to deplore the darkness of the Middle Ages, dark not because they lacked men of talent or noble acts, but because the light of eloquence had not illuminated and so preserved them. Hence they languished *in tenebris*.

The humanists followed the Ciceronian tradition also in their portrait of the orator as hero. The true orator, they maintained, should combine wide learning, extensive experience – and, according to most humanists, good character with persuasive capacity. His role was to instruct, to delight, and to move men toward worthwhile goals. His eloquence would represent a unity of content, structure, and form, without ever losing sight of the sovereignty of substance or of the didactic aims which were to be realized, and could only be realized, through the cooperation of argument and style. Without his eloquence, truth would lie mute, knowledge would never serve the reality of human affairs or speak to the needs of worldly existence. The other arts would be lost, society ill-organized; justice might not triumph nor evil be vanquished. The humanists' *uomo universale*, if such there was, is to be found in their picture of the ideal orator, master of many arts and governor of his fellowmen, through the force of his eloquence forging a link between the intellectual and practical spheres of human experience.

In Cicero's *De Oratore*, the influence of the great orator had been described in these terms:

> It is the part of the orator, when advising on affairs of supreme impor-
> tance, to unfold his opinion as a man having authority; his duty too is
> to arouse a listless nation, and to curb its unbridled impetuosity. By
> one and the same power of eloquence the deceitful among mankind
> are brought to destruction, and the righteous to deliverance. Who more
> passionately than the orator can encourage to virtuous conduct, or more
> zealously than he reclaim from vicious courses? Who can more austerely
> censure the wicked, or more gracefully praise men of worth? Whose
> invective can more forcibly subdue the power of lawless desire? Whose
> comfortable words can soothe grief more tenderly?

These and similar ideas were repeated over and over in humanist writing; another commonplace, but a commonplace taken seriously. Its truth, the humanists believed, had been proved in antiquity [. . .] [Such] assumptions grew out of the conviction that knowledge should serve practical ends, that human learning ought to have utility for human life, that education should instruct both will and intellect, and that in persuasion and eloquent discussion lie the effective means of conveying truth. In turning to rhetoric as the teacher of these means, the humanists derived from it more than literary formulae, slogans about education, or aesthetic satisfaction. The subjects which seemed to them of interest were just those which, according to the ancient rhetorician, fell within the province of eloquence. Equally important, rhetoric provided a source for the humanists' basic modes of argument and analysis. Ancient doctrine held that it was the function of rhetoric to argue over matters which presented alternative possibilities, problems about which different points of view could be maintained, questions open to debate because they could be judged only in terms of probable truth and were not susceptible to scientific demonstrations of irrefutable validity. The principal questions to which the humanists addressed themselves could be ascribed to this category. Thus they developed their ideas in the framework of rhetorical argumentation not only because of their artistic and didactic ideals, but also because their discussions appeared to fall naturally within the area to which rhetorical analysis was applicable.

[. . .]

Their presuppositions about eloquence identified the humanists with no one school of philosophy. The same general assumptions could be adopted and developed by men who maintained quite different positions on the role of human will and reason, the relative value of the active and contemplative lives, or the relationship between secular learning and religious concerns. However, in reflecting on such issues the humanists recognized certain common boundaries, outlined by their concern with rhetoric and by the structure of belief which underlay it, and these in turn influenced both the form and the substance of their theoretical discussions. For the majority of humanists, philosophy signified ethics or practical philosophy as opposed to pure logic or metaphysics. It belonged to the liberal arts, to the studies of eloquence, and it required, in return, the support and the voice of eloquence. Moral philosophy was connected with poetry, which taught ethical truths under the guise of fiction, and with history, which showed how its precepts had actually been, and should always be, applied in practice. The other branches of speculation had value especially in their relation to ethics, or should at least be directed toward the problem of how to find and lead the best life; studied for their own sake, they became merely academic.

For consigning moral philosophy, understood in its widest sense as including political and social theory, to the hands of the "orator," the humanists could find precedents in a number of ancient sources. When they turned to other aspects of philosophy, they usually attempted to apply, to some degree at least, the tools and concepts of rhetoric. Their efforts were ordinarily directed at simplifying, or even popularizing, the philosophical systems of antiquity. They were more interested in showing essential similarities and compatibilities among ideas than in making close discriminations among different schools of thought, and they were typically eclectic in their views. All these tendencies were reinforced by the humanists' rhetorical–didactic concerns. It was regarded as the task of eloquence to take what was at hand, to make it generally intelligible and useful. Over-attention to precise contrasts could be criticized as word-splitting and concentration on points of little import. Virtue and vice, prudence and folly might, after all, be described in different languages and exemplified in a variety of ways while remaining substantially the same for all. The moralist had, of course, to declare what was unacceptable and erroneous, what could not be reconciled with the true standards of ethics and religious teaching, but his major aim must be to instruct by constructive synthesis.

[. . .]

In dialogue, the humanists found the most flexible form for discussing issues of all sorts. In their view, dialogue could bring to life and dramatize with persuasive effect the actual process of exposition, analysis, and debate appropriate to the matters under discussion. Rational thinking about such subjects was regarded as in itself a mental dialogue; the form, through externalizing, could help to teach the method of thought. The development of a dialogue could demonstrate how questioning was essential to the illumination of truth. The humanist, presenting his interlocutors as men of firm reputation and experience, could attach at once authority and a concrete, personal tone to the ideas which he had them express. Otherwise he might employ invented interlocutors, or stage a simple question and answer session between himself and some disciple or friend, again on the assumption that to "see" and "hear" individuals engaged in discourse would have a greater effect on the audience than would the reading of a straightforward treatise. In dialogue, a humanist could state a clear position or refuse to take one. Some dialogues were left deliberately without explicit conclusion, either because the author wished to point out what could be said on different sides of doubtful or complex matters, not to assert one final decision, or with the purpose of allowing the reader to render his own judgement. It was possible in dialogue to take up a number of issues, sometimes quite unrelated ones, without sacrificing its unity. Dialogue, according to humanist practice, should show busy men engaged in thoughtful leisure, it should be non-formalistic, ostensibly casual; in setting and atmosphere it should be natural and unhurried. All this required careful design.

To dialogue as to the other types of eloquence the humanists applied the principle that form and content must be fused, that language and tone must suit both the speaker and his argument. In Erasmus' *Ciceronianus*, we have a humanist dialogue which provides both an example of and a rumination on that tradition [. . .]

Rhetoric has been called "the greatest barrier between us and our ancestors." Too often, the attempt is made to destroy that barrier by regarding rhetorical form as the chaff which can be separated from the wheat of humanist thought. "What subject," asked Melanchthon, "can possibly be richer than that of the dignity and utility of eloquence?" The question was, of course, rhetorical, but the answer was clear. It was the pursuit of eloquence which united humanists of all shades. To ignore the impact of eloquence and of the ideas associated with it is to distort the mentality of humanism and to disregard a vital dimension of Renaissance thought and method.

Chapter 4

Robert Black

■   from **HUMANISM**, in C. Allmand, ed., *The New Cambridge Medieval History*, VII, Cambridge, 1998, pp. 243–277

A DISCUSSION OF RENAISSANCE HUMANISM must begin with Burckhardt, whose *The Civilization of the Renaissance in Italy* has set the terms of debate and analysis from the time of its publication in 1860 up to the most recent scholarship. Burckhardt's interpretation of humanism was not particularly novel, but he stated his views with powerful simplicity and systematic logic. No scholar can now accept Burckhardt's thesis as a whole, but it must be conceded that he raised the crucial historical issues concerning humanism.

For Burckhardt, the Renaissance was not fundamentally about the revival of Antiquity: "the essence of the phenomena might still have been the same without the classical revival," which had "been one-sidedly chosen as the name to sum up the whole period." In Burckhardt's view, instead, the "characteristic stamp" of the Renaissance was a new spirit of individualism. What was reborn in Italy from the mid-thirteenth to the early sixteenth century was not classicism but rather man himself.

> In the Middle Ages both sides of human consciousness — that which was turned within as that which was turned without — lay dreaming or half awake beneath a common veil. The veil was woven of faith, illusion and childish prepossession, through which the world and history were seen clad in strange hues. Man was conscious of himself only as a member of a race, people, part, family or corporation — only through some general category. In Italy this veil first melted into air; an *objective* treatment and consideration of the state and of all the things of this world became possible. The *subjective* side at the same time asserted itself with corresponding emphasis; man became a spiritual *individual*, and recognized himself as such.

With typical consistency, Burckhardt painted a portrait of the humanists in which the colours and contours of his subjects were not academic or scholarly but anthropological: superficially the humanists might have been "mediators between their own age and a venerated antiquity," but their essential definition was human and personal: "malicious self-conceit," "abominable profligacy," "irreligion," "licentious excess." It was not their devotion to Antiquity which in the sixteenth century resulted in their fall from grace, according to Burckhardt, but rather they were "the most striking examples and victims of an unbridled subjectivity."

Burckhardt thus powerfully articulated several fundamental problems about Renaissance humanism which ever since have preoccupied scholarship. Was humanism essentially concerned with reviving the culture of classical Antiquity, or did it represent something more fundamental – a change in the very nature of man, in his view of himself, or at least a new philosophy of man? And what was the relation of humanism to the preceding historical period, to the Middle Ages? Did it represent a decisive break from previous cultural traditions, or is it more appropriate to speak of continuity and evolution rather than of revolution?

Burckhardt's thesis dominated the interpretation of humanism for at least half a century after the publication of *The Civilization*. His definition of humanism and the Renaissance in human, not in scholarly or literary, terms was adopted by influential figures such as Symonds, Villari, Goetz, Taine and Müntz. Burckhardt had posited a political explanation of the origins of Renaissance individualism, which in his view was the product of the egoistic and amoral political world of the Italian city-states; this particular facet of the Burckhardtian synthesis was soon challenged by a succession of writers, such as Renan, Thode, Gebhart and most eruditely by Burdach, who saw the origins of the Renaissance in the religious world of medieval spirituality. Yet despite their disagreement over the sources of the Renaissance, these early revisionists still carried on with Burckhardt's anthropological approach to the nature of humanism. Similarly Burckhardtian in conception was much of the so-called "revolt of the medievalists" which gained momentum particularly in the first half of this century; their continued emphasis on the precocious discovery of the world and of man, on a "truly Renaissance spirit," individualism, sensuality, rationalism, realism are all obviously Burckhardtian categories of analysis. Even the attempt to deny to the Renaissance the status of a genuine new historical period, devaluing it instead as the decaying after-life of the Middle Ages – a type of *histoire des mentalités* most famous in the writings of Huizinga – is still painting with a Burckhardtian brush. Despite all this revisionism, moreover, it is important to remember that Burckhardt has continued to have his unabashed champions well into the twentieth century, not least two of the most famous German refugees in modern American academic life – Ernst Cassirer and Hans Baron. Individualism is a central theme of Cassirer's study of the philosophy of humanism; moreover, his emphasis on the inter-relation of the elements of a culture and an historical period – "society, state, religion, church, art, science" – is pre-eminently Burckhardtian in conception. It might seem paradoxical to connect Baron, who of course highlighted the republican strand of humanism, with Burckhardt, who saw despotism as the determining political influence in Renaissance Italy; nevertheless, Baron's preoccupation with a sharp contrast between the Middle Ages and the Renaissance ("a fundamental transformation in *Weltanschauung*"), with the emergence of modern secular and lay values, with the decline of medieval concepts such as Guelphism and Empire, not to mention his denigration of pure classicism and his attempts to link together the various strands of cultural history (political and historical thought, artistic realism, positive valuation of wealth) – all these features of his interpretation of early Italian humanism are solidly within the Burckhardtian tradition.

However, it is particularly in the Italian scholarly tradition – most notably in the field of the history of philosophy – that Burckhardt has continued to enjoy the most powerful resonance. This is in one sense ironic, since Renaissance philosophy was egregiously ignored in *The Civilization*. Yet Burckhardt had declared that "Every period of civilization which forms a complete and consistent whole manifests itself not only in political life, in religion, art and science, but also sets its characteristic stamp on social life," and it has been irrefutably demonstrated by Gombrich that Burckhardt derived this concept of the spirit of the age from the idealist historical philosophy of Hegel. Bertrando Spaventa introduced Hegelian idealism into Italian philosophical circles in the 1860s, and his approach was a determining influence on the two giants of Italian philosophy in the early twentieth century – Croce and Gentile. Croce gave little detailed attention to humanism, although his support for a Hegelian literary historian such as De Sanctis and his implicit criticisms of a pro-Catholic revisionist such as Toffanin added weight to the Burckhardtian tradition in Italy. It was above all Gentile who developed an Hegelian/idealist interpretation of Renaissance humanism in Italy: the Middle Ages had devalued man and life in this world; Italian humanism, by contrast, restored the dignity of man, the potential of the human mind and the value of earthly existence. Gentile thus effectively bolstered the Burckhardtian view of Renaissance Italians as "the first born among the sons of modern Europe." This Burckhardtian/Hegelian approach continues to find powerful support in contemporary Italian philosophical circles. Indeed, the leading Italian post-war Renaissance scholar, Eugenio Garin, was Gentile's protégé; it is not surprising that he has emphasised a coherent outlook in Renaissance humanism, which he sees as a new philosophy of man, in sharp contrast to medieval devaluation of humanity. It also comes as no surprise that Garin has embraced many of Baron's views, including his "civic humanism"; indeed, Garin finds Burckhardt himself particularly sympathetic:

> Humanism consisted in a renewed confidence in man and his possibilities and in an appreciation of man's activity in every possible sense . . . Burckhardt's old and vigorous conception which linked the reaffirmation of man with the reaffirmation of the world, the reaffirmation of the spirit with the reaffirmation of nature, ought to be connected without fear of rhetoric to the old notion that the Renaissance succeeded in bringing about a new harmony. This ideal of the harmony and the measure of a complete man runs . . . through those centuries.

It is also ironic that the most effective and powerful challenge to the Burckhardtian approach to the Renaissance and humanism has come from another of Gentile's protégés from the 1930s. It is no exaggeration to say that Paul Oskar Kristeller has revolutionised the study and interpretation of Renaissance humanism in the last fifty years. This is not only because of his now completed vast, six-volume catalogue of unpublished humanist manuscript collections, *Iter italicum*, a work which has rightly concentrated scholarly attention on the study of unpublished primary sources in intellectual history, but also because of his fundamental repudiation of Burckhardt's thesis that Renaissance humanism represented a new philosophy of man. In the single most influential article on Renaissance humanism written this century [Chapter 2 above], Kristeller refuted the interpretation of "humanism as the new philosophy of the Renaissance, which arose in opposition to scholasticism, the old philosophy of the Middle Ages," declaring "that the Italian humanists on the whole were neither good nor bad philosophers, but no philosophers at all." Instead, he saw Renaissance humanism as a literary movement, focusing on grammatical and rhetorical studies; the excursions of humanists into the realm of philosophy were often erratic, amateurish and superficial. Humanism could not have replaced scholasticism as the new philosophy of the Renaissance for the simple reason that scholasticism and Aristotelian philosophy continued to thrive in Italy until the mid-seventeenth century. Because humanism was not a philosophical movement, it could not, for Kristeller, represent a new vision of man:

> If we think or hear of such a topic as "renaissance concepts of man," we are immediately reminded of a view of the Renaissance period that is widespread and has often been repeated: the Renaissance, according to this view, had a special interest in, and concern with, man and his problems. Very often, and in my view mistakenly, this notion is associated with the phenomenon called Renaissance humanism, and in stressing the difference which distinguishes the Renaissance from the period preceding it, it has been pointedly asserted that the thought of the Renaissance was man-centered, whereas medieval thought was God-centered.

For Kristeller, the essential focus of Renaissance humanism was precisely what Burckhardt had rejected: the revival of Antiquity. In undermining one foundation stone of the Burckhardtian edifice – the anthropological definition of humanism – Kristeller did not ignore the other central tenet of Burckhardt's thesis; besides stressing the importance of humanism's new classicism, Kristeller also emphasised its great debt to the Middle Ages: to the French medieval grammatical tradition of classical studies, to the Byzantine heritage of Greek scholarship and, above all, to the Italian medieval rhetorical tradition of *ars dictaminis*.

The great merit of Kristeller's interpretation of Renaissance humanism – indeed the key to its lasting appeal – is his philological study of primary sources; unlike some of his German and Italian predecessors and contemporaries, his studies have not been preconditioned by adherence to an anachronistic philosophical school or methodology. Discarding modern meanings whereby "almost any kind of concern with human values is called 'humanistic'," Kristeller returned to contemporary usage of the late fifteenth century when the term *humanista* was invented to designate teacher of the humanities on the analogy of such medieval university labels as *legista, jurista, canonista* or *artista*. Although the term humanism was a nineteenth-century coinage, Kristeller connected *humanista* with a defined group of subjects, the *studia humanitatis*, which in the late 1430s had been equated by the future

Pope Nicholas V, in planning a library for Cosimo de' Medici, with grammar, rhetoric, poetry, history and moral philosophy. Moreover, Kristeller cited
a number of fifteenth-century texts by Bruni, Ficino, Antonio Benivieni, Alamanno
Rinuccini and Pontano (to whom can now be added Salutati, Barzizza and Traversari), not to mention the above library canon, in which it is clear that the *studia
humanitatis* were regarded as a literary programme, focused on grammar and
rhetoric and clearly distinguished from philosophical, mathematical, medical, scientific and theological studies. Kristeller finally indicated how the phrase *studia
humanitatis* was revived by fourteenth-century humanists (in fact first by Salutati
in 1369) on the basis of Ciceronian usage (in his oration *Pro archia*) to mean a
literary or liberal education. All this suggested that humanism was a self-conscious
cultural and literary movement which extended back at least to the days of
Petrarch's discovery of *Pro archia* in 1333.

Subsequent scholarship has continued to confirm the philological accuracy of
Kristeller's definition of humanism. A recent collection of usages of the term *studia
humanitatis* from 1369 to 1425, with selected examples to 1467, substantiates its
meaning as a literary and cultural programme, albeit not always precisely spelled
out. Here it is perhaps worth pointing out that the ancients too had some difficulty with Cicero's meaning, to the extent that Gellius offered this gloss on the
meaning of *humanitas*:

> Those who have spoken Latin and have used the language correctly do
> not give to the word *humanitas* the meaning which it is commonly
> thought to have, namely, what the Greeks call φιλανθρωπία, signifying
> a kind of friendly spirit and good-feeling towards all men without
> distinction; but they gave to *humanitas* about the force of the Greek
> παιδεία; that is what we call . . . education and training in the liberal
> arts . . . That it is in this sense that our earlier writers have used the
> word, and in particular Marcus Varro and Marcus Tullius, almost all
> the literature shows.

The correct antique meaning of humanism in the sense of *paideia*, not philanthropy,
was universally adopted by fifteenth-century writers when using the phrase *studia
humanitatis*, indicating the philological soundness of Kristeller's definition, as well as
the anachronism inherent in associating humanism with humane values or a new philosophy of man. Moreover, a number of texts in which leading figures such as Bruni
and Poggio speak of the *studia humanitatis* as their particular specialism ("nostra
studia," "nos omnes qui prosequimur studia hec humanitatis," "nostra studia humanitatis") confirm humanism as a self-conscious movement, with a genuine *esprit de
corps*. Finally, although it has been doubted that the *studia humanitatis* were associated at first with the five disciplines of grammar, rhetoric, poetry, history and moral
philosophy, it needs to be pointed out that Petrarch himself identified these as his
particular areas of interest. In his list of favourite books [. . .] Petrarch wrote, "My
specially prized books. To the others I usually resort not as a deserter as a scout."
Besides the actual titles, this list is significant as indicating how Petrarch defined his
particular area of academic specialism. The scholastic, philosophical disciplines are
limited to one volume each, and dialectic is given only a grudging place: "Tractat(us)

(et) n(ichi)l ult(ra)." The rest of the list falls under the headings "Moral(ia)," "Recth(orica)," "ystor(ica)" (with its usual subsection "ex(empl)a"), "Poet(ica)" and "Gram(matica)." It does not need to be emphasised that these are the five divisions of the *studia humanitatis* as found first in Parentucelli's [Nicholas V's] canon and then with increasing frequency in the second half of the fifteenth century.

Kristeller's work with thousands upon thousands of humanist manuscripts has made him wary of generalising on the basis of a few texts, or of highlighting one or several famous humanist texts, in the Burckhardtian or idealist fashion, at the expense of numerous less well-known or even unpublished works.

> Renaissance thought [he writes], when seen in its entire range, say, from 1350 to 1600, presents a very complex picture. Different schools and thinkers expressed a great variety of views, on problems related to the conception of man as on others, and it would be extremely difficult if not impossible to reduce all of them to a single common denominator.

Although he himself, writing in 1979, still acknowledged that "there is at least a core of truth in the view that Renaissance thought was more 'human' and more secular, although not necessarily less religious, than medieval thought and that it was more concerned with human problems," older as well as recent research has made it impossible to make even this small concession to the Burckhardtian tradition. In the first place, it has been established that the Renaissance emphasis on man was consciously borrowed from classical, biblical, patristic and medieval authors; there was no lack of medieval authors (for example Honorius of Autun, Peter Damian or Hugh of St Victor) who used arguments (such as God's choice of man for the Incarnation, the creation of man in His likeness or man as the binding force of the universe) later favoured by Renaissance proponents of the dignity of man. Moreover, there was no consensus among Renaissance humanists whether to lament the misery of the human condition or applaud the dignity of man. Famous treatises exalting human dignity by Fazio and Manetti have of course been spotlighted, whereas the alternative view, as developed for example in Poggio's *De miseria humanae conditionis*, has been passed over in silence. Indeed, human misery versus dignity had been conceived as a type of *paragone* (rhetorical arguments on both sides of a question) in the classic medieval treatment by Innocent III, who had failed to deliver his promised treatise on the dignity of man to complement his *De miseria humane conditionis*; in fact, Poggio "not only borrowed Innocent's title but also elaborated many of the themes he had discussed," highlighting there (as well as in *De varietate fortunae*) the frailty, the miserable destiny and the stupidity of mankind. Indeed, it would be hard to find a more dismal portrait of the human race than in the youthful *Intercoenales*, as well as in the more mature *Toegenius* and *Momus* written by the so-called "universal man of the early Renaissance," Leon Battista Alberti. Another important fact is that the anti-intellectualism and fideism of much humanist moral philosophy represented a serious limitation of man's potential. Petrarch's *Secretum* taught knowledge alone could not achieve Christian virtue, which could be gained through will and experience only with grace. For Valla in his *Collatio Novi Testamenti* and *Adnotationes in Novum Testamentum*, theological understanding was enhanced by philology, but, as he also argues in *De libero arbitrio*, ultimately human free will and predestination were concepts that had to be accepted as acts of faith. Similarly, in his *De vero falsoque bono*, Valla makes no effort to sustain the conclusions of religion through rational philosophy; in portraying the after-life, he seeks the help of faith and imagination, not knowledge. Another fact which is frequently overlooked is the relation which would develop between humanism and the Reformation in the early sixteenth century. It would be impossible to go further than Luther and Calvin in denying human potential and dignity; according to the former, for example, "If we believe Christ redeemed mankind by his blood, we are forced to admit that man had been entirely lost," a view strongly supported by the latter: "Wherever you turn, you understand you are nothing except squalor, vice, sickness, crime, and so worthy of every kind of loathing; all help, all salvation and dignity must be expected from God." The older view that this Reformation anthropology was rejected by Renaissance humanism, speaking through Erasmus, is no longer acceptable; scholarship has demonstrated that countless reformers had been and continued to be humanists, and indeed it was largely by their efforts that the Reformation was able to spread throughout Europe [see Chapter 19 below].

As a general definition of humanism, the anthropology of Burckhardt and his innumerable successors must be discarded; indeed, attempts to reduce humanism to some kind of philosophical formula, to attribute to it a universal philosophical content or doctrine, will always fail. Just as scholasticism can never be defined in terms of a given body of propositions or views, so humanism did not represent one overall intellectual theme or perspective. It is often said that humanism implied a new historical consciousness which was lacking in the Middle Ages, and it is true that much revolutionary philological work of the humanists rested on new historical insights about texts, manuscript affiliations and translations. However, it is a fact that many humanists, as chancellors, secretaries or teachers of grammar and rhetoric, did not engage in original or significant philological activity. Moreover, the proposition that the Middle Ages lacked a sense of history, which then characterised the activity of Renaissance humanists, is patently false. In some areas, for example, in ecclesiology, medieval authors had a powerfully developed sense of historical change and periodisation; such a view ignores the graphic historical contrast between the primitive and the contemporary Church drawn by writers such as St Bernard, Ptolemy of Lucca, Dante or Marsilius of Padua. Similarly, it would be hard to find an approach less historical, yet one more powerfully supported by Renaissance humanists, than the ancient theology – the view that a body of mystical doctrines were transmitted to Moses and Hermes Trismegistus and then preserved miraculously unchanged through the Egyptians, Persians, Greeks, Romans, church fathers and medieval Byzantines to reach the contemporary world of fifteenth- and sixteenth-century Europe. These types of generalisation – just like Panofsky's famous but equally false formula of the union of form and content in the Renaissance (who would seriously argue that clothing classically modelled figures in antique garb was a characteristic of fifteenth- or sixteenth-century art?) – are simply variations on the Hegelian theme of the spirit of the age; no one will ever identify the "characteristic stamp" of the Renaissance, because it exists only in the minds of Hegel, Burckhardt and their followers, not in historical reality. Not even antipathy to scholasticism was entirely characteristic of humanism; the attacks by Petrarch, Bruni, Valla or Erasmus are famous, but it should also be pointed out that Poggio praised and admired Aquinas, and that his successor as Florentine chancellor, Benedetto Accolti, in contrast to the previous generation of humanists, showed a renewed interest in scholasticism and in natural, speculative and metaphysical philosophy, finding many scholastics to praise, while rejecting Cicero, who had been assigned the highest rank among philosophers by his Florentine predecessors; moreover, these views are shared by a number of Accolti's contemporaries, including Alamanno Rinuccini, Donato Acciaiuoli and Ficino.

Kristeller's definition of humanism as *studia humanitatis* tells us how humanists themselves described their particular field of learning, but of course the nature of every historical phenomenon is not clearly articulated by contemporaries, if only because for them its essential features were so obvious as to require no explanation. In the case of humanism, any moderately informed researcher can detect the presence of a humanist text simply through its Latin; by attempting to show his readers that he is affiliating himself, however imperfectly, with the Latin style of the ancients as opposed to the moderns (or medievals in modern parlance), a writer is making an implicit declaration of his affinity with the humanist movement. A humanist is thus someone who acts like other humanists; this is how contemporaries would have identified humanism, and such a definition, stripped of historicist paraphernalia, will work equally well for us. To take the limiting case, consider Machiavelli, who, because of his unconventional and hardly humanitarian views, not to mention his exclusively vernacular literary production, has frequently been denied the status of humanist. But by education, beginning scholarly and literary activity, early latinate epistolography and classicised orthography Machiavelli showed all the traits of a humanist, and, by appointing him as successor to other humanist types such as Alessandro Braccesi as second chancellor, his Florentine contemporaries obviously regarded him as a qualified humanist. When in the dedication of *The Prince* he pointed to his "continual reading of the ancients," he was identifying himself in a way that his contemporaries could never have misunderstood.

The *studia humanitatis* developed out of medieval traditions of grammar and rhetoric; the activities of the Paduan, Aretine and Bolognese pre-humanists, as well as of Petrarch himself, all have roots in Italian *ars dictaminis* as well as in the classicism of northern Europe, particularly France. Nevertheless, the mixture of elements was unprecedented: medieval French grammatical studies did not have a preponderant rhetorical emphasis, whereas the *ars dictaminis* had had little direct connection with the reading and imitation of classical authors. Although the origins of humanism have been intensively investigated, no entirely satisfactory explanation for the change of direction taken by Italian grammatical and rhetorical studies at the end of the thirteenth century has emerged. Various hypotheses have been advanced: for example, almost all the pre-humanists had a legal background which put them in immediate contact with the antique heritage through ancient legal texts and compilations; alternatively, the actual change instigated by the first pre-humanist, Lovato Lovati, has been reduced to the imitation of classical verse, which in turn has been explained by the lack of a medieval Italian tradition of Latin poetry, so that Lovato encountered fewer obstacles in imitating ancient metrical models. All this is enlightening and doubtless provides valuable contexts for this fundamental change of taste; and yet it is impossible in the end to provide a complete historical explanation for the birth of humanism, precisely because this classical literary taste, implying the absolute superiority of ancient models in both grammar and rhetoric, was unprecedented in the Middle Ages. Ultimately, any fundamental change of style in the arts is inexplicable. Context and circumstances can fill in the background of why the Greeks in the fifth century BC made the decisive move from hieratic to naturalistic art; of why Giotto moved beyond the expressionism of Cimabue to genuine illusionism; of why Masaccio turned his back on the International Gothic to found a new monumental *gravitas*; of why Donatello rediscovered the human anatomy; of why Leonardo invented the High Renaissance style. But in the end we come up against genius and trend setting. Thus it is with Lovato, Mussato and Geri d'Arezzo: their new feeling for ancient literary style was their own creation.

If the ultimate origins of humanism are beyond the realm of historical research, more can be said of its achievements by the end of the fifteenth century. Many humanists were highly skilful or even professional scribes and copyists, and they launched a reform of script which has lasted to the present day. Rejecting the Gothic bookhand which had come to dominate Europe in the thirteenth and fourteenth centuries, they created humanist script, believed to be an imitation of ancient Roman handwriting but in fact based on the script of the Carolingian revival which had been used both north and south of the Alps up to the early thirteenth century. The humanists also reformed cursive writing, distancing themselves from Gothic chancery hands and creating what has come to be known as Italic script. These were great and lasting achievements, but, in terms of their own aim of reviving *littera antiqua*, they were not fully successful. The humanists' idea of palaeographic chronology was primitive; their identification of Caroline with ancient Roman script must seem about as quaint as the widely held belief in the fifteenth century that the Florentine Baptistry was the Roman temple of Mars. Moreover, their imitation even of Caroline script was hardly a complete success: the characteristic rotundity of humanist bookhand is an adaptation of the round Gothic script of the fourteenth century; the humanists never realised that the Caroline "t" had been a low letter like the "c," rising above the half-line level only in the course of the thirteenth century; they also never understood that Caroline copyists wrote usually above the first ruled line of the manuscript, not below as in Gothic manuscripts; they also preferred the more square page layout of Gothic manuscripts to the more normal oblong shape of Caroline codices. These are only some of the criteria according to which modern palaeographers distinguish humanist manuscripts from their Caroline precursors, and they demonstrate the limitations of the humanist reform of script; moreover, it must be remembered that Italic script is a hybrid creation, based on Gothic chancery cursive with elements adopted from Caroline writing, the likes of which never existed in the pre-Gothic period, much less in Antiquity.

In their central aspiration, the revival of the Latin language, humanist success was inevitably incomplete. The humanists wished to restore "to light the ancient elegance of style which was lost and dead," but modern scholarship has often been too much influenced by their own claims; in fact, the "vocabulary, spelling, syntax of early humanist Latin, and even of certain late Quattrocento authors, have numerous features without parallel in classical Latin, but which are found in medieval Latin." The fifteenth-century controversy over neologisms demonstrates the extent to which coinages, just as in the Middle Ages, were still taking place; rare words, not really characteristic of classical Latin, were turned into normal usage by fifteenth-century humanists, desperate to widen the restricted classical vocabulary. Especially significant was the humanist failure to distinguish in practice between the language of classical poetry and prose, although certain critics (such as Valla or Cortesi) made theoretical objections to a practice which was founded in medieval habits. In some cases, it is even difficult to determine whether the unclassical practices of the humanists were the result of direct influence of the vernacular or were based on traditional practices, developed in late ancient Latin and compounded in the Middle Ages, particularly by the *ars dictaminis*. In fact, the concept of Latinity itself inherited from the Middle Ages died only a slow death in the fifteenth century. The medieval view (as stated characteristically by Dante in *De vulgari eloquentia*) was that there had been two languages in Antiquity, the vernacular and Latin – the former learned and spoken naturally, the latter invented by the great authors as an artifice for their works of literature and philosophy and subsequently acquired at school. This view (upheld by early humanists such as Petrarch and Bruni) was finally challenged in the mid-fifteenth century by such figures as Biondo, Alberti, Poggio, Guarino and Filelfo, who maintained that there was only one language in ancient Rome and that the medieval vernaculars developed from Latin as it was corrupted by the barbarian invasions. This dispute had vast importance not only for the birth of vernacular grammar but also for the humanists' attitude to the revival of Latin. On the one hand, if all languages were natural – Latin as well as the vernacular – then they all had a rational structure; it is no accident that the first grammar of the Italian language by Alberti emerged from this changed view of the history of Latin. On the other hand, as long as it was believed that the ancient Romans were in an analogous position to the moderns, then the revival of Latin was not an insurmountable task: if the Romans had had to learn Latin artificially, there was no reason why the moderns could not do the same. It was only necessary to clear away the corruption caused by the Middle Ages and to arm oneself with all possible purified texts; it is no accident that the most fervent upholder of the traditional, medieval concept of Latinity was Valla, whose *Elegantiae* were premised on the belief that there had been an ancient vernacular and that true Latin was universal and eternal, only to be rediscovered and purified. However, when it came to be taken for granted by the end of the fifteenth century (for example by Poliziano) that Latin was a natural language, humanists realised that they could never again step into the ancients' shoes. Many now felt they had to resort to extreme measures, abandoning the eclectic imitation typical of the early Quattrocento, and slavishly following just one model – hence the Ciceronianism prominent at the turn of the sixteenth century. The humanists finally realised that their fundamental goal was an impossibility: as Silvia Rizzo has aphoristically put it, "Latin became a dead language only when it was realised that it had been a living language."

The return to antique rhetoric was a fundamental goal of the Renaissance humanists, and here they faced fewer problems than in the revival of classical Latin; eloquence had had to be learned by the ancient Romans too, who bequeathed to posterity a number of excellent textbooks, including the pseudo-Ciceronian *Rhetorica ad Herennium*, Cicero's genuine *De inventione* and Quintilian's comprehensive *Institutio oratoria*. Rhetoric had been practised during the Middle Ages by means of the *ars dictaminis*, a debased derivative of the classical art, which itself continued to be studied and taught on a theoretical and academic level, although not put to practical use, by medieval commentators on the two Ciceronian textbooks. The early signs of humanism can be seen in the commentaries by a number of Bolognese *dictatores* on the *Ad Herennium* and *De inventione* at the turn of the fourteenth century. Cicero's orations had been neglected in the Middle Ages, and the classical emphasis of early humanism was enhanced by the recovery of almost all of Cicero's orations between the 1330s and the 1420s, as well as of full texts of his other rhetorical works, not to mention Quintilian's *Institutio*, works which had been either unknown, little used or available only in corrupt versions during the Middle Ages. By the early fifteenth century, the humanists had largely turned their backs on the *ars dictaminis*, reunited classical rhetorical theory and practice, not only by commenting on the ancient manuals, but also by using them as guides to rhetorical practice, which was also now based on the imitation of the Ciceronian orations – something which had never taken place in the Middle Ages. Moreover, the humanists began to gloss Cicero's *Orations*, even before the recovery of Asconius Pedianus' ancient commentary; here they diverged somewhat from ancient practice, going beyond purely philological annotation to a discussion of rhetorical structure, reflecting their new concern to imitate ancient models.

All this was far beyond the achievement of the Middle Ages, and yet even in rhetoric the humanists were unable to put the medieval heritage fully behind them. As in the Middle Ages, the *Rhetorica ad Herennium* remained the most widely used textbook. The humanists added little in the way of new theoretical works, preferring to compose epitomes of the antique art; the only significant new large-scale rhetorical treatise to have been composed by the end of the fifteenth century was George of Trebizond's *Rhetoricorum libri V*. More significant was the inability of the humanists to revive classical rhetoric as it had been practised in the days of Cicero. The ancient treatises had divided rhetoric into three genres, judicial, deliberative and epideictic, but in later Antiquity and the Middle Ages, the first two, representing the oratory of the law courts and of public debate, had fallen into disuse, leaving only the rhetoric of praise and blame, as practised for example in speeches at weddings and funerals, university functions or on formal civic occasions. Although the humanists continued to give theoretical attention to judicial and deliberative oratory, the social functions of rhetoric remained unchanged from the early days of the Italian communes in the thirteenth century, with the result that the humanists have bequeathed an exiguous oratorical literature apart from *epideixis*. Even more notable was the continued humanist emphasis on letter writing, which had been the principal focus of the *ars dictaminis*. The recovery of Cicero's letters in the fourteenth century provided new models for epistolography; putting aside the invented or contemporary letters used by the *dictatores*, the humanists could now let Cicero show the way, not only in epistolary imitation but also in publishing their own letter collections. However, they never succeeded or possibly never even attempted to tip the balance of rhetorical literature again in favour of the oration; the numerous humanist treatises on epistolography written during the fifteenth century show that their overriding interest was to supplant the *ars dicta-minis*, not to restore to rhetoric its principal classical function of oratory.

History, as one of the five disciplines of the *studia humanitatis*, was a principal concern of the humanists, who not only assiduously studied the ancient Roman histories but also wrote histories of their own, usually of the post-classical period, where their models were especially Livy and Sallust. The latter had been widely read and even imitated in the Middle Ages, whereas the former had been copied and read but had not served as a model. In this sense, Leonardo Bruni, with his *History of the Florentine People*, was an innovator, writing the first post-antique history explicitly imitating Livy; similarly Livian was the inspiration of a second great pioneer of humanist historiography, Flavio Biondo, who recounted the aftermath of the fall of the Roman Empire *ab inclinato imperio* just as Livy had written of the rise of Rome *ab urbe condita*. It has sometimes been argued that the achievement of early humanist historians went beyond formal classical imitation to philological research. This is certainly true of sections concerning the foundations of cities and states; Bruni for example subjected his classical sources to critical analysis to prove that Florence had been founded not under Julius Caesar but rather under the Republic. This was a kind of research closely related to the humanists' philological study of classical texts, and so it is not surprising that they applied their new critical techniques to this aspect of historiography. It has also been maintained that they carried this kind of philological critique of sources over into the main body of their historical works. However, it is doubtful that early humanists adopted new critical working methods for the writing of post-classical history. Not only did Bruni, Biondo and Accolti fail to synthesise or compare the material in their sources; they also invented extensive passages in their histories. They adhered to the time-honoured medieval method of following one man chronicle, whose account was elaborated and embellished with additional material according to the requirements of classical imitation. Bruni's occasional use of archival documents here seems to have had the same purpose as older chronicles used by Biondo and Accolti: to supplement, not to displace or check, the account of the main chronicle source. History was regarded as a branch of rhetoric, where truth was defined not as absolute fidelity to sources but rather as verisimilitude or probability. The adoption of more critical methods of historiography came much later for humanist historians under the influence of changed attitudes to the rules of history. In the earlier Renaissance, humanist historians followed Cicero's views, as stated in *De oratore*, that history required no special theoretical study, but in the wake of the debate at the very end of the fifteenth century over how to achieve a truly classical style, it began to be argued that, in addition to imitation, rules were needed. This idea was immediately applied to history, with a succession of new and lengthy *artes historicae* emerging from the turn of the sixteenth century. A number of historians, including the Florentine chancellor Bartolommeo Scala, became unsure how to write history in the absence of rules and in this changed critical climate; others, such as Tristano Calco, became highly critical of the achievements of their predecessors and began to rethink historical method afresh. The new *artes historicae* which emerged discussed not only style but also historical method and truth, often ranking types of historical sources in order of reliability. This new climate affected the historical outlook and method of the greatest humanist historian, Francesco Guicciardini, whose scrupulous research methods could not have been further removed from the rhetorical practices of the early historians such as Bruni or Biondo.

As grammar teachers, one of their principal professional activities, it has been asserted that the "humanists of the fifteenth century changed the Latin curriculum, a major academic revolution," "one of the few in the history of Western education, in the relatively short time of about fifty years — 1400 to 1450." It is true that humanist educators attacked the curriculum of their medieval predecessors; however, the reality is that the changes they effected in the classroom were often far more complex and gradual than is believed by some modern scholars, misled by the humanists' exaggerated tendency to self-advertisement.

The grammar curriculum in the Middle Ages and the Renaissance was divided into two relatively distinct phases: elementary education, which consisted of learning to read and write; and secondary education, in which Latin was learned properly, including both prose composition and the study of literature. As far as elementary education is concerned, the basic textbook in Italian schools both before and after the coming of humanism was a treatise on the parts of speech, attributed to the Roman grammarian Donatus but actually a compilation of material mainly from Priscian, which is conventionally known as *Ianua* by modern scholars after the first word of its verse introduction. There was complete continuity here between the Middle Ages and humanism, not only in textual but also in methodological terms: from the beginning of the fourteenth century the learning of *Ianua* was divided into two stages, first reading phonetically without meaning, then re-reading and memorising the text with meaning. Accompanying *Ianua* as further reading material were a collection of verses preceded by an introduction and collection of moral aphorisms, the *Disticha Catonis*, a late ancient text which continued in heavy use throughout the sixteenth century and even received a commentary from Erasmus. Learning *Ianua* meant memorising the basic Latin forms, so that the pupil, having left elementary school, was now in a position to learn Latin syntax, culminating in prose composition and letter writing. This was accomplished through *Regulae grammaticales*, a generic name for treatises written by medieval grammarians such as Goro d'Arezzo, Filippo di Naddo of Florence or Francesco da Buti of Pisa, just as by humanist teachers such as Guarino Veronese, Gaspare da Verona or Perotti. Again the most prominent feature of this genre of schoolbook, from Filippo di Naddo to Perotti, is continuity: the medieval concept of governance, developed in northern France during the twelfth century, was used without change to teach the relation between the parts of the sentence; mnemonic verses were employed to fix rules in the pupil's memory; medieval grammatical terminology was omnipresent; completely unclassical syntactical rules of thumb (such as the ubiquitous analysis of

grammatical function according to word order (*a parte ante* and *a parte post*))
remained in constant use; invented sentences rather than quotations from classical
authors continued to provide normal examples of grammatical usage. The claim that
humanists such as Guarino pioneered the abbreviated grammar textbook is unfounded, given that such works were already in circulation in the thirteenth (e.g.
the *Regule* of Tebaldo of Siena) and fourteenth centuries (e.g. the *Regule parve* of
Goro d'Arezzo). Even the supposed new departure of Perotti in ending his treatise
with a section on epistolography is in fact traditional practice: many manuscripts of
Francesco da Buti's *Regule* also end with a treatise on letter writing.

Matching continuity in formal grammar at this school level was continuity in
reading matter. For school purposes in both the Middle Ages and the Renaissance,
the Latin authors were divided into two groups: the *auctores minores*, a cycle of late
ancient and medieval texts, mainly in verse; and the *auctores maiores*, mainly the
Roman poets but also a few prose writers. Despite the harangues against them by
the humanists, the minor authors continued to be read at school throughout the
fifteenth century in Italy, as is attested by many manuscript copies which either
originated or were actively glossed throughout the Quattrocento in Italy; even
Pietro Crinito, Poliziano's disciple, continued to teach Henry of Settimello's *Elegy*.
The most intensively read school text in the fourteenth and fifteenth century was
Boethius' *Consolation of Philosophy*, a work which often stood at the threshold
between the minor and major authors. It is true that this text, like the minor
authors, suffered a decline with the rise of the printing press at the end of the
Quattrocento; nevertheless, manuscript copies, as in the case of the minor authors,
continue to show intensive school use until the end of the century.

The Roman classics had been read at school in Italy throughout the Middle Ages,
as is clear again from the study of surviving manuscript schoolbooks. However, they
were subject to significant changes of fashion and interest, and here the humanists
did often play a significant role. The grammar curriculum in twelfth-century Italian
schools finished with a study of the poets Vergil, Lucan, Ovid, Juvenal, Persius,
Horace, Terence and Statius, as well as of prose texts by Cicero and Sallust's two
histories. In the thirteenth century some authors such as Vergil, Persius and Cicero
(apart from the suppositious *Ad Herennium* and the genuine *De inventione*, which were
commented on as part of the study of rhetoric) seem to have dropped out of the
curriculum with the rise of new, particularly northern European school texts such
as Geoffrey de Vinsauf's *Poetria nova*, Alexandre de Villedieu's *Doctrinale* and Evrard
de Béthune's *Graecismus*. In the course of the fourteenth century, a number of classical texts, including Seneca's *Tragedies* and Valerius Maximus' *Facta et dicta*, first
entered the curriculum, possibly under the partial influence of pre-humanists such
as Lovato. However, the most significant curricular change was the recovery of
Cicero, not to mention Vergil and Persius, for the schoolroom at the turn of the fifteenth century. Cicero's shorter moral treatises (*De amicitia, De senectute, Paradoxa
stoicorum* and *De officiis*) had had a place in the twelfth-century Italian curriculum,
and after nearly two centuries of neglect they once more became widely studied at
school in the fifteenth century. Moreover, Cicero's letters, unknown in the Middle
Ages, now became widely adopted as stylistic models in fifteenth-century Italian
schools, although they were never subjected to philological commentary in the
schoolroom like other classical texts.

As far as the classical authors are concerned, therefore, the picture is complex: neither revolution nor evolution is an adequate description, but continuity does describe the prevalent use of verse grammars from the thirteenth to the end of the fifteenth century. No classical grammar was written in verse, but it was found in the Middle Ages that versification was an essential method of prodding the memory of schoolboys. Works such as *Doctrinale* and *Graecismus* continued in constant use in Italy throughout the fifteenth century, and when Lorenzo Valla, himself a grammar teacher, wanted to replace the *Doctrinale*, he began to compose a thoroughly unclassical verse grammar himself. Similarly, there was continuity in methods used to teach the authors in the grammar schools from the Middle Ages to the end of the fifteenth century. Humanist teachers such as Guarino may have declared that their aim was to turn their pupils into better men, but the reality of pedagogic practice was far more mundane: the study of hundreds of manuscript schoolbooks and their glosses in Florentine libraries dating from the twelfth to the end of the fifteenth century has confirmed the view that the overwhelming fare of humanist as well as of medieval grammar schools was simply philology (history, mythology, grammar, simple rhetoric, figures of speech, geography, paraphrase), not moral philosophy.

In fact, if there was a pedagogic revolution in the Italian classroom, it took place not at the turn of the fifteenth but rather of the fourteenth century. It was at this point that the vernacular began to be used extensively as a pedagogic tool to teach Latin, not only to clarify vocabulary but also as a means to teach Latin prose composition; previously pupils had been taught to write in Latin through the medium of Latin, but at the beginning of the fourteenth century, possibly first in Bologna and then in Tuscany, Latin prose composition began to be taught by the use of *themata*, or passages to translate from the vernacular into Latin. This practice continued throughout the fifteenth and sixteenth centuries, and was even used by a humanist such as Poliziano to instruct his pupil, the young Piero di Lorenzo de' Medici. A complementary change in the curriculum, which seems to have taken place at the turn of the fourteenth century as well, and which also represented a concession to the growing numbers who wanted to make use of education skills in a culture increasingly dominated by the vernacular language, was the abbreviation of the *Ianua* text to allow the minimum treatment of Latin grammar and the maximum amount of practice in reading skills. The text was still taught in Latin, often now by specialist elementary school teachers (*doctores puerorum* as distinct from *doctores grammatice*) with knowledge of Latin hardly extending beyond the texts taught, in preparation for abacus or arithmetic schools, where the language of instruction would be the vernacular, and for eventual entry into the world of business and commerce, also exclusively conducted in the vernacular. It hardly needs to be pointed out that this new and significant role for the vernacular and for its culture in education had nothing to do with Italian humanism.

Poetry, in the medieval and Renaissance tradition, primarily meant the study of the ancient poets and so, in terms of the curriculum, was subsumed usually under the discipline of grammar. Some consideration remains due, therefore, to *moralia* or moral philosophy, the final constituent of the *studia humanitatis*, which, in a typical humanist assertion, were claimed to "perfect and adorn man"; the human-

ists castigated their scholastic rivals for arid learning and for failing to inspire virtue
in mankind and yet there was little novel in the humanist contribution to ethics.
Humanist moral philosophy was overwhelmingly based on ancient ethics, much
of which had been extensively studied in the Middle Ages. The main sources
of Aristotelian *moralia* were all translated into Latin and received commentaries at
universities during the thirteenth century; moreover, Stoic ethics, as expounded
by Seneca and Cicero, had been a characteristic ingredient of medieval moral
thought. These two traditions provided the core of most humanist moral philosophy too, although in the fifteenth century there was some attempt by humanists
to revive philosophical sources weakly represented in the Middle Ages. These
included, in the first place, Platonism, which however failed to stimulate a synthesis
of ethics, unlike Aristotelianism, partly because Plato's writings were themselves,
unlike Aristotle's, unsystematic and partly because most Renaissance Platonists,
like their ancient, medieval and Byzantine forerunners, were more interested in
cosmology and metaphysics than in ethics; even the Platonic doctrines of the
contemplative life and the theory of love, ostensibly part of ethics, tended to form
the backdrop to spiritualism, mysticism and metaphysical speculation in the hands
of fifteenth-century Platonists. In the Middle Ages, Epicureanism had been even
less known and understood than Platonism, although it had been handled with
surprising subtlety by Abelard and Aquinas, and the sympathetic treatment of
Epicurus by Lucretius and Diogenes Laertius gradually came to the attention of
humanists. His ethics, which propounded intellectual pleasure as the goal of life,
convinced Cosma Raimondi and even appealed to Filelfo, but his unfavourable
treatment at the hands of Cicero prejudiced most humanists; even Lorenzo Valla,
who preferred Epicureanism to Stoicism, in the end conventionally advocated
Christian morality above all other systems.

Humanist political thought, strictly speaking a division of moral philosophy,
has particularly preoccupied modern scholarship. According to Baron's theory of
"civic humanism," Bruni and his followers initiated the republican strain of thought
which became a feature of some – though by no means all – Renaissance political
thought. However, it is now clear that a fully developed republican ideology existed
in the Italian communes long before Bruni, whose political ideas were only one
phase of a long tradition, inaugurated by the growth of the communes and their
struggle against the Empire and tyranny. The early communes produced such
outspoken republicans as the translator of the *Fet des Romans*, Rolandino of Padua
and Brunetto Latini, and the translation and assimilation of Aristotle's *Politics*
encouraged republican overtones in the political thought of Aquinas and Marsilius
and inspired the militant and categorical republicanism of Ptolemy of Lucca. The
classical texts at the disposal of medieval civic republicans had been limited largely
to Aristotle, Sallust and Cicero's *De officiis*, a text which probably underwent a
decline of influence in the course of the later thirteenth and earlier fourteenth
centuries, as attested by sharply falling manuscript circulation of the Ciceronian
moral treatises possibly caused by the rise of Aristotelian scholasticism. Bruni's
original contribution to republicanism was to restore its Ciceronian foundations –
a process which had already been begun by his mentor Salutati, who had directly
cited *De officiis* when advocating political equality. Followers of "civic humanism"
have also overstated Bruni's commitment to the merits of the active over the

contemplative life. It is true that he went further than many of his predecessors in championing active citizenship, but like previous thinkers he did not see the question in black and white terms, as is clear from one of his most significant assessments of the problem, the *Isagogicon moralis disciplinae*, where he states: "Each of these ways of life has its own qualities worthy of praise and commendation." This kind of qualified judgement has its source in the tenth book of Aristotle's *Nicomachean Ethics*, an analysis which Bruni approached even more closely at the end of his life in a letter of 1441; Bruni's vacillations and qualifications echo the complex analysis of the problem found in the writings of his mentor, Salutati, as well as in the thought of Aquinas, who actually went very far in justifying the active life. Bruni has claim to some originality in the energy with which he puts the arguments for the active life, but the overall pattern of his political thought on this question is a development of Aristotelian thinking, along the lines already established by Aquinas and Salutati.

The contrast between Middle Ages and Renaissance – the cornerstone of the Baronian school – is particularly out of place in studying the political thought of the Italian communes, whose actual history showed notable continuity between the fourteenth and fifteenth centuries; more fruitful has been the approach which attempts to relate the political ideals of humanism to the ambitions of particular regimes, political groupings and diplomatic needs, regardless of meta-historical concepts. It is clear, for example, that an emphasis on both equality and elitism are simultaneous features of the political thought of Salutati in the years after the defeat of the anti-oligarchic regime in Florence in 1382. It would be easy to accuse the Florentine chancellor here of inconsistency and insincerity, but this would ignore the close connection of Salutati's political ideas with the facts of Florentine political life. After 1382, in fact, the Florentine constitution was able to accommodate the ambitions of the wider political class to hold public office and yet at the same time enable a restricted oligarchy to retain a tight grip over real political power. This balance was achieved by qualifying ever-larger numbers of citizens for the highest public offices, while giving preferential treatment to the oligarchs through the use of constitutional manipulations such as the *borsellino* and the *accoppiatori*. Such practices not only account for Salutati's emphasis simultaneously on democracy and elitism, but also explain Bruni's definition of political liberty as the equal hope of winning office in his *Oratio* for Nanni Strozzi of 1428, a view which reflected the realities of the Florentine political world between 1382 and 1434, when "many were elected to offices but few to government." Similarly, Salutati's advocacy of monarchy as the best form of government in *De tyranno* was interpreted by Baron as "political quietism," reflecting his allegedly residual medieval and conservative belief in world empire as opposed to the truly Renaissance republicanism of his pupil, Bruni, whose views in the *Laudatio Florentinae urbis* were supposedly more in tune with the needs of Florentine liberty in the struggle against Milanese tyranny. However, it is now clear that in fact Salutati's monarchism was more closely related to Florentine diplomatic interests than Bruni's generic republicanism; Salutati was actually upholding the inviolate imperial majesty of Florence's ally, the Emperor-Elect Rupert of the Palatinate, whose dignity had been debased by the sale of the imperial duchy of Milan to Florence's enemy, Giangaleazzo Visconti. A less schematic approach explains Italian political thought much more sensitively than Baron's formula of a conflict between Florentine liberty and Milanese tyranny, when in historical fact both were imperial powers involved in a struggle to establish their respective territorial empires by extinguishing the political liberty of their neighbours.

It has been necessary to emphasise the limits of humanist achievements in order to dispel the notion – rooted in Burckhardt and ultimately in Hegel – that humanism somehow represented a new period in intellectual history. The fact is that change in the central disciplines of the *studia humanitatis* was irregular and uneven, alternately limited or facilitated by many distinct inherent traditions and differing external circumstances. Indeed, just because the humanists fell short of effecting intellectual revolutions in grammar, rhetoric, history and moral/political philosophy does not mean that in other areas they did not achieve a more decisive break with the medieval past. In Latin scholarship, the fifteenth-century humanists, with their discovery or rediscovery of texts either seldom read or completely unknown in the Middle Ages, virtually completed the corpus of the Latin classics such as is known today; as far as scholarship of Tacitus, Lucretius, Catullus, Propertius or Cicero's letters is concerned, therefore, humanism represented a decisive break with the Middle Ages. Similarly, the notion of the public library was a creation of the Renaissance. Before the invention of printing, humanists such as Petrarch became acutely aware that the process of preservation and dissemination through copying inevitably implied textual deterioration; the foundation of public libraries in Florence, Rome, Venice, Urbino and Cesena during the fifteenth century was therefore intended to provide scholars with authoritative versions in order to counteract the further corruption of texts. The procedures of textual criticism were vastly improved by the humanists. Few medieval scholars went beyond collation of manuscripts to secure a superior text, but the humanists now engaged in sometimes successful and even inspired conjectural emendation. Moreover, Poliziano inaugurated the ranking of manuscripts according to age, and his efforts perhaps even anticipate modern stemmatics; in this sense, the humanists were the remote ancestors of modern classical philologists. Another important new contribution was antiquarianism; in the Middle Ages, classical artefacts had been prized mainly because they were precious, not because they were ancient. Petrarch, in contrast, began to collect ancient objects because they evoked for him the lost world of classical Antiquity; his antiquarian efforts remained largely romantic, but his humanist successors Poggio and Biondo actually did begin the critical study of ancient remains, providing the distant foundations of modern archaeology.

Without doubt, however, the greatest single achievement of the fifteenth-century humanists was the revival of Greek, an endeavour with few precedents in the western Middle Ages. There had been no tradition of Greek scholarship in the medieval west, few Greek manuscripts in western libraries, no place in the school or university curriculum for the Greek language. The Latin translations from the Greek were limited to a few authors and to a restricted range of disciplines; with rare exceptions, leading medieval scholars had no Greek. The precedent for the humanists' Greek revival came from Byzantium, where the study of classical Greek language and literature had continued throughout the Middle Ages. Although Petrarch and Boccaccio had engaged Greek teachers, the renewal really began only with Chrysoloras, called to teach Greek in Florence at the end of the fourteenth century; his pupils formed the first extensive circle of western Greek scholars since Antiquity, inaugurating the study of Greek as a major activity both of education and scholarship. Most important here were the copying and dissemination of Greek manuscripts in the west and, above all, the translation of the classics of Greek literature, philosophy and science into Latin, including the retranslation in a less literal manner of authors such as Aristotle who had been available in the Middle Ages. It remains the greatest achievement of Renaissance humanism that almost all classical Greek literature became available to the west, both in editions of the original texts and in Latin translations.

The most original aspect of humanist Greek scholarship in the fifteenth century was undertaken by Valla with his philological study of the New Testament; indeed, to subject the Bible itself to critical textual analysis was a genuine innovation in western history, without precedent either in Antiquity or the Middle Ages. Valla compared the Vulgate with the Greek text, bringing to bear all the philological knowledge of the ancient languages accumulated by the humanists – a revolutionary step as Jerome's translation had been revered as divinely inspired and authoritative for more than a millennium. Erasmus regarded himself as the continuator of Valla's work, which also profoundly influenced Luther's interpretation and general approach to the Scriptures, and yet in his own century Valla's biblical criticism remained an aberration, unpublished and without impact until Erasmus's edition of 1505. In fact, despite its vast importance for future history, the Greek revival remained in the fifteenth century a limited enterprise. Many important humanists never learned Greek, a language which very few were capable of writing proficiently (Filelfo's letters and Poliziano's verse were exceptional). Many Greek authors were hardly appreciated or known, even in Latin translation, and it is almost bizarre that a spurious text such as the pseudonymous letters of Phalaris was far more widely circulated in translation than Homer. The taste for Greek literature in the fifteenth century tended to be Hellenistic, rather than classical, which is not really surprising, in view of the fact that the Roman authors with whom humanists were most familiar had been the direct heirs not of classical, but rather of Hellenistic Greece. Despite the Greek revival, Antiquity in the fifteenth century on balance still meant largely Roman Antiquity.

In one way, the humanist movement, as developed by Petrarch and many of his successors, represented, in negative terms a narrowing, more positively a deepening, of knowledge. This can be seen, for example, in Petrarch's list of favourite books. Petrarch's interests are almost exclusively in the *studia humanitatis*; the ancient and medieval heritage in science, philosophy (apart from ethics) and theology are virtually put to one side. Even his favourite, Augustine, author of more than a hundred works of theology and philosophy, is represented by a mere four titles – *The City of God, The Confessions* and two devotional works, demonstrating a notable deviation from the medieval view of Augustine as a philosophical and theological authority and suggesting that he had become a figure of more personal and moral inspiration. On the other hand, the classical works listed constituted a specialist collection, including works and authors (e.g. *De oratore*, Cicero's orations, Livy) far removed from the mainstays of the medieval literary canon;

indeed, Petrarch's library was later to include many recondite works almost unknown in the Middle Ages.

Of course, not all humanists shared Petrarch's distaste for metaphysics and speculative philosophy; his most notable immediate successor, Salutati, had a wide knowledge of scholastic philosophy, including the latest trends in nominalism and Scotism. Although a number of other humanists, such as Manetti, devoted many years, after their grounding in the *studia humanitatis*, to the study of philosophy and theology, it is clear that there was no intrinsic connection between the humanist and scholastic disciplines; attempts to connect Petrarch's or Valla's emphasis on will rather than intellect with developments in late medieval nominalism showing similar tendencies have revealed only links of the most generic nature, demonstrating at best that such voluntaristic colourings were a common currency in much late medieval thought from mysticism, pietism and devotionalism to nominalism and humanism. Nevertheless, the philosophical and speculative poverty of the *studia humanitatis* worried a number of fifteenth-century humanists. Alamanno Rinuccini, for example, criticised the generation of humanists before the 1450s for taking no more than a small sip from the cup of philosophy, thinking it was more than enough to have dabbled in ethics. The most powerful (and amusing) assertion of this view came from Giovanni Pico in his famous letter to Ermolao Barbaro of 1485, when he ridiculed humanism as mere playing with words, in contrast to the sublime study of philosophy.

Salutati's formulation of the *studia humanitatis* as a prelude to the *studia divinitatis* was repeated in so many words by Pico in his famous *Oration*, a text only incidentally and initially concerned with the dignity of man; in fact its actual purpose was to underpin the traditional hierarchy of learning from grammar and rhetoric to dialectic and philosophy and finally to theology (the subject of Pico's 900 theses which the oration was meant to justify) as the queen of the sciences. If the overall shape of knowledge remained so traditional in the fifteenth century, then it was inevitable that the programme of learning envisaged in the *studia humanitatis* would eventually come to be regarded as incomplete. It is against this background that the great Platonic revival of the fifteenth century must be considered. Attempts have been made to see this landmark in the history of thought in political terms, particularly with reference to Florence, where the new emphasis on the contemplative life propounded by Platonists such as Landino and Ficino have been related to growing Medicean hegemony and to the narrowing possibilities for real political participation; however, this thesis has now been decisively refuted by the simple fact, overlooked by scholars keen to invert Baron's "civic humanism," that the turn to speculative philosophy in Florence actually began in the mid-1450s, a time when Medicean control in Florence was near to collapse. Another equally unsuccessful explanation has focused on the lectures of Argyropoulos, who, having begun teaching in Florence in the mid-1450s, supposedly championed Plato over Aristotle; many scholars have subscribed to this thesis, first propounded by Garin, evidently without a close reading of Argyropoulos's actual writings, where it is clear that he was an Aristotelian who regarded Plato as a crude forerunner of his greater pupil. Nevertheless, the role of Argyropoulos was decisive for the origins of a philosophical culture in Florence, if not for Platonism itself. The Byzantine learned tradition, of which he was a notable product, extended beyond rhetoric, grammar and literature to philosophy, science, mathematics and theology; there were almost no Byzantine scholars without developed interests in some of these areas. When Argyropoulos came to Florence, it was natural for him to range beyond the narrow limits of *studia humanitatis* and to criticise humanists such as Bruni for their ignorance of philosophy, for their insistence that philosophy and eloquence were necessarily linked and for their disdain of speculation. Some seeds of this favourable attitude to speculative philosophy may have been sewn at the University of Florence by Marsuppini, who seems to have himself ranged more widely than usual in his lectures in the humanities, and there are other important preliminary figures such as the scholastics Lorenzo Pisano and Niccolò Tignosi, Ficino's teacher; moreover, the undoubted growing elitism of Florentine society in the later fifteenth century provided a receptive clientele for Ficino's "special esoteric form of Christianity." Nevertheless, the seeds of the new philosophical culture of later Medicean Florence, with the essential critical attitude to humanism which underlay Ficino's and Pico's Platonism, must have come from Argyropoulos and the Byzantine tradition which he represented.

Fifteenth-century humanism was overwhelmingly an Italian phenomenon, but it has long been recognised that the Renaissance began to cross the Alps well before the turn of the sixteenth century. Patriotic scholars earlier this century were keen to find indigenous roots for northern humanism, but their attempts were largely in vain. Recent research, for example, has demonstrated that the Dutch *devotio moderna* was a devotional, not an educational, movement, which only coincidentally shared a distaste for scholastic theology with some (but not all) Italian humanists. Moreover, humanism, like scholasticism, had its roots in the earlier medieval study of the liberal arts; while in Italy this ultimately led to a more intensive study of the classical Latin authors beginning at the end of the thirteenth century, in northern Europe the tendency was to direct the grammatical/rhetorical aspects of the curriculum as much as possible to the eventual study of logic, philosophy and theology. Nevertheless, the Latin classics were never completely abandoned in the north, and there were moments – for example among a few English friars at Oxford and Cambridge in the second quarter of the fourteenth century – of more intensive classical study. However, these English mendicants, whose interest in the classics was mainly directed towards preaching, shared none of the Italian humanists' rejection of medieval learning, and the same can be said of a number of classically minded French clergy of the fourteenth century.

Humanism was imported from Italy to the north. At first there were a few native scholars who, although influenced by Italian humanists, did not quite manage to establish the movement firmly across the Alps. Such, for example, were Jean de Montreuil, secretary of the French king and friend of Bruni and Niccoli, or the earlier imperial chancellor, Johannes von Neumarkt, correspondent of Petrarch's. In fifteenth-century England, the brief residence of Poggio led to no lasting results, while the great patron, Humfrey, duke of Gloucester, who engaged Italian secretaries, collected a huge library of classical and humanist texts and numbered Italian humanists among his correspondents, nevertheless failed to establish an indigenous English humanist movement: in the mid-fifteenth century, English humanism was limited to men such as Tiptoft, Grey, Flemmyng or Free, all of whom acquired

their humanist inclinations while studying in Italy and who never managed to establish a solid institutional basis at home.

In the fifteenth century, humanism made its greatest inroads north of the Alps
in the Germanic regions of the continent. An early figure of note was Peter Luder,
another Guarino pupil, who taught the *studia humanitatis* at Heidelberg, Ulm, Erfurt
and Leipzig. Much more significant was Rudolf Agricola, who spent more than a
decade in Italy, mainly in Pavia and Ferrara; his treatise on dialectic, albeit un-
influential until its publication in the early sixteenth century, became a landmark
in the humanist reform of logic, emphasising probability and persuasion rather than
certainty, and placing Cicero and Quintilian above Aristotle as authorities [see
Chapter 17 below]. Particularly important for the establishment of the movement
in Germany and the Netherlands was the foundation of humanist grammar schools,
the most renowned of which was St Lebwin's in Deventer, headed by Alexander
Hegius, whose pupils included the German mystical humanist Mutianus Rufus and
Erasmus himself. Hegius was an archetypal transitional figure: he used the traditional medieval verse grammar, the *Doctrinale*, but possibly also introduced the
study of Greek and criticised the use of medieval, logically orientated speculative
grammar in favour of the simplified grammatical methods current in Italy.

By the close of the fifteenth century, there were humanists – some indigenous, some Italian trained – throughout Germany. A number were conservative,
such as Jakob Wimpfeling, an outspoken nationalist, who, like Hegius, called for
a simplification of grammar and supported the teaching of some pagan authors such
as Cicero and Vergil, while banning others, including Ovid and Catullus; after
some dithering, Wimpfeling upheld the value of scholastic learning. A figure of
greater significance, albeit strictly conservative in religion, was Johann Reuchlin,
who made three long visits to Italy, where he came into contact with Lorenzo de'
Medici, Ficino, Pico and Ermolao Barbaro; well before the end of the century,
following the path of his idol Pico, he began to study Hebrew, of which he published
the first usable grammar in 1506, so becoming the first northern scholar of the
three ancient languages. From Ficino and Pico he adopted the Ancient Theology,
and he also took up the latter's view that the Cabbala embodied a hidden wisdom
revealed directly by God to Moses; his own cabbalistic works provided an essential link between Florentine occultism and later developments in northern Europe.
More iconoclastic than either Wimpfeling or Reuchlin was Conrad Celtis, an
outstanding Latin poet who on an Italian trip met Battista, son of Guarino, Ficino
and Pomponio Leto; on his return he founded humanist societies or academies,
possibly inspired by the example of Florentine and Roman academies, in various
German cities including Ingolstadt, Heidelberg and Vienna. Equally important was
the patronage he gained while teaching poetry in Vienna at the close of the century,
from the emperor, Maximilian. A fervent German patriot, Celtis published a
student edition of Tacitus' *Germania* in 1500, which helped to link humanism with
frustrated German nationalism.

By the end of the century humanism was fairly well rooted in Germany, with
numerous local groups, humanist schools and a firm, if subordinate, position in
the university curriculum, not to mention several outstanding indigenous representatives. The movement's progress in France was more marginal. In the fifteenth
century, the Parisian colleges of Navarre and Montaigu remained strictly

conservative. An Italian humanist, Gregorio Tifernate, had been appointed to a professorship of Greek in the mid-fifteenth century, and the scholastic philosopher Guillaume Fichet had lectured on classical authors, besides establishing France's first printing press, whose output included a number of classical and humanist texts, as well as work by Fichet himself. But it was not until Robert Gaguin that France had its first genuine humanist. After several Italian visits, not only did he gather round himself a modest classical academy, but he also published vernacular versions of Livy and Caesar as well as his own history of Frankish origins in 1498. Particularly significant was his encouragement of the youthful Erasmus, whose first two publications appeared in works by Gaguin. Another important late fifteenth-century development was a scheme to replace medieval translations of Aristotle with those by Italian humanists. The great personality here was Jacques Lefèvre d'Etaples. Inspired by Ermolao Barbaro, he aimed to paraphrase essential ideas from Aristotle's metaphysics and natural philosophy, deliberately leaving to one side the accumulated tradition of scholastic commentary. After several Italian visits on which he met both Ficino and Pico, Lefèvre took up Platonism and Hermeticism; significant for French national sympathies was his publication of the late ancient neoplatonic mystic, Dionysius the Areopagite, erroneously identified with a convert of St Paul's and also with France's patron saint, Denis. Despite these important inroads, nevertheless, it is clear that by the end of the century humanism had made greater progress in the Netherlands or Germany than in France, where there is little convincing evidence of influence on grammar school education.

The picture is not dissimilar in the rest of western Europe. Spanish humanism produced only one figure of note in the fifteenth century, Antonio de Nebrija, educated at Bologna and the author of perhaps the most successful humanist Latin grammar, a work which soon achieved a notable circulation throughout Europe, including Italy. In England, the claims for humanism have tended to be exaggerated, mainly owing to the misunderstood affiliations of John Colet. Recent research has demonstrated that, although he visited Italy and admired the Florentine Platonists, his educational reforms demonstrated antipathy to most classical literature, which had little place in his curriculum for St Paul's school, which was only given a genuine humanist direction by its first high master, William Lily. Other figures of some note were Thomas Linacre, a physician who had studied with Demetrius Chalcondyles and Poliziano, whose other pupil, William Grocyn, gave the first established lectures in Greek at Oxford before the end of the century. Particularly significant for future developments was Erasmus's brief stay in England in 1499. Recent research has suggested that the English universities, although dominated of course by the traditional scholastic syllabus, allowed greater scope for the development of humanism than had previously been assumed. At Oxford, Cornelio Vitelli, a minor Italian humanist, taught grammar at New College in the 1480s, while also tutoring privately in Greek; Magdalen College school, founded before the end of the century, also stressed from the start the reading of classical authors. Greater early progress was made at Cambridge; Lorenzo Traversagni taught rhetoric and moral philosophy there between 1472 and 1482, while another Italian humanist, Auberino, taught classical authors, together with John Fisher, later bishop of Rochester. Most notable was a statute of 1488, reinforced in 1495, establishing a public lectureship at Cambridge on "humanity."

While the achievements of ultramontane humanists in the fifteenth century are thus limited, their Italian counterparts had certainly accomplished great things; nevertheless, in its core areas humanism preserved many traditional features and showed marked continuity with medieval learning. Many of its genuine innovations, such as textual criticism or the revival of Greek, were esoteric pursuits, not even practised and certainly not mastered by the majority of humanists. The query remains, therefore, why humanism was so successful as a cultural movement: if it shared so much in common with medieval learning, what was the secret of its undoubted appeal not only in Italy but eventually throughout Europe? This fundamental question is never asked, much less answered, by Kristeller; pointing to the continuity and development of traditional Aristotelian studies throughout the Renaissance, as well as emphasising humanism's literary rather than philosophical focus, provides only a negative response: humanism's success could not have been due to its alleged appeal as the new philosophy of the Renaissance, because in fact it offered no genuine philosophical alternative to scholasticism [see Chapter 2 above]. Hanna Gray goes further and asks why the humanists "failed to recognize, indeed disclaimed, continuity with medieval practice," questioning why they should have been so highly valued by their "particular age." Her answer focuses on "the subjective consciousness of novelty": the humanists succeeded because they were convinced, and were able to convince the world at large, that their studies – particularly the pursuit of eloquence – offered a surer path than scholasticism to virtue and the good life [see Chapter 3 above]. Gombrich similarly stresses the subjective appeal of humanism, its one-upmanship: like a fashion, it succeeded by giving its adherents a sense of superiority.

These kinds of interpretations are the inevitable response to the "revolt of the medievalists" – whose ranks Kristeller must to some extent join: if humanism was not objectively so different from medieval learning, then its appeal must have been subjective. There is doubtless much to recommend this approach, and yet it could hardly be the whole story. Humanism swept Italian society in the Quattrocento, to be followed by overwhelming success throughout Europe in the sixteenth century. It became impossible to get a job as a schoolmaster, private tutor or public servant without humanist credentials. Hard-headed Florentine businessmen paid large sums of money to humanist teachers to educate their children, to booksellers to fill their libraries with classical and humanist texts, to dealer and agents to adorn their palaces with enormously expensive antiquities. Was this no more than just fashion, and indeed a fashion which was to last for centuries? Surely they must have expected something more tangible than just virtue or one-upmanship for all the money, effort and time spent.

One solution to this problem focuses on the "civic" world of late fourteenth- and fifteenth-century Italy, suggesting that humanism's success was due to its practical political lessons. Scholasticism, it is argued, offered only intellectual knowledge; humanism, in contrast, taught men how to make hard political and moral decisions in the real world. Humanism appealed because Italian citizens found its lessons to be of greater practical use than those offered by the scholastics. This view not only accepts literally the humanists' own claims for their wares, but also is far removed from the realities of Italian political life. In fact, humanist treatises, like their Ciceronian or Senecan models, offered few, if any, lessons in political reality; their moral platitudes and banalities could hardly have helped any Italian politician faced with decisions about war or peace, alliances, factional conflict, taxation or government of subject territories. This kind of interpretation in fact depicts the ideal political world "of republics and principalities which have never been seen or known to exist," so scathingly ridiculed by Machiavelli in Chapter 15 of *The Prince*. Evidently misleading has been the discovery that some debates of the Florentine delibera- tive council, the *Pratica*, contained more elaborate speeches, more citations from classical authors and more references to history in the 1410s; however, these changes coincided with new chancery personnel in Florence, and may have represented bureaucratic elaboration, known to have occurred at other times in the fifteenth century, rather than an actual different style of debating. Most importantly, the records in the Florentine archives demonstrate that humanist moralising hardly concerns the speakers; at issue instead were the real problems of political life and even survival. Humanism appealed far beyond republican Florence or Venice: to suggest that in a time of growing elitism and loss of political liberty there was still scope for significant civic participation in the vestigial communal institutions of Milan, Mantua, Ferrara or in the host of subject cities such as Padua, Vicenza, Arezzo or Pisa is inappropriate; subjects in such cities were only too aware of the fact that they had lost their liberty and any kind of meaningfully active political life. Humanist educators promised to teach morals and create worthy citizens; the fact that they made no attempt to live up to these claims in the actual classroom must funda- mentally undermine the thesis that humanism succeeded because of the practical benefits offered to society. No republican or "civic" interpretation can adequately explain humanism's triumph for the simple reason that in the age of humanism civic and republican life were rapidly becoming anachronisms.

One historian has written that "the acceptability of the new culture as the common currency of élite society rather than as the hobby of a few eccentrics depended on the conclusion by hard-headed Florentine oligarchs that humanistic studies were useful to a ruling class." The truth of this statement depends on the definition of the word "useful." If useful means teaching practical or even rela- tively more practical lessons for everyday political and social life, then it is patently false. If, however, "useful" means fulfilling the interests of the ruling class, then we have at last arrived at the reason for humanism's success. For centuries Italy had been a snobbish, elitist society; even the Florentines, who stopped short of establishing a constitutionally privileged and exclusive aristocracy as in Venice, had never allowed rapid and extreme fluctuations of wealth, characteristic of the medieval Italian economy, to level the gradations of the social hierarchy. Traditionally, a classical education meant nothing to the Italian upper classes. What they wanted for their children was enough literacy and numeracy to carry on the family business, to maintain and improve the family's patrimony: for them, in Alberti's words, "it is enough to know how to write your name, and to know how to add up how much money you are owed." It was along these lines that one patrician Florentine, Bernardo Manetti, provided for the education of his son:

At a young age, he sent him, according to the custom of the city, to learn to read and write. When, in a brief time, the boy had mastered the learning necessary to become a merchant, his father took him away from elementary school and sent him to arithmetic [abacus] school, where in a few months he similarly learned enough to work as a merchant. At the age of ten he went into a bank.

Another Florentine, a member of an ancient Florentine family of illustrious feudal descent, Messer Andrea de' Pazzi, gave his son Piero little encouragement to pursue his education:

Being the son of Messer Andrea and a young man of handsome appearance, devoted to the delights and pleasures of the world, Piero gave little thought to the study of Latin letters: indeed, his father was a merchant and like those who have little education themselves, he had scant regard for learning nor did he think that his son would show much inclination in that direction.

Similar were the views of one famous humanist's father, a man who was "in accordance with the custom of the city, more given to earning than to learning," and who therefore refused to sanction his son's classical studies.

The Italian (and European) idea of a gentleman, however, was redefined by the circle of patricians who had originally gathered round Salutati and who became even more influential after his death. For such men as Palla Strozzi, Niccolò Niccoli, Roberto Rossi, Antonio Corbinelli and Agnolo Pandolfini, classical learning was an essential ingredient of gentility, a necessary qualification for membership of the social élite – a view which they derived from the study of the ancients themselves. The classical texts which provide the most compelling portrait of the ideal Roman gentleman – Cicero's *Orator* and *De oratore* and Quintilian's *Institutio* – were either studied for the first time or with renewed vigour at the turn of the fifteenth century; from such sources the Florentine avant-garde was confirmed in its view that no one should command a high social position, no one could rightfully call himself a gentleman, no one was qualified to rule, without a classical education. Such ideas were the core of the first and most influential of all humanist educational treatises, Vergerio's *De ingenuis moribus*, written *c.* 1402 in the wake of the author's stay in Florence and of his association with Salutati's circle as a pupil of Chrysoloras. Vergerio's work aimed to guide the education of society's leaders, whether citizens, princes or courtiers; it established classical learning as an essential qualification to merit or retain political power and social leadership. This new humanist ideal of education could be associated with any leader or élite, republican or monarchical, and therefore was adaptable throughout Italy and ultimately throughout Europe. The greatest humanist teacher, Guarino, who frequented Chrysoloras's lessons too, later teaching in Florence from 1410 to 1414, was also soon advertising the humanist claims to educate society's rulers, as in this letter to a *podestà* of Bologna in 1419:

I understand that when civil disorder recently aroused the people of Bologna to armed conflict you showed the bravery and eloquence of a soldier as well as you had previously meted out a judge's just sentence . . . You therefore owe no small thanks to the Muses with whom you have been on intimate terms since your boyhood, and by whom you were brought up. They taught you how to carry out your tasks in society. Hence you are living proof that the Muses rule not only musical instruments but also public affairs.

The crucial change from the traditional medieval to the Renaissance ideal of education is revealed with great clarity by Alberti:

> And who does not know that the first thing useful for children are Latin letters? And this is so important that someone unlettered, however much a gentleman, will be considered nothing but a country bumpkin. And I should like to see young noblemen with a book in hand more frequently than with a hawk . . . If there is anything which goes beautifully with gentility or which gives the greatest distinction to human life or adds grace, authority and name to a family, it is surely letters, without which no one can be reputed to possess gentility.

Humanism succeeded because it persuaded Italian and ultimately European society that without its lessons no one was fit to rule or lead. The common misconception about this educational revolution is that it involved a change in substance, in curriculum, as well as in ideology. A change in the practical benefits of education never could nor did occur; better Latinity could never mean superior morality or greater political expertise. A change in curriculum only developed very gradually, slowly in the fifteenth century and then more quickly in the sixteenth. But the change in ideology was rapid and decisive.

What then was the appeal to the upper classes of this humanist educational programme? Italian society, since the rise of the communes, if not before, was always in flux; in an economy where wealth and prominence depended not just on land but also so much on commercial and industrial fortunes, on local as well as far-flung international and overseas trading adventures, families and individuals rose and fell with amazing rapidity. In this world, society was always on the look out for better definitions of social and political acceptability. This was particularly true in communal Italy during the fourteenth and fifteenth centuries, when traditional definitions of nobility had been devalued by association with mercenaries and with politically ostracised groups such as the Florentine magnates. Humanism's particular definition had the best of all possible seals of approval – it was endorsed by the ancients. The crucial texts by Cicero and Quintilian had been little known in the Middle Ages; moreover, Cicero's moral philosophical works in general had suffered a serious decline during the preceding century and a half. It is here that the subjectivity stressed by Gombrich or Gray comes into play. It did not matter that the equation between Latinity, virtue, social leadership and political power did not really add up. It suited everyone – humanists as well as the social elite. Nor could anyone say that a humanist education was empty, for its products emerged as outstanding Latin and ultimately Greek scholars. No one questioned the equation between a classical education and moral and political virtue: if it was good enough for Antiquity, it was surely good enough for the Renaissance.

PART TWO

Renaissance Scholarship and Learning

Chapter 5

Ian Thomson

■   from **MANUEL CHRYSOLORAS AND THE
EARLY ITALIAN RENAISSANCE**, *Greek, Roman
and Byzantine Studies*, 7 (1966), pp. 63–82

FROM AT LEAST the eighteenth century, when scholars first began to
discuss the "Italian Renaissance" as a cultural phenomenon, the importance of
Manuel Chrysoloras, the first notable professor of Greek in Western Europe, has
been widely recognized. Writers such as Carlo Rosmini, Jacob Burckhardt, John
Addington Symonds, and Remigio Sabbadini have given him deservedly honorable mention as the teacher of a number of influential humanists, whose interest
in classical studies did much to bring about the Renaissance as a whole. It was not
until 1941, however, that Professor G. Cammelli produced a full-length study of
Chrysoloras' career and its effect upon the early Renaissance. This excellent work
has made information on the external events of Chrysoloras' life, especially for
the period 1397–1415, readily accessible.

The purpose of this article is [. . .] to assess the extent of Chrysoloras' influence
on his pupils and the nature of their admiration for him, with particular reference
to Guarino da Verona [. . .]

Chrysoloras was not without honor in his own lifetime, as is well attested in
the letters and orations of his pupils and friends.

Indeed, during the eighteen years between his arrival in Florence in 1397 and
his death at or near Constance on April 15, 1415, his considerable intellectual gifts
and excellence as a teacher won him almost universal respect and inspired in some
of his pupils a sense of gratitude that survived him for almost half a century.

His most direct contribution to the Revival of Learning was made in the years
1397–1400, during which he taught Greek to a small number of humanists in
Florence. These men not only set the cultural tone of their own city but were
able eventually to make their influence felt all over Italy. It should be noted that
since Petrarch and Boccaccio there had existed among the more intellectually radical
scholars in Florence and throughout northern Italy at least a theoretical desire to
learn Greek, but few of them did much about it. Guarino, we are told by the so-
called Anonymous Veronese, was "urged by the wise men whose company he often

sought" to learn Greek, but he was the first important scholar intrepid enough to visit Constantinople for that specific purpose. Many scholars paid lip service to Greek as an interesting and harmless bagatelle, but the majority of professors and students were simply not interested or were actively averse. At the end of the fourteenth century only Coluccio Salutati, Palla Strozzi, Niccolò Niccoli and a few others – probably no more than ten in number – were really enthusiastic about learning Greek. Mere numbers, however, are unimportant; what matters in cultural history is breadth of influence and contribution ultimately recognized.

Leonardo Bruni, for instance, contributed to the spread of Greek culture by a series of important translations. He had cut his teeth as a translator of Greek with Latin versions of Basilius' *Homilia* and Xenophon's *Hieron*. By 1403 or 1404 he had produced a translation of Plato's *Phaedon*. The list continued to grow over the next three decades, and embraced versions of Aeschines, Plutarch, Demosthenes, and Aristotle. Already by 1418 he was able to boast in a letter: *Tam multa etiam ex Platone, Demosthene, Plutarcho, Xenophonte in latinum traduximus.*[1] His most important translations were those of the *Ethica* (before 1416), *Politica* (1438), and *Oeconomica* of Aristotle, Book I of the (pseudo-) Aristotelian *Oeconomica* being completed on March 3, 1420, and Book II being added between March 25, 1420 and March 24, 1421.

Roberto Rossi also translated Aristotle, although his work was not as influential as Bruni's. The only extant version by Rossi is that of the *Analytica Posteriora*. It is worth noting, however, that in 1411 Guarino praised Rossi's translations of Aristotle and spoke of them as being in use throughout the "gymnasia"[2] of Italy. [. . .]

In 1404 Pier Paolo Vergerio wrote his famous essay *De ingenuis moribus et liberalibus studiis adolescentiae*,[3] the very title of which suggested a break with the traditions of mediaeval education. Vergerio proposed a return to the balanced, liberal curriculum of later Greek education – in effect, to the so-called *enkyklios paideia*, although he does not use that term – in which the individual's physical and mental aptitudes were to be equally developed. By giving physical education such prominence and by insisting that the cultivation of good morals was the sovereign aim of education, Vergerio pointed the way that Barzizza, Guarino and Vittorino were to follow. Admittedly so far as intellectual training was concerned, his "revised" curriculum, consisting of syntax, dialectic, rhetoric, poetry, music, mathematics, astronomy, natural history, drawing, medicine, law, ethics, and theology, is little more than a rehashed list of the subjects of the mediaeval *trivium* and *quadrivium*; nor does Vergerio add any recommendations as to how these subjects should be taught, or for how long, or in what order. But he did show that a balanced education designed to produce a whole man was desirable; and the inspirational effect of this upon the great humanistic educators cannot be doubted. What was implicit in Petrarch was explicit in Vergerio.

It is possible to argue [. . .] that Vergerio's treatise owes nothing to the teaching of Manuel Chrysoloras and that "we may reasonably assume that he was putting on paper the principles that had guided him throughout his career," but there is no evidence to support such an assumption, except for a disputed dating of the *De ingenuis moribus*. Vergerio spent most of his life teaching logic, and never opened an independent school in which he could have implemented his ideas. It is more reasonable to regard the *De ingenuis moribus* as Vergerio's reaction to the teaching of Chrysoloras, especially since he is able to cite Greek authorities directly [. . .] Through Vergerio, then, Chrysoloras may be said to have given educationalists in the West a new and clearer inspiration to implement the ideals of Greek education, which led to the translation by Guarino in 1411 of Plutarch's *De liberis educandis*[4] and the remarkable experiments by Barzizza at Padua (1408–1420), Vittorino at Mantua (1423–1446), and Guarino at Venice (1414–1419), Verona (1420–1429), and Ferrara (1430–1460).

There can be no dispute, moreover, about the effect of Chrysoloras' teaching methods upon Bruni, for the latter's *De studiis et litteris*[5] (*c.* 1425) addressed to Battista Malatesta, daughter of the count of Urbino, was the first detailed exposition of the new pedagogic technique that Chrysoloras had brought from Constantinople. This technique stressed accurate pronunciation, the use of mnemonics, constant and regular revision of subject matter and the preparation of copious notes under the headings of *methodice* (grammar, syntax and vocabulary), and *historice* (what we should call "background material"). Bruni recommended minute attention to linguistic detail and imitation of classical models through the use of these techniques. Chrysoloras left no account of his methods, the culmination of centuries of Byzantine experience, but we know what they were from Bruni's treatise, and in even finer detail from Battista Guarino's *De modo et ordine docendi et discendi*,[6] which was read and approved by his father Guarino in 1459. Guarino himself wrote nothing on educational method save for sundry recommendations scattered throughout his letters; the honor must go to Bruni for having been the first humanist to summarize Chrysoloras' ideas in a convenient form.

Chrysoloras' work at Florence had yielded excellent fruit in Bruni, Rossi and Vergerio, not to mention such minor contributions to learning as Jacopo Angeli da Scarperia's translations of Plutarch's lives of Brutus (1400) and Cicero (1410) and Ptolemy's *Chorographia*.[7] But his influence cannot be measured only in tangibles. Such men as Poggio, Traversari, Salutati, Marsuppini, Niccoli and Palla Strozzi acquired, in addition to some knowledge of Greek, a deeper understanding of antiquity and an increased confidence in themselves. It would be mistaken to underestimate the force of this self-confidence in shaping the political and humanistic literature that glorified Florence as true heir of republican Rome and the champion of popular liberty Italy.

Those pupils who benefited from Chrysoloras' instruction at Florence naturally expressed their gratitude. One indication of the value they attached to him was the fact that his salary was raised on two occasions, the final sum in 1400 standing at 250 gold florins. More important, however, was the devotion they expressed in letters, the literary form most favoured by the humanists. Vergerio, for instance, in a letter of 1406, deplores the possibly permanent loss of Chrysoloras to students in Italy and refers to him as "the best and most learned man whom your city (Florence) had called from the heart of Greece to disseminate Greek studies in Italy" [. . .] Poggio, too, was conscious of a deep personal debt to Chrysoloras and expressed as much in letters to other scholars. The same is true of the other Florentine pupils, with the possible exception of Niccoli. On the whole, however, the Florentines' praise of Chrysoloras did not run to luxuriance. They were grateful for his willingness to answer their call for a good teacher of Greek, and aware of the benefits they had reaped from his instruction, but they did not make a cult of him, as did Guarino. This may have been because they were a proud breed of men, over-partial to their own achievements and given to intellectual pretensions that often irritated the citizens of other states. But more probably their political pre-occupations had something to do with it. As Baron has pointed out, the dramatic struggle in the war against Giangaleazzo Visconti produced a series of humanistic works glorifying Florence and her political and cultural heritage. The Florentine attitude to great men varied with the political climate. For example, Salutati's treatise *De Tyranno*, written in 1400, was a defense of Julius Caesar and the rule of a single man, but the *Invectiva in Antonium Luscum Vicentinum*[8] shows that within the next few years he had radically altered his opinions. Again, in Bruni's *Dialogus ad Petrum Paulum Histrum*[9] *I* Niccoli is depicted as a militant classicist with little time for Dante, Petrarch and Boccaccio, and Bruni himself seems ranged on Niccoli's side, whereas in the *Dialogus II*, composed about three years later, in 1403 or 1404, Bruni, Niccoli, and Salutati join in defending the Trecento tradition. As is well known, Bruni later produced lives of Dante and Petrarch in Italian. The immense pride felt by the Florentines in their cultural tradition may have detracted somewhat from their appreciation of Chrysoloras. It certainly saved them from the excesses of Guarino da Verona.

Guarino did not begin his study of Greek until after Chrysoloras had ceased to be active as a teacher in Italy. In March or April of 1403, the latter had returned with the Emperor Manuel II Palaeologus to Constantinople. Guarino followed him shortly afterwards, and studied under Manuel and his nephew John until about 1406. Manuel was absent for part of the time, but one cannot doubt that his was the guiding spirit of the school, and that he made an overwhelming impression upon his young Italian student. By the end of 1407, Manuel moved permanently to the West and Guarino returned to Italy in 1408. Thereafter, the two men seem to have remained in touch, although at probably sporadic intervals. The extant correspondence between them is limited to three letters, one in Latin from Guarino and two in Greek from Chrysoloras. It is known, however, that they met in Italy on at least two occasions.

In the first of Manuel's Greek letters, dated January, 1412, he congratulates Guarino on his success in disseminating in Italy what he had learned in Greece, and refers to the Σύγκρισις τῆς παλαιᾶς καὶ νέας Ῥώμης[10] which Guarino had received from him in October of the previous year [. . .] It appears that Guarino had been distributing copies of this work – a comparison between Rome and Constantinople, designed in essence to foster good relations between the East and West – throughout Northern Italy. Chrysoloras was signally grateful for this service, but Guarino probably felt that he was only fulfilling the demands of *pietas*.[11] Most humanists felt obliged to spread the fame of their friends and teachers as widely as possible. For that reason, Guarino rarely missed an opportunity, both during and after Chrysoloras' lifetime, of reminding his fellow scholars in letters, conversation, orations, and lectures of their debt to Chrysoloras.

It is noteworthy, however, that in his correspondence, in which the bulk of these tributes appears, Guarino seldom refers to Chrysoloras specifically as a teacher of Greek, but rather as the one man most responsible for the restoration of the "best studies" to Italy. By "best studies" (*optima studia*), the "rebirth of letters" (*renata humanitas*) and other such expressions the humanists – and Guarino was no exception – generally meant that critical approach to the content of ancient literature and the close, prescriptive study of classical Latin which we associate with the Revival of Learning. At first sight, then, Guarino's praise seems paradoxical, for Chrysoloras' reputation in cultural history rests upon his success as a teacher of Greek. It is known that he never mastered Latin as well as did some of the Greek émigrés later in the fifteenth century, and certainly could never have taught it at a professorial level to Italians. Guarino must have been thinking more of the good effect that Chrysoloras had exerted upon classical studies in general. He believed, undoubtedly, that Chrysoloras had given the Italians much more than a narrow specialty. Further, he believed that a proper understanding of Latin could not be achieved without a knowledge of Greek.

[. . .] It seems that both Guarino and his son thought that the Latin and Greek languages, not merely their literatures [. . .] are more intimately related than modern philologists would concede; but this does not invalidate the point that to them Chrysoloras appears to have made possible a fuller understanding of the Latin tongue itself. It was natural for Guarino to see the spread of Greek as marking the dawn of a new era in Latin studies and to invest Chrysoloras with a special significance, as not merely having supplied a knowledge of Greek, but also the humanizing spirit and sovereign stimulus needed to rouse Italian scholarship out of its long sleep.

Guarino's insistence that Chrysoloras had been the harbinger of a new age did not go without notice. In the first place, his prestige as a scholar enabled him to command the attention of the educated public. Although his letters were not collected and edited for publication in his own century, they were nevertheless passed around as models of style and collectors' items. Any praise of Chrysoloras contained in them was thereby assured of a fairly wide circulation. This helped to keep the name of Chrysoloras alive in the later fifteenth century and brought it again to the fore in the eighteenth and nineteenth centuries when Guarino's letters began to be collected and published in small batches. Second, and perhaps more important, is the fact that from 1436 at least, Guarino was the most influential teacher in Italy, if not in Europe. He was in a unique position to pass on his reminiscences to large numbers of young students who could never have seen or met Chrysoloras. Some of these pupils were inevitably affected by Guarino's admiration for Chrysoloras and referred to him in their own writings.

[. . .]

Shortly after Chrysoloras' death, Vergerio suggested to the Venetian Niccolò Leonardi, a physician with humanistic leanings, that their common friend, Guarino, ought to write a formal *commemoratio* of the great Byzantine. Guarino, however, claimed that his own powers were unequal to such an undertaking, and referred it to Vergerio himself [. . .] Vergerio composed a very fine epitaph, and the Venetian Andrea Zulian wrote a funeral speech which had a wide circulation and is extant in many manuscripts. The lack of some worthwhile memorial to Chrysoloras, however, weighed upon the consciences of his pupils and friends for many years. Guarino, for example, wrote in July, 1416, to Giacomo dei Fabbri: "Many a time I have set myself to write a splendid work in praise of this man . . . for I think it unfair and a mark of ingratitude that he whose industry helped us not merely to speak but to speak with eloquence, should be immersed in silence

. . . but I am overwhelmed by the amount there is to say and the importance of the subject, and I give up." He goes on to praise the funeral speech by Zulian, and concludes: "After Zulian, silence would seem the better course, unless one had a mind to unfold in detail the life of the aforesaid Manuel from the cradle up" [. . .] No one, however, wrote the projected biography, perhaps because details of Chrysoloras' earlier life were lacking, but more likely because most scholars did not consider him important enough to warrant a detailed biography. It is perhaps surprising that Guarino never fulfilled his own suggestion. Poggio shared something of Guarino's hero worship of Chrysoloras, and as late as June, 1455, was still sufficiently disturbed by his own failure to write at length in praise of Chrysoloras that he confessed to Guarino: "As to your writing of a rumor that I had composed a laudation of the late brilliant and learned gentleman, Manuel Chrysoloras – I wish it were true!" Guarino did, however, make some reparation by collecting a series of works about Chrysoloras, which he edited and disseminated in 1452 under the title of *Chrysolorina*. This collection helped to preserve the fame of Chrysoloras, as did the fact that his *Erotemata*, a Greek grammar that followed the usual method of question and answer, continued to be widely used until well into the sixteenth century. Its first printing was at Venice in 1484, but it had been used in manuscript long before that; in fact, until the publication of Constantine Lascaris' *Erotemata* at Milan in 1476, it had been the sole Greek grammar in general use in Italy.

In a letter to Vergerio in 1415 Guarino remarks that Chrysoloras had provided the perfect example to follow in leading "the good and blessed life," and even advances the extravagant notion that if Homer had been fortunate enough to have had Chrysoloras as his hero in the *Iliad* instead of the bloodthirsty and uncouth Achilles, he would have been inspired to write a better poem! [. . .] Ludicrous as this may seem to us, Guarino probably meant it seriously, for he subscribed to the ancient and mediaeval notion that the aim of literature is moral edification and for that reason interpreted the *Aeneid* and the Homeric epics allegorically. Thirty-eight years later, Guarino's devotion had not been diminished, for in complimenting his son Battista on a literary sketch of Chrysoloras he says: "You set him before my eyes in such a way that as I behold Manuel's stature, expression, beard, complexion, mannerisms, and the whole set of his body, I almost shout for joy, 'even such his eyes and hands, and such the face he showed.'" It is not perhaps surprising that a man capable of such loyalty should have exaggerated his master's true importance.

It is interesting to note that in the entire epistolary of Guarino, which runs to over 700 letters from him and about 200 from others to him, there is no mention of Dante or Boccaccio, and only one passing reference to Petrarch [. . .] Any reader of Guarino's letters must be struck by the fact that he was either blind to or willfully ignorant of the achievements of scholars in the fifteenth century. Presumably he had read some at least of Petrarch's works, but his silence prompts one to conclude that he did not consider them important. Nor does he ever mention that other great precursor of the Renaissance, the celebrated Giovanni Conversino da Ravenna, to whom he probably owed a great deal. Typical of Guarino's patronizing attitude to scholars of the previous century is the sneer he casts at the Latin style of Salutati's mentor, Pietro da Muglio: *Adeo enim inepte, obscure et inusitate dicit, ut non tam loqui quam mugire videatur*.[12] There is here a play upon "Muglio" and *mugire*. The fact is that to Guarino and many of those he influenced, their predecessors seemed little better than cattle lowing in the darkness. The figure of Chrysoloras, by contrast, assumed the proportions of a colossus ushering in a new and better age.

Historical perspective has enabled us to assess Chrysoloras' contribution to learning more accurately. His instruction in Greek certainly led to the translations made by the Florentine pupils and by Guarino, and in a less direct way helped to stimulate the recovery of lost manuscripts and the study of Latin; but it could be argued that these advances would have been made in any case. Further, there was a demand for Greek in Florence and if the Florentines had not secured Chrysoloras they would probably have found some other teacher of Greek. If Chrysoloras made a unique contribution to the humanistic movement, it surely lay in the protreptic force of his personality and the educational methods to which he introduced the Italians. He obviously used those methods in his teaching at Florence, because Bruni refers to them, but none of his pupils there, except for Vergerio, was a practising teacher, and if Guarino had not passed on the methods to Vittorino and others they might not have become widespread; but as it was, thousands of students in the Renaissance were enabled to absorb massive amounts of grammar, syntax and cultural background. The fountain-head of all this activity was Chrysoloras. Bolgar is surely right when he says that in the last analysis the difference between the age of Petrarch and that of Guarino was "the appearance and widespread adoption of a pedagogic technique."

[. . .]

Editor's Notes

1   We have translated into Latin so many works by Plato, Demosthenes, Plutarch and Xenophon too.
2   schools
3   *On Character and Gentlemanly Studies during Youth*
4   *On the Education of Children*
5   *On Studies and Letters*
6   *On the Method and Order of Teaching and Learning*
7   *Geography*
8   *Invective against Antonio Loschi of Vicenza*
9   *Dialogue to Pier Paolo Vergerio of Istria*
10   *Comparison of Old and New Rome*
11   duty
12   His style was so inept, obscure and strange that he seemed not so much to speak as to bellow.

Chapter 6

Anthony Grafton

■   from **ON THE SCHOLARSHIP OF POLITIAN AND ITS CONTEXT**, *Journal of the Warburg and Courtauld Institutes*, 40 (1977), pp. 150–188

F OR AN INDETERMINATE PERIOD between 1513 and 1521 Claude Bellièvre, that amiable traveller and amateur of papyri, stayed in Rome. Among the many sights he saw there was the Vatican Library, where he examined the Codex Romanus of Virgil with considerable care:

> In the inner library of the Vatican we saw a very old codex of Maro, which Angelo Poliziano boasts in chapter 77 of his century of *Miscellanea* that he saw. There he uses many pieces of evidence to prove that one should say "Vergilius" with an *e* and not "Virgilius," though the latter is more commonly used. And amid the other evidence he particularly cites that of the old codex of Maro, in which "Vergilius" is written throughout with an *e*. I too, while I was carefully studying this manuscript – which by no means everyone is allowed to handle – noticed something else worth remembering. Now there are some recent writers, who try to write all too eloquently, who maintain that "Explicit liber primus" is improper Latin. We, in order that we may agree with Poliziano and many other good men, who think that this very old codex should be considered very trustworthy, shall also think that "Explicit liber primus" is proper Latin. For it is written in this same manuscript, at the end of each book, in clear letters, to serve as the numbering of the books. This manuscript is written in capital letters, and the story is illustrated throughout. And if by chance you wish to see the true form of the script, it is this, which I have drawn as accurately as I could.

What is new here is the way that Bellièvre seeks to use the codex. His interest in palaeographical and orthographical details, his careful description of the manuscript's location and appearance, his precise citation of Politian's work – these interests and practices are new. And it is clear that he has derived them from one source: Politian's *Miscellanea*, his carefully annotated copy of which is still extant.

I do not know if Bellièvre ever met T. Diplovatacius. They would probably have enjoyed one another's company. Each of them was both lawyer and anti-quarian; each of them had intellectual roots in both humanistic and juristic traditions. And they had another link as well. Diplovatacius's *De claris juris consultis* derived just as directly as did Bellièvre's note from the work of Politian. Diplovatacius could never have reconstructed the lives and writings of the ancient jurists had he not been able to draw on Politian's letters – especially the famous letter to Jacopo Modesti da Prato, which summarized much of what could be learned from the *Index Florentinus*. Nor could he have reconstructed the *fortuna* of the Digest without the information given in the *Miscellanea*. To be sure, he had his troubles with Politian's Latin; but he nevertheless ransacked Politian's works to the best of his ability.

What these two cases show – and there are many more – is that Politian brought about a revolution in philological method. For before Politian we find no such work being done in the criticism of texts and sources. In this paper I shall try to sketch the course of this revolution, drawing chiefly, but not exclusively, on the *Miscellanea*. I shall also try to put the revolution in context by comparing Politian's work in some detail with those of his immediate predecessors.

The humanists of the period 1460–80 tended to employ one standard medium for recording and communicating the results of their researches. They commented on classical texts, line by line and often word by word. At first, they gave their commentaries merely as university lectures, and many of them have come down to us only in the form of *recollectae* – students' notes. From the 1470s on, however, it became more and more common to revise such commentaries after delivery and to publish them either independently or along with the texts they concerned.

This style of commentary had a number of advantages. In the first place, it was the traditional style. There were many ancient or old line-by-line commen-taries on standard authors: Servius on Virgil, Donatus on Terence, Porphyrio and Pseudo-Acro on Horace, the scholia on Juvenal and Persius. These works pro-vided the starting point for the earliest humanist commentaries on the works they dealt with; indeed, very often the humanists did little more than repeat what their ancient predecessors had said, merely taking care to conceal the extent of their indebtedness. The first humanist commentary on Virgil, that by Pomponio Leto, relied very heavily on an interpolated text of Servius; Gaspare de' Tirimbocchi, the first humanist commentator on the *Ibis*, relied equally heavily on the extant scholia. Where there was no ancient or pseudo-ancient commentary, there was sometimes a later one of similar form and method – for example, the twelfth-century commentary by "Alanus" on the *ad Herennium*, which Guarino sedulously pillaged for his lectures. Moreover, even for those commenting on texts that were not adorned with ancient scholia, the ancient commentaries provided an obvious model for style and method, one that was both readily accessible and at the same time satisfactorily different from the style of the late medieval classicizing friars.

This style had other advantages as well. Line-by-line commentaries inevitably bulk as large as or larger than the texts they deal with. The commentator, in other words, was expected to fill a large amount of space. His audience expected him to turn any suitable word or phrase into the occasion for an extended digression: into the etymology of a word, into the formation of compounds from it, into its shades of meaning; most often, perhaps, into the justification in terms of formal rhetoric for its appearance in the passage in question. Many digressions departed even farther from the text, into mythological, geographical, antiquarian, and even scientific matters. A commentary on almost any ancient author could thus become an introduction to ancient language, literature, and culture. In short, the commentary was a highly flexible instrument of instruction. Here too, of course, the humanists were following their ancient models. Servius, in particular, used the medium of a commentary on Virgil to impart quantities of information on almost every conceivable subject.

Finally, this style was attractive to students. Since the commentator felt obliged to gloss every word that might present a difficulty, he generally made his text accessible even to students of mean intelligence or poor preparation. At the same time, the student who could write quickly enough to keep up with his teacher ended up with an invaluable possession. When he himself went out to teach, he could simply base his lectures on those of his teacher and so avoid the trouble of independent preparation. It is hardly surprising that students came to demand lectures of this kind; what student would not have his teacher do all the work? As M. Filetico, an unwilling practitioner of this style of commentary, wrote:

> At that time [c. 1468–73] certain very learned men had made the young accustomed not to want to listen to anything unless they added a definition on almost every word. . . . I therefore had to follow their customs.

The style long continued to endure. Politian himself employed various forms of it in his lectures, adapting the content of the excursuses to the needs of his hearers. Its most preposterous result did not appear until 1489 – namely, Perotti's *Cornucopiae*, in which a thousand folio columns served to elucidate one book of Martial.

But the style had disadvantages as well as advantages. It forced the commentator to deal with every problem, the boringly simple as well as the interestingly complex. It also forced him to waste time and pages on the donkey-work of listing synonyms – which is all that thousands of the humanists' short glosses amount to. Worst of all, in a period of intense literary competition the commentary made it impossible for its author to shine. For the most noticeable aspect of all the humanists' commentaries is their similarity to one another. Especially in their printed form, the so-called "modus modernus," the commentaries are nearly indistinguishable. Waves of notes printed in minute type break on all sides of a small island of text set in large Roman. Even numerous digressions into one's field of expertise could not make one commentary distinctively superior to its fellows, for they were hidden by the mass of trivial glosses.

Characteristically, it was Domizio Calderini, one of the first to have one of his commentaries printed, who was also the first to break away from the commentary tradition. In 1475 he decided that he had found a new medium. "Hereafter," he wrote, "I shall not be much concerned with commentaries." Rather, he said, he would concentrate on translation from Greek and on another work

which we have entitled "Observations," in three books, of which the
first contains explications of three hundred passages from Pliny, the
second whatever we have noticed that others have omitted in [expli-
cating] the poets; the third what we have gathered and observed in
Cicero, Quintilian, Livy, and all other writers.

This, then, was to be the new style: books written by and for scholars, books that
dealt selectively with difficult and interesting problems.

Calderini published only a few notes "ex tertio libro Observationum." But they
were soon followed by a number of similar works: M. A. Sabellico's *Annotationes
in Plinium* (finished *c.* 1488, published 1503); Filippo Beroaldo the Elder's
Annotationes centum (1488); Politian's *Miscellaneorum centuria prima* (1489). Politian's
work, then, belonged to a solidly-established, if modern, genre, and to that extent
the *Miscellanea* did not represent a break with the immediate past.

As soon as we look beneath the surface, however, the differences become far
more striking than the similarities. Calderini did not claim explicitly that his
Observationes were inherently more interesting or useful than commentaries. In fact,
the work is for the most part an advertisement for himself and for his previous
writings, and Calderini quoted passages from his own commentaries at length and
with relish. Sabellico said that he was publishing a selection from his notes on
Pliny; he did not say that a selection was preferable to a full commentary. Even
Beroaldo was defensive about the selective and structureless character of his
Annotationes:

> Indeed, in making these annotations we did not keep any order in the
> contents. For we were dictating them extemporaneously . . . This
> offspring was clearly premature, as it was both conceived and brought
> forth in less than a month's time.

For Politian, on the other hand, the very disorder of his work was its principal charm. In phrases carefully adapted from Gellius, Clement of Alexandria,
and Aelian, he boasted of the variety of subjects treated in the *Miscellanea*, for
variety was "fastidii expultrix."[1] Unlike his predecessors, Politian was explicitly
proclaiming the merits of the new genre, which he regarded as a revival of the
ancient antiquarian miscellanies. He was the first to make the break with the
commentary tradition an open one.

The method that Politian employed in the *Miscellanea* was even more novel
than the claims he made for its form. First of all, he placed a new emphasis on
the quality and quantity of his sources. As early as the preface he attacked the
methods of his predecessors and set up his own method as exemplary. He claimed
that he had cited only genuine works by genuine ancient authors:

> But lest those men who are ill employed with leisure think that we
> have drawn [our conclusions] . . . from the dregs, and that we have
> not leapt across the boundaries of the grammarians, we have at the
> outset followed Pliny's example. We have put at the beginning the
> names of the authors – but only ancient and honorable ones – by whom

these [conclusions] are justified, and from whom we have borrowed. But [we have not put down] the names of those whom others have only cited, while their works have disappeared, but those whose treasures we ourselves have handled, through whose writings we have wandered.

At the same time, Politian argued that his predecessors had consistently misused their sources. He used Calderini's commentary on Ovid's *Ibis* as one example of incompetent work. Calderini's claim to have drawn on numerous arcane sources he refuted with contempt:

> Domizio expounded Ovid's *Ibis*. He began by saying that he wrote matter drawn from Apollodorus, Lycophron, Pausanias, Strabo, Apollonius, and other Greeks, and Latins as well. In that commentary he invents many vain and ridiculous things, and makes them up extemporaneously and at his own convenience. By doing so he proves either that he had completely lost his mind, or that, as someone says, there was so great a distance between his mind and his tongue that his mind could not restrain his tongue.

[. . .]

Now there was nothing new in accusing one's predecessors of misusing or inventing sources. Calderini had done just the same. In his commentary on Quintilian Valla had cited an oration of Cicero *pro Scauro*. "Indeed," wrote Calderini,

> I have read in Valerius Maximus and Pedianus that the case of Scaurus was tried in Cicero's presence. But I have never read that Cicero delivered the oration on his behalf from which Lorenzo claims that he drew these words. Nor do I believe that it exists. And I am afraid that Lorenzo, following some ignoble grammarian, recited these words rather than reading them anywhere in Cicero.

So much Politian might have said. The difference lies in two things: in the truthfulness of the attacks, and even more in the consistency of them with the actual practices of the attacker. Calderini's attack was not in fact justified, for Valla had taken his quotation from the *pro Scauro* from a fairly reliable source: Isidore's *Etymologiae*. Moreover, the commentary of Asconius Pedianus – which Calderini himself cited in his attack – clearly indicates that Cicero delivered a speech *pro Scauro*. More important, Calderini's attack on Valla was inconsistent with his own practice. For in the very next section of the *Observationes* he enthusiastically retailed what he had read about Simonides "in a Greek writer" – "apud Graecum scriptorem." One whose own references were so slipshod had no business correcting other people's footnotes – and can hardly have been upholding a personal ideal of full, clear, and accurate citation.

Politian's new standards for the use of sources represented a clear break with the methods of the last generation. Their methods were formed not in the study but in the lecture-hall. They never acquired the habit of full or precise quotation from their sources, for such precision was impossible to attain if they were to lecture comprehensively on the wide variety of topics that their texts suggested.

In particular, they seldom engaged in extensive quotations in Greek, which would have been unintelligible to most of their students and unmanageable for most printers. Instead, they usually provided vague paraphrases, together with imprecise indications of the sources from which they were drawing. Worse still, like their ancient exemplars, they often invented explanations by back-formation from the texts they claimed to be elucidating: "misinformation is often elicited from the text by aid of unjustified inferences."

When the members of this generation turned from the commentary to the collection of precise *Annotationes*, they did abandon one bad habit which had characterized their lectures. They no longer set out two alternate solutions of a given problem without choosing between them – a maddening habit which had characterized the classroom lecture since the Hellenistic period. Indeed, the whole point of their new genre was to show off their ability at solving problems once and for all. Unfortunately, however, they did not abandon their other habits of sloppy, inaccurate citation and unjustified back-formation. Even Perotti, who tried to be honest, abbreviated the names of the authors he cited even when the resulting forms were ambiguous – for example, "Lu." Moreover, he usually failed to inform his readers whether the verses he cited came to him at first or second hand, even though on many occasions he was citing not a line from an extant work but a fragment preserved by Festus or Nonius Marcellus, and on many other occasions he was citing even verses from standard works at second hand. Calderini [. . .] knew Plautus only at second hand, though his own words suggest first-hand knowledge. Most of Perotti's contemporaries were dishonest as well as sloppy. Pomponio Leto gave it out in his lectures that he had a complete text of Ennius. Calderini falsified his notes on Martial in order to refute a justified attack by Perotti. Worst still, he invented a Roman writer, Marius Rusticus, from whom he claimed to derive disquieting information about the youth of Suetonius.

Politian's practices could not have been more different. Not only did he list his sources; even when he quoted a fragment at second hand, he generally pointed out that he was doing so and identified the intermediary source [. . .] Politian's attacks on the practices of his predecessors were traditional only in form. Unlike the earlier ones, they stemmed not only from a desire to gain a reputation and to destroy those of others, but also from genuine desire to reform the current method of citation.

Politian's use of his sources was also different in kind from that of his predecessors. He was the first to compare and evaluate sources in a historical way – that is, in the way which is still employed. Now Politian's sources presented him with various kinds of problem, some of which were fairly trivial. For example, he not uncommonly encountered ancient sources that contradicted one another about historical or mythological details. The solution in such cases was usually obvious. It was only natural for him to follow the most authoritative source, which in most cases simply meant the oldest one. And that was just what Politian did when, for example, he preferred Homer's testimony about the ages of Achilles and Patroclus to those of Aeschylus and Statius.

So far there is nothing new here. Petrarch had encountered contradictions in his ancient sources while compiling the *De viris illustribus*. Salutati and Bruni had uncovered discrepancies in the ancient histories of republican Rome. Flavio Biondo had found ancient authors contradicting one another about the functions of certain ancient buildings. And all of them had found it possible to resolve such contradictions. They assumed that the more authoritative source, or the one which was itself based on more authoritative sources, was correct. The divergent accounts in other texts must have resulted either from scribal errors, in which case they could be emended, or from simple slips on the part of the less authoritative writer, due to bias or bad memory.

Politian, however, arrived at a novel insight. He saw that even a group of sources that agreed still posed a problem. Given three sources A, B, and C, all of which agreed on a given point; if B and C depended entirely on A for their information, should they be considered to add any weight to A's testimony? Politian insisted that they should not. In other words, even a group of concordant sources must be investigated, and those which were entirely derived from others must be identified and eliminated from consideration. The way to perform such an investigation was to arrange the sources genealogically, and then to pay attention only to the source from which the others were derived.

Politian stated this principle in *Miscellanea* I.39, while explaining a riddle in a poem by Ausonius. Ausonius had employed the expression "Cadmi nigellas filias" – "little black daughters of Cadmus." Politian explained that it referred to the letters of the alphabet: "For Cadmus was the first to bring letters into Greece from Phoenicia." Since the Latin letters were directly derived from the Greek, Ausonius could refer to them too as "daughters of Cadmus." Politian cited Herodotus as his authority for stating that Cadmus had imported the alphabet. He admitted that other ancient writers had said the same. But he argued that all of them were simply repeating what they had read in Herodotus. Since their testimony was entirely derivative, it must be ignored:

> I omit Pliny and very many others, who say that Cadmus brought them into Greece. For since these different men recalled indiscriminately what they had read in Herodotus, I think it enough to have restored these matters to his authority. For in my opinion the testimonies of the ancients should not so much be counted up, as weighed.

It is easy to show how original Politian's thinking is here. Beroaldo discussed the same riddle from Ausonius in c[h]ap. 99 of the *Annotationes*. He solved it in the same way. And he too cited the sources which had informed him about Cadmus and the alphabet:

> He [Ausonius] calls the letters "daughters of Cadmus" because Cadmus is said to have been the inventor of letters. In Book vii of the *Natural History* Pliny says that he brought sixteen letters from Phoenicia into Greece. Therefore the ancient Greeks called the letters Phoenician, according to Herodotus in Book v. The same writer says that he saw "Cadmean letters," very similar to Ionian letters, incised on certain tripods in the temple of Apollo. Furthermore Cornelius Tacitus avers that Cadmus was the author of letters, while the Greek peoples were still uncultured.

Beroaldo is completely unconcerned with the dependence or independence of his sources. Pliny is evidently as reliable as Herodotus, and Herodotus no more reliable than Tacitus. Since they all agree on the main point in question, he cites all of them. And he omits other accounts not because they are derivative but because they seem irrelevant to him.

What Politian has done is to view the problem of the reliability of sources from a new direction. For him the question is no longer, as it was for Beroaldo, to amass evidence indiscriminately, but to discriminate, to reduce the number of witnesses that the scholar need take into account. It was this new approach to source criticism that made possible Politian's revolutionary transformation of philology.

Politian's most sweeping innovation in philological method was [. . .] to treat textual criticism as a historical study. When he found what seemed to him to be corrupt passages in recent manuscripts or printed texts of classical writings, he did not try to emend them by conjecture. He went back to the oldest sources – that is, to the oldest manuscripts. He recognized that they were not free from errors; but he insisted that they were the closest extant approximations to what the ancient authors had really written. The newer texts were removed by more stages of copying from antiquity, and any apparent correct readings they contained were merely the results of attempts at conjectural emendation. Such alluring but historically unjustifiable readings were less valuable to the textual critic than the errors of the old manuscripts, for at least their errors "preserve some fairly clear traces of the true reading which we must restore. Dishonest scribes have expunged these completely from the new texts."

Politian employed this method throughout the *Miscellanea* [. . .] This new method could not have been more in contrast with the practices of Politian's predecessors. Beroaldo, for example, relied almost exclusively on conjecture. And even when he cited manuscripts he identified them only in the vaguest terms [. . .] Politian's description includes the name of the manuscript's owner and a classification of its script. Beroaldo's citation – which is, if anything, unusually precise for him – gives neither.

In most cases the old manuscripts were more trustworthy than the new merely because they were older, and therefore fewer stages of transmission intervened between them and the author. But there were some textual traditions which Politian was able to analyse in a more complex and more decisive way. He applied his genealogical method of source criticism to the manuscripts of certain texts and proved that one extant manuscript was the parent of all the others. In such cases, he showed, the extant archetype must be the sole source used in establishing the text.

One case [. . .] was that of Cicero's *Familiares*. Politian had at his disposal in the library of St. Mark the ninth-century Vercelli manuscript [. . .] and a fourteenth-century manuscript which he wrongly believed might have been written by Petrarch [. . .] He also consulted an unspecified number of more recent textual witnesses. In *Miscellanea* I.25 he proved that the fourteenth-century manuscript, in which a gathering had been transposed because of an error in binding, was the parent of all the more recent manuscripts, for the same transposition occurred in all of them, without any evidence of physical damage to account for it. He also asserted, without giving the evidence, that the fourteenth-century manuscript was itself a copy of the ninth-century one. And he concluded that since the ninth-century manuscript was the source of all the others, it alone should be employed in correcting the text of the *Familiares*. As he wrote:

> I have obtained a very old volume of Cicero's *Epistolae Familiares* . . . and another one copied from it, as some think, by the hand of Francesco Petrarca. There is much evidence, which I shall now omit, that the one is copied from the other. But the latter manuscript . . . was bound in such a way by a careless bookbinder that we can see from the numbers [of the gatherings] that one gathering has clearly been transposed . . . Now the book is in the public library of the Medici family. From this one, then, so far as I can tell, are derived all the extant manuscripts of these letters, as if from a spring and fountainhead. And all of them have the text in that ridiculous and confused order which I must now put into proper form and, as it were, restore.

A second case was that of Justinian's *Digest* or *Pandects*. Here Politian used a different method to identify the extant archetype. He received permission through his patron, Lorenzo, to collate the famous Florentine manuscript of the *Digest*. He noticed certain erasures and additions in the preface, which, he thought, must have been made "by an author, and one thinking, and composing, rather than by a scribe and copyist." He therefore decided that this must be the very manuscript which Justinian's commissioners first wrote. If the Florentine manuscript was the authors'-copy, it must obviously be the archetype. Consequently, all texts of the *Digest* ought to be emended in accordance with the text of the Florentine manuscript [. . .] For Politian [. . .] there was no problem at all here; there could not be one. If the reading of the archetype made grammatical and juristic sense, then it must be right. Divergent readings in later codices could by definition be nothing but alterations introduced by scribes or jurists. As Politian put it,

> in those Florentine Pandects, which, indeed, we believe to be the original ones, there is no negative at all. Therefore the Florentine jurisconsult Accursius, who also had a faulty codex, torments himself – I might almost say wretchedly.

In this case elimination of *codices descripti*[2] seems to lead to the elimination of medieval legal science. There was nothing new in attacking medieval jurists – Valla and Beroaldo had done the same. But the method underlying the attack was unprecedented.

[. . .]

Now reliance on old manuscripts was not completely unprecedented. Gellius frequently consulted older manuscripts in order to correct errors in newer ones. Thus, he defended a reading in Cicero's fifth oration *In verrem* in part because he had found it so written in "a copy of unimpeachable fidelity, because it was the result of Tiro's careful scholarship." Again, he argued that scribes had replaced the unfamiliar archaic genitive "facies" with the later form "facei" in a work by Claudius

Quadrigarius. In the oldest manuscripts, he said, he had found the old reading "facies"; in certain "corrupt manuscripts," on the other hand, he had found "facies" erased and "faciei" written in. Thus, Politian's chief literary model had insisted that old manuscripts were more reliable than new ones.

Moreover, Renaissance humanists from Petrarch on had also sought out and copied or collated old manuscripts. Some of them had even studied the genealogy of manuscripts. Giovanni Lamola was a friend of Guarino. In 1428 he set out to collate the codex of Cicero's rhetorical works which had been discovered seven years before in the cathedral archive at Lodi. This manuscript contained complete texts of Cicero's *De oratore* and *Orator*, which had previously been known only in mutilated texts, and of his *Brutus*, which had previously be unknown. All these works were fundamental for the rhetorical teaching of the humanists. Consequently, the discovery attracted attention immediately: Poggio Bracciolini, who was then in England, knew of it within a year. And many copies of the new texts were soon in circulation. But as the Lodi manuscript was written in what the humanists called "Lombardic script" – that is, an unfamiliar miniscule – they found it hard to read. Consequently, they made their copies not from the original but from other humanists' copies. As a result both of inevitable mistakes in transcription and of equally inevitable attempts at conjectural emendation, the texts in circulation soon became extremely corrupt. Lamola declared that it was necessary to return to the original source. He wrote to Guarino that he had "restored the whole work according to the earlier text." He knew that the Lodi manuscript was very ancient from its unusual script [. . .] More important, its discovery had created a sensation only a few years before, and no other complete manuscript of the works it contained had been discovered. Therefore, Lamola, like every other humanist of his time, knew that the Lodi manuscript must be the archetype of all the other complete manuscripts: "from that accurate exemplar," he said, "they copied the text which is now commonly accepted." He decided that any attempt to emend the text must be based on a collation of this manuscript. He even maintained that the errors in the Lodi manuscript were worthy of preservation and study. For even the errors of so old a manuscript were preferable to the conjectures of later scribes:

> I also took care [he wrote] to represent everything in accord with the old [manuscript] down to the smallest dot, even where it contained certain old absurdities. For I'd rather be absurd with that old manuscript than be wise with these diligent fellows.

Giorgio Merula was a prolific editor and commentator of the generation just before Politian's. In his edition of Plautus, which appeared in 1472, he pointed out that all the extant manuscripts of twelve of Plautus's comedies were descended from one manuscript: "There was only one manuscript, from which, as if from an archetype, all the extant manuscripts are derived." The archetype to which he referred was the eleventh-century Orsini manuscript of Plautus [. . .] This manuscript had been brought to Rome in 1429 by Nicholas of Cusa. Like the Lodi manuscript, it had created a sensation among the humanists, for twelve of the sixteen plays which it contained had previously been unknown. Hence, it too was widely known to be

the archetype of the other manuscripts. Merula was unable to collate the Orsini manuscript himself and had to content himself with restructuring its readings by collat-
ing copies of it. But even though he failed to act on his knowledge of the textual
tradition, Merula too understood that the manuscripts of one text could be arranged
genealogically, and that the text should be based on the extant archetype.

Both Lamola and Merula, then, had noticed that all the manuscripts of some
works were descended from one archetype. Both had agreed that in such cases the
text should be based on the archetype. And one of them, Lamola, had made a full
collation of the archetype, recording even its errors.

Politian, however, showed how to examine a group of manuscripts and discover
how they were related to one another. He showed that in some cases such an examination could identify an archetype which was not commonly recognized as such. He
insisted that such an examination must be performed in all cases. He maintained that
even where no archetype could be identified, "conjectural emendation must start
from the earliest recoverable stage of the tradition." And he backed up his statements about the history of texts with precise identifications and evaluations of the
manuscripts which he used. Politian's genealogical method went far beyond the isolated insights of Lamola and Merula. In fact, he arrived at the same set of principles
with which modern scholars still set about editing classical texts.

It was Politian's passionate need for rigour and completeness that enabled him
to surpass his predecessors. For it led him to study many textual traditions; hence
he found that there were many instances where later manuscripts were derived
from extant earlier ones. And the genealogical criticism of sources which he had
established for the myth of Cadmus enabled him to see the descent of manuscripts
as a particular case of a general rule about sources – that they should be weighed
rather than counted up and that derivative ones should be ignored. No previous
scholar had even come close to formulating the set of critical principles which
Politian considered to be generally valid.

Politian also applied his genealogical method to literary works themselves as
well as to manuscripts. He realized that the Latin poets – whose works were his
primary interest – had drawn heavily on Greek sources in a variety of ways. And
he came to insist that only a critic who had mastered Greek literature could hope
to deal competently with Latin.

The Romans, first of all, had frequently employed Greek words – sometimes
transliterated, sometimes not – when there was no appropriate Latin one. They
had employed a Greek adjective or common noun when Latin had no word for
the shade of feeling they desired to express – or when there was a Latin word,
but it did not fit the metre. From Hellenistic pastorals they had borrowed Greek
names of shepherds and nymphs. Along with Greek mythology they had taken over
some Greek names of gods and heroes. And only someone who knew the original Greek could know the proper forms of these words.

Politian was able to correct many corrupt Greek words in Latin texts and to
defend many genuine Greek words from attempts at emendation [. . .] With great
sense of occasion he produced the Greek authorities that supported his thesis:

> We shall set out from the stock-pile of Greek, as if from a store-room,
> authorities whose creditability can neither be derogated nor taken away.

By them the reading is preserved intact and the fog of explanation is dispelled.

[. . .]

The restoration of corrupt Greek words to Latin texts was not an innovation in itself. Guarino had made something of a speciality of filling in the spaces in Latin texts where Greek words or passages had dropped out, and of correcting the nonsense medieval scribes had made of the Greek words they had tried to copy. Calderini had stated just as clearly as Politian that "some Greek words have been accepted for our use". [. . .]

What was new in Politian's work was the completeness of his mastery of Greek. When Beroaldo or Calderini explained a Greek word in a Latin text, they tended to explain fairly obvious words and to draw their explanations from obvious sources. Even when their results were the same as Politian's, the contrast between their methods was clear. Beroaldo knew the story of Hecale from Pliny and from Plutarch's life of Theseus. Politian knew the passages from Pliny and Plutarch. But he also had relevant passages from Statius, the *Priapea*, the *Suda*, an anonymous Greek epigram which accompanies certain codices of Callimachus's hymns, and the old scholia on Callimachus's *Hymn to Apollo*. And he used them not only to tell the story of Theseus and Hecale, but also to establish just what Callimachus's *Hecale* was and why he had written it (Callimachus's detractors had claimed he could not write a long poem; the *Hecale* was his answer to their charges). For Politian, then, the comparative study of Greek and Latin could shed light on both languages; it could even lead to the partial reconstruction of lost works.

The Romans, however, had not confined themselves to borrowing words and names; they had also translated long passages – sometimes even whole poems. And Politian took advantage of this fact too in his text-critical method [. . .]

Yet the most striking effects of Politian's comparative method were not in the field of textual criticism but in that of exegesis. Politian was the first humanist to insist that most Latin poets had drawn very heavily on Greek models for both content and style. Proper exegesis must therefore begin from identification of the philosophical theories and myths which Latin poets had borrowed, and the metaphors and grammatical constructions they had imported.

[. . .] For example, Politian pointed out that Ovid, *Fasti*, i.357–8 was adapted from an epigram in the Greek Anthology [. . .] Ovid had translated the Greek "as literally as possible" – "quam potuit ad unguem" – but he had still failed to capture all the nuances of the original:

> The Latin poet did not even touch that – if I may so call it – trans-marine charm.

Since Ovid himself was "poeta ingeniosissimus," this episode led Politian to formulate a playful judgement about the Latin language. Quintilian had characterized Ovid's style as "lascivus" – "abundant," "Asiatic." Politian argued, on the basis of his comparison, that Ovid was unable to equal his Greek model not from lack of ability, but because the Latin language itself ran counter to his special stylistic gifts:

> This is the fault of the [Latin] language, not so much because it is lacking in words as because it allows less freedom for verbal play [. . .]

In other cases Politian was able to combine the study of verbal borrowings with that of intellectual borrowings. He discovered, for example, that Persius had modelled his fourth satire on the Platonic dialogue *Alcibiades I*. Persius had drawn the entire philosophical message of his poem from the dialogue:

> it is clear that Persius . . . drew from it the discussions which Socrates there holds with Alcibiades about the just and unjust, and about self-knowledge.

Indeed, Politian said, the words "Tecum habita," with which Persius's poem ended, were a good summary of the dialogue as well:

> When he says "tecum habita," doesn't he seem to have understood the meaning of that dialogue clearly – if indeed, as the commentator Proclus affirms, Plato here had in mind precisely that Delphic writing which admonishes every man to know himself.

At the same time, Politian was able to point out that Persius had made some direct allusions to individual lines in the dialogue. Persius is an extremely obscure and allusive poet. Medieval readers, completely at a loss to understand the satires, had invented wild explanations for them. Persius was said to be attacking "leccatores" – gossips, gluttons, bishops and abbots who failed to live up to their vows. Only after Politian's explanation could Persius's poem be read as its author had intended. Politian, of course, was hardly the first to point out that Latin poetry was heavily dependent upon Greek models. Latin poets themselves generally claimed to be not the first to write a particular kind of poetry, but the first to introduce a particular Greek style or verse-form into Latin. Moreover, Politian's model, Gellius, had actually compared passages from Latin poetry with the Greek originals from which they had been adapted. For example, he compared Virgil's adaptations of certain passages from Theocritus and Homer with the originals. He pointed out that Virgil had omitted a good deal, and he argued at some length that such omissions were necessary. Mere literal translations, he argued, would be clumsy, and would therefore lack poetic effectiveness. Virgil's practice of selective translations should therefore serve as a model for future Latin poets:

> Whenever striking expressions are to be translated and imitated from Greek poems, it is said that we should not always strive to render every single word with literal exactness. For many things lose their charm if they are translated too forcibly – as it were, unwillingly and reluctantly. Virgil therefore showed skill and good judgement in omitting some things and rendering others when he was dealing with passages of Homer or Hesiod or Apollonius or Parthenius or Callimachus or Theocritus or some other poet.

Similar information and arguments were available in other works as well – for example, the *Saturnalia* of Macrobius, where Virgil and Homer are compared at length, and the commentaries of Servius on Virgil.

These texts, in turn, attracted the attention of various medieval and Renaissance scholars before Politian. Richard de Bury, Bishop of Durham in the fourteenth century, had read his Gellius and Macrobius. In consequence, it is not surprising to find him asking, in his *Philobiblon*,

> What would Virgil, the chief poet among the Latins, have achieved, if he had not despoiled Theocritus, Lucretius, and Homer, and had not ploughed with their heifer? What, unless again and again he had read somewhat of Parthenius and Pindar, whose eloquence he could by no means imitate?

And it was a commonplace among humanist teachers in the fifteenth century that only those who had a sound knowledge of Greek literature could properly understand Latin literature.

Calderini, moreover, had given detailed attention and much effort to the comparative study of Greek and Latin. In his brief commentary on Propertius, for example, he arrived several times at novel and interesting results. He pointed out that Propertius i.20 is to some extent modelled on Theocritus XIII: "In this passage his particular aim is to imitate and adapt Theocritus, on the story of Hylas." And his wide reading in Greek poets, scholiasts, and historians enabled him to unravel a number of Propertius's mythological and geographical allusions. For example, he rightly interpreted the phrase "Theseae bracchia longa viae" in Propertius iii.21.24:

> He means the long walls, which were called ["long legs"] in Greek. They ran from the city [of Athens] up to the Piraeus; a careful account is to be found in Thucydides.

He also noticed that Propertius often made use of variant forms of well-known myths. Thus, in i.13, 21 Propertius described the river-god Enipeus as Thessalian. Calderini rightly pointed out that other ancient writers located Enipeus not in Thessaly, but in Elis.

Yet it is just this commentary that best enables us to grasp how different Calderini was from Politian, for we can see here how lacking he was in Politian's special qualities of judgement and reflection. In iv.I.64 Propertius calls himself "the Roman Callimachus." The phrase is not so simple as it appears; when a Roman poet claims a particular Greek poet as his model, he may mean that he has derived his subject or his metre from the Greek, but he may also mean simply that he is as innovative, learned, and subtle as the Greek had been. Calderini, however, took Propertius's phrase in the most literal way possible. He assumed from it that Propertius must have written direct adaptations from Callimachus:

> [Propertius] calls himself the Roman Callimachus. For he sets out Callimachus, a Greek poet, in Latin verse.

And he applied his interpretation at least once in a most unfortunate way. In i.2,
1 Propertius calls his mistress Cynthia "vita" – "my life." "The word," wrote
Calderini,

> is drawn from Callimachus, who is Propertius's chief model. For he
> too, while flattering his mistress, calls her by the Greek word [for life
> (i.e., ζωή)].

Calderini's arguments clearly found some acceptance, for Beroaldo repeated
them – without acknowledgement – in his own commentary on Propertius, which
first appeared in 1487. He too argued that Propertius had taken Callimachus as
his model, his "archetypon." And he too described Propertius's use of "vita" in i.2,
1 as done in imitation of Callimachus.

The notes of Calderini and Beroaldo stimulated Politian to produce a splendid
rebuttal in *Miscellanea* I.80, where he raised a crushing objection to both Calderini's
general interpretation and his reading of i.2, 1 – namely, that there was not one
shred of evidence that Callimachus had written any love poetry at all, much less
a love poem in which ζωή was used as an endearment:

> I find it astonishing that Domizio and some others after him . . . dare
> to write that Propertius says this or that in imitation of Callimachus.
> For beyond a few hymns nothing at all remains to us of that poet, and
> certainly there is nothing at all that treats of love.

Politian certainly had the best in the exchange. There is no reason at all to think
that Calderini had found evidence to back up his theory. As a commentator on
Juvenal, Calderini knew from *Sat.* VI, 195 that ζωή was sometimes used as an
endearment. As to the notion that Callimachus had used the word in that sense,
it was no doubt Calderini's own invention. But Politian's rebuttal is even more
significant when it is seen in the context of the chapter in which it occurred.
For in addition to attacking Calderini, Politian there gave a demonstration of the
proper way to use Greek poetry to elucidate Propertius. In iv.9, 57–58 Propertius
alludes to the myth of Tiresias's encounter with Pallas while she was bathing.
To illustrate the myth Politian published, along with much other material, the
editio princeps of Callimachus's entire poem on the Bath of Pallas, which he
also translated word-for-word. The Alexandrian poets, in other words, could be
used to explicate Propertius's mythological allusions, but not, except where the
parallel was certain, to explain verbal details. In *Miscellanea* I.80, then, Politian
showed that he understood more than just the virtues of the comparative method
in exegesis – he understood its limitations as well. He understood that different
Latin poets had used their Greek sources in different ways, and that the exegete
must take these differences in poetic method into account when making his comparisons. For all Calderini's wide reading in Greek sources and genuine sensitivity to
the nuances of Latin poetry, he could not rival Politian in the methodical application of source criticism. Yet he was the most sophisticated of Politian's
predecessors. In exegesis as in textual criticism, Politian's methodological innovations created a revolution.

Modern scholars still begin the study of Latin poems by looking for possible Greek sources and models. To be sure, when they find a model they compare it with the Latin in a far more detailed manner than Politian did. We want to know not only that Ennius translated Euripides, and that in doing so he made alterations, but also what specific changes he made, and what purpose they were meant to serve. But it would be unhistorical to reproach Politian for not carrying his comparisons far enough. After all, he took them as far as had Gellius, his model. Rather, Politian's work on the comparative method should be seen in the same perspective as his work on manuscripts: as the lineal ancestor of the methods which are still employed.

[. . .]

Politian's principles did not triumph at once [. . .] Even Politian's disciple, Pietro Crinito, seems to have learned relatively little from his master. His own method, at least as embodied in the *De honesta disciplina*, rested on the study of the ancient Latin grammarians rather than on that of manuscripts and Greek sources.

But Politian's new methods survived his contemporaries' lack of insight. By the middle of the sixteenth century, scholars were employing them throughout Europe. The comparative study of Latin and Greek flourished especially in France; systematic recension of manuscripts preoccupied scholars in Florence and Rome. And isolated insights from his work appeared in the writings of many others besides Bellièvre and Diplovatacius.

[. . .]

Editor's Notes

1   anathema to boredom.
2   Subsequent manuscripts since the authorial version.

CHAPTER 7

Victor Scholderer

■   from **PRINTERS AND READERS IN ITALY
IN THE FIFTEENTH CENTURY**, in *Fifty Essays in
Fifteenth- and Sixteenth-Century Bibliography*,
ed. D. Rhodes, Amsterdam, 1966, pp. 202–215

DURING THE FIRST GENERATION of its existence, that is to say, down to the end of the fifteenth century, the Italian printed book had won for itself a primacy scarcely in any respect to be questioned, and the Italian genius was at the height of its scientific achievement. Yet the printing art itself, so far-reaching in its consequences, was invented and perfected entirely by northerners, and it did not penetrate to the south for some ten years after the 42-line Bible had been struck off at Mainz. It might well, we think, have been otherwise. Leon Battista Alberti, that "uomo universale" who flourished at the very same time as Gutenberg, "acquired," as we are told, "every sort of accomplishment and dexterity, cross-examining artists, scholars and artisans of all descriptions, down to the cobblers, about the secrets and peculiarities of their craft." Did none of the scholars whom he interviewed complain of the difficulty and expense of obtaining the books necessary for their studies, and did nothing seen in the shops of the metal-workers ever suggest to him the possibility of a way of artificial writing prompter and less liable to error than the scriveners' pen and ink? We are told, again, that the most populous cities of Italy were full of political exiles who, in the words of Gioviano Pontano, "took their virtues with them wherever they went." Such precisely was the status of Gutenberg, expatriate at Strasburg, where his first experiments in typography were made; but if any among the crowds of well-meriting refugees mentioned by Pontano proposed to himself a similar end, assuredly nothing came of it. It may be that a chronic shortage of books was after all a more grievous handicap in the north than under a southern sky, where ease of personal contact and oral instruction could to some extent mitigate it; the academy and the learned society were characteristically Italian institutions. And there can be no doubt that the literati of Italy looked for patronage in the first instance to princes and nobles who deemed worthy of their attention only manuscripts of the finest quality, such as even the most careful typography must despair of rivalling. Vespasiano Bisticci, book-purveyor to Federigo of Urbino, tells us that the Duke his master would have held it shame to own a printed book, and many of his rank will have shared his opinion; in such company technical improvements in book-production could scarcely expect much consideration. It might be added that the fever of political tension in which the major powers of Italy had their being would be likely to attract inventive genius to the arts of war rather than of peace – we know from our own experience how widely Mars may so usurp upon the Muses. But Gutenberg can no more be imagined recommending his type-casting instrument to Ferrante of Naples than offering a new kind of gun to the burghers of Mainz for use against their Archbishop.

Be this as it may, the printing art was already familiar to at least three different places in Germany before it crossed the Alps, and the first book printed for the Italian market, a meditation in Italian on the passion of Christ, was produced in Germany during that early period, to be conveyed to its destination by colportage. A full decade probably separates the first books of Mainz from the first books printed on Italian soil, which, as is universally agreed, were the work of two German clerics in minor orders, Conrad Sweynheym and Arnold Pannartz, at the Benedictine monastery of Subiaco, some thirty miles due east of Rome. This house was under the special patronage of the Spanish Cardinal Juan de Torquemada, who was now in his seventy-sixth year but whose mind was still commendably open to new ideas, since it must have been at his invitation that the printers set up their press in the monastic precincts. Four books were completed by them at Subiaco, and the three most substantial of these reflect very exactly the mixed ecclesiastical and humanistic preoccupations of a prelate of the High Renaissance: they are the *De oratore* of Cicero, the works of Lactantius, an apologetic writer of the third century known from the purity of his Latin as "the Christian Cicero," and St. Augustine's *City of God*. The fourth book catered for quite another class of reader, being the elementary Latin grammar of Aelius Donatus, which, after enjoying almost unchallenged supremacy as a schoolbook during the Middle Ages, was now considered a mere relic of barbarism by the new learning. It must, nevertheless, have still been in demand among old-fashioned educationalists, as no copy of the Subiaco edition is known to exist to-day.

The two partners were occupied at Subiaco for barely three years, moving on to Rome itself in 1467. The Cardinal, for whatever reason, had lost interest in their doings, and when in the same year he determined to make public a work of his own, a series of meditations on the life of Christ, the contract went to a rival craftsman from Germany, Ulrich Han, who adorned it with woodcuts reputed to reproduce the frescoes which Torquemada had caused to be painted in the church of Santa Maria de Minerva; these cuts are the earliest in any Italian printed book and among the very first in any printed book whatsoever. Meanwhile Sweynheym and Pannartz, establishing themselves in the palazzo of the brothers De' Massimi, embarked on a programme of work which had taken on the character of a library of classical literature when in the spring of 1472 they were pulled up short by the imminent threat of bankruptcy consequent on an overstocked market. The story is well known how, starving in a palaceful of unsaleable print, they appealed for help to the newly elected Pope Sixtus IV (luckily a humanistic enthusiast), and how he afforded them sufficient relief to carry on for another twelvemonth before their partnership was dissolved for good. The frustration of a venture celebrated from the first for the beauty of its productions, which incidentally have inspired some equally splendid typography in modern times, was no doubt in part due to want of commercial foresight, but its main cause must be considered to be the disequilibrium of Roman society in the Quattrocento. The printers depended all but completely on the patronage of the Curia; when the interest of popes and cardinals in the novel experiment languished, as was sooner or later inevitable, there was no alert and moneyed middle class, such as existed in Venice or Milan, on which they could fall back for fresh custom. This is the true reason why printing at Rome in the early period "cannot be said to have either fulfilled the promise of its enthusiastic beginning or produced a total output worthy of so great a City." Here and there a book such as the Ptolemy of 1478 with maps engraved by Sweynheym or the Missal printed by Stephan Plannck in 1496 redeems it, but few illustrated works and very little in the vernacular is found in it, while the typography is seldom distinguished and sometimes sinks to very low levels. Law books, generally of unprepossessing appearance, and short occasional tracts form its staples, and it is noticeable that the list of its printers contains very few Italian names. The total number of editions issued in Rome to the end of the century is probably not less than 1,500 but this figure loses its impressiveness when analysed, since it is blown up by a multitude of thin pamphlets containing the matter of innumerable sermons preached before the Pope on Sundays and at high solemnities, or of the loyal addresses presented to him on his accession by the spokesmen of official deputations from all over Europe. The obligation to sit through so many harangues was felt to be very irksome, and a sermon briefer than the ordinary was greeted with universal satisfaction, but the orators, who had put forward their very best Latin for the occasion, were naturally desirous of making the most of themselves in print, so much so that two of the Roman presses were kept constantly busy on this ephemeral literature, which accounts for well over one-tenth of the statistical grand total. Others about the papal court were not content with so simple a form of advertisement, and a Sicilian named Giovanni Filippo di Legname, who described himself as a "familiar" of Sixtus IV, seems to have set up what corresponded to the private press of modern times mainly for the purpose of printing the writings of the Pope himself and of others in authority, and provided them with suitable dedications, directed where they might fructify. His editions, as befits a private press, were very small, averaging no more than 125 copies, but in the case of the Pope's own work this number was increased to 300, a fact of which the dedication was careful to inform His Holiness.

Printing was already a matter of history at Subiaco and had taken firm root in Rome at the moment of its introduction into Venice, where it was soon to flourish incomparably. Here, in the bourgeois atmosphere of a great mercantile centre, its development took a very different course. John of Speyer, a well-to-do italianized German who had long been resident in Venice, opened the first printing office there in 1469, doubtless with the assistance of experts from the country of his origin. The processes of typography, which Gutenberg was still able to treat as a trade secret, were by this time common property; mindful of this fact, John endeavoured to safeguard himself from competition by securing a patent of monopoly from the Signoria. From Sweynheym and Pannartz he probably took over the practice of ending his books with a colophon in verse, in which, more fortunate than they, he had no need to apologise for his uncouth Teutonic surname, but he was indebted to them for little else. The appeal of his work is to the general public and not to the aristocracy, while his fount of roman type, so different from the angular masses of the first founts used at Rome, already foreshadows in its unobtrusive flow those qualities which were to recommend the "literae venetae" of twenty years later to readers all over Europe.

John of Speyer died in 1470, only a year after he had set up his press, and his privilege, which was personal to himself, lapsed before it could become a serious check on enterprise. The Signoria, aware of its mistake in granting it, henceforward extended its protection only to specific books or technical innovations — a first step towards the modern system of copyright. John's brother Wendelin continued the business, which before the end of 1470 had already two rivals and two years later not less than a dozen; the total output from them all had probably reached 200 editions by the end of 1472. As at Subiaco and Rome, the first text selected for printing was Ciceronian, John of Speyer starting with the *Epistolae ad familiares* and reprinting them immediately, so that 600 copies of this text were on the market before the last quarter of 1469. The emphasis continued to be on humanistic literature — classical texts, grammars to enable them to be understood, and contemporary exercises in the ancient manner — so much so that pretty well two-thirds of the books produced in these years (1469–1472) belong to this class. It thus comes as no surprise when we find that the glut of humanistic books hit the Venetian book-trade almost as hard as the Roman in the critical year 1472. We can easily imagine with what exuberance the devotees of the new learning clamoured for the multiplication of their beloved classical texts. The printers, foreigners as most of them were, had allowed themselves to be taken off their guard by so much southern *brio*, and now they were paying the penalty. In the north there was never a similar crisis; more sober reading habits prevailed, to which publishing found it easier to adapt itself. A successful appeal to the Pope had tided Sweynheym and Pannartz over the worst, but this form of insurance was not available at Venice, and thus the printers were happily induced to enlarge the scope of their appeal so as to embrace every section of the reading public. The promptitude with which they turned over to this as the only satisfactory long-term policy redeemed their initial failure in business acumen, and Venetian publishing was soon as much to the fore in almost every subject as it had originally been in respect of the classics. What was destined to be perhaps its most lucrative line, editions of the *Corpus juris* and canon law with commentaries, now showed a rapid increase. Wendelin of Speyer must have the credit for striking this vein when as early as 1471 he realized that there was a certain prejudice amongst lawyers against the humanistic associations of roman letter and deferred to it by providing himself with a gothic fount suitable for legal work. He was, however, soon surpassed by the famous Frenchman Nicolas Jenson, who, employing two beautifully harmonious gothics and taking great pains to ensure the accuracy of his texts, helped Venice, not without good profit to himself, to a pre-eminence in this field which for some time came near to a monopoly. A little later Baptista de Tortis started on a series of such books which became known all over Europe and for which the words "volumen de Tortis" on the title-page constituted a sufficient advertisement; so well considered were they in Spain that "letra de tortis" passed into the language as the equivalent of "gothic letter." Of one of these editions we know that it was struck off in no fewer than 2,300 copies, totalling little short of 1,500,000 large folio pages. While it is probable that jurisprudence supplied the Venetian printers with what were on an average their bulkiest texts, they were never reluctant to put in hand works of substance in any department of literature, and this makes all the more impressive the figure of some 4,500 editions credited to them in the thirty-two years from 1469 to 1500. As the total of all editions produced in Europe during the period is conjecturally placed at rather more than 30,000, the contribution of Venice does not fall far short of one-seventh of the whole, and if we assume an average of 250 copies of the edition – which is possibly an understatement – we arrive at the impressive total of 1,125,000 printed books offered by Venice to the reading public by the beginning of the sixteenth century. These figures may be commended to the attention of historians as helpful in estimating the degree of literacy, as well as the desire for learning, in Italy at this time, and they may be reinforced by 1,500 editions from Rome, over 1,000 each from Milan and from Florence, and nearly 700 from Bologna.

While no fewer than 150 "presses" can be distinguished as having worked at Venice during the early period, analysis of this formidable total shows, as we might expect, that a minority of powerful firms was in real control of the trade. At first the two associations of foreign craftsmen represented respectively by the Germans John and Wendelin of Speyer and their successors and by the Frenchman Jenson were paramount, and they became still more influential when at the end of the 1470s they amalgamated under the title of De Colonia, Jenson and Company. A little later, anticipating the now-familiar tripartite organization of publisher, printer, and book-seller, the syndicate concentrated on the book-market, leaving the actual typography to others; its stationers were to be found all over Italy, and abroad as well. By this time the Italians had taken the measure of the situation, and the leading enterprises were from about 1480 onwards almost all controlled by Italians. Printing nevertheless continued on the lines originally laid down by the foreign craftsmen. The influence of Jenson's celebrated roman, immediately recognized as an unsurpassed model, can be felt in many later types more economical for ordinary book-work, and his four gothics, the two later rather more florid than the earlier, were subsequently much modified but never quite forgotten. Another foreigner, Erhard Ratdolt of Augsburg, came forward in 1480 with the first of a series of more "modern" gothics which left their mark both on Venetian printing and on that of his own country when he returned thither in 1486, while earlier his partner and fellow townsman Bernhard Maler had designed for his type-pages the well-known decorative borders unsurpassed until the days of William Morris, than which scarcely anything, one might think, could be more Italianate. Native craftsmen were largely content to follow the foreign lead until Aldus Manutius produced, as the century drew to an end, a roman of much originality which later became a favourite model; his best-known innovation, the italic, falls outside the period. The Italian-designed borders are generally of the "Renaissance" or classicizing kind less suitable for surrounding print than Maler's and with one striking exception are not so carefully executed.

The contrasting patterns of the book-trade as developed respectively at Rome and at Venice have been described at some length, since the histories of other

Italian printing centres generally follow either the one or the other. In the great cities the pattern is the Venetian one of a few large concerns, or it may be a single powerful combine; Milan is the most important instance of these, being, *longo intervallo*, the only rival of Venice; below it rank Bologna and Naples. In the smaller places, on the other hand, all as a rule depended upon individual patrons or small interested groups, and local printing was a transient phase in consequence; of this I shall say more presently. There is, however, one city which, in this as in other respects, stands apart, and that is Florence. The first press there, of which we know little save that it started work in 1471, immediately strikes a new note by printing three of the love-romances which are among the parerga of the great Alberti, then nearing the end of his life. In the following year comes a very remarkable book, the *editio princeps* of Servius's commentary on Virgil, in large folio. It was the work of Bernardo Cennini, the goldsmith "skilful beyond all others" in his own estimation, who executed some of the splendid reliefs on the reredos of the Baptistery at Florence, and he undertook the task in the true Renaissance spirit to show that he could do this also. Without regular training as a printer and with only his son Domenico, a youth of nineteen, to assist him, he designed, cut, and cast the type and put his folio of 230 leaves through the press apparently in little more than a twelvemonth. "Florentinis ingeniis nihil ardui est"[1] boasts the sentence which concludes the second part, and we feel no inclination to demur. So strikingly inaugurated, humanistic printing at Florence continued to be touched to different issues than elsewhere. While little was added to the common run of classical editions, a number of Greek texts testifies to the efforts of her scholars, headed by Marsilio Ficino, to track Hellenism to its source. Ficino, the leading spirit of the Florentine Academy over which Lorenzo the Magnificent himself presided, was a neo-Platonist rather than a Platonist proper, but he deserved eminently well of the Master by his complete Latin version of the dialogues which he succeeded with some difficulty in getting printed in the year 1485; although the edition consisted of no fewer than 1,025 copies, another was prepared at the cost of Lorenzo himself only six years later, but this time at Venice. These two books, together with an edition of Ficino's commentaries on five select dialogues, are practically the only publications directly connected with Plato which were put forth by the new art during the 1400s; the Greek originals, except for the Letters, remained unprinted until 1513. In the forefront of the other texts printed in the Greek tongue at Florence stands the magnificent *editio princeps* of Homer, which we owe to the joint efforts of two Florentines, a Milanese Cretan (so he styles himself), and an Athenian. Below this come the first editions of Euripides – four plays only – of Lucian, of Callimachus, of Apollonius Rhodius, and of the Anthology, the last-named printed throughout in capitals; the editor, Janus Lascaris, found the available Greek cursives not to his mind. The eagerness which the Florentines brought to classical studies is illustrated by a passage from a letter of Jacobus Antiquarius to Politian in 1489. "When I went the other day into one of our public offices," writes Antiquarius, "I found the clerks quite neglecting their proper business, engrossed in reading a book which had been distributed in sheets among them. I asked what new book it was, and they said: 'Politian's *Miscellanies*.' So I too climbed up to their desk and began eagerly to read." The volume which so bemused these old-time civil servants was a collection of observations on obscure passages in the Latin classics; one can scarcely imagine an officeful of their present-day successors yielding to a like distraction. Turning from ancient to Italian letters, we find that the earliest effort to provide readers of the *Divina commedia* with a worthily illustrated edition was made at Florence in 1481. It took the shape of a large folio in which the text is surrounded by Landino's commentary, and a space is left at the beginning of each canto, destined to be filled by an etching based in each case upon a design from the hand of Botticelli. The attempt was for technical reasons a failure, and the etchings were discontinued after the nineteenth canto of the *Inferno*. Had it succeeded, no other of the fifteen editions of Dante's epic produced in the early period could have compared with it. It may be noted that this is the only Florentine edition among the fifteen, and there was possibly in the minds of its promoters (of whom Landino himself was no doubt one) the idea of an *amende honorable* posthumously offered on behalf of the city to the illustrious exile.

The most remarkable episode in Florentine printing, however, pertains to quite different matters. Everywhere in Italy, though to a somewhat lesser extent than in Germany, religious literature was a staple of the typographical output, but that of Florence suggests from the very beginning somewhat less than unmisgiving orthodoxy. Her presses were conspicuously neglectful of the patristic and exegetical texts and the service books which formed part of the cleric's professional library and which printers elsewhere showed no reluctance to undertake. The venerated Archbishop of Florence, Saint Antonine, who died in 1459, is represented by occasional editions of his manuals of confession in the vernacular, but his great *Summa theologica*, many times published in Venice and the north, is ignored at home. On the other hand, books appealing to everyman rather than to his pastors, devotional tracts, and controversial pamphlets by local authors, distinguished or obscure, make constant appearances in the book-lists, all finally centring upon the personality of Savonarola and on the reformation in little which flourished and died with him. Savonarola first appeared in Florence in 1489 and became Prior of St. Mark's only two years later. Thenceforward, up to his execution in May 1498, he was the dominant figure in the life of the city, and the stream of revivalist and polemical literature grew ever greater until it bade fair to swallow up every other kind of printed matter. The editions of the Friar's own exhortations and manifestoes cannot be put at fewer than 150, and those published by supporters or opponents add largely to this total. Tracts, sermons, and pamphlets were hurried off to press as soon as written and most were doubtless in circulation within a few days. This is, in fact, the first occasion in the history of printing when the art was pressed into the service of a propaganda campaign appealing to the public at large. And propagandist literature has surely never been presented in so beautiful a dress. The letterpress, it is true, is undistinguished – the Florentine type-faces being of no great merit as a rule – but nothing could be more admirable than the simply executed woodcuts with their skilful use of black in both design and frame which adorn so many of these modest quartos. Like the clay figurines of ancient Tanagra, they are the products of an artistic awareness so general that even the humblest craftsmen seems to partake of it almost instinctively. Yet these little books, now so much sought after, sold in their day for a few grossi and their printers did not even trouble to name themselves in the colophons.

Clerics, especially those in minor orders, played a great part in early typography all over the West, but they seem unusually numerous at Florence. One of them, Francesco Buonaccorsi, was probably a kinsman of Savonarola himself, and another, Bartolommeo de' Libri, was the most prolific printer engaged in his cause. Florence also supplies the most picturesque example of the monastic presses met with here and there both in Italy and the North, namely, that of the Convent of Dominican nuns of San Giacopo di Ripoli in the Via della Scala, which was managed by the conventual procurator and in which the nuns themselves, who were already well known for their skill in calligraphy and illumination, worked as compositors. The day-book of the press is still extant to show that it was run on strictly business lines, and secular reading is well represented among the eighty or so editions which issued from it during the eight years of its existence.

Since typography is in its very essence a means of mass-production it was logical to consider first the most important centres of the early book-trade. But the art was practised on a smaller scale and less continuously in many other Italian towns, where its history is often of considerable interest. Very nearly eighty names require to be marked on the typographical map of Italy in the fifteenth century, whereas that of Germany, including her outliers, is complete in sixty-four, and that of French-speaking territory in some forty-five. If, however, we draw a line across that map so as to pass through Rome and Subiaco, we find only eight names, just one-tenth of the total, lying to the south of it, while of these eight only one, that of Naples, can be linked with more than a mere handful of editions. The farther north we look, the more crowded becomes the map, and it is above a line drawn just south of Bologna that the names cluster thickest – in Lombardy, in Emilia, in Venetia, and in Piedmont. We are thus left in no doubt at all as to that part of the country in which the greatest economic and intellectual energy was being put forth, just as on the German map the tracts south and west of Nuremberg bear similar witness. Many of these provincial and up-country presses were set in motion on the initiative of particular groups of students or scholars, others on that of some religious house, yet others by the local authorities, who were usually ready to extend an invitation to any craftsman recommended to them [. . .]

The decade of the 1470s, during which Venice and the other major centres had not yet deployed their full resources, was the natural playground of local and occasional typography, and during those years the art found its way to quite fifty of the eighty Italian towns made acquainted with it before the century closed. How transient were many of these visits may be gathered from the fact that twenty of the fifty had already dropped out of the lists for good by the end of 1480, while in several others the press was thereafter only intermittently active. As we reckon up the modest score of this scattered output and confront it with the thousands of Venice, Milan, Rome, and Florence, we see that control of the market by big business was inevitable from the first, and we cannot but acknowledge that the boons of variety and cheapness of reading matter were thereby conferred on an ever-increasing multitude of readers. Yet the earlier, wayward children of an art only just come to maturity – the true incunabula – are attractive as their more exactly standardized successors rarely contrive to be. Theirs is the charm of the experimental and the idiosyncratic, and of a happy diversity of type-faces conceived in a still vital tradition of fine calligraphy. Such books as the Subiaco Lactantius of 1465 or the Foligno Dante of 1472 (to mention only these) are noble things, and if they lack the "exhibition finish" of the finest modern printing, we must remember not only that the technique which produced them was primitive compared with that of today but that they were originally the very contrary of high-price *éditions de luxe*. Their purpose was to supply the wants of the ordinary reader more quickly and cheaply than could pen and ink, and so they manage to avoid that touch of the *trop voulu* which is somehow apt to haunt the technically flawless productions of our own century. Circumstances, however, were already changing when Jenson died, rich and full of honours, in the autumn of 1480, and before the new decade closed type-faces were fast settling down, as it were, to a greatest common measure, with a short range of roman patterns for humanistic texts, another of gothics suitable for law books, and so forth, until the founts in each class end by differing so little from each other that variants can be detected only by the specialist. It becomes possible for several offices to share the printing of a long text and the average reader to be none the wiser, and one facsimile may in a modern catalogue be not inadequate to represent material used by twenty-five or thirty presses. This does not mean that such utility faces are of poor quality, or that there is any serious decline in typographical standards; in some respects the contrary is true. But it does mean that a book of a given kind is no longer likely to be very different from another of the same kind, and the present account can accordingly turn at this point to a more general evaluation.

The appetite for classical literature soon recovered from its early surfeit of print at Rome and Venice. To this there can witness editions of the Latin classics to the number of some 900, and possibly more; purely scientific texts, like the *Natural History* of Pliny the Elder, are additional to this count. In the forefront of them all stands Cicero, whose prestige fluctuated during the Renaissance but who during the later 1400s had become the very god of prose composition. More than 200 Italian editions of his writings are known, and they include the first edition of his complete works, published at Milan in 1498 and 1499 – no small under-taking, with its four volumes in large folio, of nearly 800 leaves altogether. The primacy of Cicero as a letter-writer was at no time in doubt, and the ability to compose an epistle as close to the Ciceronian model as possible was an accomplishment indispensable to every humanist, whose daily bread might depend upon his command of the commendatory, laudatory, gratulatory, petitory, regratiatory, or, in the last resort, vituperative letter, as the case might be (the nomenclature is that of a popular "ready writer" of the time, the *Modus epistolandi* of the Venetian Franciscus Niger). It is thus no surprise to find on record as many as fifty-four editions of Cicero's own *Epistolae* (chiefly those *ad familiares*) and to read that one of these, published at Rome in 1490, consisted of no fewer than 800 copies. Apart from Cicero, the Roman masters of prose were less popular than the poets, at the head of whom stands Virgil, with something like seventy editions of his complete works. If many of them offend by continuing the *Aeneid* with the thirteenth book which Maffeo Vegio ("the egregious Vegius," as Saintsbury called him) had the presumption to add to Virgil's text, we cannot blame their printers, who were only giving a not-too-discriminating public what it wanted. As for the Greek writers, they enjoyed a *succès d'estime*, indeed, but most students fought shy of them when presented in their original tongue; there were, after all, a number of translations made by famous scholars, such as Laurentius Valla, which might be held to satisfy all reasonable demands. The two most important series of Greek printed texts were that of Florence, which has already been spoken of, and that published at Venice by Aldus Manutius between 1495 and 1499, and including the "philosophy," natural and otherwise, of Aristotle and Theophrastus in five great volumes, nine comedies of Aristophanes, and the *Idylls* of Theocritus. But Aeschylus and Sophocles were never printed at all, any more than Herodotus or Thucydides, while a collection of the speeches of Isocrates, very handsomely printed at Milan in 1493, went off so slowly that a remainder was re-issued with a fresh title-page as late as 1535. Grammars and dictionaries were numerous, and included the vast *Lexicon* of Suidas, but most of them were apparently designed for conversation with Greeks, either in Italy or in their own country, where Venetian traders and officials must have often found a knowledge of the language indispensable. Greek type-faces suffered from the lack of a good calligraphic tradition, the contemporary cursive script being entirely unsuited to reproduction in type; while one or two have never been improved upon save in detail, others are so barbarous as to be almost unreadable, and the best known, the Aldine cursive, is of very indifferent quality.

All in all, the humanists were well served by the printers to whom they had given so much encouragement from the beginning, and relations between them were generally cordial, in spite of a natural tendency to blame all errors on the press-men, who were not in a position to reply. It is nevertheless remarkable that the writings of the humanists themselves make no great show in the book-lists, except in so far as they contributed commentaries to the classical texts or prefaces and dedications of particular editions of these [. . .]

If the length and size of the books rather than the mere number of editions were made the statistical criterion, there is little doubt that the law would outdistance all other subjects with which the earliest Italian printers concerned themselves. The fundamental texts of both civil and canon law were long, the explanatory glosses with which they were provided were no shorter, and the commentaries written upon them by a host of jurists were interminable. But the demand for them all, even for the most prolix, was constant. This may seem at first sight surprising, but its explanation lies in the crowd of independent authorities, ecclesiastical and secular, into which sovereignty in medieval Italy was comminuted. Each of these, from the Curia downwards, had of necessity its chancery and its legal experts, and a training in canon law was almost indispensable to a cleric in high office. The need for law books was correspondingly great, and their circulation extended across the Alps, where Germany was in much the same political condition; the national anarchy was the printers' opportunity. It has already been said that Venice specialized in editions of the *Corpus juris* and the *Decretals*, but the treatises of the commentators were printed everywhere, and at Bologna, famous for its school of law, legal texts apparently account for more than a quarter of the total output. The learned writers were practically without exception southerners, and we need no further testimony than that of the book-lists to be assured that in jurisprudence as in so much else Italy stood at this time in the forefront of the western nations.

Not less pre-eminent were the Italian presses in respect of scientific literature, which would make a poor show indeed without their contribution. This is especially true of medical texts. Such editions as were published of the physicians of antiquity, especially of Galen and Celsus, are virtually all Italian, and the same applies to Avicenna, Mesue, Rhasis, and the other Arabians whom contemporary medicine still regarded as its guides. In addition, there were the minor medical classics of the Italians themselves, together with a handful of monographs [. . .] which are evidence of more modern trends of thought. Outside Italy only Lyons, stimulated by contacts with the faculty of Montpellier, had anything of importance to show in print; the German offices dealt only with texts of the "family doctor" class. Along with the study of medicine went of course the study of the natural sciences, which were little considered in the north. The biological writings of Aristotle were four times printed at Venice in a Latin version, and Aldus's great Greek Aristotle, already mentioned, afforded an opportunity for their further study. Six more or less complete editions of the Aristotelian corpus in Latin, also printed at Venice, testify to a more comprehensive interest in his works than in Germany or France, where he appears rather as a logician than a scientist, and it is surely not without significance that the edition of his *Politics* with a commentary printed at Rome in 1492, and making up a good-sized folio of 256 leaves, should have been struck off in as many as 1,500 copies. The *Natural History* of Pliny had entirely superseded such medieval compilations as the *De proprietatibus rerum* of Bartholomew the Englishman, still unchallenged in the north; the records are instructive, inasmuch as they show Pliny printed fifteen times in the original and thrice in an Italian translation, in every case in Italy, but Bartholomew twenty-four times north of the Alps and not once south of them. It would probably be fair to say, in sum, that the only departments of secular knowledge in which the northern presses catered at all comparably with the Italian for their readers were astronomy, astrology, and scholastic philosophy and logic. And such landmarks as six editions of the *Geographia* of Strabo, two editions of the *De architectura* of Vitruvius, that of Alberti's *De re aedificatoria* (1485), commended by Politian to Lorenzo de' Medici for help in its distribution, or the famous edition, so magnificently illustrated, of the *Hypnerotomachia* of Francesco Colonna (1499), containing a theory of art in guise of an allegory – these, to name only a few, show the Italian intellect at home in regions as yet quite beyond the purview of the rest of Europe. It is a commonplace that "in the fifteenth century, 'educated Europe' is but a synonym for Italy"; bibliographical facts and figures help us more exactly to assess its truth.

There remain to be considered the services rendered by the early printers of Italy to the national literature. Here they were given an opportunity beyond the reach of their colleagues in other parts by the unquestioned primacy of this literature over those of the other Western vernaculars. The work of its three great masters, Dante, Petrarch, and Boccaccio, was alive and calling for dissemination; in France and Germany the great epics and lyrics of an older time were all but forgotten, and scarcely anything of value had since been produced to take their place, while England had as yet only Chaucer. The idea of putting into print the earliest and greatest Italian classic, the *Divina commedia*, must have occurred almost simultaneously to three different persons as early as 1471, since in the following year the three first editions appeared within a few months of each other, one at

Foligno, one at Mantua and one at Venice. All are worthy books, but that of Foligno, printed with a monumental roman, copes best with the grandeur of its contents. These three were followed before the century closed by twelve others, and the nine latest include one or other of the current commentaries of Benvenuto D'Imola and Landino. Some contain illustrations, but only those of the Florentine edition of 1481 spoken of above are valuable. Of the rest of Dante's writings the *Convito* was printed once, but the *Vita nuova* not until half-way through the next century. An average of one edition every other year of so exacting a masterpiece as the *Divina commedia* is perhaps no bad record, and even if the Foligno edition consisted of only 200 copies, as there is some reason to suppose, this figure was no doubt greatly exceeded by its successors. But we cannot wonder that a much wider circulation in print accrued to the *Canzoniere* and the *Trionfi* of Petrarch, of which there are counted no fewer than thirty-four editions, nine of them comprising only the *Trionfi*. The earliest, of 1470, is one of the earliest Venetian essays in vernacular printing, while that completed at Padua in 1472, which describes its contents somewhat slightingly as "rerum vulgarium fragmenta,"[2] reproduces the text of Petrarch's own manuscript, now in the Vatican, the same that also served for the first edition in the Aldine italic in 1501. As in the case of the *Divina commedia*, the latest editions included a commentary. It was natural for a generation that took such delight in elaborate allegorical pageants to call for many editions of the *Trionfi*, and from 1488 onwards these were made additionally saleable by woodcuts of the triumphs of Love, Chastity, Fame, Time, and Divinity. Petrarch's crowded visions, however, are not easily illustrated within the compass of a smallish folio page, and these pictures satisfy us as little as those provided for Dante. The other writings of the great humanist were strangely neglected, and the only comprehensive early edition of his Latin works was actually not printed in Italy at all, but at Basel in 1496. A wider typographical field was covered by Boccaccio. While the *Decameron* heads the list with eleven editions, the *Filocolo* runs it close with as many as eight, and there were twenty-two editions of eight of his other romances, if we include the *Urbano*, then still considered to be his work, so that, statistically, he overtops Petrarch as well as Dante. Apart from the three great names only one other from the earlier time makes any show, that of Cecco d'Ascoli, the ill-fated contemporary of Dante, whose epic *L'Acerba* went through at least ten editions; but its appeal was in fact scientific and not literary, like that of Brunetto Latini's *Tesoro*, which in its Italian adaptation was once printed in 1474, or Fazio degli Uberti's *Dittamondo*, also printed in the same year.

    As the first half-century of the printed book drew to its close Italian literature was beginning to flower afresh. Ariosto, the greatest poet of the age, belongs, indeed, only by birth to this period, but two lesser masterpieces fall within it – Luigi Pulci's *Morgante maggiore* and Boiardo's *Orlando inamorato*. Of the former, first published in its entirety in 1482, nine editions are known, of the *Orlando*, in its several stages, four, and the extent of its popularity may be gauged from the fact that of altogether 2,000 copies of its four editions only two can actually be read today – all the rest have perished, thumbed to pieces by eager readers. Not but what the romances of chivalry which these two epics satirized were quite as popular; witness *Guerino il Meschino*, reputed the work of one Andrea da Barberino, of which twelve editions are known to us. Another kind of story-telling is represented by the *Novellino* of Masuccio Salernitano: copies of five editions have survived, but in this, as in the case of so much popular literature, others may well have perished completely. Devotional poetry, some of it of considerable merit, was frequently printed; such as that of Iacopone da Todi, Leonardo Giustiniani, and Antonio Cornazzano, whose *Vita della Vergine* in *terza rima* passed through at least a dozen editions. Lorenzo de' Medici himself wrote poems both religious and secular, which were several times printed; an edition of his *Ballatette* includes also those of Politian and others of this circle. A complete list would include many other names, now forgotten; but enough has been said to show that by the end of the fifteenth century no new book of any quality was likely to fail of the permanency conferred by print.

Editor's Notes

1   Nothing is arduous to Florentine talents.
2   fragments of vernacular things

PART THREE

Political Thought and "Civic Humanism"

Chapter 8

Charles Davis

■ from **PTOLEMY OF LUCCA AND THE ROMAN REPUBLIC**, *Proceedings of the American Philosophical Society*, 118 (1974), pp. 30–50

"WHAT IS HISTORY BUT THE praise of Rome?" Petrarch's famous question seems to epitomize the enthusiasm of the Renaissance for the classical past. Petrarch himself is often regarded as the first great herald of that enthusiasm and, in particular, as the curator of the humanistic cult of admiration for the pagan republic. Hans Baron, for example, asserts that a "profound break with the medieval mode of thought had been effected by Petrarch's youthful redis-covery of pre-imperial Rome and of the human and national forces – the *virtutes Romanae* – which in the time of the Respublica Romana had made Rome great, but had afterwards declined." Is this a tenable affirmation?

Beryl Smalley thinks that it is not. In a paper on "Sallust in the Middle Ages" she points out that a good deal of information about the Republic can be found in some medieval chroniclers and that there were many readers and imitators of the author of the *Jugurthine War* and the *Conspiracy of Catiline* during this period. They "knew perfectly well that the Roman people had flourished and had won their most striking victories in the good old days of early Roman tradition."

Whether republican victories were really considered more striking than those of Julius Caesar or Trajan is a moot point. But much evidence could be brought forward to support Smalley's general thesis. In the Middle Ages such authors as Florus, Lucan, Virgil, Servius, Cicero, Juvenal, and Valerius Maximus were popular, and whether or not they attacked the Empire, they all praised pristine virtue and republican heroes. The latter were also eulogized by some medieval historians: for example by Paul the Deacon in the lengthy section of his *Historia Romana* that he copied from Eutropius. Perhaps the most eloquent of all in cele-brating them was the twelfth-century rhetorician, John of Salisbury. He extolled such famous names as Camillus, Fabricius, Marcus Cato, Regulus, Gneius and Aemilius Scipio, Curius, and Lucius. It is of course true that in the same chapter John also extolled the virtues of kings, emperors, and non-Romans: Alexander, the sons of Aristides, Hannibal, Augustus, and Masinissa, and, in the next chapter,

Trajan, whom he praised most lengthily and fervently of all. At the same time, his general verdict on the Romans, though not directed specifically toward the Republic, applied most naturally to it. He asserted that "by devotion to justice and tranquil liberty, by reverence for the laws, by friendship with neighboring peoples, by maturity of counsel and gravity of words and deeds the Romans achieved dominion over the world."

In his erudite acquaintance with a large number of classical authors and in his sympathy for their ethical outlook John was exceptional. But interest in the Republic was not confined to intellectuals. For example, Arnold of Brescia was able to stir up people in Rome, according to Otto of Freising, by "putting forward the examples of the ancient Romans, who made the whole world theirs through ripe counsel of the senate and the courage of their youths." In the same period (first half of the twelfth century) an epitaph was set up in the cathedral of Pisa for a consul of that city named Henricus which compared him with Cato, Hector, Cicero, Fabricius, and Regulus. By the early thirteenth century an account of ancient history up to Julius Caesar had been written in French, as well as the *Fet des Romains*, a compilation of Sallust, Suetonius, and Lucan with insertions from Caesar's *Commentaries*. Both the history and the compilation were subsequently translated into Italian. Probably before 1250 another Italian translation had been made of a work dealing, among other matters, with Roman republican history and heroes. This was the Latin *Multe Ystorie et Troiane et Romane*, which drew heavily on Paul the Deacon. It was translated, probably at Rome, under the title *Liber ystoriarum romanorum*, and seems to have enjoyed considerable popularity for a limited time, until it was smothered by the influence of the *Fet des Romains* and of the chronicle of Martin of Troppau. In view of all this, how can Baron speak of Petrarch's "rediscovery of pre-imperial Rome"? Surely only by dismissing evidence contrary to his concept of "the medieval mode of thought" (which he postulates but, understandably, does not define) as either an exception or an anticipation.

One may feel uneasy at the dogmatic way in which Baron formulates his thesis. At the same time one can hardly deny that an obsessive interest in the Roman republic was not characteristic of pre-fourteenth-century Christian intellectual life. Earlier historians and moralists sometimes imitated Sallust's rhetoric and related a few republican *exempla*. But it was natural, as Smalley herself acknowledges, that they should find the Empire more relevant. Had not Augustus established the universal peace that facilitated the spreading of the Gospel? Had not Constantine bestowed sovereignty in the West on the Papacy? When Christ was born the Republic no longer existed. To the Middle Ages it seemed remote. Moreover, if precursors of Christ were sought, they were looked for not among Roman republican heroes but among those of the first chosen people, the Jews.

Due weight should be given to the impressive evidence furnished by Smalley about Sallust's medieval importance and to her suggestive dictum, "Orosius and Sallust supply the twin keys to medieval historiography." But surely Orosius, together with his great master St Augustine, was far more influential in shaping attitudes and providing information both about republican and imperial Rome. Orosius accepted Augustine's advice that he should try to show that the tribulations of the pagan past were even worse than those of the Christian present. It is true that he followed Origen and Eusebius to the extent of making Rome's dominance part of God's plan. At the same time he emphasized how unpleasant the process of acquiring such dominance had been for the subjugated peoples. Orosius was in the curious position of denying that Roman rule constituted, as Cicero had said, a *patrocinium*,[1] but asserting that it was providential in a special way, because the order it provided helped Christ's messengers. So the process was hateful but the end was glorious. Remorselessly polemical, Orosius had little attention to spare for examples of pagan heroism. Why had God picked the Romans and not another people to establish a universal peace? The answer lay hidden, Orosius seemed to believe, in His unsearchable will.

Augustine was more drastic. All rule, he said, came from God, but he refused to adopt the theory that the Roman *imperium*, even after it controlled the world, was necessarily desirable. Ideally, he thought, it would be possible to have as many kingdoms on earth as families in a city, and rulers should be like fathers reflecting the fatherhood of God and not like despots as the Romans had been to those in their power. Augustine was not dazzled, like Eusebius and Orosius, by the Roman "mission" and the Augustan peace, or even by the Christian Empire.

Both Augustine and Orosius presented a rather unsympathetic picture of Roman republican heroes, while furnishing the medieval world with most of its information about them. Augustine, it is true, praised their virtues far more eloquently than Orosius, but he did so for the most part in an extremely sardonic way. Their discipline, he admitted, was admirable. They scorned wealth and gladly faced hardship and danger. But this discipline did not come from love of the true God or of their fellow men. It came ultimately from love of themselves. They suppressed all lesser vices in the service of the supreme vice, pride. They lusted for sovereignty and glory. They were not citizens of the City of God but of that opposite mystical entity, the City of Man or the Devil. As for their own earthly realm, it was never a true republic since it did not serve the common good. How could it serve the common good when it taught its citizens to worship false gods or demons and thereby consigned them to Hell? It inspired in them a devotion that was ultimately self-destructive, since it pandered to their own self-love. Yet what feats of bravery and sacrifice the ancient Romans performed, hypnotized though they were by glory and bound for Hell! Such feats should kindle, St Augustine thought, a spirit of emulation in the breasts of Christians predestined to membership in the true republic and *patria* of Paradise.

The influence of Orosius and St Augustine tended to inhibit medieval sympathy for the Roman Republic. The prevalence of monarchy must also have played its part in damping enthusiasm. One would expect it to flare up again exactly where Baron has found it: in places where republics existed and had become selfconscious. The first happened in Italy. There the development of republican institutions and ideology naturally led to a patriotic reaffirmation of the glories of the Roman Republic, which, as Baron says, was a striking and significant cultural breakthrough. The aggressively Italian Petrarch was certainly its incomparable publicist. Even John of Salisbury seems detached when we compare his praises of Roman heroes (warmest of all, we should remember, in regard to Trajan) with Petrarch's passionate advocacy. But was Petrarch really the first to make, if not the "rediscovery of pre-imperial Rome," at least the rediscovery of specifically republican values?

It is possible to argue that he was not, and that this was the work of a previous generation. Baron himself provides a clue that leads us backward toward a pre-Petrarchan figure. This was the Dominican Ptolemy (or Tolomeo or Bartolomeo) of Lucca (*c.* 1236–1326), a member of the prominent Fiadoni family of that city, a notable civic and ecclesiastical historian, and a warm advocate of the hierocratic theory of papal power. In his *Crisis of the Early Italian Renaissance* Baron quotes from Ptolemy's continuation (*c.* 1302) of Aquinas's *De regimine principum*. "Ptolemy," Baron says, "at that early date, had formed the clear-cut judgment that the power of Rome had been built up under the consuls and free councils of the Republic, when 'no one among the Roman leaders wore a crown or was adorned with the purple, for his personal glorification.'" So Ptolemy, unlike John of Salisbury, compared the Republic with the Empire to the detriment of the latter.

Baron does not mention an even more significant departure by Ptolemy from earlier medieval writings on the Republic. He was the first, both in the *De regimine* and in another treatise written some twenty years earlier, the *Determinatio compendiosa*, to attack the Augustinian verdict on Roman self-love. Starting from Augustine's references to Roman heroes, particularly in Book V, chapter 18 of the *City of God*, Ptolemy turned Augustine's moral on its head. He did not attack the great African father directly. Instead he demonstrated an obsequious respect, together with a shameless flair for misquotation. Ptolemy made Augustine say that Roman rule was just and benevolent and motivated by *sincerus amor pro patria*.[2] In the *De regimine principum* he went even farther and affirmed that this patriotism was derived from *caritas*, the highest of all the virtues. Nowhere in these discussions did Ptolemy mention Augustine's words about the egoistic self-love of the Romans and their lust for power and glory. He said on the contrary that the Romans were intent on the good of their *patria* and their subjects. They were, in short, not a scourge but a blessing for the human race.

Probably Ptolemy was influenced by John of Salisbury's words about Roman justice and Roman friendship with neighboring peoples, for he quoted in the *Determinatio* from the *Policraticus*. But John did not have Ptolemy's intensity. In his rather meandering chapter he mixed together Romans and non-Romans, kings, emperors, and republicans. He felt no need to quote Augustine in this context, for he was primarily interested in presenting *exempla* rather than in justifying the Roman historical mission.

Perhaps Ptolemy had *Policraticus* V, 7 in mind when he wrote his three chapters in the *Determinatio* about Roman patriotism, zeal for justice, and civil benevolence or *pietas*, chapters that were later incorporated in expanded form in the *De regimine principum*. But they were not merely an expansion of John's words. They were primarily an answer to St Augustine's. In their comprehensiveness and passionate enthusiasm they represented a new departure. Their most striking characteristic was their attribution of so selfless a patriotism to the Romans that it could be described under the heading of the supreme Christian virtue of *caritas*.

One reason why Ptolemy prized Roman patriotism so highly may have been his membership in the upper class of Lucca, a great Italian republic. It is a curious and interesting fact that his use of *De civitate Dei* V, 18 and his twisting of Augustine's moral were soon echoed by two citizens of another important Tuscan city-state, Florence. One was the Dominican theologian and lector of S. Maria Novella,

Remigio de' Girolami; the other was the lay poet, intellectual, and politician Dante Alighieri, after 1302 an exile from his city. Both emphasized the patriotism of the Romans and regarded it as the basis of their moral and political virtue.

Probably only a year or two after Ptolemy had finished his continuation of the *De regimine principum*, Remigio wrote his remarkable treatise *De bono communi*.[3] In it he quoted at great length from *De civitate Dei*, V. 18. But far from indulging in Augustinian irony over the spectacle of Roman heroes conquering the world but still condemned to Hell, Remigio said that a citizen should be willing to go to Hell rather than see his commune there, if this could be done without offending God. Perhaps he was thinking of the famous sacrifice of Marcus Curtius, mentioned by Augustine and Ptolemy. Remigio was interested enough in it to copy out the fairly long passage about it that Paul the Deacon had previously copied from Eutropius into his *Historia Romana*. This account said that the great hole that opened up in the middle of Rome could be seen to reach "ad infernum."[4] So when Marcus Curtius armed as a soldier leapt into it, causing it to close over his head, he was literally leaping down into Hell (or at least into Hades) for the safety of his city. Therefore Remigio's idea of patriotism went considerably beyond the "pugna pro patria"[5] of the *Disticha Catonis* that he and many other medieval writers quoted. He even cited with apparent approval a favorable verdict on Cato's suicide and a rather striking anticipation of Dante's view that Cato had died for liberty. According to it, Cato killed himself because he thought the triumph of Julius Caesar "had brought the *res publica* into great danger." But Seneca in his letters to Lucilius and John of Salisbury in the *Policraticus* connect Cato's suicide specifically with his zeal for liberty and are therefore more likely to have been, on this point, among Dante's sources.

In passages of the *De via paradisi*[6] [. . .] Remigio followed Valerius Maximus (III, 4) in eulogizing Manilius Torquatus for giving judgment against his own son and in affirming that Brutus was equal in glory to Romulus; the latter established the *urbs romana* and the former established *libertas romana*, by ending Tarquin's sway. Evil kings, said Remigio, and evil prelates, too, ought to be confounded.

At the same time, the basis of Remigio's political ethic was not pagan history but Christian theology. Remigio quoted St Paul's words, "Charity seeketh not its own," and St Augustine's exposition of them in his Rule, "Charity places common things before private ones." So, like Ptolemy, Remigio identified patriotism (which he defined in Aristotelian terms as devotion to the common good) with *caritas*.

St Augustine, on the other hand, had identified Roman patriotism with self-love. Since the Romans did not cherish the true God but rather demons, men, and the idols of sovereignty and glory, there was among them no true justice and no true *res publica*. But without justice what were conquests but great thieveries? Augustine told the story of the pirate who had hailed Alexander as a colleague, saying that what he did on a small scale Alexander did on a large one. Dante, too, had thought for a time that the Roman conquests had been based only on violence. Evidently then he was a faithful disciple of Augustine, at least in his attitude to Rome. But Dante wondered why the Roman primacy had not been resisted. By the date he wrote the *Convivio* (1304–1307) he had abandoned the Augustinian view entirely, though he drew a large part of his catalog of Roman heroes in

Convivio IV, v (and also later in *Monarchia* II, v) from *De civitate Dei* V, 18. In the *Convivio* he said that the primary cause of Roman success was divine providence but the secondary cause was the political genius of the "gente latina."[7] He praised it for its ability to gain power with subtlety, to maintain it with strength, and to exercise it with gentleness, qualities especially apparent in the descendants of Aeneas. For this reason God made them ruler of the world. As for the Roman heroes, they loved their city not with human but with divine affection, inspired in them by God. "O most holy breast of Cato," exclaimed Dante, "who shall presume to speak of thee?" In the *Monarchia*, he opposed Augustine's contention that the Roman conquests had been lawless and asserted on the contrary that they had been intended to fulfill the end of law, the public good.

Three Tuscan contemporaries, Ptolemy, Remigio, and Dante, were the first medieval writers to meet Augustine on his own ground and stand his moral on its head. For Augustine, Roman patriotism was ultimately based on the sin and folly of egoistic pride. For Dante it was holy, for Remigio it was rational, and for Ptolemy it was charitable. One is naturally impelled to ask what the relationship between these three latter-day Roman patriots may have been.

In a learned article published in 1938, Theodore Silverstein attempted a partial answer. He suggested that Ptolemy was a major source for Dante's eulogies of republican heroes [. . .] Of course, another hypothesis is possible: enthusiasm for the Roman republic may have been in the air in late thirteenth-century Tuscany. Common use, and even distortion, of a famous chapter in St Augustine need not imply direct dependence. Certainly, as we shall see, this common use was directed toward very different purposes.

[. . .]

We know now that our authors at least sometimes used different classical texts. As we shall soon see, they also used them for different purposes. Their approaches to the republican past were therefore essentially independent. Even on the basis of this brief investigation, we can say with confidence that the current of classicism in late thirteenth- and early fourteenth-century Tuscany was not drawn from one source. Nor, as we shall observe, did it run towards one destination.

This current was also fed by a parallel stream, which in fact was older than the revolt against Augustine. Ptolemy had no part in it. It was focused on Cicero, and not merely on his rhetoric and philosophical thought, which had been popular in western Europe for many centuries, but also on his deeds. It was characterized by praise for Cicero as a brave and patriotic statesman, who defended Rome against the evil conspiracy hatched by the aristocratic demagogue Catiline. Augustine, Orosius, and their followers had not been interested in Cicero as a republican hero. Authors like Otto of Freising and John of Salisbury read his works and agreed with his theoretical judgments but never eulogized his acts. Although a rather full account of Cicero's role in defeating Catiline was given by Sallust, most medieval readers seem to have been more interested in Cato and Caesar, as indeed Sallust was himself. It was in thirteenth- and fourteenth-century Florence that this attitude changed, and Cicero began to be admired as a republican patriot. Here, again, one must take account of a sweeping verdict by Hans Baron. In substance it is basically correct. This time, however it seems to fall short not merely by fifty years but by more than a century in its attempt to determine the temporal point at which crucial cultural change took place.

For the Middle Ages, Baron says, Cicero was mainly "a stoic sage, a model of aloofness and suppression of those passions that govern public life. For a thousand years there had been no room for Cicero's civic doctrine that man is meant to play an active part in his community and in the state, and not to pursue mere solitary contemplation." It is well known that Petrarch reproved Cicero for his interest in politics. According to Baron, a new attitude to Cicero as a statesman came to fruition only in late fourteenth-century Florence, when Salutati praised his patriotism.

Similar eulogizing did occur, however, in Florence much earlier than the end of the fourteenth century. Its chief source, oddly enough, was the previously mentioned French compendium the *Fet des Romains*. Written, according to its editors, between 1213 and 1214, probably by a cleric from the Ile de France, it was primarily concerned with providing tales of Caesar and his wars. Yet its author showed considerable sophistication in combining, abridging and rearranging the classical works on which he drew (Sallust, Suetonius, Lucan, and Caesar), as well as considerable stylistic talent in translating them. He was not a republican or a Roman patriot, but rather an apparently devoted subject of Philip Augustus. He left out Sallust's long-winded description of the pristine virtues of the Romans and also some of Lucan's strictures on Caesar. But Cicero, for some reason or other, seems to have caught his fancy, and he rendered Sallust's rather grudging praise with an exuberance that sometimes went beyond it. For example, about the election of Cicero as consul, Sallust said merely that, although many aristcrats thought that it lowered the dignity of the consular office to elect an outsider, however outstanding his deserts, they had to suppress their envy and arrogance in time of peril. The author of the *Fet* added "the city had need of good counsel in such necessity, and in it there was no other man so sagacious." About Cicero's crucial speech against Catiline in the Senate Sallust said, "Cicero gave a brilliant oration that was useful for the *respublica*." The author of the *Fet* said, "And Cicero spoke so well for *le preu dou coumun*[8] that everyone marvelled." He also translated Lucan's judgment that, in the civil war between Caesar and Pompey, Pompey's cause would have triumphed if it had not been for the sins of the Romans and the luck of Caesar. He noted that Cicero and Cato were among those who favored Pompey. Not least among Italians, his compendium had great success.

About fifty years after the composition of the *Fet*, and about twenty years before Ptolemy wrote his *Determinatio*, the Florentine notary, rhetorician, and politician Brunetto Latini was in exile in France (1260–*c*. 1265). While there he composed his *Tresor*, an encyclopedia for laymen written in French, and his *Rettorica*, a commentary on and translation of part of Cicero's *De inventione* written in Italian. In both Brunetto drew on the *Fet*'s portrait of Cicero the statesman in order to paint an even more glowing one of his own. In the *Tresor* he used "sagacious," the same adjective employed by the author of the *Fet*, to describe Cicero, and went on to affirm with enthusiasm, "By his good sense he vanquished the conspirators, and captured and destroyed many of them on the advice of the good Cato, who judged them worthy of death. . ." Brunetto also observed in the *Rettorica*:

and there [in the *De inventione*] where he [Cicero] says . . . "our commune," I read "Rome," since Tully was a citizen of Rome, new and of no high rank [*nuovo e di non grande altezza*], but for his wisdom he held such a place that all Rome was controlled by his voice, and . . . for the good of his country he was completely opposed to Catiline. And then, in the war between Pompey and Julius Caesar, he sided with Pompey, like all those wise men who loved the state of Rome. Perhaps he calls her "our commune" because Rome is the head of the world and the commune of everyone.

Brunetto's political experience in the councils of Florence, his love for his city and hatred of faction, sharpened by the bitterness of exile, and his first-hand knowledge of some of Cicero's orations combined to make him respond more directly and emotionally to the figure of the Roman statesman than did even the author of the *Fet*. Brunetto went as far beyond the latter in eulogizing Cicero as Ptolemy had gone beyond John of Salisbury in eulogizing other heroes of the Republic. The author of the *Fet* had translated *res publica* interestingly but rather abstractly as *preu du commun*. Brunetto, citizen of a republic that boasted its descent from Rome, spoke of the latter as the "commune of everyone." Florence was closer to Rome than was France. Brunetto could identify his patriotism with Cicero's in a way that was new, at least in its immediacy and intensity.

He was followed in this by a number of his Florentine compatriots. Dante in *Convivio* IV, v was adapting Brunetto's phrase "new and of no high rank" when he called Cicero "a new citizen of low estate" who "defended Roman liberty against so great a citizen as Catiline." The chronicler Giovanni Villani also said that Cicero was "a new citizen in Rome" and referred to the "sagacity and foresight" that enabled him to expose Catiline's plot. As for Remigio, he did not mention Catiline, but he called Cicero "the best among the Latins" because he tried to allay the strife of the factions. Perhaps Remigio was thinking of the Ciceronian orations translated by Brunetto into Italian (*Pro marcello, Pro ligario*, and *Pro deiotaro rege*), for these were all appeals to Caesar's clemency on behalf of his opponents. Remigio, too, was praising him for his political acts. All this was a remarkable anticipation of the later Florentine admiration for Cicero the statesman, whose beginning Baron connects with Coluccio Salutati and his pupils.

Italian translations of the *Fet* and of Sallust must have made the Roman republic seem less remote. A translation of the former work was executed, perhaps at Florence, in the latter part of the thirteenth century, perhaps not much later than the appearance of Brunetto's *Tresor* and *Rettorica*. About 1300 a direct translation of Sallust's *Catiline* (and also of his *Jugurtha*) was brilliantly achieved by the Tuscan Dominican Bartolommeo da San Concordio, who also composed the famous book of moral lore *Ammaestramenti degli antichi*. Bartolommeo's translation of Sallust was already being drawn on in a codex of 1313 in an attempt to improve the earlier Italian translation of the *Fet*. When Dino Compagni sought a literary model for his description of Corso Donati, the leader of the Black Guelf party he hated, he could find it easily in Sallust's portrait of Catiline. It is doubtful whether Sallust ever had so wide and knowledgeable a medieval audience as in late thirteenth- and early fourteenth-century Tuscany.

Here streams of classical influence flowed together, and all dealt with subjects that concerned the Roman Republic. Perhaps it is at this point that we find the "re-discovery of pre-imperial Rome" which Baron defers until Petrarch, and in regard to Cicero, until Coluccio Salutati. In Tuscany around 1300 interest in the Roman Republic was remarkably intense and widespread. Even if we accept Smalley's contention that the latter did not need to be rediscovered, one must admit that earlier medieval references to it seem scattered and on the whole coolly detached when compared with the enthusiasm and combativeness of our Tuscan phalanx.

No doubt Tuscany, with the exception of Arezzo, contributed very little to the development of humanistic philology. But to the development of what we may call humanistic history it contributed a great deal. The rewriting of Augustine, the re-evaluation of Cicero, and the translations of Sallust and other classics helped to prepare the way for later devotees of the Roman Republic. The extent to which humanistic theories of history were indebted to those of their medieval predecessors is a question that still needs exploration. Such a task will not be attempted here. The present paper is intended to show that there was a significant wave of enthusiasm for the Roman republic in late thirteenth- and early fourteenth-century Tuscany, and to examine the motivations of its protagonists.

Its first purpose has hopefully already been accomplished. Its second must now be attempted. Perhaps the latter task can best be approached by comparing Brunetto, Remigio, Dante, and Ptolemy first as to their historical and then as to their political attitudes. We shall find Ptolemy the most enigmatic and in some ways the most interesting theorist of the group. Trying to account for his curious combination of high papalism and communal patriotism will occupy much of our attention in the remainder of this essay.

The historical views of Brunetto and Remigio need not detain us long. Brunetto, in fact, crammed Romulus and Catiline into one chapter of his *Tresor*, omitting everything between, and went on to speak of Julius Caesar (whom he, like Dante, regarded as the first emperor), Augustus, Titus, Justinian, Charlemagne, Otto of Freising, and Barbarossa. Probably he was not really much interested in Roman history, except where it seemed immediately relevant to his own city, its government, and its factional problems, as in the part of the *Fet* that translated Sallust's account of the conspiracy of Catiline. Brunetto's ideal, of which he thought Cicero had been the supreme exemplar, was that of the virtuous rhetorician who was the teacher and civilizer of his fellow citizens.

Remigio, too, was a local patriot who sought by his rhetoric to calm factional passions and promote a love for the commune on the part of its citizens. He said that the fullness of time had come under Octavian, when secular power was universal and peace was complete, and he praised Julius Caesar as well as the heroes of the Republic. His eulogy of the latter as servants of the common good was, to be sure, very strong. But he placed alongside them Moses, David, and Judas Maccabeus, who served the common good of the Jewish people, and Pope Leo I, Archbishop Thomas a Becket, and King Louis IX of France, who served the common good of the Church. There was no emphasis by either Remigio or Brunetto on the unique political virtues and talents of the citizens of Rome.

Dante and Ptolemy, however, said that those talents were testified to by Rome's success. They thought the Romans were a chosen people, superior to all others, characterized by austerity, patriotism, justice, and civic benevolence. But their ideas of the purpose of the Roman mission differed almost as sharply as their reasons for extolling it. Dante was an apologist for the Empire. He condemned the Donation of Constantine as an illegal act that had made the clergy rich and arrogant. He denounced the meddling of popes in temporal and particularly imperial affairs. He hoped that Rome would once again become the capital of an empire that was world-wide in fact as well as in law. Ptolemy, on the other hand, was an apologist for the Papacy. He thought that Christ's royal as well as His priestly authority had been inherited by the Pope. He regarded the Donation as only a recognition of what St Peter and his successors already rightfully possessed. He rejoiced that Christ's Vicar had Rome firmly in his grasp.

Dante's idea of Rome was more complicated than Ptolemy's. Her mission, he believed, stretched from Aeneas to Henry VII and beyond, and from Troy to Heaven. It included such diverse figures as King Numa, Fabricius, Cato, Julius Caesar, Trajan, Justinian, and Charlemagne. It embraced the kingdom, the republic, the empire in both its pagan and Christian stages, and also the papacy in so far as the latter was willing to remain in what Dante considered its proper sphere. All these aspects were connected. Dante said that Aeneas's journey to the underworld was the cause both of Rome's victory (her world-wide *imperium*) and of the "papal mantle" (the Pope's jurisdiction over the Church).

Under greedy and corrupt pontiffs Rome also had a sinister dimension. Dante compared the papal city of his own day to the Great Whore of the Apocalypse, fornicating with the kings of the world. But he prophesied that "the high providence that with Scipio defended the glory of the world for Rome" would soon bring help. Probably he looked for a future emperor; at any rate for someone who would cleanse the throne of Augustus and the chair of Peter from the filth of the Beast. Dante eulogized republican heroes warmly. He believed that they were filled with divine love when they demonstrated patriotic passion for their homeland. Like John of Salisbury and unlike Ptolemy, Dante hailed Cato's devotion to liberty, sealed by suicide. Yet Dante said that liberty was most complete under imperial rule. He regarded Julius Caesar (whose triumph made Cato kill himself) as a legitimate emperor. He assigned him to Limbo among the virtuous pagans, and placed his assassins in the lowest depth of Hell. He celebrated Augustus's peace and Trajan's justice, as well as Justinian's revision of the law and Charlemagne's succour of the Papacy from the Lombards. For him the Republic was a preparation for the Empire, and the virtues of republican heroes simply made more understandable the divine choice of the Romans as the rulers of the world.

Ptolemy's view of Rome was simpler. He was interested only in the republican and papal stages of her history. Julius Caesar was a usurper; Augustus was Christ's deputy; Christ and his successors the popes were the true emperors. But the republican heroes who preceded Him demonstrated virtues that made them worthy to be His precursors. Especially praiseworthy was their poverty. Although Aristotle was right to say that in general paupers were likely to be more rapacious than rich men when elected to public office, he was only speaking of involuntary poverty. Men like Fabricius could have been rich and chose to be poor. This free choice foreshadowed the poverty of Christ and the early Church. It pointed, in fact, not only forward in time but also backward: to that state of innocence enjoyed by man before the Fall.

It recalled the purity of Eden. It also recalled the *regimen politicum* that existed before Adam committed the first sin. It was more suitable than the *regimen regale* to the *status integer* of human nature. It was this state of innocence that wise and virtuous men like the ancient Romans tried to imitate, directing their *regimen politicum* as completely as possible towards the common good.

In his historical theory Ptolemy, unlike our three Florentines, was a self-conscious republican. He alone drew a sharp line between the Roman Republic and the Roman Empire. He alone said that Julius Caesar was a tyrant, and that because of his tyranny he was soon killed by the senators. As for Augustus he was modest and ruled with circumspection and wisdom; the whole world deferred to him. But he was only the vice-regent, however unknowingly, of Christ. In his *Determinatio compendiosa*, in his continuation of Aquinas's *De regimine principum*, and in his *New Ecclesiastical History* Ptolemy said that world rule, enjoyed successively by the Assyrians, Persians, Macedonians, and Romans, passed with the birth of the Saviour to Him and His deputies. From one point of view this marked the end of the Roman supremacy. Ptolemy explained the vision of the statue in the Book of Daniel as signifying the succession of the four world empires. Its golden head and neck represented the Assyrians, its silver breast and arms the Medes and Persians, its brazen belly and thighs the Greeks, and its iron shanks and feet the Romans. But part of the feet was made of earth, which will not mix with iron, symbolizing the Roman civil wars. The statue was then pulverized by a stone [Christ] and grew into a great mountain that filled the world. This was the fifth world monarchy. It was superior to the other four in three ways: the dignity of its potentate Christ and of His vicars the popes, the length of its rule (whether computed from Christ or Constantine Ptolemy said that its duration was greater than that of the other four), and the universality of its extent (had not Christianity been preached almost everywhere?). Its supremacy was the distinguishing feature of the last temporal age of the world.

From another point of view, however, this fifth empire marked not so much the end as the apotheosis of Roman authority. In his *Determinatio* Ptolemy said that the Pope and the cardinals had replaced the consuls and the Senate, as Constantine recognized when he removed himself to the East. In the *De regimine principum* he remarked that Christ established his lordship in humility and poverty, like the rulers of the Roman Republic. He thought that the Rome of Fabricius had prepared the way not for the Rome of Augustus but for the Rome of Christ.

Christ permitted pagans to rule for a time, but their authority was legitimated only by his sufferance. With Constantine, the open lordship of the Church began, and from Jovian to Charlemagne almost all emperors were obedient to it. As for the Pope, he was superior to any emperor, and could depose him not only for crime, but also for the good of the church and the peace of the Christian people. From the papacy every other jurisdiction depended, regal and imperial as well as ecclesiastical. The Pope had transferred royal crowns from one dynasty to another. He had translated the Empire from the Greeks to the Germans and could transfer it to a different race when he chose. He had even established the German college of electors. Not only did the Pope prescribe the manner in which the King of the Romans should be nominated, but by coronation raised him to the imperial office. All such acts were expressions of his full power (*plenam potestatem*) as Christ's Vicar over the whole world. Subject to no human law he had by his own authority reversed or changed or added to the statutes of his predecessors. He was, in short, a monarch, a sovereign who carried the law in his own breast. But, strangely enough, his authority in a temporal sense was prefigured not by that of Augustus but by that of Fabricius and his peers: the republican heroes of Rome who had been the servants rather than the masters of their state. Ptolemy asserted that the authority of the Roman Republic had been legitimate, but that the Roman emperors had ruled only on sufferance and without real right. This was something new. So was Ptolemy's postulation of a Fifth Monarchy, that of the popes, as the direct successor of the Rome whose government had been free before it was overturned by the usurping ambition of Julius Caesar.

One of the sources of this surprising historical theory was the hierocratic view of the Donation of Constantine, set forth in the curial pamphlet *Eger cui lenia*. According to it Constantine had bestowed nothing whatever on the Papacy. He had simply recognized its authority, an authority that extended over the whole church and the whole world and that had been given to St. Peter and subsequent pontiffs by Christ. Ptolemy quoted from the *Eger cui lenia* in the *Determinatio*. If one accepted its thesis, as Ptolemy did, the only way to salvage the myth of the providentiality of Roman world power was to push it backward into republican times. Moreover, a heartfelt eulogy of the indifference of the old Romans to wealth and luxury might serve as a salutary reminder to lordly popes that they ought to imitate not the pomp of the Empire but the modesty and austerity of the Republic.

Ptolemy seems to have been genuinely drawn to the latter, despite his acceptance of the view that the Pope was a monarch, and a rather absolute monarch at that. Ptolemy was also attracted (and this is reflected in his political theory) by the positive analysis of popular government in Aristotle's *Politics*, newly translated from Greek into Latin. In some ways he showed a more perceptive appreciation of this treatise, and also of Roman history, than did Remigio and Dante. They admired Cicero the civic statesman, in whom Ptolemy was apparently uninterested. But only Ptolemy produced a reasoned defense of the kind of government that Cicero preferred. They echoed Aristotle's definition of man as a political animal and reproduced, either partially or completely, his governmental categories (monarchy, aristocracy, and polity and their perversions, tyranny, oligarchy, and democracy). But only Ptolemy pointed out the essential difference between a government of laws and one of men. He applied this distinction both to ancient Roman and contemporary Italian history, illustrating it with specific examples. He also weighed the advantages and disadvantages of various kinds of rule and decided that on the political level, at least in Rome and northern Italy, government limited by law was superior.

Nothing similar is found in the writings of his older contemporary Brunetto Latini, who copied much of John of Viterbo's political treatise *De regimine civitatum* into his *Tresor*. Like John, Brunetto was more interested in political common sense and political etiquette than in political theory. He said, to be sure, that French cities with appointed officials were less fortunate than Italian cities with elected ones. He mentioned Aristotle's three main categories of legitimate governments (*des rois, des bons, des communes*) and remarked that the last was "la tres millour entre ces autres."[9] He never bothered, however, to explain why. Evidently he felt no hostility for the Empire, at least on a theoretical level. He dedicated his *Tesoretto* to the imperial claimant Alphonse of Castile, and hailed him as lord of the whole world, of all the land visited by the sun and encompassed by the earth-girdling sea. But Brunetto's political interests seem to have been confined mainly to his own experience. He loathed the factionalism that had driven him into exile, but never, so far as we know, tried to philosophize about the commune or to discuss the proper relationship of the secular and spiritual powers, or the difference between legitimate government and tyranny.

This Remigio did. He analyzed very acutely the causes of dissension in his own commune and tried, both in treatises and sermons, to convince his fellow Florentines that they should shun faction and serve the good of the commune, which was the same as the common good. "From the good of the commune," Remigio said, "comes all a citizen's honor and prestige and every civic good." It was an expression of rational love on the part of "innumerable virtuous Romans" to be willing to expose themselves to death so frequently "for the sake of the *res publica*, that is, for the common good of the people." Remigio denied that the good of the commune could ever conflict with the good of the individual, for the latter was contained in the former. Remigio, following Aristotle, went so far as to say that a man who was not a citizen was not a man, just as a hand severed from the body was no longer a hand, for in each case the function, and consequently the individuality, of the part had ceased to exist. The commune, like God, should be loved more than oneself, since it also bestowed being: God created man, the commune the citizen.

The latter's good was therefore overriding, when compared with the false, selfish goods pursued by individuals. At the same time the good of a province, and much more of a kingdom, and still more of the universal church, was to be preferred to that of any individual city. The head of the universal church was the pope. Yet Remigio did not wish to regard the Pope as a universal sovereign, with direct power over temporal as well as spiritual affairs. Here he was somewhat inconsistent, for on the one hand he said that "secular power was derived from ecclesiastical" (*potentia secularis oritur ab ecclesiastica*), but on the other he denied that Christ had, as the hierocrats maintained, bequeathed all his temporal power as lord of the world to his vicar St Peter. Indeed, said Remigio, he had not given St Peter full power even over spiritual things. Could a pope establish a new article of faith or ordain a new sacrament? Obviously not. Certainly he could not intervene regularly, but only occasionally, in secular affairs: in cases involving sin or where a regular judgment could not be obtained. At the same time Remigio seems to have believed that such interventions were ultimately at the discretion of the Pope. Remigio thus occupied a middle position between hierocrats like Ptolemy on the one hand and opponents of hierocratic claims like Dante and John of Paris on the other. Since he did not, like the latter, attribute different origins to secular and ecclesiastical power (Dante said that the one was based on law and the other on Christ), and since he still tried to distinguish between their functions, his position was bound to seem hesitant and inconclusive. But it is worth noting that in practice he was ready to put what he regarded as the welfare of his commune above the specific command of the Pope. In his treatise *De bono pacis*[10] he declared that even injustices to clerics and even papal excommunication should be ignored if this were essential "for the common good and for peace."

He was not dogmatic about what kind of government could best pursue, on the temporal level, this common good. In the *De via paradisi* he mentioned, in the course of a eulogy of God's sovereignty, Aristotle's threefold classification of governments. Remigio said that the rule of many *mediocres* (*tymocratia*) was good, the rule of a few *excellentes* (*aristocratia*) was better, and the rule of one (*regnum*) was best. But when he came to compare this last form of rule to God's, he invoked not a king or a *signore* but law as the sovereign. What the law was to a political community (*civitas*, a more abstract term than *commune*), what the captain was to a ship, what the charioteer was to a chariot, what the fluteplayer was to a dance, what the general was to an army, that he said, God was to the universe. The law of the *civitas*, he believed, should be applied with discretion, always keeping in mind the *bonum commune*[11] of peace. In a sermon to the priors of Florence apparently delivered in the second half of 1294 he urged them not to forget the common good "pro Iano"[12] (the popular leader Giano della Bella) and in his *De institia* he said that though it was easier to punish a magnate (*magnus*) in a *civitas* ruled by a popular regime ("ubi populus dominatur") than elsewhere, still deferment of such penalties might sometimes be wise. He revealed the same attitude when he contrasted the characteristics of a king and a tyrant in a sermon in commemoration of King Louis X of France who died on June 5, 1316. He said that a king imposed penalties reluctantly on behalf of the common good, while a tyrant delighted in punishments. A king gave rewards to those who were "utiles rei publice,"[13] while a tyrant bestowed his favors on flatterers. A king loved the good of his subjects, but a tyrant his own profit. Remigio thus made no sharp distinction, at least in theory, between royal and constitutional government, but rather between tyrants and those rulers who were useful to the *res publica* and served the common good of peace. The highly abstract way in which Remigio formulated the purposes of secular and ecclesiastical government is significant. The king or prince of the political community ("rex vel princeps civitatis": the term no doubt also includes the podestas, priors and councils of regimes "ubi populus dominatur") should lead all the artisans and citizens ("omnes artifices et omnes cives") to the goal of temporal peace, just as the prelate should guide them to spiritual peace and Heaven.

Dante, as well, agreed that peace was the end of government and the prerequisite for human happiness. But he thought it was useless to seek peace on any but the highest political level. Only a universal and all-powerful emperor, he said, would be free from cupidity, the besetting vice of mankind. Already possessing everything, he could desire no more. Under his rule bounds could be placed on the greed of cities and kingdoms. Such order would maintain peace, which in turn would enable individuals to enjoy happiness and liberty and to develop their moral and intellectual capacities. Man was most free under Monarchy (universal empire), since then his infirm will was guided by the Emperor's just law. This law should consist of general ordinances in accordance with right reason and not of specific regulations, which Dante seems to have felt were in the competence not of the Empire but of subordinate governments.

No doubt Dante thought that under such an imperial regime most communal privileges could be retained. Indeed, such a regime would, in his view, promote liberty on the municipal level, since it would help to guard against the tyranny of faction. But on the municipal level, what sort of government was best? A *signoria*, an aristocracy, or a polity? Dante did not say. For him, as for Remigio, the essential difference was not between forms of governments, but between their purposes: whether they were directed toward the common good or toward the selfish ambitions of a tyrant.

In the *Commedia* Dante lamented the fact that in his day Italy was "full of tyrants" and he seems to have watched with melancholy the passage of cities like Cesena from "stato franco"[14] to "tirannia." A tyrannical government might be single or collegial. Obviously Dante considered Florence under the Black Guelfs to be under such a regime; he called Florence, in fact, the "tyrant of Tuscany." The essential marks of tyranny for Dante were the perversion of public laws to private ends, and violence. It is mainly with their crimes of blood against their relatives, their neighbors, and their fellow citizens that Dante reproaches the tyrants in the seventh circle of his Hell. Julius Caesar is not among them, but is in the Limbo of virtuous pagans instead. Evidently Dante thought the moderation of his exercise of power excused the violence with which he seized it, just as the concern of the Romans for the common good of the human race justified their wars of conquest.

One suspects Dante thinks that it is primarily the attitude of subordinate rulers to the emperor and of the emperor to them that determines whether their authority is legitimate or not. For assertions of autonomy by cities and kingdoms Dante had no patience. When Florence rebelled against Henry VII, Dante urged him to crush her. She was, in his eyes, a tyrant. On the other hand, Dante probably thought that the government of the Scala family in Verona, supported by the people and confirmed by the emperor, was legitimate, and that even their aggressive wars were legitimate, however much they tried to impose their will on neighboring cities like Padua, hitherto living "in stato franco." Was not Cangrande the ally of the emperor? Any government was tyrannical and should be destroyed if it tried to interfere with the divinely ordained march of the eagles towards "that Rome in which Christ is a Roman."

Dante himself was neither a reactionary magnate like Corso Donati nor a democrat like Giano della Bella. On the one hand he maintained, like Brunetto and Remigio, that an individual's nobility was based not on his birth but his virtue, and he did not like the arrogance and ostentation of some of the hereditary aristocrats of his city. On the other hand, he took part in the softening of Giano's laws against the magnates that occurred in 1295, and he was scathing about the rise of low-born immigrants from the *contado* to civic positions of wealth and authority. He was also scathing about the volatile quality of political life in Florence, the rapidity with which laws, money, regimes, and customs were changed, and the eagerness of Florentine citizens to become office-holders. Despite the fact that he himself had held a number of positions in various Florentine governments, he was much more a moralist than a politician. His enthusiasm for the emperor as the saviour who alone could impose right order was so great that in it whatever interest he may have had in the merits and faults of various kinds of subordinate governments seems to have been swallowed up.

Can Remigio and Dante be regarded as republicans in their political theory? Certainly, if by "republican" is meant a concern for the *res publica*, for the common interest rather than private advantage. They had moved far beyond the feudal notion of a ruler as a personal lord. Rather he was the holder of a public office, which existed for the sake of promoting the welfare of a community. The Roman people had formed such a community. So did the people of Florence. In the Middle Ages the term *res publica* could be used with perfect propriety for both pre- and post-Augustan Rome, for the Church (which could also be called *imperium romanum*), for kingdoms, and for individual cities. In the late thirteenth century the Aristotelian term *polity* was sometimes used as a synonym for *res publica*; Aquinas, commenting on the *Politics*, said that any government directed towards the common good, could be called a *politia* [. . .] Any legitimate government, whether monarchy, aristocracy, or a popular regime, was a *politia* or *res publica* and their perversions were tyrannies. This point was clearly grasped by Remigio and Dante. There is no evidence, however, that they grasped another fundamental Aristotelian distinction basic to our notion of republicanism: that between government in accordance with popularly sanctioned law and government by the ruler's sovereign will.

Aristotle said in the *Politics* that rule over slaves (and also over some servile barbarian peoples) was despotic, but that rule over free men was either regal, like that of a father over his children, or political, among equals, where there could be rotation between the rulers and the ruled, and the true sovereign was the people. Whether the government was aristocratic or popular it was still limited by law. A king, however, promulgated the law himself. Aristotle's definition of political rule will serve admirably as a definition of the modern concept of a republic, which need not be a democracy but must depend ultimately on a public and popularly supported law.

Aquinas saw clearly what Aristotle meant by political government. Aquinas himself preferred kingship, on the ground that it approximated more closely to the unity and absolutism of divine rule, and was more likely to provide peace and justice. Yet he tried to give political government its due. Like Augustine before him and Ptolemy after him he quoted Sallust's famous words: "It is amazing to remember how quick and great was the growth of the Roman *civitas* after liberty had been attained." Aquinas said that this was so because under such an aristocratic regime the private and public good could be more easily equated than under monarchy. But Aquinas did not eulogize the heroes of the Roman republic. Nor did he comment on the existence of a number of municipal republics in Italy. Nor, for that matter, did he have anything specific to say about contemporary monarchies. Despite the fact that his treatise *De regimine principum* was dedicated to a particular king of Cyprus, its discussion of regal government has a timeless and utopian quality, more suited to the classroom than to the political arena. At the same time it, together with his and other commentaries on the *Politics*, was important in introducing the full range of Aristotle's political thought to the late medieval world.

Aquinas contrasted political with regal government. Ptolemy of Lucca adopted a different terminology. He drew a sharp line between political rule on the one hand and both royal and despotic rule on the other. In fact, he even classified royal rule under the general heading of despotism. He said he took this distinction from Aristotle. Aristotle, however, in *Politics* III, xvii, 1 made a threefold division of the forms of government into despotic, royal, and political. N. Rubinstein observes that William of Moerbeke in his translation of the *Politics* (*ca.* 1260) left out the regal category and mentioned in this passage only the despotic and political. Ptolemy, however, as Rubinstein notes, was perfectly well aware of Aristotle's distinction between despotic and royal rule, for in his *Exaemeron* he said that the former term should be applied to the supervision of slaves and the latter to the supervision of a family. But for Ptolemy the crucial political distinction was between arbitrary rule and rule regulated by statute. However much the virtuous king might strive to follow the dictates of natural law and of his conscience he was still above positive law. No court could call him to account. In this sense he was as sovereign over the law as a despot. Officials administering a *principatus politicus* could, however, be punished if they contravened the legislation of the *civitas*.

Ptolemy, alone among his contemporaries, produced a reasoned defense of *principatus politicus* as, under optimal conditions, the best form of government. It was true, said Ptolemy, that a ruler bound by statute was less free to use his prudence than one who could proceed according to the law within his breast. It was also true that many modern podestas were more interested in their salaries than in the *res publica* and would flee like mercenaries if wolves came. Moreover, regions whose inhabitants had servile natures, like southern Italy, Sicily, Sardinia, and Cyprus, were more suited to a despotic than to a political regime. But the latter was superior in cases where citizens were not degenerate, and where governors like Samuel and the Roman republican heroes put the good of those they ruled before their own. Some men, "those of virile spirit and brave heart and confident in their intelligence," could be governed only by a political regime. This was true, for example, in northern Italy and especially in Rome (Ptolemy was ominously silent about Tuscany, probably because when he wrote his continuation of the *De regimine* about 1301 or 1302 that province was a prey to faction and lived under the shadow of a foreign prince, Charles of Valois). In the former regions, Ptolemy said, even "counts and other princes, unless they rule despotically through violence, are compelled to reign over their subjects in a political and civil manner." Partial liberty was also enjoyed by cities in some foreign lands, but there in general monarchy and despotism held sway. Political self-reliance for Ptolemy was primarily Italian. It had also existed in Israel under the judges. Neither Samuel nor Scipio, observed Ptolemy, confiscated the property of others, for they recognized the authority of the laws. It was not, however, the prophets and martyrs of Israel but rather the poor and ascetic republican heroes of Rome that Ptolemy made the precursors of Christ, perhaps because it was not at Jerusalem that the successors of Christ, the popes, had established their see.

In terms both of historical and political theory, we can say that Ptolemy was the first self-conscious medieval republican. He thought that it was political and not regal government that was most appropriate to unfallen man and also to those historical societies like Rome that had had the most virtuous, intelligent, and enterprising citizens. *Political* government could be called *dominium plurium*, but this did not mean that the actual administrators need be numerous. These governors could be many ([. . .] *politia* [. . .]), few (*aristocratia*), or one (*dictator*). Had not the Romans often chosen dictators, and modern Italian cities *signori* to deal with difficult situations? Ptolemy was no more dogmatic than Remigio and Dante about the relative advantages and disadvantages of Aristotle's three forms of political government. But he did point out in a baldly straightforward way that government by law was different from government by will, whether the wills were many or few. In Ptolemy we already see in embryo the crucial distinction between the *pars principans* and the *legislator* that Marsilius of Padua would put forward in the *Defensor pacis*. The *pars principans* may be very small, but the *legislator* represents what Ptolemy called *dominium plurium*.

Ptolemy was thus a republican in the political sphere. Even if he saw the advantages of regal rule, he still said that Romans and northern Italians could best be governed by a *principatus politicus* since they were too virile and self-confident to put up with kings and despots. But Ptolemy was a monarchist in the ecclesiastical sphere. Even if he urged the Pope to consult his cardinals, just as the ancient Roman consuls had consulted the Senate, he still believed that the Pope was the fount of law, and, ultimately, the master of the world.

How can these seemingly opposed positions be reconciled? Through Ptolemy's theory of history. He was a Roman and Italian patriot. He thought that the Roman Pope was the direct successor of the Roman republic. So the Empire (after all, presently in foreign German hands) was irrelevant to Italy, unless a shortsighted pontiff should permit this pseudo-emperor to meddle in Italian affairs. The world-lordship of the Pope, Ptolemy seemed to say, was not only ordained by God to give guidance to the whole human race; it was also the particular protection of Rome and Italy from foreign, absolutist government. Ptolemy's hierocratism, his republicanism, and his patriotism were therefore complementary. They were probably encouraged by the example of Pope Nicholas III, himself both a hierocrat and a Roman patriot. There are grounds for supposing that the *Determinatio* was addressed to him, in admiration of his lordliness but also in fear that he might allow Rudolf of Habsburg to administer Tuscany. Perhaps the continuation of the *De regimine* was written in a more pessimistic mood. Perhaps its more explicit republicanism was, at least in part, a reaction against the imperialistic policies of Boniface VIII and against his naming of Charles of Valois "peacemaker" in Tuscany, count of the Romagna, and captain of the march of Ancona and the papal patrimony [. . .] Ptolemy's ecclesiastical, political, and historical theories were closely linked. He was the first modern republican theorist. Unlike Dante and Remigio, but like Aquinas, he grasped the Aristotelian distinction between governments of laws and of men. He diverged from his fellow Dominican, however, in favoring the former over the latter, at least as the most suitable regime for intelligent and self-respecting Italians.

Ptolemy, Remigio, and Dante all took *De civitate Dei* V, 18 as the starting point for their appreciation of the heroes of the Roman Republic. They all praised their patriotism without a hint of irony, thereby transforming Augustine's sardonic moral. If we looked only at this apparent literary link between them we might conclude that Ptolemy's *Determinatio* and/or his continuation of the *De regimine* had an important effect on the historical views of Remigio and Dante in regard to pagan Rome. But we have seen that the purposes of their eulogies were diverse and reflected differing historical and political theories.

Our findings illustrate the danger of attempts to isolate and sketch the merely literary history of cultural concepts. How easy it would be to distil something called "historical humanism" or "Roman republican patriotism" from the writings of the authors we have examined and to present later eulogies of pre-imperial

Rome as scenes in an unfolding Renaissance drama. How tempting (and from one point of view how accurate) it would be to say that there was a wave of enthusiasm for the Roman Republic in Tuscany about 1300 that not only made earlier medieval praise seem superficial but also symbolized the birth of a new cultural ethos.

As we have seen, however, Brunetto, Ptolemy, Remigio, and Dante did not constitute in any sense a unified republican "school." One finds, to be sure, striking similarities in some of their references to Rome. These are probably due at least in part to lines of influence that run from Brunetto to Remigio and Dante in regard to Cicero and from Ptolemy to Remigio and Dante in regard to Augustine. The latter, however, have proved impossible to trace. Ptolemy, Remigio, and Dante used different classical sources, and responded to different contemporary motivations. Their Roman loyalties (if we may use such a term) were also diverse and cannot be understood apart from the other elements that contributed to the formation of their political and historical views.

It is important to emphasize the fact that this Tuscan sympathy for republican Rome had both personal and municipal roots. It was developed in Lucca and Florence by two Dominicans with a lively interest in civic affairs, and by two lay writers who were also politicians. None of them would have gone so far as to say with Petrarch, "What is history but the praise of Rome?" At the same time a common political background seems to have helped them all to feel a new closeness to that remote period of the City's life before Christ had come.

Editor's Notes

1   protection
2   sincere love for country.
3   *On the Common Good.*
4   to Hell.
5   fight for country
6   *The Way to Paradise*
7   Latin people.
8   the common good
9   the best of the rest.
10 *On the Merits of Peace.*
11 common good
12 on behalf of Giano
13 useful for the public good
14 free status

Chapter 9

C. C. Bayley

■ from **PETRARCH, CHARLES IV, AND THE
'RENOVATIO IMPERII'**, *Speculum,* 17 (1942),
pp. 323–341

I

[. . .]

[**F**OR DANTE AND PETRARCH, T]HE *deus ex machina*, whose coming
was to restore Rome to its old status as *caput mundi*, to compose the endemic
disorders if Italy, and to impose the beneficent yoke of the *imperium* on all mankind,
was, of course, the Emperor-Messiah. The necessary bond between city and
emperor, in appearance broken by the translation of the empire beyond the Alps,
was conceived symbolically, by both Dante and Petrarch, as a marriage, a sacrament, and hence not subject to nullification.

Scarcely less potent in moulding the political philosophy of Petrarch was the
dream of a *renovatio Romae*, the re-assertion of the ultimate sovereignty, not of the
princeps Romanus, but of the *populus Romanus*. The political program of the Arnoldists
in the twelfth century – the proclamation of Rome as the *caput mundi*, the assertion of the sovereign right of the Roman people to elect the emperor, the return
of the emperor to Rome, the traditional seat of the *imperium* – was adopted *en
bloc* by Cola di Rienzo in the fourteenth, with one significant addition: the unification of Italy under the aegis of Rome. Petrarch's enthusiastic support of Rienzo's
cause, though confined to epistolary admonition, amply revealed his conviction
that a revival of the ancient *virtù* of the Roman people might yet restore them to
political leadership in Italy, if not in Europe.

To these disparate and sometimes conflicting elements in Petrarch's intellectual inheritance may be added his Ghibellinism, a *damnosa hereditas* which had caused
the uprooting of the poet's parents from Florence, condemned them to perpetual
exile, and had left a permanent imprint on the youthful mind of their son. As the
son of the exiled Florentine notary Ser Petracco, he led a peripatetic existence
during the first eleven years of his life, in Arezzo, in Incisa, in Pisa. Then the

emigrant family quitted Italian soil altogether in favor of Avignon; and Petrarch pursued, albeit languidly, the study of Roman law for four years at Montpellier before venturing to Italy, to the university of Bologna. Thus Petrarch, in common with Dante and Machiavelli, experienced to the full that "exile's mood" which, in all three, produced a passionate desire for the stabilization and internal pacification of their native land [. . .]

The sensitiveness of Petrarch to the oecumenical claims of the Roman people, heightened by his acceptance of the poet's laurels from the Senate (1341), and by his first meeting with Rienzo in Avignon (1343), crystallized his repugnance towards the existing political *ordo* in Italy into a positive program centering on the revival of Rome's ancient eminence [. . .]

The establishment of the tribunate of Rienzo in Rome (1347) seemed to the poet to be the realization of his ambition. A stream of jubilant letters hailed the advent of the *saeculum aureum*, the new golden age of the world which had been ushered in by the energy and skill of the new Brutus. The fall and exile of the tribune (December 15, 1347) revealed to Petrarch the inability of the Roman people to become the architects of their own future greatness. The political prophet of a new age, Rienzo, had been cast forth without honor from his own country. Petrarch, therefore, a Ghibelline and a supporter of the imperial idea by circumstance of birth and education, fell back perforce upon a second possible agent of the renovation of Rome – the emperor.

II

Charles IV, the coldly realistic son of an irrepressibly romantic and endlessly intriguing father, could scarcely be viewed as a receptive object for Petrarch's enthusiasms. Born May 14, 1316, at Prague, Charles made his *début* in Italian politics at the early and impressionable age of fifteen (1331), acting as regent for his father in Lombardy. Two years of residence in Italy, crowded with incident and happily crowned by the victory of S. Felice (1333) over the rebellious Lombards, gave him an insight into the Italian *bellum omnium contra omnes*[1] which goes far to explain his subsequent caution. Thus, by the time that the good offices of his former tutor, Clement VI, had contributed to elevate the young prince to the German kingship (1346), he had already become a statesman in the tradition of his contemporary, Charles V of France. In politics an inveterate follower of the golden mean, measuring his opportunities in the light of his resources, eminently cautious, his feet firmly planted in the soil of reality, Charles displayed almost invariably an almost diabolic diplomatic *expertise* to which modern historians are beginning to do full justice [. . .] The literary and theological interests which he had acquired in early youth at Paris, under the painstaking guidance of his tutor, the future Clement VI, proved, however, more than a veneer, and provided the all-important point of contact between the realist, Charles, and the idealist, Petrarch.

The flight of Rienzo after the collapse of the republican experiment in Rome (December, 1347), first to the solitude of the Apennines, then to Charles IV at Prague (July, 1350), gave a new orientation to the political thought of Petrarch. The weakness and disunion of Italy, and the translation of the Empire from the

Romans to the Teutons were alike the result, in the poet's view, of the incurable fickleness of the goddess *Fortuna*, who was no longer controlled by the antique and long-lost *virtù* of the *populus Romanus*. The meteoric career of Rienzo, however, inspired the hope that the ancient civic virtues were not dead in Italy, and might yet be applied to the twofold program of Italian unification and the restoration of the *imperium* to Rome. Thus Rienzo's energies were directed towards the formation of a federation of Italian cities on the one hand, and to the re-establishment in Rome of the emperor, chosen by an electoral college of twenty-four representing the Roman people, on the other. The weakening of Rienzo's position in Rome, and his consequent flight, naturally undermined Petrarch's confidence in the civic virtues of the Roman people as the driving force of political revival, and caused him to turn to the Emperor as an alternative means to the same ends.

The first letter to Charles IV (February 24, 1351), possibly inspired by rumors of the immediate descent of the Emperor on Italy and by the memory of Dante's exhortations to Henry VII, Charles' grandfather, may be regarded as the firing of the opening gun in Petrarch's campaign for enlisting Charles' interest in the project of an Italo-imperial revival [. . .]

A marvellously polished literary production, the letter failed to advance sensibly the cause of Petrarch, or of the exiled Rienzo. When Charles received it, his envoys, Nicholas, duke of Troppau, and Ernest, archbishop of Prague, had returned unsuccessful from Avignon. Clement VI was not inclined to complicate the Italian problem by smoothing the way to Rome for his former pupil, and thus presenting him with a valuable piece on the European chessboard, without first securing something in the nature of a *quid pro quo*. In any event, Charles' temperament was not receptive to idealistic enthusiasms; and in his answer to Petrarch's winged words the imp of realism grins between every line [. . .]

Not for two years and a half did the king's reply reach the volatile and restless poet, and meanwhile still another kaleidoscopic change in Italian affairs caused Petrarch to pen a renewed appeal to Charles. The despatch of cardinal Albornoz to Italy by the new pope, Innocent VI, following the conclusion of an alliance between Charles and the envoys of the Tuscan cites at Prague (May, 1352), showed that both imperial and papal policy were swinging into the same path. Milan, under the careful and ruthless guidance of Giovanni Visconti, was approaching perilously near a hegemony of the Lombard cities; and the spectacle aroused apprehensions in the new pontiff concerning the safety of his Italian revenues. Charles, for his part, felt that the re-assumption of the regalian rights of the Empire in Italy, coupled with a coronation in Rome, would swell both his money-bags and his prestige. Hence Petrarch despatched his second letter to Charles, in which he adverted to the favorable situation in Italy for a decisive intervention, and repeated his former arguments in terms still more urgent and supplicatory (Spring 1352). Late in 1353, having received at long last the reply of Charles to his first *cri du coeur*, he was able to embark on the congenial task of refuting Charles' arguments point by point [. . .]

The arrival of Charles on Italian soil (October, 1354) evoked an enthusiastic letter from the poet to the new Messiah, enshrining one deliciously equivocal compliment which unmasked for a moment his real opinion of the transalpine barbarians: "Neque vero magni interest ubi sis natus, sed ad quid."[2] Charles promptly expressed a desire for a personal interview at Mantua, when the difficulties between the Tuscan League and Milan – minimized by the timely death of Giovanni Visconti – had been composed. A four days' ride through the icy countryside brought the poet face to face with the King (December 15, 1354). The boundless egotism of Petrarch emerged in high relief in his account of the interview, which he preserved for an admiring posterity in a short letter to Zanobi da Strada, and in a longer, more elaborately embroidered narrative addressed to his friend Laelius. Charles, for example, submitted a request to his guest for a manuscript of the the the *De viris illustribus*, in the transparent hope that his name would be found worthy of inclusion in that distinguished roll. He received the bold retort (according to Petrarch's version of the interview) that only when he had enrolled himself in the ranks of famous men through the renown of his deeds and the splendor of his fame would that culminating honor be awarded him. Petrarch, with rather naive diplomacy, had brought with him some gold and silver coins of the later Roman Empire, which he presented to Charles with a short lecture identifying the imperial effigy on each, thus attempting to strike from the cautious monarch a few sparks of emulation. An effort of Charles to attach the poet temporarily to his entourage as a kind of animated Baedeker having failed, Petrarch returned to Milan shortly before Christmas. Two weeks later Charles made his ceremonial entry into the city, and received the iron crown of Lombardy in the basilica of St Ambrose (January 6, 1355). When Charles left Milan, where he had enjoyed practically an honorable captivity, Petrarch accompanied him to Piacenza, though he refused a renewed offer to ornament the court of Prague (January 12).

The withdrawal of Charles from Rome immediately after the imperial coronation (April 5, 1355), and his hasty retreat through Tuscany, brought down the high hopes of Petrarch to the dust. He knew nothing, of course, of the agreement between Charles and Innocent VI which provided for this rapid retirement, and the news came to him out of a seemingly clear sky. His bitterness and disappointment overflowed in the remarkable letter of June 1355, impressive even in translation:

> What thy grandfather and numberless others have striven for with so great sacrifice of blood and with so much labor, thou, O Emperor, hast attained without difficulty and shedding of blood. Italy was peaceful and open, accessible to the threshold of Rome, the sceptre easy to wield, the Empire calm and tranquil, thy crown bespattered with no blood. But, ungrateful for such great rewards, or incapable of rightly estimating their value, thou dost abandon it all and return again to thy barbarous kingdom. I dare not tell thee clearly what my heart and the matter did bid me, lest I should sadden thee with my words, thou, who hast saddened myself and the world with thy deed. Not that I feel compelled to laud him who has merited cursing and satire, or that I fear to tell the truth for any reason. I refrain from so doing because I believe that no one is more grieved at thy hasty departure, which, truth to tell, resembled flight, than thyself.

Unheeding, Charles continued his journey northwards [. . .]

The career of Petrarch, compact of contradictions, was never better epito-mized than by his diplomatic errand of two years later, when he was sent by his patrons the Visconti to the diet of Metz in order to assuage the mounting annoy-ance of Charles at the renewal of hostilities between Milan and the Lombard cities. The temporary inability of the Emperor to appear in Metz persuaded Petrarch to seek him in Prague. A stay of four weeks effected very little solid progress in the matter in hand; it was probable enough that Charles failed to take the poet as diplomat very seriously (June–July, 1356) [. . .]

In 1361 Charles took up again the thread of their correspondence, but merely requested the opinion of Petrarch on two privileges produced by Rudolf IV of Austria, emanating, according to Rudolf, from Julius Caesar and Nero. Petrarch's keen sense of style, coupled with the exercise of a little common sense, enabled him to expose the documents as clumsy forgeries. An accompanying invitation from Charles pressing him to take up permanent residence at the court of Prague was refused with the tact and the finesse that were always at the poet's command; though Petrarch was encouraged thereby to adopt his familiar role of *advocatus diaboli*, and to urge the cause of Italy once again to the Emperor's averted ear. Charles was reminded, with abundance of apt quotation, that Time steals all things from poor mortal longingness [. . .]

It is useless and pointless for Charles to plead that he is Bohemian by birth; he has become Italian by his coronation in Rome, which Petrarch envisages, in organic connection with his older theory, as a ceremony of rebirth. Even the capit-ulations made by Charles to Clement VI and Innocent VI, which bound him never to return to Rome without express papal permission, were swept away like straws in the flood of the poet's eloquence – Charles must secure dispensation from these engagements. The letter closed with a veritable trumpet-call: "Vale, Cesar invic-tissime, et sepe, oro, cogita quid viro debitum, quid principi!"[3] The Emperor, impressed as ever, by the manner rather than the matter of the Petrarchian epis-tles, renewed his invitation on two occasions in the course of this same year (1361) [. . .] Finally, however, Petrarch, having exhausted the possibilities of polite evasion, declared himself prepared to make an indefinite stay at Prague. It was almost symbolic that he should find the route through Upper Italy barred to him by wandering bands of *condottieri*, stirred up by the recently constituted league of the Church, the della Scala, and the d'Este against Bernabo Visconti. Petrarch, whose studies of the worthies of ancient Rome had not inspired in him the *robur*[4] which they esteemed the chief of the masculine virtues, and not ill-pleased, perhaps, to leave the barbarians to their cold, their fog, and their cultural degradation, retraced his steps and settled temporarily in Venice (1362). From there he directed still another exhortation to Charles; but the overtone was one of despair, and the voice of Italy was a voice crying in the wilderness.

As yet, however, hope still glimmered under the ashes; and the events of Spring 1365 fanned it to a renewed glow. A long series of "conversations" at Avignon between Charles and Urban V culminated in a large measure of agree-ment on the two crucial issues of the restoration of the Papacy to Rome and the suppression of the "companies," the bands of *condottieri* which ravaged the penin-sula. Acquainted with the progress of these negotiations by his faithful Sagremor di Pommiers, Petrarch believed that the time was ripe for him to take up the pen which he had thought to have cast aside forever. His letter to Charles (December 11, 1365) was strung on the theme of "gloriosus finis lentum principium excusabit"[5]; and the threadbare arguments of yesteryear were repeated *ad nauseam*.

[. . .]

III

Debate concerning the ultimate political ideals of Petrarch, though far from recent in origin, still appears unable to resolve itself into even a moderate degree of harmony. The fluidity of Petrarch's opinions, the complexity and contradictions of his character, his chameleon-like adaptiveness to environment, undoubtedly serve in some measure to account for the varying interpretations of his political philosophy. What common factor, if any, linked his appeals to Cola di Rienzo and the emperor Charles IV? And how can his patriotic *canzone* be fitted into the framework of the imperial idea? Further, tendentious interpretation has increased the obscurity. Italian scholars from Ugo Foscolo to the present have viewed Petrarch in the reflected light of the Risorgimento and of the heightened nationalism of the post-war era. Others, viewing him as the first great humanist, have striven to emancipate him from the political climate of his age, and to transform him into an apostle of *Realpolitik*, a forefunner of Machiavelli. Yet a third school, seeking firm ground under the flux and reflux of Petrarch's political idealism, and finding none, condemn him at the bar of History as a political Hamlet, pursuing a policy of romantic occasionalism.

Any attempt to imprison the plastic and impressionable intelligence of Petrarch within the iron cage of formula and definition seems likely, therefore, to defeat its own purpose; the clash of learned opinion is in itself an indication of the inadvisability of such efforts. Actually, Petrarch's political system existed on three planes – the Roman, the Italian, and the imperial – and tended towards three objectives: the *renovatio Romae*, the *renovatio Italiae*, and the *renovatio imperii*. The restoration of the city of Rome to its long-lost position as *caput mundi*; the cessation of the civil strife which was ravaging the fair body of Italy and rendering her easy prey to transalpine "barbarians"; and the transference of the *imperium* from Germany to Rome, constituted a highly idealistic but integrated political program, the sources of which, both antique and mediaeval, are not far to seek. The decay and degradation of Rome; the hopeless anarchy into which Italy was plunged; and the reversion of the Empire into the hands of unlettered barbarians constituted a political present which Petrarch found intolerable. Thus, exactly as the arid scholasticism of the day caused him to seek a more congenial intellectual climate in the age of Cicero and Seneca, so the distressing political conditions of the age impelled him to turn, for relief and inspiration, to the *saeculum aureum* of Rome's world dominance. The enormous contrast between past and present, however, was viewed through mediaeval spectacles, and down the perspective of more than a thousand years; for no man can live, like a god, remote and isolated from his century. Petrarch, therefore, with no sense of incongruity, could look for the realization of his threefold political ideal from any one of the major forces competing in Italy. The threefold *renovatio* might be set in motion by an efficient tyrant like Robert II of Naples; or by an unexpected revival of the antique *virtù* of the Roman people, inspired by the tribune Cola di Rienzo; or by an emperor-messiah such as Charles IV, transformed into a Roman by the ceremony of coronation; or even by a union of the *grandi*, combining to thrust the barbarian from Italian soil. Petrarch, therefore, may appear to posterity as a republican, an imperialist, and a patriot in turn; but the apparent inconsistency arose from the adoption of different means to attain his objective: the realization of the threefold *renovatio*, in whole or in part. The practicability of the program is, of course, open to the gravest criticism; but the charge of Utopianism levelled against Petrarch need not be seconded by the accusation that he was an unscrupulous opportunist, untroubled by an ultimate idealism. The hopes reposed by Petrarch on Charles IV, then, represented something more than a hasty and unprincipled trimming of the sails to catch a favorable political wind. Their relations constituted, rather, an episode, long drawn out, in the persistent efforts of the poet to transform into reality his ideal of a triple revival of Rome, of Italy, of the Empire.

Editor's Notes

1   war of all against all
2   Nor does it greatly matter where you were born, but for what.
3   Farewell, unconquered Caesar, and think often, I ask, what is the duty of a man, what of a prince!
4   hardness
5   a glorious end will excuse a slow beginning.

Chapter 10

Ronald Witt

■ from **THE *DE TYRANNO* AND COLUCCIO SALUTATI'S VIEW OF POLITICS AND ROMAN HISTORY**, *Nuova rivista storica*, 53 (1969), pp. 434–474

[Note: Translations of the Latin, Italian and Old French quotations in this article have been made by the editor and can be found in the notes at the end of this chapter.]

A STUDENT OF THE POLITICAL IDEAS of Coluccio Salutati cannot be blamed for wishing that one of the humanist's tracts, the *De tyranno*, had been proven spurious or that it could be counted among the "lost" works of the author. Yet this puzzling little tract, which contains a defense of Caesar's rule and of monarchy as the best form of government, was without question written by the Chancellor of the Florentine Republic and must be considered one of the fixed points of Salutati's biography. The *De tyranno* raises the question of Salutati's position on the best form of constitution in general and on the relationship between the Roman Republic and the Roman Empire in particular. In the following pages an attempt will be made, first, to give an analysis of the text and to define its purpose; and second, to view the issues raised by this work in terms of Salutati's writings and of the intellectual life of Florence in the late fourteenth and the early fifteenth centuries.

I

A response to a letter from a student in arts at Padua, Antonio of Aquila, the *De tyranno* was finished not later than August 31, 1400. On that date it was dispatched to Francesco Zabarella in Padua for delivery to the student. Antonio had asked Salutati two questions. The second was: Were Antenor and Aeneas traitors to Troy? The nature of the first was not specifically stated but according to the structure of Salutati's reply it most probably was: Were Cassius and Brutus traitors to Rome? Like the second, the first question concerned the problem of treason but, unlike the second, it involved a very delicate issue for a Florentine: Was Dante right or wrong to place the two murderers of Caesar in the lowest depths of Hell? Furthermore, to judge the act of Cassius and Brutus and hence the opinion of Dante, one must first determine whether Caesar had been the father of his country or merely a tyrant. If the father of his country, then Caesar was unjustly killed and his murderers justly damned. If, on the other hand, he had been a tyrant, then before acquitting Brutus and Cassius of murder, one had still to decide whether tyrannicide was justified. Even preliminary to this discussion, a definition of tyranny was required. Consequently, in reply to the Paduan student's questions on treason, Salutati first directed himself to a consideration of the problem of tyranny.

The treatise is divided into six parts, each designed to answer a different problem: (1) Who is a tyrant? (2) Is it lawful to kill a tyrant? (3) Was Caesar a tyrant? (4) Was Caesar justly killed? (5) Was Dante justified in placing the murderers of Caesar in Hell? (6) Were Antenor and Aeneas traitors to Troy?

A statement on the nature of tyranny from the *Magna moralia* of Gregory the Great occupies a central place in Salutati's effort to arrive at a definition of tyranny. [. . .] Salutati distinguishes two general types of tyranny, the one of character, the other of action. Salutati is careful to specify that he is concerned only with the second sort, that of action. Obviously for him tyrannical impulses of the heart which remain unexpressed in action, transcend the categories of law and politics. Then follows a discussion of Gregory's views on tyrannical action. According to Salutati, Gregory suggests the existence of three forms of tyranny, each corresponding to one of the three legitimate forms of government, the royal, the constitutional or political, and the despotic [. . .] Specifically attributing definite forms of government to the various levels of political life, Salutati assigns the royal to the level of the *respublica*, the political or constitutional to that of the province or the city, and the despotic to the level of the house [. . .]

Having given his gloss of Gregory's statement on tyranny, Salutati observes that a tyrant is the prince who does not rule according to law. Either he does not have legal title to rule and is a *tyrannus ex defectu tituli* or, while possessing legal title, he rules *superbe*[1] and is a *tyrannus ex parte exercitii*. Part II of the treatise is devoted to the problem of tyrannicide in respect to the two different situations. Salutati obviously considers usurpation of public power as one form, the most serious, of usurpation in general. If by Roman law individuals are authorized to kill usurpers of private property, they have an even greater right to kill those attempting to occupy the state.

But it is possible for a *tyrannus ex defectu tituli* to legitimize his power. In cases where the community has no overlord, the usurper must obtain popular approval either implicitly or explicitly; in communities where there is an overlord he needs both this approval and the overlord's sanction. If this overlord lives abroad and does not assert his authority (obviously the case of many of the political societies in Italy), then the election is probably valid until the overlord declares to the contrary. But until the *tyrannus ex defectu tituli* has a title and consequently ceases to be a tyrant on these grounds, he is nothing but a dangerous criminal and can be killed by anyone.

In regard to the *tyrannus ex parte exercitii* the problem of tyrannicide is quite different. This is the case of the ruler who, although he has legitimate title to rule, abuses his power. According to Salutati, if the community has an overlord and that overlord sanctions his deposition or punishment, there is no question that the community may act to dispose of the tyrant. If the community has no superior, it is empowered to punish its legitimate lord turned tyrant as it decides. But private citizens cannot take matters into their own hands. The ruler's title has the sanction of the community and of the overlord (where this is necessary) and only by the action of the duly constituted authorities can such a ruler be deposed.

With Part III begin those lively sections of the work which are of greatest interest to most modern readers. Both John of Salisbury and Cicero have accused Caesar of being a tyrant. Salutati's procedure is to focus on Cicero and to disprove his criticism of Caesar by the remarks of Cicero himself. While Caesar lived, Salutati begins, Cicero praised him and accepted benefits from his hand. Even when allied with Pompey, Cicero realized that the struggle between Pompey and Caesar was "quidem non omnino ne quisquam, sed uter regeret et rerum summam et moderamen assumeret . . ."[2] It was, Salutati says, an act of God that caused Caesar to triumph in this struggle. Even Cicero admits that once in power Caesar "mira clementia teterrimum bellum ac arma civilia, quibus nihil potest esse crudelius, compensavit."[3] All supported his rule [. . .]

Salutati sees Caesar raised to power by the gratitude of his fellow citizens. Immediately after this he directs his attention to the murderers. Did they not accept offices at his hands? Did not the Senate confirm all his acts and carry out even his unaccomplished projects after his assassination? Did they not recognize his legitimacy by these very things? Would the Roman people have so favored a dead tyrant? Not only was this murder displeasing to men but it was also a heinous act in the eyes of the Gods. Within three years all the conspirators perished violently. Is this not a sign of divine displeasure?

Immediately following there is a long series of justifications for his power based on counsels of prudence: the conditions of the Empire given the civil strife required the rule of one man. Revolution against the man who was attempting to bind up the wounds of the state was a crime. Revolution in any case is a dangerous thing [. . .]

In connection with this emphasis on the magnanimity of Caesar toward his enemies and his efforts to bring peace and justice to the state, Salutati launches into a defense of monarchy as the ideal form of government. Do not all authorities agree, Salutati asks, that "monarchiam omnibus rerum publicarum conditionibus preferendam, si tamen contigat virum bonum et studiosum sapientie presidere?"[4] Just as the heavens are ruled by one God, so human affairs are better managed the nearer they imitate this divine order. Where many command "non unum erit, sed plura regimina."[5] If there had been monarchical rule in Rome, there would never have been a civil war. The aristocratic government was "wholly unsuited to the times." Proof of this is what happened after the murder of Caesar. The civil war which broke out again could only be ended when Octavius united the imperial power in the hands of one man.

The reader would assume that Salutati is arguing that Caesar's rule, originally *ex defectu tituli*, became legitimate through the tacit or express consent of the community: its worth was proven *ex parte exercitii* and the condition of the times led the Roman people to sanction it. This, however, is definitely not the conclusion Salutati draws. At the opening of Part V before taking up the work of Dante, Salutati gives us specifically the conclusion that he has been aiming as throughout his analysis of Caesar's rule: "Quoniam ergo Cesar, ut luculentissime probatum est, tyrannus non fuit titulo, quem grata non coacta patria sibi delegit in principem, non fuit et superbia, qui clementer et cum humanitate regebat, clarum est quod sceleratissime fuit occisus."[6] There can be no question of Salutati's position. The Florentine chancellor's justification of Caesar's rule is that he was neither a *tyrannus ex defectu tituli* nor a *tyrannus ex parte exercitii* and therefore was treacherously and unjustly murdered.

Certain modern interpreters of Salutati have been very unclear on this point. Salutati's defense of Caesar is not a veiled defense of the Trecento *signore* regime. There is, of course, an unmistakeable similarity between the Trecento tyrant of Salutati's day and Caesar as he is depicted by the author. It is also very probable that *in actual fact* the "legitimacy" of Caesar was as questionable as that of the tyrants of Italy in the fourteenth century. It might even be contended that in justifying Caesar on the basis of necessity and plebiscite Salutati was actually lending weapons to the arsenal of those defending the Italian tyrants. According to all his definitions Caesar for Salutati ought to have been a *tyrannus ex defectu tituli* who removed his illegitimacy through the beneficence of his rule and consequently ceased to be a tyrant.

But this is not Salutati's conclusion. The Chancellor of Florence had no intention of justifying tyranny in any way [. . .] He specifically makes Caesar a legitimate monarch without any stain whatsoever on his title. As far as Salutati was concerned there was no suggestion in the *De tyranno* that Caesar had anything in common with Trecento tyrants nor his rule with Trecento tyranny.

Thus, by vindicating Caesar Salutati can in Part V free Dante completely from the charge of error in placing the murderers in the lowest depths of Hell. Dante was wholly right in his judgment [. . .] In brief, we finally have Salutati's summary of how Caesar rose to power: it was the Senate and People of Rome who called him to become their ruler and to bring an end to the civil war.

Just as Judas betrayed the God-man, so the other two betrayed Caesar, "the image as it were, of divinity in the rightfulness of his rule," the defender of the fatherland and their own benefactor. Dante's judgment, moreover, is supported (1) by the authority of Virgil, (2) by the fact that the conspirators were defeated and (3) by the manifestation of the will of God, who with Augustus brought the world under the rule of one man [. . .] The last section of the *De tyranno*, Part VI, is a mere appendage to the treatise. In answer to the question of whether or not Antenor and Aeneas were traitors to Troy, Salutati replies that the old histories are at variance and no definite judgment can be drawn [. . .]

The general significance of the text in terms of Salutati's intellectual biography can only be ascertained at the conclusion of our investigation of the humanist's other political writings. At this point, however, it can be said that the *De Tyranno* is a literary work designed as a defense of the reputation of the immortal Dante. Salutati wrote both as a lover of the poet's work and as a Florentine citizen who felt one of the great glories of his city under attack [. . .]

Certainly his predominantly favorable attitude toward Caesar and the beginning of the Roman monarchy in the *De tyranno* has some parallel in Salutati's other writings at this period. Only in this tract Salutati's doubts about Caesar's position have been erased: the hesitations about Caesar's rise to power, which Salutati had throughout most of his life and even in these very years around the turn of the century, are barely perceptible in the *De tyranno*. Carried away by the need to defend Dante and by his conviction of the justice of Dante's general position, Salutati was led to simplify an attitude which was fundamentally more complex for him [. . .] What I am suggesting, therefore, is that beneath Salutati's rhetoric there were genuine, if sometimes contrasting, intellectual commitments. These were sources both for the force of conviction with which he argued his case in the *De Tyranno* and for the psychological limitations hampering his freedom of action as a rhetorician.

[. . .] Not so easily explained, however, is the relationship of this work with its praise of monarchy and of Caesar to Salutati's other works. Granting that Salutati spoke with conviction in the *De tyranno*, in what way is one to reconcile its statements with Salutati's republican pronouncements elsewhere? Or within the treatise itself to resolve the apparent conflict between the monarchism of Part IV and the implications of Part I that republican government is the most suitable constitution for the *civitas* and the *provincia*?

II

The figure of Caesar evoked ambivalent feelings in the men of the thirteenth and fourteenth centuries. His military prowess, his intelligence, his clemency made him very attractive. As founder of the Empire under which ideally, at least, Europe still lived; as the immediate predecessor of that Augustus under whom Christ was born, Caesar seemed to the men of these centuries to be an instrument of God. Realistic thinkers, moreover, could look back to the corruption of the republican state and regard Caesar as having offered the only hope for Rome. Yet, considered as the author of the civil wars, which took the lives of hundreds of thousands of citizens, as the dictator whose rise to supreme power in the state was of doubtful legality, Caesar was certainly objectionable to the medieval mind. There is no need in this article to present a history of the "mantle of Caesar." Graf, Parodi and Gundolf have sufficiently established the existence of pro-Caesarist sentiments in the Middle Ages. Anti-Caesar feeling, on the other hand, has not received comparable attention.

Among the Roman authors who were largely anti-Caesarist and who were widely read in the Middle Ages we could number four: Cicero, Lucan, Florus and Eutropius. Two early Christian writers, Lactantius and Eusebius, whose works had an enormous diffusion throughout the Middle Ages, also offered criticism of Caesar. Lactantius brands Caesar the parricide of the *patria* while Eusebius in his *Chronicle* declares that Caesar "summum imperium invasit."[7]

Of the medieval critics of Caesar's political activity one of the earliest would certainly be John of Salisbury. In his work called the *Policraticus* the twelfth-century ecclesiastic writes: "Hic tamen quia rempublicam armis occupaverat, tyrannus reputatus est, et magna parte senatus consentiente, strictis pugionibus occisus in Capitolio."[8]

Given the long passage leading to this statement in which Caesar's immense talents are detailed and extolled, one might interpret the above reference to Caesar's tyranny as an opinion ascribed by John to the Senators as a motive for their action. However, in the following description of Caesar's successors the analysis shows that this is John's view as well. Specifically exempting Augustus from the charge of tyranny, John discusses Tiberius (*a Julio tertius*)[9] and then Caligula and brands the latter as "*tertius tyrannus*."[10] In any case Salutati considers John of Salisbury's opinion to be adverse to Caesar and in the opening lines of his discussion of Caesar's rule he quotes the above passage to refute its charge.

Even as Dante was growing up in Florence, he must have heard vigorous debates over the assassination of Caesar. Brunetto Latini, Dante's teacher, in his *Tresor*, in classifying types of arguments, after discussing a general-type argument and illustrating it with the proposition: "I praise women vs. I blame women," takes up the particular-type argument and illustrates it with an example: that some say that Caesar was "mout preus et mout vaillans,"[11] others say, "non fu, mais traitres et desloiaus."[12] At the same period St. Thomas declares in his *In Secundum librum sententiarum* in answer to the question whether Cassius and Brutus were justified in murdering Caesar: Yes ". . . qui ad liberationem patriae tyrannum occidit, laudatur, et praemium accipit."[13] It is essential to realize the extent of this anti-Caesarist feeling in the thirteenth century to appreciate the fact that Dante in the *Divina commedia* in defending Caesar was taking sides on a very controversial subject.

Aquinas' disciple and the continuator of the *De regimine principum*, Ptolemy of Lucca, is no easier on Caesar than is his master. At one point Ptolemy writes: "Duravit consulatus [. . .] usque ad tempora Julii Caesaris, qui primus usurpavit imperium; sed parum in ipso supervixit, a senatoribus quidem occisus propter abusum dominii."[14] A little before this Ptolemy speaks of ". . . Julio Caesare et Hannibale, qui propter abusum dominii diro necati sunt exitu . . ."[15] The anti-Caesarist tendencies of the young Petrarch are well-known but even the aged Petrarch, who becomes decidedly favorable to Caesar's political rule as he grew older, is not completely convinced of the injustice of Caesar's assassination. In 1366–67, a few years before his death, in spite of his eloquent praise of Caesar during this period, Petrarch still declares parenthetically in one letter: "Legisti ut Cassius eorum unus, qui Julio Caesari non dico impias ac scelestes [. . .] sed audaces certe manus intulerant . . ."[16]

The Trecento commentators of Dante's poem reflect as well the various currents of opinion in their remarks on certain crucial passages. Jacopo della Lana, one of the earliest and best-known commentators, shows himself to be hardly of one mind on the figure of Caesar. In writing on *Inf.* IV, 123, he calls Caesar "quello sopradetto imperadore, il quale fu molto vivo e armigero uomo."[17] On *Inf.* XXXIV, the canto describing the punishment meted out to Brutus and Cassius, Jacopo explains that these two murderers belong where they are because they had received "molte grazie a giurisdizione da lui"[18] and then "a tradimento l'ucciseno."[19] On *Parad.* VI, however, Jacopo makes a very un-Dantean observation on Caesar's murder: "Stando costui (Caesar) in tanto onore fue tentato da molti vizii si in lussuria come in avarizia. La giustizia di Dio che non comporta Cesare in quella sedia, mise in quore ai senatori di doverlo uccidere."[20]

Here Caesar is actually said to have attained power without God's sanction and to have been put to death because of the justice of God [. . .]

Unfortunately, Boccaccio's commentary on Dante, made at the very end of his life, was not set down beyond the close of Canto XVI of the *Inferno*. His comment on the central passage, Canto XXXIV, consequently, is not known and perhaps was never made. What remains, however, is sufficient to permit us to say that Boccaccio is unfavorable to Caesar and has to resort to a symbolic interpretation in order to avoid criticizing Dante. While in other works Boccaccio expresses either a favorable or ambivalent attitude toward the Roman dictator, Boccaccio in the *Commento* is clearly no friend of Caesar. In his comment on *Inf.* II Boccaccio identifies Caesar as "il quale recò nelle sue mani violentemente tutto il governo della republica."[21] Commenting on *Inf.* IV, 123, after describing the circumstances of Caesar's origin, the great qualities which he possessed (courage and military ability, eloquence, the gift of poetry and the virtue of clemency) and his great vice of lust, Boccaccio goes on to describe how Caesar "occupò la republica, e fecesi fare, contro alle leggi romane, dittatore perpetuo . . ."[22] He also demanded the right to wear the laurel wreath continually (Boccaccio sarcastically says that this was to cover up his baldness). Because Caesar wanted to become king, he was slain by a conspiracy in the Senate.

[. . .]

Perhaps outspoken criticism of Dante's judgment on Caesar was in circulation decades before Salutati took up his pen to defend the great Florentine poet. Benvenuto da Imola, Boccaccio's disciple, in his own commentary on *Inf.* XII might be alluding to such an accusation when he writes: "Vade nunc et praefer Alexandrum Caesari si potes, aut quaere, quare Dantes non posuit, Caesarem hic, qui altra alias virtutes multas et magnas fuit sobrissimus hominum . . ."[23]

The justification of Alexander's fate for Benvenuto seems to be that not only was he violent to his enemies but also, when drunk, he raged against his friends. Caesar, Benvenuto is saying, was not a drunkard or a violent man and should not be compared with Alexander [. . .]

His own attitude to Caesar was, nevertheless, as ambiguous as that of some of his contemporaries. While emphasizing at various points in his analysis the idea that God ordained the creation of the Roman monarchy and that Caesar's death was "indignissima,"[24] at others he expresses opposite feelings just as strongly. Speaking of Caesar's assault on the Republic, for example, Benvenuto writes: ". . . quod arma Caesaris hucusque fuerant magnifica et gloriosa, amodo vero impia potius iniusta, quia contra patriam nulla possunt ratione excusari."[25] A few pages later he continues his indictment of Caesar with the admission that

> . . . Caesar, sicut dicit Livius de Hannibale, habuit vitia paria virtutibus magnis, et maxime fecit multa enormia cupiditate dominandi; nam contra patriam bellum civile movit cum tanto sanguine civium: in suo consulatu omnia ad arbitrium fecit expulso armis collega Bibulo, et prius tentaverat multis modis facere aliquam novitatem in urbe ut veniret in statum. Solus fuit defensor coniuratorum Catalinae: omnium reorum erat refugium, dicens, quod tales erant apti bello civili. Bis spoliavit aerarium Romae, primo fraudulenter, secundo violenter: summum sacerdotium emit magno pretio: fecit se dictatorem perpetuum, immo, ut ait Lucanus, omnia Caesar erat.[26]

Earlier in the *Purgatorio* Benvenuto explains that Metellus, the tribune who barred the way to Caesar into the treasury, is called "the good" "quia ausus est contraire Caesari violatori libertatis."[27] Benvenuto, moreover, is ostensibly pained to have to identify as Marcus Brutus that Brutus who is between the jaws of Satan. For Marcus Brutus was a man of great soul and literary genus: "tamen mihi videtur quod debeat intellegi potius de Decimo Bruto . . ."[28]

The purpose of this brief discussion of anti-Caesarism in the Duecento and Trecento was to offer some idea of the general background against which Salutati's own writings are to be judged. To the mind of these generations the ancient Roman was a union of such a series of incongruous qualities that he could provoke the most contradictory and extreme judgments even in the same people. Expression of hostility to Caesar, however, does not necessarily imply a republican attitude either to politics in general or to the interpretation of Roman history in particular. Cola di Rienzo's commentary on Dante's *De monarchia* serves as an example of the way men of these centuries could condemn Caesar yet praise his successors. Contrasting Caesar and Augustus, Cola writes: "Qui quidem Octavianus non ut Caesar predictus armata manu a senatu reque publica ad seipsum renovavit imperium, sed multis violentatus precibus a senatu et populo et coactus sceptrum assumpsit."[29] Just as Nero and Caligula could be condemned as tyrants without bringing criticism on the other Emperors or on the institution of the Empire, so could Caesar be added to their number without condemning the whole imperial period.

In fact, criticism of the institution of the Empire is not easy to find in the Trecento [. . .] Amazing as it might seem, St Thomas, in this work [*De regimine principum*] praising monarchy as the best form of government, was nevertheless able to view the history of Rome from a republican point of view [. . .] Whereas in most writers of these centuries criticism of Caesar stopped with a moral judgment of his actions, St Thomas' anti-Caesarism in the *Sentences*' commentary developed into a general critique of the Empire as an institution. It would be difficult, I think, to find a clearer statement than that of Aquinas on the importance of liberty to the vitality of Rome and on the effects of one-man rule on Rome's development. Most of the emperors became tyrants and "brought the Roman commonwealth to naught"; compared to Rome's growth under the kings, Rome of the Republic (in Sallust's words) "waxed incredibly strong and great in a remarkably short time." For Aquinas the explanation for these phenomena is based on the nature of men: when men know they are working for the common good and have a voice in making decisions, they are willing to make sacrifices which they will not make in a state ruled by a king [. . .]

It is difficult to say at this point in research how influential this statement of Aquinas was in the Trecento. That it was not entirely ignored, however, is certain. At least one Portuguese writer, the pro-papalist Alvaro Pelagius, incorporated Aquinas' words almost literally into his widely-diffused *De planctu ecclesiae* published in 1332 [. . .] Pelagius repeated the passage once again in his less well-known *Speculum regum*. It is probable, on the other hand, that the definite republican flavor of Ptolemy of Lucca's remarks on Roman history owes more to his experience in the northern Italian communes than to these paragraphs of his master [. . .]

III

[. . .] Whereas in Aquinas and Pelagius assertions of the effect of liberty on the human mind and the analysis of Roman history were made casually in works defending monarchy as the best form of government, Salutati used these ideas to support an extreme republicanism in which government of one *per se* was equivalent to tyranny.

Perhaps the clearest example of this is to be found in a public letter written by Salutati in the early winter of 1377 during the war that Florence was waging with the Papacy. The policy of Florence since the beginning of the struggle two years before had been to excite the communes of the Patrimony to revolt against their papal overlord. The attempt had been enormously successful. The Florentine troops took the field bearing a red banner with the word *Libertas* inscribed in gold upon it and one commune after another took up the standard in revolt. But the city of Rome continued to resist Florentine seduction. Because the revolt of that city would have been a profound embarrassment to the newly returned Papacy, Florence was eager to convince the Romans to follow the action of many other cities in the papal domains.

On November 6 the Otto di Balia tried once again to encourage the Romans to revolt. Salutati wrote to Rome in their name:

> non putetis, excellentissimi domini, quod maiores vestri et nostri, [qui] communibus quidem parentibus gloriamur, serviendo domi, tantum tamque memorabile Imperii de[c]us [. . .] fundaverunt nec dimictendo suam ytaliam sub externea vel domestica servitute. Illa quidem moles imperii, assistendo sociis et pro eorum libertate pugnando, vobis primo subegit ytaliam, yspaniam vicit, affricam superavit, demum vero in tantam est imperium vestrum sublimitatem evectum quod romanum nomen cunctis nationibus prefuerit.[30]

But with the coming of the emperors and the loss of liberty Rome eventually lost its power:

> Sublata autem sub cesaribus libertate – extollant quicumque volunt laudibus cesarem et usque ad divinitatis honores subliment augustum, celebrent mira commendatione vespasianum, trahiani iustitiam et rei militaris gloriam summo laudum preconio referant, denique constantinum, pium antonium, iustinianum et ceteros quibus volunt laudibus efferant – in ipsorum manibus certe vastitatem recepit ytalia et illud imperii culmen effluxit. Solum itaque libertatis studium et imperium et gloriam (et) omnem romanis peperit dignitatem.[31]

While the word "libertas" is an elusive one for the fourteenth century, at least when Salutati speaks of liberty in these passages, he surely means republican liberty as opposed to government of a lord no matter how beneficent his rule. Against the backdrop of Roman history Salutati conceives of the struggle with the Church in this letter as a battle between republican freedom and lordship. History for

Salutati justifies the revolt of Florence and Rome both because of the common heritage of freedom and because of the dire consequences of subjection for any people. The "moles imperii"[32] in this text suggests a type of spiritual power residing in people who live in liberty.

It is in the correspondence of the Signoria with Bologna in 1376 and 1377 that Salutati developed in most detail the relationship between republican liberty and flourishing civic life. Bologna revolted against the Church in March 1376. This city, the most important in the Romagna, was a great loss to the Church and Florence was constantly fearful that the Papacy would try to retrieve its former possession. In July 1376, bands of mercenaries under the command of the Cardinal of Geneva, the later Clement VII, made an assault on the city. Weakened by internal dissension, the city was in danger of falling to the assailants. The situation was perilous and Salutati's letters to the city reflect very well the anxiety of the Florentines.

Out of the scores of surviving letters to Bologna written during these summer months two stand out. While most of the others merely appeal to the Bolognese to defend their "liberty," the letters of July 1 and 28 give us a clearer idea of what this word implied for Salutati. In the letter of July 1 Salutati began with the description of the first Brutus, who expelled Tarquin, the last of the Roman kings, from the city and gave liberty to the Romans. He knew that the liberty of the patria was of priceless value and was prepared to sacrifice his own sons who thought of bringing back the "dignitatem regiam."[33] Salutati then procedes to contrast the lot of those subjected to the will of a lord with the situation of free peoples. "Subiecti" are forced to make war for the benefit of the lord; the taxes are levied for his needs. They can never be certain of their own property nor can they protect their wives and daughters from the lusts of the ruler. Most important perhaps: "In quo vigor virtutis apparet, cum dominanti incipiat esse formidini, securim sue sentit semper iminere cervici aut proscriptionem aut exilium preparari?"[34] It was for this very reason that, while Tarquin ruled, Brutus "regem metuens se vanum et fatuum simulavit."[35]

[. . .]

It might be that Salutati himself was not quite aware on July 1 how far he would go. In any case, by July 28 Salutati in another letter to Bologna consciously made an attack on government of one *per se*. First, he traced in some detail the relationship between liberty and civic life.

> Quid autem honestius, quid securius quam optata perfrui libertate? Hec quidem sola, civitates exaltans, populos mirabilibus multiplicat incrementis, res familiares amplificat, statumque et maiestatem civium decore mire venustatis exornat. Hec est mater legum cum non ad libidinem et voluntatem unius sed ad utilitatem publicam referantur. Hec est magistra virtutum quoniam nemo dubitat in sua republica que libertate floreat, quantum quidve virtuosum efficere possit, ostendere, ad quod etiam adeo optimorum civium animi concitantur quod non verentur morte pulcerrima pro salute patrie animas expirare.[36]

The passage concludes with a complete condemnation of the institution of kingship:

> Cogitate ut divinarum scripturarum attestantur oracula reges ob peccata populorum ab initio constitutos qui, quantumcunque iusti, populos non regerent sed punirent. Quicumque se domino dignum putat se reum magnorum scelerum confitetur cum constet dominos non fore civitatibus ornatui sed supplicio et populorum oneri fore propositos non honori.[37]

For Salutati writing on July 28, 1376, there was a sharp contrast between a government of liberty and any government of one.

It is natural for men to be free but Italians have a hereditary right to freedom based on their history [. . .] Salutati at various points in his correspondence in these years recalls to the cities of Italy their original freedom. In February 1376, he wrote in some detail about this freedom to the commune of Ancona.

> Maiores nostri, omne quidem genus italicum, quingentis annis contra romanos continuatis proeliis, ne libertatem perderent, pugnaverunt. Nec potuit totius orbis princeps populus italiam armis subigere donec in societatem imperii pene omnes italos receperunt iungentes eos sibi federibus libertate atque civitate donantes.[38]

[. . .] Salutati places emphasis on [the early Etruscan states'] independent existence. He conceives of these states as republican. Remember your ancestors, Salutati writes. They fled "servitutem Grecorum"[39]: guided by their desire for liberty, they sought freedom in exile and founded a city which "olim inter nobiles totius latini civitates fuit habita celebris . . ."[40] You know what slavery means: "eius cui quod libet contradicere non valetis voluntati ac cupidini subiacere."[41] Will you then accept the yoke of the Church and of their barbarian mercenaries?

Out of this letter emerges a vision of ancient Italy covered with prosperous republican city-states not much inferior to the city-state of Rome itself. In his attempt to stir up the communes of Italy against the Church and her soldiers Salutati appealed to this heritage of republican freedom and the historically proven superiority of Italians over other peoples.

In March of the following year a letter, which again betrays the uneasiness of the Florentines over the political stability of the communal regime in Bologna, illustrates how the concept of republican liberty was for Salutati specifically tied to the "middle classes" of the Italian communes, i.e. the *mercatores* and the *artifices* [. . .]

Self-government, Salutati is saying, is most feasible where there is a feeling of equality in the community. This sense is strongest among merchants and artisans. The feudal nobility, on the other hand, with their pride of race and their powerful connections, are with difficulty integrated into republican life. The nobility think they have a natural right to rule, Salutati writes in another letter in the following year: they will do anything that they can to gain power over others.

We appear to be confronted with an absolute contradiction between Salutati's attitude in the public letters of 1376–77 in regard to Roman history and monarchy and his position in the *De tyranno* in 1400 on these same matters. Even though the *De tyranno* manifests internal contradictions in the categories used to discuss

constitutional forms, nevertheless, the principal impression conveyed by this literary work is that Salutati considered the rule of the "optimus princeps"[42] to be
ideally the best form of government. In these letters of 1376–77, on the contrary,
the greatest of the Roman Emperors were regarded as incapable of saving the Roman
state from destruction once liberty was lost. How is this contradiction to be
explained?

The simplest means of resolving the apparent conflict would be to regard the
divergence between his republican statements in 1376–77 and his monarchical
assertions of 1400 as indicating a development in Salutati's thought. A second
approach, and one fairly common today, is to view Salutati's political remarks as
rhetorical. He appears to contradict himself frequently because, like any orator,
he consciously adjusts his words to the necessities of the situation. When circumstances change, Salutati shifts his position accordingly in order to win his listeners
or, in this case, his readers. While questioning the sincerity of the Florentine
humanist in general, this position especially casts doubt on his honesty in the public
letters: one has, of course, no problem in finding examples in these documents of
empty flattery and obvious duplicity.

[. . .]

As a general rule, it is fair to assume that political opinions expressed by
Salutati in his private letters in situations where there is no cause to suspect
ulterior motives are genuine reflections of his feelings at the moment of writing.
Accordingly, to cite an example, when a harsh statement on monarchy occurs in
a private letter in the early thirteen nineties, it is a good indication that Salutati's
attacks on monarchy as a form of government in the public correspondence years
earlier were sincere from his point of view. As we will see, moreover, almost
every theoretical statement in the *Missive* or in Salutati's propaganda tracts like the
Invectiva contra Antonium Luschum has a counterpart in private letters where Salutati
has no need to dissemble.

[. . .]

A study of the *Missive* during the years 1375–78 suggests that the extreme
republican interpretation of liberty, implying that the rule of one man was a
tyranny, is only one of three different usages occurring in these documents. A
second usage of the word suggests a liberty which is essentially freedom from
outside intervention. During the long war with the Church, Salutati incessantly
brands the ecclesiastical officials sent out by Avignon with their mercenaries as
foreign tyrants. He writes, for example, to Galeazzo Visconti urging him to fight
for "libertas Italie."[43] Couched in these terms the conception of liberty relates
directly to an Italian patriotism which can be felt by lord and commune alike.
Between Italian powers this vocabulary is used when one power unjustly attempts
to seize the lands of another. In the case of attempted or successful usurpation the
invader is considered a tyrant and the rightful possessor's "liberty" is said to be
affected. Because the Chancery is so occupied with the "foreign tyrants" in the
War of the Eight Saints, this latter usage does not appear until later in the *Missive*.
But at work in both these general cases is a notion of the right to autonomous
existence on the part of one or more political power units. This right, however,
is modified by the implicit assumption that the ruling power is legitimate, that it
is the "natural" authority (*dominus naturalis*). Possession *de facto* is insufficient: it is

a contradiction in terms to speak of the liberty of a lord whose authority is based on usurpation. He is himself a tyrant.

There is an obvious connection between this idea of liberty as the right of legitimate powers to autonomous existence and another notion which conceives of it as life under the law. Every state, if governed by just laws, is a free state. This conception of the *Rechtsstaat* had been deeply engrained in Salutati and in the men of his age. At times the *Missive* seems to suggest that world order is based on a series of diverse magistracies, each one administering justice in its proper sphere and each presiding over the actions of free men. As Salutati writes to the King of Aragon in 1379: "Invente sunt a mortalibus diversissime potestates ut moribus atque legibus in equitate et rectitudine iudicantes cunctos sub iustitie regulis continerent."[44] The nature of the constitution is a matter of indifference provided that law rules. Salutati is not simply playing on the word "Franci" when he addresses the King of France in a public letter in 1376 as "rex liber"[45] ruling over a "populus liber."[46] Granting that any state where the law prevails is a free state, Salutati opposes monarchy to tyranny. Where justice does not exist, there tyranny rules. In a letter of late June 1376, just a few days before his strongly-worded republican letter of July 2, Salutati in the course of giving advice to the beleaguered Bolognese ally distinguishes between tyrants and kings. He speaks of the rulers who fear and suspect their subjects: "Solus metus cum dominationi coniungitur nomen regium in tirannidem horrendam impellit."[47] Only a few days later, of course, he seems to see no distinction between "nomen regium"[48] and "nomen tyrannicum."[49] For this very reason, when Salutati writes in the *Missive* to a communal government describing the horrors of arbitrary government, it is not easy to know whether his words should be interpreted in a republican or in a more general *Rechtsstaat* sense where tyranny and monarchy are clearly distinguished one from the other [. . .]

Both in his public and private correspondence there can be no mistaking Salutati's obvious pride in the republican institutions of the city. When the Papacy accuses the leaders of Florence of lying to the people about the causes of the war, Salutati replies that "non est ista communitas sicut cetere quas paucorum regat ambitio et que factione modica comprimatur."[50] He proceeds to detail how decisions of the Florentine government are really those of the Florentine people. In other letters he emphasizes the fact that the Florentines are merchants and depend on trade. Living from commerce, they are peace-loving and hate war if only out of self-interest. Through their labors, moreover, they benefit not only the patria but every country where they practice commerce. Given its communal government, Florence can only be certain of safety if she is surrounded by other republics with similar interests in preserving their states. Florentine liberty is more assured "quanto latius se liberi populi circumfundant."[51]

Traces of this limited, non-revolutionary republicanism can be found throughout Salutati's life. In a public letter to the commune of Siena in October 1390, Salutati reiterates his earlier reference to a "ring of liberty." We Florentines have always defended liberty

> nec unquam magnanimitati maiorum nostrorum satis visum fuit, liber-
> tatem habere domi nisi et ipsam per circuitum in populis ipsam

diligentibus atque volentibus aut restituerent amissam aut aliunde concussam suis viribus tuerentur.[52]

The same sentiment is in evidence fifteen years later when, promising Florentine protection for the newly liberated commune of Forlì, Salutati writes in the name of the Signoria, that Florence desires "celeste bonum istud (liberty) cunctos populos consolari."[53] Perhaps this feeling is expressed in its most succinct form in Salutati's public letter of August 21, 1390, congratulating the new doge of Genoa on his election and giving thanks "illi eterno numini per quod reges regnant et principes dominantur cuique, teste Cicerone, nichil est quo (sic!) quid (sic!) fiat in terris acceptius quam concilia cetusque hominum iure sociati que civitates appellantur."[54]

    There is no contrast between liberty and monarchy in this statement, no attack on other forms of government, no claim that men can have freedom only where they have political liberty. Yet in this letter Salutati expresses what is obviously a deeply felt conviction that republican government, characteristic of the *civitas*, is most acceptable to God. While recognizing the God-willed rule of emperors and kings, he still insists on the intrinsic worth of republican city-government. Furthermore, the statement intimates that the appropriate area of republican government to Salutati's mind is the *civitas*. The categories of constitutions found in the opening pages of the *De tyranno* reflect something of this same notion. In that work, as was pointed out, Salutati assigned monarchy to the level of the *respublica*, the *politea* to that of the provinces and *civitas* and the despotic constitution to the household. This restricted, unbelligerent republicanism consequently seems to have insinuated itself even into what appears to be Salutati's most complete defense of monarchy [. . .]

    Together with this limited republican sentiment, it is easy to trace through Salutati's public and private writings from 1378 to his death in 1406 the presence of the term liberty used in reference, first, to freedom in a civil society ruled by law and, secondly, to the right of any state to security from outside agression. In 1381, a few years after the War of the Eight Saints, Salutati in a letter to Charles of Durazzo, the new King of Naples, distinguishes between a king and a tyrant:

> unde et tyranni iniusti domini dicti sunt. sive ergo iniuste intraverit sive iniuste regat, tyrannus est . . .[55]

The true king must obey the laws:

> si [. . .] cum servis clementer vivendum est comiterque sunt et in sermonem et nonnunquam in necessarium consilium admittendi, et denique conandum est quod colant te potius servi tui quam timeant; quidnam debes facere, gloriosissime princeps, quid non servis imperas, sed liberis antistaris?[56]

Similarly, Salutati, writing to the Romans in 1405 on behalf of the Signoria, urged them not to fear Ladislaus of Naples:

> Unum nostris mentibus est grave quod videamus nomen gloriosissimi principis regis Ladislai rebus istis, ne cum infamia dixerimus, nimium permisceri qui, cum ingenuis [. . .] populis imperet et citra libertatis offensionem didicerit presidere, credere non possumus unquam de servitute romani cogitasse.[57]

Perhaps the clearest definition of this concept of liberty to be found in Salutati's writings occurs in his *Invectiva contra Antonium Luschum* where Salutati refers to "dolce libertatis frenum, quod est iure vivere."[58] In the same work Salutati attempts to defend Florence's choice of allies in the struggle with Milan. Again Salutati characterizes the King of France as enjoying "libertas regia"[59] and contrasts his rule with that of the Visconti.

As already mentioned, the idea of liberty as freedom from outside aggression is frequently found in the later correspondence. Examples of such usage occur at the beginning of the second phase of the Visconti Wars when Florence calls upon the Malatesta, the Lords of Ferrara, Mantua and Padua to defend the liberty of Italy against Giangaleazzo and, somewhat later in the same year, when in the name of the Signoria Salutati urges the lord of Padua to support Mantua against the "libertatis hostem."[60] In one public letter of this period, reporting a communication of the Pope, Salutati writes to Bologna:

> pro defensione libertatis italice sibi [the Pope] necessarium videbatur quod sua sanctitas et omnes itali tam populi quam domini singulares se pro defensione statuum colligarent contra quoscumque qui vellent ab ultramontanis partibus invadere latium vel statum alicuius bellaciter perturbare.[61]

The independent existence of the Italian states must be defended both against foreign aggressors and those from within Italy who would extend their rule.

By contrast, in the public letters following the War of the Eight Saints until Salutati's death, there is never again a clear condemnation of government of one as harmful *per se* to a people. As has been said, this does not mean that in these later letters there is less expression of pride in Florence's constitution and faith in the republican way of government. But one no longer perceives the aggressive republican spirit which clearly identifies monarchy with tyranny. Would one, however, expect to find it in the wars against Giangaleazzo Visconti? While the dangers of the second long struggle were just as menacing for the Florentine liberty as the first had been, the nature of Florence's alliance system in the later conflict made impossible a clear articulation of a truly republican idea. Whereas Florence found its allies in the war against the Church mainly among the Italian communes, the alliance system of the Visconti Wars, involving leagues with lords, kings and Emperor, impeded an extreme republican statement on war aims. Probably for this reason Salutati usually described the war with convenient ambiguity as being a war between "liberty and tyranny." I do not intend, of course, to suggest that Salutati consciously avoided such extreme republican statements; rather, my meaning is that emotionally the nature of the protagonists made an aggressive republicanism literally unthinkable.

Just as Salutati attained his deepest republican visions in the War of the Eight Saints under the stimulus of a war basically between communes and the Church, so Salutati's one extreme anti-monarchical statement in his private correspondence is found in the period just following his discovery of a codex containing new letters to Cicero, the *Epistolae familiares*, in 1392. For the first time in his life, Salutati writes in this letter to the Milanese chancellor, Pasquino dei Capelli, the true meaning of the Civil Wars of Rome is clear. Now he realizes "quid caput illud orbis terrarum de libertate populica in monarchie detruderit servitutem."[62] This is the first and only time in Salutati's existing private correspondence that monarchy is considered as a government of servitude. The excitement of the discovery doubtless leads Salutati, still under Cicero's influence, to equate monarchy with tyranny, therefore returning to a position which he himself articulated sixteen or seventeen years before under quite different conditions.

While Salutati's extreme position on monarchy as the best form of government in 1400 was also the product of a strong stimulus, there are definite monarchical tendencies in Salutati's writing before the *De tyranno*. The humanist's usual reverence for monarchy as an institution is very apparent in his public and private writing. One indication of these monarchical sympathies is found in a letter written to Giovanni Boccaccio by the young Salutati in Rome in 1368. In this letter he describes to the older man his impressions of the imperial coronation of Charles IV by the Pope which had just taken place in the city.

> ego autem tanto gaudio perfusus sum, ut vix meimet capax forem, aspiciens quod nostrorum parentum memoria et temporibus invisum forte et insperatum fuit, papatum cum imperio convenire, carnem obtemperare spiritui, et denique terrenum imperium celesti obsequi monarchie. o, utinam, dixi, talis concordia ligaret singulos, uniret principes, coniungeret populos, nectaret universos! crede michi, bene irent res humane, rediret cite maiestas imperii . . .[63]

In the same vein in 1379 Salutati writes to the Romans regarding the forthcoming election of a pope. After describing the Eternal City as the seat both of the Empire and the Church, he relates how this came about through the wisdom of God. Rome, the center of the Roman Empire became the head of the Church as well, in order that the whole world "ydolorum superstitione ac abominatione sublata verum deum humiliter adoraret."[64] Obviously at work in Salutati's mind is the same combination of history and Divine Providence which twenty-one years later will be used to justify Caesar and monarchy.

Salutati's *Rechtsstaat* concept of liberty was a two-way street. Just as it posed no challenge to a moderate republicanism, so it was adaptable to advocacy of the monarchical principle. This is precisely what occurred in the *De tyranno*. In this work Salutati asks: "Nulla libertas maior quam optimo principi cum iusta precipiat obedire?"[65] While any government where law rules is a free government, might one not still inquire: What government is most likely to realize the ideal of justice? In the *De tyranno*, where Salutati was intent on justifying Dante, he was prepared to find the ideal in the rule of the best prince.

What I am suggesting is that certain monarchical sentiments and ideas were always alive in Salutati's mind. Under proper conditions these tendencies could result in a basically honest defense of monarchy, especially in a case where Salutati was engaged in an argument which for him had no reference to contemporary political life. In the case of the *De tyranno* Salutati's essential sincerity can be shown by the fact that in the year or so just preceding its composition the influence of Dante on him was at its highest and the world vision of the Florentine poet reinforced in Salutati certain intellectual tendencies which had always been present but in more moderate form.

IV

Like every other writer of the Middle Ages, Salutati never wavered in his condemnation of many of the Roman emperors as tyrants: Caligula and Nero especially were branded along with Dionysius and Tarquin as paradigms of tyranny. In the case of Caesar, Salutati generally displayed the usual ambivalence. At the point in the letter of 1377 to the Romans he went beyond his generation to an assessment of Caesar in terms of the whole history of liberty in its struggle with lordship but even then he made no direct criticism of Caesar as an individual ("extollant quicumque volunt laudibus cesarem . . .")[66] In his private correspondence, furthermore, we must wait until Salutati is in his sixties in order to see him take such a direct critical approach to the Roman dictator.

Characteristic of Salutati's mixed sentiments of admiration and disapproval is a reference to Caesar in a letter written to Francesco Guinigi of Lucca in December 1374:

> Caesar ipse, qui nefas rempublicam invasit, cum bis et quinquagies in acie pugnasse tradatur et pene hostium undecies centena millia delevisse, absque his quos bella civilia rapuerunt, non tamen tantam et tam solidam gloriam de victoriis infinitis accepit, quantam etiam cum sui capitis periculo de clementia in victos hostes et conservatione civium reportavit. hinc primus pater patrie dictus est: hinc clementia sua ipsam dicebatur vicisse victoriam.[67]

In this passage written in 1374 there seems to be no incongruity between Caesar's having usurped power in the Roman state and his rightful claim to the title of *pater patriae*.

The same apparent confusion of attitudes can be illustrated by a second passage taken from a letter written nine years later. In this letter Salutati writes:

> at Caesar dictator, cuius, sicut aliorum Romanorum, finis erat amor patrie laudumque immensa cupido, post victas Gallias, victum et occisum Pompeium superatumque Senatum et post rempublicam patriamque subactam dicere solitus fertur, quasi eum vivendi satietas teneret: vixi satis nature, vixi satis et glorie.[68]

Salutati seems again to feel no inconsistency involved in ascribing a love of country to Caesar at the same time as he describes his destruction of the Roman state.

With the discovery of the *Epistolae familiares*, however, Salutati's attitude toward Caesar in his private correspondence becomes definitely critical. The letter of September 1392, announcing to Pasquino the discovery of the new collection, does not mention Caesar specifically but one senses the implicit accusation that it was he who plunged the Roman Republic into "the servitude of monarchy." In another letter, written two months after this one, Salutati's criticism of Caesar becomes explicit. This time Salutati speaking through the mouth of Cicero brands Caesar the "patricida patrie."[69] But if we called this "patricida patrie," the "pater patriae," Cicero is made to say, we never became so servile as to address him plurally (vos). Yet again at this second high point in Salutati's anti-Caesar sentiment Cicero's influence is not enough to bring the humanist to praise Caesar's murderers – at no point, for that matter, in any of Salutati's writings is such praise found. The only statement referring to Brutus during these years comes in a letter dated [. . .] between 1392–94 and this is a fairly neutral one. In the process of justifying Cicero's participation in politics, Salutati refers to Cato and Brutus, who committed themselves to the Civil War but on opposing sides. Brutus had fought faithfully for Caesar against Pompey but "nec obscurum est ad Cesarem apud Emathiam inclinante victoria, Brutum de ipsius cede cogitasse, ut quem consilio vel potentia a tyrannide se videbat prohibere non posse, ferro saltem arceret." [70] Salutati's conclusion was, however, that this was not to be the case: quoting Virgil he writes: "'Fortuna omnipotens et ineluctabile fatum' ut rerum eventus edocuit, obstiterunt."[71] It is important to stress this conclusion in order to bring attention to the tensions at work within Salutati even in this republican interpretation of the Civil Wars and their aftermath. Brutus' intention to bring an end to tyranny was thwarted, according to this passage, by *fortuna et fatum*; in the *De tyranno* it is to be Dante's *Providentia* which plays this role.

Probably directly connected with the Cicero discovery and its emotional repercussions is a statement of Salutati made in a public letter to Genoa in 1394. It is the second and last time in the public correspondence that Salutati severely criticizes Caesar. Both the dictator and his nephew are branded the "principium perpetui servitutis."[72] Salutati uses the example specifically to warn Genoa of the evils of civil disturbances and, unfortunately for our purposes, makes no general observations on monarchy. The statement, nevertheless, re-emphasizes his earlier judgment of 1377 on the evil consequence of the coming of the emperors.

In the years between 1392 and 1395 a number of other brief references to Caesar are found in the private correspondence: Caesar is called the "fondator imperii"[73] without further comment; and at one point Salutati notes parenthetically that Julius Caesar "primus invasit imperium."[74] It is difficult on the basis of these statements to judge how consistently Salutati held to his anti-Caesarism in these years.

It is only in February 1398, in a letter to Astorgio Manfredi that Salutati gives evidence of a definite shift in his interpretation of Julius Caesar. In this letter Salutati speaks of the "Bruti sacrilegium."[75] Caesar is said to have attained the *dominium*[76] in Rome "concedente patria."[77] Moreover, Salutati adds that "Cesar civibus, ingratissimis percussoribus suis, plurima bona fecit."[78]

As was said above, Salutati had never spoken in praise of the murderers of Caesar but neither had he condemned them. His strong statement here that the *patria* recognized Caesar's dominion and this manifest condemnation of the dictator's murderers, therefore, are unexpected developments. The line between this letter of early 1398 and the defense of the legitimacy of Caesar's rule in 1400 is obviously direct. But how is one to fill in the steps involved in this change between 1392 and 1398?

In order to find a partial answer to this question, it is necessary to turn from a consideration of Salutati's correspondence to his treatise, *De fato et fortuna*. If we are to accept the dating assigned to the five parts and the introduction of the work by Walter Ruegg, we conclude that Book II was completed sometime before mid-July 1396; Books I, III and IV between 1396 and the beginning of 1398; and Book V and Introduction were written between March 1398 and September 1399. Ostensibly designed to define and discuss the nature of fate and fortune, the work is infused with a deep sense of the omnipotence of the Christian God and the Providence of that God working in history. While insisting on the integrity of the freedom of the human will, Salutati nevertheless creates the impression of the presence of a higher power lying behind human history which uses men for the satisfaction of its eternal purposes.

In contrast to the Brutus of the Manfredi letter of 1398, the figure of Brutus, the future assassin of Caesar, is very sympathetically treated in Book I of this work (written between 1396 and 1398). Here Salutati speaks of Brutus "qui morte cesaris tollere tyrannidem de republica cogitans, successioni tyrannidis aditum patefecit."[79]

Still in this period Brutus is considered the defender of liberty against the tyranny of the Caesars. Yet for all of Brutus' nobility Salutati conveys the impression that it was right that he be crushed. As his letter of 1392–94 already intimated, tyranny at Rome could not be prevented. Higher purposes were working their way out in history. While acting from his own free will, Brutus was still the agent of these forces.

In the previously written Book II Salutati had referred to the murder of Caesar by Brutus in some detail: "Providit enim deus fore non simpliciter quod Brutus interficeret dictatorem sed quod eum interficeret non necessario sed prorsus contingenter et libera voluntate."[80]

[. . .]

That Salutati had been meditating for a long time on the problem of fate and fortune is evident from his rather elaborate discussions of these matters at other times in his correspondence. Nor do his theories in this work seem to differ in any appreciable degree from those discussed in less developed form elsewhere. But the central example, the murder of Caesar, is not to be found associated with these earlier treatments. In the *De fato et fortuna*, whose composition spreads out over a number of years, the historical events connected with Caesar's murder appear throughout as the central illustration for the arguments. Salutati, moreover, seems to realize fully that Brutus' intention in killing Caesar was honorable. There appears, consequently, a tension between sympathy for the noble Brutus and knowledge of the fate God had in store for him. While God's ends must prevail and Brutus' will be thwarted still the final conclusion is unsatisfactory. It might be asked: Granted God set the world under the domination of one man for his own purposes, was Brutus justly punished? Was the man he murdered a usurper or was he a legitimate ruler in constitutional terms?

In the two years between the finishing of the *De fato et fortuna* and that of the *De tyranno* Salutati's argument in support of the belief in the divine origin of the Roman Empire was developed to include an answer to these questions. God in bringing the world under the rule of one did not use as his representative of the imperial order a man whose claim to power rested on usurpation. The letter to Manfredi in 1398 already indicates the basic argument which Salutati will use in the *De tyranno*: Caesar did not usurp power in the Roman state but came to domination "concedente patria."[81]

Intimately connected with the rise of Caesar's credit in Salutati's eyes was Salutati's growing attachment to the figure and writings of Dante in the last years of the Trecento. Earlier in his life he had explicitly stated his preference for Petrarch. This happened in the year of Petrarch's death and, while we might suspect that the estimate was a product of his immediate grief at the loss of the poet, nevertheless, the fact that Salutati did not quote Dante until 1383 would suggest this to be a considered judgment. Indeed, only in the last half of the nineties, when Salutati was already in his sixties did Dante's name and opinions occur with any frequency in the pages of Salutati's work.

Yet from the very first discussion of Dante's *Divina commedia* to appear in Salutati's letters, Dante seems to be under attack and Salutati to be the poet's defender against criticisms which have been made "a multis indocte."[82] The *De fato et fortuna*, finished as has been said sometime before the fall of 1399, really indicates the degree to which Dante found a champion in Salutati. Not only does Salutati explicitly follow Dante's interpretation of a divinely-willed Roman monarchy but Dante's authority is repeatedly invoked to give direction to the discussion of fate and fortune and to support the conclusion. Book III of the treatise is principally a defense of Dante's opinion on fate and fortune as opposed to those who have criticized him "non inerudite solum sed stulte et temerarie."[83] Especially Cecco d'Ascoli, who in his *Acerba*, written soon after Dante's death, had criticized Dante's view on these matters, comes in for severe criticism [. . .] Salutati, moreover, makes a point of defending the Florentine idiom as a superior literary language while at the same time including his own Latin translations of portions of two cantos from the *Divina commedia* itself.

The reader of the *De tyranno* has the distinct impression that in this work the vision of Dante, "divinissimus compatriota noster,"[84] has largely become that of Salutati. Dante's influence, of course, had little to do with generating Salutati's conviction that God was constantly at work in history. This [. . .] had been a confirmed article of Salutati's faith for decades. In the early 1390s, moreover, Salutati applied this principle to an explanation of the events surrounding the creation of the Roman Principate but without developing the idea. Even at the height of Salutati's expression of anti-Caesarism in his private letters, the humanist recognized the inevitability of events and the helplessness of Brutus before the forces of destiny. How long this idea had been in Salutati's mind cannot be determined. The *De fato et fortuna*, moreover, still showed the same inward struggle in Salutati: the knowledge supported by Dante's authority that the Empire had to be and yet the realization that Brutus was noble and Caesar a tyrant. As has been shown, this inner battle reached the pages of the *De tyranno* itself. But unquestionably in the foreground of this latter work was Salutati's sympathetic depiction of Caesar. Under Dante's influence in this period the rule of Caesar was considered not simply inevitable but also acceptable. To state the situation briefly: at the time of writing the *De tyranno* Salutati was genuinely on Caesar's side. Dante had converted him. Yet in part exaggerating in order to vindicate Dante's opinion and in part unconsciously carried away by his own rhetoric, Salutati went beyond what, under other circumstances, would probably have been his usual opinion of the Roman dictator even in 1400.

There is no way to determine from Salutati's writings after 1400 whether or not he remained basically favorable to Caesar. Most of his references to the dictator in these last six years of life suggest neither praise or blame. There are, however, a number of indications that he qualified his extreme statements of mid-1400. In a letter most probably written late in 1400–1401, Salutati expresses a general view of Caesar's character which closely resembles that of earlier years.

> fuit in Caio Cesare dictatore, L. Cesaris filio, mirabilis et summa clementia, fuit et ingens ambitio, fuit et in eodem etiam ab hostibus laudata sobrietas, fuit et in ipso etiam ab amicis reprehensa libido; unde fertur dixisse Cato nullum qui sobrius esset preter Cesarem aliquando rempublicam invasisse.[85]

This attempt to balance the great vices and virtues of Caesar is another manifestation of the humanist's usual feeling of ambivalence toward the figure of the great conqueror. Bruni's presentation of Salutati in the second book of the *Dialogi ad Petrum Paulum histrum*, written a few years after the above statement, also lends support to the suspicion of a movement away from the extreme position on Caesar of 1400. True, Bruni has Salutati say that he has never been able to criticize Caesar as a parricide (this is literally true – Cicero had spoken the words "patricida patrie"[86] in 1392), but the whole tone of the speech is one of uncertainty in the overall assessment of Caesar's career and personality. Salutati was still alive at the time of writing and, if the aged humanist had still been extremely favorable to Caesar, the speech attributed to him by Bruni would have been a gross misrepresentation of his views.

V

In the matter of politics, Salutati's mind, cluttered and untidy, sheltered within its compass a mass of contradictory traditions and brilliant insights. The humanist seemed to hold them together *in potentia*, expressing now one, now the other, depending on the circumstances of the moment and the direction of his own thought processes. Salutati could be characterized as a republican, as a monarchist, or as neither, depending on the conditions in which he happened to be writing and the train of ideas he was pursuing [. . .] [H]is political ideas seem to have had no real history. All the various meanings of liberty were always present to his mind during his years as chancellor. Under the influence of Dante, or Cicero or of a war in defense of communal liberty, he could give vent to most extreme positions. Yet in the following year, the next letter, perhaps in the next sentence, he could back away, qualify or absolutely contradict himself. Essentially, what I have attempted to describe is a plasticity of mind [. . .]

Throughout his life Salutati was always an enemy of tyranny and a defender of liberty. Even in his most pro-monarchical work, the *De tyranno*, there can be no serious question as to Salutati's position regarding the rule of a tyrant. Still Salutati's political ideas are confusing because he had a series of rather diverse notions of the meaning of "liberty" and by contrast of "tyranny." He himself never seemed bothered by the confusion. Unconsciously he was able to move with great ease by means of this ambiguous general term from republicanism to a monarchical defense. From our point of view, of course, the most significant notion of liberty articulated in his work was that which I have labelled "extreme republican" because it took such an uncompromisingly hostile view toward all forms of one-man government [. . .] In the 1370s under the stress of a war he related the republican interpretation of Roman history and the general principle of the relationship between freedom and human nature to a call for communal freedom and expulsion of the ecclesiastical tyrants. The letter to the Romans in 1377 is possibly the clearest expression of his insight. During these same years criticism of the nobility's anti-republican temperament and analysis of "bourgeois" republicanism complimented these attacks on the evils of monarchical rule. The need to present Salutati's extreme republican views in comprehensible form, however, caused me to create a false impression of consistency. These few letters are included among hundreds of others out of which quite other visions of politics and history can be drawn. Salutati's extreme republican statements were sporadic outbursts of mental energy which in depth of insight carried Salutati intellectually into the next century.

[. . .]

Editor's Notes

1   proudly
2   indeed not that no one but which of these two should rule and assume the reins of power
3   made up with admirable clemency for the horrifying war and the civil conflict, than which nothing can be more cruel.
4   monarchy is to be preferred to all forms of government, provided that a good and wise man rules?
5   there will not be one, but many governments.
6   Therefore Caesar, as has been proved most clearly, was not a tyrant in name, since his country gratefully and without coercion made him its prince, nor through pride, since he ruled with kindness and humanity, and so it is clear that he was killed with the utmost wickedness.
7   usurped the highest authority.
8   Nevertheless since he overturned the republic by armed force, he was branded a tyrant and, with the approval of the majority of the senate, was killed by daggers drawn in the Capitol.
9   the third after Julius (Caesar).

10   the third tyrant

11   was very valiant and very strong.

12   he was not, but treacherous and disloyal.

13   whoever kills a tyrant in order to liberate his country is praiseworthy and deserves to be rewarded.

14   The consulate lasted up to the time of Julius Caesar, who was the first to usurp power; but his rule was short, killed as he was by the senators on account of his abuse of power.

15   Julius Caesar and Hannibal, who on account of their abuse of power each suffered a harsh death.

16   You have read that Cassius was one of those who raised their hands, I do not say disloyally or wickedly, but certainly boldly, against Julius Caesar.

17   that above-mentioned emperor, who was a very energetic and warlike man.

18   many favorable commissions from him

19   treacherously killed him

20   Caesar, raised to such high honor, was tempted by many vices including luxury and avarice. God's justice, which did not tolerate Caesar's remaining in such a position, inspired the senators with a duty to kill him.

21   the one who violently took into his own hands the entire government of the republic.

22   seized the republic and made himself, contrary to Roman law, perpetual dictator.

23   Go on now and prefer Alexander to Caesar if you can, and ask why Dante did not place Caesar here, someone who beyond other numerous and great virtues was the most sober of men.

24   most unworthy

25   that Caesar's military achievements up to this point were great and glorious, but thereafter wicked and unjust, since such things against one's country cannot be excused for any reason.

26   Caesar, just as Livy said of Hannibal, had vices equal to his great virtues, and he achieved many great things especially through his desire for conquest; for he waged civil war against his own country shedding much blood of citizens; in his consulate he suited only himself, having removed his colleague Bibulus by force of arms, and he attempted in many ways to achieve a revolution in the city so that he could come to power. He was the only defender of the Catilinarian conspirators: he was the refuge for all guilty men, saying that such persons were prone to civil war. Twice he despoiled the Roman treasury, the first time fraudulently, the second violently; he sold this highest sacred office for a high price. He made himself dictator for life; indeed, as Lucan says, Caesar was all things.

27   since he dared to opposed Caesar, the violator of liberty.

28   nevertheless it seems to me that one ought to understand Decimus Brutus here instead.

29   Unlike Caesar, who seized power with armed forced for himself from the Senate and the republic, Octavian, forcibly compelled by the imprecations of the senate and people, assumed the scepter of monarchy.

30   you should not think, most excellent sirs, that your and our ancestors, whom we proudly share as relatives, founded such a memorable and glorious empire by being slaves at home nor by placing their own Italy under foreign or domestic servitude. On your behalf, that vast empire, by helping its allies and by fighting for their liberty, first subdued Italy, conquered Spain, overcame Africa, and

finally your empire was lifted to such sublime heights that the Roman name presided over all nations.

31   with liberty removed under the Caesars – let all who want extol [Julius] Caesar with praises and raise Augustus up to divine honour, let them celebrate Vespasian with admiring commendation, let them hail the justice of Trajan and the glory of his military achievements with the highest praise, let them finally exalt Constantine, Antoninus Pius, Justinian and the rest with whatever praises they want – in their hands Italy was certainly devastated and the empire descended from its highpoint. Only the pursuit of liberty, therefore, achieved empire, glory and dignity for the Romans.

32   the great mass of empire

33   royal dignity

34   In whom does virtue appear vigorous, when he begins to fear the ruler's axe, when he always feels its threat on his neck, or proscription or exile to be looming?

35   fearing the king, pretended that he was a empty and foolish person.

36   What is more honest, what more secure than to wish for and enjoy liberty? This alone exalts cities, causes their population to multiply prodigiously, enhances family wealth, decorates the government and majesty of citizens with ornament and admirable beauty. This is the mother of laws which do not reflect the desire and will of one man but rather the public good. This is the mistress of virtues, since no one doubts, in a republic, where liberty prevails, how much and what that liberty can lead a virtuous man to do; indeed, the best citizens are inspired to such an extent that they consider death something beautiful nor do they fear to relinquish their lives for the welfare of their country.

37   Consider, as witnessed by the testimony of divine scriptures, that kings were instituted from the beginning on account of people's sins so that they, however justly, would not rule but punish peoples. Whoever considers himself worthy of being a lord betrays himself as guilty of great crimes, since it is clear that lords are not placed over cities for ornament but for punishment and to burden, not honour, peoples.

38   Our ancestors, the entire Italian race, fought for five hundred years against the Romans in continuous warfare in order not to lose their liberty. Nor could the ruling people of the whole world reduce Italy by force of arms until they had formed a free imperial alliance with almost all Italians.

39   Greek servitude.

40   once among all noble Latin cities was celebrated

41   unwillingly you have to submit to his desires and will nor can you contradict him.

42   best prince

43   the liberty of Italy.

44   Various types of government have been invented by mortals so that, judging all men by custom and law in equity and rectitude, they can restrain them under the rules of justice.

45   free king

46   free people

47   Fear alone, when it is joined to dominance, turns the royal name into a horrendous tyranny.

48   royal name

49   tyrannical name

50   it is not this community but the rest that are governed by the ambition of the few and oppressed by petty factionalism.

51   in so far as the city is surrounded by free peoples.

52   nor ever did it appear to our magnanimous ancestors that liberty could be maintained at home unless they restored it to surrounding freedom-loving peoples or, if threatened, protected them with their strength.

53   to comfort all people with the heavenly gift of liberty.

54   to that eternal power by which kings rule and princes dominate, and to which, as Cicero testifies, there is nothing more acceptable on earth than for the councils and communities of men to be lawfully joined together in societies which are called cities.

55   Hence tyrants too are called unjust lords. Whoever therefore unjustly obtains power or unjustly rules is a tyrant.

56   if servants must be indulgently treated and courteously addressed and sometimes even consulted, and finally an effort must be made for them to cherish rather than to fear you; what must you do, glorious prince, in order not to command slaves but to preside over free men?

57   One grave matter as far as we are concerned is that we see the name of that glorious prince King Ladislaus (lest we should say anything infamous) implicated in these things, whom, although he rules over free peoples and will have learned to do so without offence to liberty, we cannot believe ever to have contemplated the servitude of the Roman people.

58   the sweet restraint of liberty, which is to live by law.

59   regal liberty

60   enemy of liberty

61   for the defense of Italian liberty it seemed necessary to the Pope that he and all Italian peoples and lords should join together for the defence of their regimes against anyone who would want to invade Italy or disturb anyone's rule through warfare.

62   how that head of the world moved from popular liberty to monarchical servitude.

63   But I was filled with so much joy that I was scarcely capable of self-composure, seeing what was unseen in the memory and times of our parents and perhaps unhoped for, namely, that papacy came together with empire, that flesh obeyed spirit, and finally that earthly empire yielded to celestial monarchy. O, would that, I said, such concord bind individuals, unite princes, join peoples, link all men! Believe me, human affairs would go well, the majesty of empire would quickly return.

64   should worship the true God, with idolatrous superstition and abomination destroyed.

65   Is there any liberty greater than to obey the best prince when he gives just orders?

66   let whoever wants extol Caesar with praise.

67   when, so it is said, he had waged war fifty-two times and had slaughtered over a million one hundred thousand enemies (not counting those killed in the civil wars), Caesar himself, who had shamefully attacked the republic, did not win as much glory from his infinite victories as he earned, with danger to his own life, from clemency towards conquered enemies and from the salvation of

citizens. Hence he was named the first father of his country: hence it was said that his clemency had conquered victory itself.

68   But Caesar the dictator, whose aim, as with other Romans, was love of country and immense desire for glory, after conquering the Gauls, defeating and slaying Pompey, vanquishing the senate and subjugating the republic and his country, was reported to have been in the habit of saying, as though he had wearied of life: I have experienced enough of nature, I have experienced enough of glory too.

69   the parricide of the fatherland

70   nor is it unknown that, with victory tipping in favor of Caesar at Emathia, Brutus considered Caesar's death: if he could not prevent him from becoming a tyrant either by advice or power, at least he could stop him with the sword.

71   "Omnipotent fortune and inescapable fate", as the outcome of events shows, stood in the way.

72   the beginning of perpetual servitude

73   founder of the empire

74   was the first to seize power

75   Brutus's sacrilege.

76   rule

77   with the agreement of his country

78   Caesar did many favors for the ungrateful citizens who attacked him

79   who, hoping through the death of Caesar to remove the republic from the threat of tyranny, opened the way to a succession of tyrants.

80   For God provided that Brutus would not simply murder the dictator but that he would kill him not of necessity but indeed contingently and of his free will.

81   through the agreement of his country.

82   ignorantly by many

83   not only ignorantly but foolishly and rashly

84   our most divine fellow countryman

85   There was in Caius Caesar the dictator, son of L. Caesar, an admirable and lofty clemency; there was an enormous ambition too; there was also in the same man a sobriety even praised by his enemies; there was in him as well a lust even censured by his friends; hence Cato is reported to have said that no one more sober than Caesar had ever attacked the republic.

86   the parricide of his fatherland

Chapter 11

David Quint

■   from **HUMANISM AND MODERNITY:**
A RECONSIDERATION OF BRUNI'S *DIALOGUES*,
Renaissance Quarterly, 38 (1985), pp. 423–445

LEONARDO BRUNI'S *DIALOGUES* for *Pier Paolo Vergerio* (1401), in the dispute which Bruni stages between the fictionalized figures of Coluccio Salutati and Niccolò Niccoli [. . .] are one of the first masterworks of humanist letters, and part of their interest lies precisely in their early date. Bruni writes at a historical moment when the newness of humanism still had to be accounted for, when neither its premises nor its eventual success were taken for granted. Bruni's Niccoli, who contends at the beginning of the humanist Renaissance that there cannot, will not be a true Renaissance may, in retrospect, appear to be a false prophet. But Niccoli's criticism of the humanist project contains a strain of melancholy renunciation which, no less than the confidence voiced by exponents of modern creativity and cultural innovation, was to become part of the new consciousness that arose from the debates of humanism. Both of these attitudes – the despair and the exhilaration that accompanied the humanist's awareness of his own modernity – were largely to be submerged as humanism rapidly gained cultural ascendancy throughout the Italian peninsula and, in its moment of triumph and usurpation, forgot the novelty of its origins.

The *Dialogues for Pier Paolo Vergerio* have been at the center of a major controversy in recent Renaissance scholarship. Before proceeding further, it is necessary to give some account both of Bruni's text and of the critical debate which surrounds it.

In the first of two dialogues, Bruni describes how one day during the Easter holidays he, Niccolò Niccoli, and Roberto Rossi had gone to visit Coluccio Salutati, the Chancellor of Florence and the leading humanist scholar in the city. After greetings are exchanged, there is a lull in the conversation in Salutati's house. Salutati breaks the embarrassing silence by recalling the days of his youth when he used to visit Luigi Marsili and engage him in Latin disputations on various subjects, a practice which, Salutati regrets, has fallen into disuse. Niccoli replies that such disputations are not possible for him and for his friends because of the nature of the times in which they live. It is an age when the books and learning of the ancients have been lost, when philosophy, once so eloquent, has fallen into the hands of scholastic writers ignorant of Greek who rely on corrupt translations of Aristotle and write in an obscure and ungrammatical Latin. Niccoli remarks that Salutati alone, by some remarkable and almost divine genius, has been able to overcome the obstacles of the age and to equal, perhaps surpass, the ancients in wisdom and eloquence.

Salutati replies that the eloquence of Niccoli's very speech has disproved his contention; he has just performed the disputation that he claims he is incapable of performing. Salutati further reminds Niccoli that while much of ancient culture is indeed lost, much of it still remains. And he puts forward the examples of Dante, Petrarch, and Boccaccio, whose accomplishments in the last century belie Niccoli's assertion that the possibilities of literary creativity have been cut off from him and his contemporaries. The mention of these three *trecento* authors sets Niccoli off again in a vitriolic denunciation of their putative literary achievements. The specific charges against Dante are that he lacked Latinity – and Niccoli points to the notorious (and on Dante's part intentional) mistranslation of *Aeneid* 3, 56 in *Purgatorio* 22, 40 – that he portrayed Cato, who died at the age of 48, as a white-bearded old man in *Purgatorio* I, and, most serious of all, that in *Inferno* 34 he placed Marcus Brutus, the assassin of Julius Caesar and defender of Republican liberty, in lowest Hell, next to Judas in the mouth of Satan. Petrarch is criticized on the basis of his *Africa*, his much heralded, but universally deplored Latin epic, of his *Bucolicon carmen*, which in no way savors of the pastoral, and of his *Invectives*, which lack the art and eloquence of the orator. There is no need to discuss Boccaccio at all, since everyone acknowledges that he is surpassed by the other two writers. Salutati replies that these objections to the *trecento* writers can be answered, but defers their defense to another time, and as the dialogue ends he reiterates his conviction that disputations are both possible and profitable in the present time.

The second dialogue opens on the next day in the gardens of Roberto Rossi. Coluccio speaks admiringly of the elegance and beauty of the buildings of Florence, which remind him of Bruni's *Laudatio*, a panegyric speech on the city's excellence. Salutati remarks that Bruni, in order to commend the republican institutions of Florence, had found it necessary to attack the memory of Julius Caesar, thus contradicting the defense of Caesar's policies which Salutati had undertaken in his own treatise, the *De tyranno*. To continue this praise of Florence, Rossi urges Salutati to answer the charges against the city's great writers which Niccoli had leveled on the preceding day. "What charges are you talking about?" Salutati answers. He has, he says, understood yesterday's strategems for what they were, merely an attempt to rouse him into an encomium of the Florentine authors. Refusing to rise to the bait, Salutati gives this task instead to Bruni, who, in turn, consigns it to Niccoli. Niccoli is thus put in the position of having to argue against his own accusations. He first readily agrees that everything he had said on the day before was merely a ploy to bring Salutati out, and then performs a point-by-point refutation of his arguments in the first dialogue. Niccoli's speech is praised and Rossi welcomes him back into the fold, inviting the whole company to dinner; the dialogue ends with harmony apparently restored within the little humanist community.

The question of how to explain Niccoli's change of position has divided the scholarly interpreters of the *Dialogues*. Hans Baron has argued that this about-face cannot be accommodated into a unified reading of Bruni's work. In *The Crisis of the Early Italian Renaissance*, he concludes that the two dialogues were composed at different times, and he argues that the second is separated from the first, which appears from its dedication to have been written by 1401, by the "crisis" year of 1402, the year of Giangaleazzo Visconti's death. With the ensuing relaxation of the military threat which Visconti's Milanese "tyranny" had posed to Florence and the rest of Northern Italy, a republican "civic humanism" acquired new self-confidence and assertiveness in Florentine intellectual life. The praise of the three great Florentine writers of the *trecento* which the character Niccoli performs in the second dialogue gives voice, according to Baron, to Bruni's newfound patriotic enthusiasm for his adoptive city, the same sentiments expressed in the *Laudatio*, which Baron also re-dates. Baron finds these republican sentiments "entirely absent" from the first dialogue, and asserts that the two dialogues represent separate stages in the development of Bruni's thought, molded as it was by the decisive events of 1402.

Baron's reading and dating of the *Dialogues* have been attacked by other scholars who object to the relationship he draws between intellectual and political history, to his emphasis upon a republican ideology shaping the course of early Florentine humanist thought. In a pair of essays, Eugenio Garin has argued that Niccoli's recantation in the second dialogue of his attack on the Florentine authors in the first need not represent a change in Bruni's position; it rather forms part of a typical rhetorical exercise of arguing for and against (*in utramque partem*) a given thesis. Garin points out that the context of Bruni's work is the praise of the art of disputation, an art brilliantly exemplified by Niccoli's pro and contra speeches. The two dialogues thus fit seamlessly together into a single work.

In an important polemical article [see p. 288 below], Jerrold Seigel has challenged Baron's redatings of Bruni's works, and further argued for the unity and coherence of the *Dialogues* by comparing them to their literary model, Cicero's *De oratore*. Here, in a debate between two forensic orators, Crassus and Antonius, can be found the precedent for Niccoli's recantation. Antonius first attacks the contentions of Crassus that the orator needs a broad philosophical culture; the following day in the second book of Cicero's work, Antonius reverses himself and confesses that he had not really meant what he said (II, 10, 41). Seigel sees the *Dialogues* primarily as a discussion directed to "how persuasive speech is to be produced, and to the way in which those who aim to speak well should stand in relation to philosophy in general," a discussion carefully modeled upon Cicero's treatise. Seigel's account of the *Dialogues* omits any mention of civic or republican sentiments, and he argues that the presence of these sentiments in Bruni's *Laudatio* constitutes little more than a repetition of rhetorical commonplaces. He, in fact, demands that the humanism of the early *quattrocento* be redefined as an almost exclusively rhetorical movement, which aimed to produce public speakers and literary men on the model of Cicero. The movement grew up in a civic, urban context, but its ideas neither greatly altered nor were, in turn, decisively shaped by that context. Seigel thus rejects Baron's thesis, which insists upon the uniqueness of the humanist experience in Florence.

All these readings of the *Dialogues* share a basic understanding of their argumentative structure: Niccoli attacks the triumvirate of Florentine *trecento* writers in the first dialogue, then reverses himself and defends them in the second. His second position, which appears to restore unanimity in the little group of human-ists, has also generally been taken to represent Bruni's own attitude. The reasons for this conclusion lie partly outside the *Dialogues*. It was Bruni who in 1424 would write an attack on the historical Niccoli for the latter's disparagement of Dante and Petrarch, and who still later in 1436 would compose his admiring *Lives* of those writers. And yet the invectives of Cino Rinuccini and Domenico da Prato – however they are dated – point to an earlier Bruni who sided with Niccoli *against* the *trecento* authors. Baron, of course, wishes to see Bruni changing positions between the first and second dialogues in response to the intervening events of 1402. But Garin, Seigel, and other readers have also assumed that Niccoli's conver-sion shows Bruni already in possession of the viewpoint which he would espouse a quarter of a century later.

The temptation to read the *Dialogues* as Bruni's intellectual biography-in-the-making may be nearly irresistible. It is all the more enhanced by the prospect of saving Dante and Petrarch from the humanists and, at the same time, of saving the humanists from themselves. Modern scholarship has had to contend with the nationalist bias of nineteenth-century historiography which saw the Italian human-ists' Latinity as an aberrant chapter in an otherwise popular, vernacular cultural history. How could one respect, much less wish to study men who had cast asper-sions upon Father Dante? This question may hover in the background of discussions of Bruni's work. The *Dialogues* might appear much more attractive when read as vindication of the great *volgare* writers, placing humanism safely back inside the Italian national tradition.

This comforting picture, however, disappears or is at least greatly complicated if Niccoli's recantation is taken to be less than genuine and complete, if the second dialogue does not, in fact, reconcile the conflicting positions put forward in the first. I shall attempt to demonstrate that the Niccoli of the second dialogue gives several indications during his defense of the Florentine triumvirate that he has not really changed his positions of the first day and that he explicitly returns to them at the dialogue's close. Niccoli's attack on Salutati's position in the first dialogue, moreover, continues just as forcefully in the second, if under a different form: an attack on two of the historical Salutati's writings, the *De tyranno* and the 1379 *Letter to Giovanni Bartolomei.*

In so far as it sees the *Dialogues* as a unified work, my reading agrees with the findings of Garin and Seigel. The great divide which Baron saw between the two dialogues, and upon which he based his view of political and patriotic conversion in Bruni's thought, simply does not exist. This internal evidence does not indicate – while neither does it necessarily exclude – two separate periods of composition; the vexed dating problem is not my concern here. Notwithstanding his critics, however, Baron is, I believe, correct to have emphasized the presence in the *Dialogues* of a republican ideology that represents something more than a mere topos of Ciceronian rhetoric. This ideology is crucial to the argument staged in the *Dialogues* although it does not constitute their central subject [. . .] the prin-cipal concern of the *Dialogues* is to define the creative possibilities of humanist culture at the moment when that culture became aware of its own modernity.

The first of the *Dialogues* casts its arguments as a conflict between two gener-ations of Florentine humanists. In Bruni's model, the *De oratore*, the principal speakers Crassus and Antonius are both elder statesmen of roughly the same age performing before a younger audience. But the debate of the *Dialogues* takes place between the old and the young – the historical Salutati (1331–1406) was separated by thirty-six years and more from the generation of Niccoli (1367–1437) and Bruni (1370–1444). The fatherly Coluccio addresses Niccoli, Bruni, and Rossi as "iuvenes,"[1] and Niccoli's attempt to define himself in contradistinction to an earlier humanist tradition acquires the form of an oedipal struggle. Urging the younger men to participate in rhetorical disputation, Salutati asks them to repeat his own youthful experience in the company of the father-figure, Luigi Marsili. This repetition suggests a reassuring image of cultural and generational continuity. The wisdom which Salutati will now hand down to the young men gathered in his house he himself received from the "authority" of Marsili: "At ego multa ab eo audivi, multa didici, multa etiam, de quibus ambigebam, illius viri auctoritate confirmavi."[2] Marsili, in turn, derived this authority from the classical authors: Cicero, Virgil, Seneca. In Salutati's estimation, Marsili had so completely mastered and absorbed their writings that, in accordance with ideal humanist norms of imitation, he was able to make his use of their words a form of self-expression: "nec solum eorum opiniones atque sententias, sed etiam verba persaepe sic proferebat, ut non ab alio sumpta, sed ab ipso facta viderentur."[3] By scholarship and imitation – the kind which, according to Petrarch and subsequent humanists, conferred upon the imitator a resemblance to his ancient model like that of a son to his father – Marsili had succeeded in affiliating himself within the classical tradition. It is precisely this idea of cultural transmission – that humanism can make itself the legitimate heir of classical letters and recover an untroubled and unbroken line between itself and antiquity – that Niccoli emphatically rejects when he argues that his age has lost the "patrimony" of ancient culture: "Nonne videmus quam amplo pulcerrimoque patrimonio haec nostra tempora spoliata sint?"[4] Niccoli's declared unwillingness to participate in disputations, by which he separates himself from his humanist fathers Salutati and Marsili, thus also represents his recognition of his historical separation from the classical culture which these fathers claim both to restore and relive.

These disavowed fathers, moreover, carry with them the legacy of the great Florentine writers of the *trecento*. The historical Salutati was Petrarch's correspondent, and in the second dialogue Niccoli speaks of having learned about Petrarch's life and character from talks with Marsili. Niccoli's attack upon the Florentine triumvirate, his declaration of a decisive rupture between a new classical purism and the literary tradition of the *trecento*, should be understood as a second rejection of the older generation of humanism. Niccoli's two repudiations of the humanist fathers who offer him the cultural inheritances first of classical antiquity and then of fourteenth-century Florence proceed on different grounds, but these grounds turn out to be interrelated. Niccoli would gladly receive from Salutati the ability to perform classical disputations and to resuscitate the world of ancient culture, but he, unlike Salutati, realizes that antiquity is irrevocably lost. He further rejects the works and tradition of Dante, Petrarch, and Boccaccio precisely because those writers lacked – inevitably – a sufficient knowledge of classical letters.

And yet, Niccoli asserts, these *trecento* writers did not hesitate with "singular arrogance" ("singulari arrogantia") to label themselves respectively as poet, laureate, and *vates*.[5] They indeed assumed themselves to be equal to the ancients. By contrast, Niccoli has earlier declined Salutati's invitation to engage in rhetorical disputation because he does not want to appear "impudent"; his modesty results from his knowledge of his own limitations, which are the limitations imposed upon him by history. The conditions of learning in his age will allow no one to speak even on the smallest subject without the greatest impudence [. . .] Lack of similar historical self-knowledge appears to account for the presumption which Niccoli attributes to Dante, Petrarch, and Boccaccio. By implication Salutati, too, would be guilty of this presumption, but Niccoli carefully makes an exception of Salutati, whose extraordinary and almost divine genius ("praestantissimo ingenio ac paene divino") allows him to overcome the deficiencies of the times in which he lives. But this same genius may also allow him to remain unaware of these deficiencies – and Niccoli's praise of Salutati as the equal or surpasser of the ancients links him further with the Dante whom Salutati would rank with or above the Greeks themselves. Salutati is the exception who proves Niccoli's rule.

The declaration of Salutati's uniqueness in the present age, moreover, depends upon a complicated imitation of the *De oratore*. In Cicero's work, first Scaevola (I.17.76–7) and then Antonius (I.21.95) praise Crassus as the orator who is able to achieve true eloquence, combining philosophical wisdom and rhetorical skill. Both maintain, however, that Crassus is an exceptional case, for the orator of the law courts simply does not have the time to acquire the accomplishments of philosophy. Neither Crassus (I.17.57) nor Bruni's Salutati will admit to being classified as an extraordinary, isolated genius, both out of modesty and because such an admission would damage their arguments that their own eloquence is available to others. Salutati turns the praise back upon Niccoli, claiming that the latter's skillful disputation on the impossibility of making skillful disputations must either contradict itself or argue for Niccoli's own special genius [. . .] Here he imitates Cicero's Crassus who similarly returns Antonius's compliment by praising the exceptional genius of Antonius which allows him to win court cases without a deep study of the law. As Seigel points out, the *Dialogues* cast Salutati and Niccoli in the respective roles of Crassus and Antonius in the *De oratore*. But what complicates Bruni's imitation is that while, in terms of the plot and structure of Cicero's work, Niccoli's praise of Salutati recalls the praise of Crassus, the orator whose art is based on profound learning and philosophy, Niccoli's actual words are modeled instead on those which Crassus later used to reciprocate with the praise of Antonius, the sophistic orator who can speak as the occasion demands without the benefit of doctrine.

> You [Salutati] seem to me by your extraordinary and almost divine genius to have been able to accomplish this, even lacking those things without which others are unable to so; and thus you alone should be excepted from these remarks; let us speak of others, whom ordinary nature produced . . .

[. . .]

> Antonius' rather incredible, almost unique and divine power of genius seems, even though it be stripped of this legal learning, to be able easily

to defend and safeguard itself with the other arms of prudential wisdom. Wherefore he is to be excepted from our case; but I shall not hesitate to give my verdict and condemn the others first of laziness, then of impudence as well.

Crassus charges the orators who share neither learning nor the exceptional talents of Antonius with impudence: this is the charge which Bruni's Niccoli, disclaiming the unique gifts of Salutati, wishes to avoid. Bruni's peculiar doubling of his source material creates a subversive ambiguity about the nature of Salutati's genius: he may not be a learned Crassus, but rather a shallowly glib Antonius. The ambiguity restates the central issue that is at stake in the first dialogue. Is it possible, in the present times, for the humanist to achieve true eloquence, or has history so cut him off from the ancient sources of learning and wisdom that his speech must necessarily possess only the form and appearance, but not the substance of eloquence?

The model of the *De oratore*, where a group of orators use all their rhetorical skills to argue persuasively about the nature of rhetorical persuasion, should alert the reader of the *Dialogues* to the tactical aspects of the arguments put forth by Bruni's speakers. Niccoli's praise of Salutati may be less of a compliment than a rhetorical ploy, and indeed this is how Salutati takes it. The same may be said for Niccoli's celebrated recantation in the second dialogue. The analogous recantation of Antonius on the second day of discussion in the *De oratore* comes at the prompting of his opponent Crassus, who remarks that Antonius has now come around to his side (II.10.40). Antonius agrees that he has heretofore spoken only to counter Crassus' arguments and that he will henceforth express his own opinions. But, in fact, Antonius continues to develop a model of the orator that is quite opposed to that of Crassus; if the arguments of the two men sometimes arrive at what seem to be similar conclusions, they start from and continue to defend antithetical premises. Thus, if Niccoli's retraction of his attack on Dante, Petrarch, and Boccaccio is modeled on Antonius's recantation in the *De oratore*, it, too, may be more apparent than real.

Salutati contends that his rival disputant really shares his own views. He claims to have seen through Niccoli's arguments: they were just a ploy to make him rise to the defense of the *trecento* authors. Niccoli is now obliged to refute his own invective in the first dialogue, to argue *in utramque partem*. He begins by readily admitting that his earlier speech was indeed merely intended to draw Salutati out; in the same vein, he attests to his own personal devotion to the Florentine writers in order to show that he could not conceivably have held the opinions he expressed the day before. But these preliminary assertions may themselves be rhetorical strategems, and Niccoli may already have assumed the pose of a speaker for the defense. One way to refute an opponent's proposition is to accuse him of not believing in it himself: Niccoli argues *ad hominem* against himself. Given the peculiar rhetorical framework in which he speaks, his recantation cannot be taken at face value. In fact, Niccoli's subsequent arguments reveal, alongside expressions of praise, his continuing criticism of Dante and Petrarch – and of the Salutati who admires those *trecento* writers.

Niccoli is not the only figure in the second dialogue to be accused by Salutati of holding a rhetorical position in which he does not really believe. Salutati remarks that Bruni, in his *Laudatio*, inveighed against the Caesars in order to exalt the republican institutions of Florence. He suggests that Bruni was merely serving the cause for which he was arguing [. . .] since it cannot be truly maintained that Julius Caesar was the parricide of the Roman republic. After all, Salutati had himself defended Caesar from this charge in his *De tyranno*. The character Bruni does not respond to this assessment of his anti-Caesarean position in the *Laudatio*, but the *Dialogues* appear to contain the author Bruni's answer, for the historical and moral status of Julius Caesar is a central issue in Niccoli's defense of Dante.

In the first dialogue, Niccoli's most serious criticism of Dante had focused upon *Inferno* 34 and the placement of Marcus Brutus – who should be praised to the heavens for his assassination of the tyrant Caesar – in the mouth of Satan. When Niccoli turns around and defends Dante in the second dialogue, he contends that the poet's fiction should be read allegorically: Caesar symbolizes there the just earthly monarch, while Brutus personifies the seditious, evil-minded man who criminally kills him. But, Niccoli asserts, Dante surely knew that the *historical* Caesar and Brutus were neither of these things.

[. . .]

> But do you think that Dante, the most learned of all men of his age, was ignorant of the means by which Caesar had acquired his power? That he was ignorant of how liberty was destroyed and how, to the groans of the Roman people, a crown was placed on the head of Caesar by Mark Antony? Do you believe that he was ignorant of the great virtue with which all histories agree that Brutus was endowed? For who does not praise his justice, integrity, industry, and greatness of soul? Dante was not ignorant of this, no.

Certainly, Niccoli contends, Dante was aware of the true nature of Caesar and Brutus, upon which everyone agrees – everyone, that is, except for Salutati, who, in the fifth chapter of the *De tyranno*, argues "That Dante was Right in Placing Brutus and Cassius in Lowest Hell as Traitors of the Deepest Dye." Niccoli flatly contradicts Salutati's assertion earlier in the dialogue that Caesar was not a wicked ruler and indeed should be the object of unending praise – a statement which is itself an answer to Bruni's charges against Caesar in the *Laudatio*. By reaffirming those charges, moreover, Niccoli suggests that only ignorance of the classical sources – one should note the repetition "ignorasse . . . ignorasse . . . ignarum . . . ignoravit" – could make one advocate the cause of Caesar. Surely Dante, the "most learned of all men of his age," did not share such ignorance. Or did he? Niccoli may protest too much and this seeming defense of Dante may insinuate that the poet was the victim of the deficiencies of classical learning in his age, the deficiencies which Niccoli had attacked in the first dialogue.

In fact, Niccoli is not entirely satisfied with his allegorical reading and offers a second explanation of Dante's treatment of Brutus. There do exist, he admits, authors who attack Brutus for impiety either from party allegiances ("affectionem illarum partium") or to please the emperors. Salutati had accused Bruni of defaming Caesar in the *Laudatio* in order to praise Florence and her Guelph, anti-imperial traditions. Now Niccoli rejoins that a pro-Caesarian position – such as the one upheld in the *Commedia* and in Salutati's own *De tyranno* – could indicate a monarchical bias. Here again, the *Dialogues* group Salutati together with the *trecento* writers he praises in order that the new humanist generation of Niccoli – and here, it appears, of Bruni, too – can define itself in opposition to them. If one does not accept the rather far-fetched allegorization of *Inferno* 34 by which Niccoli seeks to argue away Dante's notorious, historically documented monarchical politics, then the poet is guilty – along with Salutati – of upholding a misguided view of Caesar, because of his and his age's ignorance, because of pro-imperial political sympathies, or, most probably, because of a combination of the two.

Because the attack on Dante's imperialism continues in both of the *Dialogues*, it is difficult to agree with Baron's contention that Bruni underwent a political conversion between the first dialogue and the second. But Baron was surely correct to identify the work as a republican document: Bruni explicitly aligns himself with Niccoli's criticism of Caesar and of pro-Caesarian sympathizers. This republicanism should not be dismissed as just so much classicizing rhetoric, but is an example of how humanism in Florence shaped itself to provide a civic ideology for the ruling circles of the city [. . .] Within the *Dialogues* themselves, republican ideology becomes one further issue dividing the younger humanist generation of Niccoli and Bruni from the older generation of Salutati.

By its very reliance on allegory, moreover, Niccoli's defense may draw one final distinction between the two humanist generations. In the first dialogue, Niccoli's criticisms of Dante – not only of the punishment which the poet allots to Brutus, but also of his depiction of Cato as an old man and of his mistranslation of "Quid non mortalia pectora, cogis auri sacra fames" – proceed according to what Garin has called a "historico-philological" method of reading, the invention and authentically revolutionary component of the humanists' cultural movement. The historical Niccoli was particularly identified with this method; in his hands it apparently assumed a drastically reduced or intolerantly "purist" form, restricted to painstaking textual emendations. The Niccoli whom Bruni depicts finds it impossible to refute his own criticism of Dante on the same philological grounds on which they were made. He is required to allegorize Dante's poem, indeed the appropriate method for reading much of the *Commedia*, but one which ties its poet to an older medieval mode of thought. And perhaps not just the poet, but his supporters as well: the historical Salutati's "addiction to allegory" in the *De laboribus Herculis* has well been characterized by Berthold Ullman. The allegory by which Niccoli defends Dante may constitute one more of the cultural traditions of the *trecento* with which Salutati still identifies but which the younger humanists criticize and seek to replace.

Niccoli's ensuing defense of Petrarch is more lighthearted in tone. Responding, it seems, to an imaginary critic who voices the very complaint that Niccoli had himself made against Petrarch in the first dialogue – that Petrarch's *Bucolicon carmen* has nothing redolent of pastoral in it – Niccoli begs to disagree [. . .] It is the carping critic who is stuffed with shepherds and sheep, a rustic ignoramus. The assembled company laughs ("Hic cum omnes arriderent . . .") at Niccoli's turning of the tables upon himself or, as he quickly explains, upon certain very stupid men whose arguments he had used, and feigned to believe in, the day before.

Niccoli continues to jest at the conclusion of his discussion of Petrarch. As Baron has documented, it became a commonplace for praisers of Petrarch in the *trecento* and *quattrocento* to point out his versatility: he excelled in Latin both as a poet and as a writer of prose. Seneca the Elder (*Controversiae* 3. Prologue 8) had discussed how difficult it is for literary genius to flourish in more than one genre: Cicero's skill left him when he turned to verse, Virgil's Muse similarly deserted him when he wrote in prose. In a letter of 1379 to Giovanni Bartolomei, Salutati had contended that even if Petrarch were surpassed by Virgil in the writing of verse, he would still outstrip Virgil because of his prose works, since, Salutati rather curiously argues, prose is a more dignified literary form than poetry, to which it bears the same relationship that a sea does to a river. He further maintains that Petrarch's prose is the equal of Cicero's and that Petrarch surpassed Cicero as a poet. Thus Petrarch is inferior to neither Virgil nor Cicero. Bruni's Niccoli alludes to this letter, which was well-known and often appended to codices of Petrarch's works in the last decades of the *trecento*, when he states that Petrarch was the equal of the most famous poets and the best orators. But he ends his praise of Petrarch with a peculiar variation upon that familiar critical formula.

[. . .]

so that I say that I would far prefer one of Petrarch's orations to all of Virgil's letters, and the poems of Petrarch to all of Cicero's verse.

Now this is not at all what Salutati had written: Petrarch is praised over Virgil and Cicero only in the literary forms in which they neither excelled nor staked their fame. E. H. Gombrich rightly calls Niccoli's concluding remark a "malicious joke" and "a very back-handed retraction." The target of Niccoli's wit has shifted from Petrarch's critics back to Petrarch. Moreover, his joke is as much at Salutati's expense as at Petrarch's.

Niccoli's defenses of Dante and Petrarch, then, both contain passages that continue, rather than refute, his earlier attacks upon the *trecento* poets. They also both contain not-so-veiled attacks on individual writings of Salutati, the *De tyranno* and the *Letter to Bartolomei*, and they thus extend the conflict between the humanist generations of Salutati and Niccoli which emerges as a continuous thread uniting the *Dialogues*. In *both* dialogues, Niccoli defines the views and aspirations of the new generation in contrast to those of the old. Linking Salutati to the writers of the Florentine *trecento*, he criticizes both for their complacent belief in their cultural continuity with the culture of classical antiquity, for what is, in fact, their lack of a sound grounding in classical culture (and Latinity), for the self-assurance and even arrogance with which they write, for their old-fashioned allegorical thought, for their imperial political sympathies. By contrast, Niccoli's own culture is staunchly republican, rigorously historicist and classicizing in outlook, so much so that it recognizes its own historical separation from antiquity, and is humbled before a classical culture whose standards it despairs ever of attaining. While the glib Salutati may confidently urge his younger friends to literary creativity, they prefer to remain in embarrassed silence rather than join a Florentine tradition from which they are alienated. At the close of the second dialogue, Niccoli sums up the position he has been developing through both days of discussion.

[. . .]

> especially since I in no way deceive myself – but I know well enough both who I am and what abilities I have. For when I read those ancient authors whom you just mentioned (which, when my affairs allow me to, I do most gladly), when I consider their wisdom and eloquence, I am so far from thinking that I know anything, recognizing the weakness of my own genius, that it seems not even the loftiest geniuses can learn anything in these unfortunate times. But the more difficult I think it, the more I admire the Florentine poets, who, by some superabundance of genius, succeeded, even against the opposition of their times, in emerging as equal or superior to those ancients.

However Niccoli's recantation is read, it is clear that he returns here to the opinions he had expressed in the first dialogue. The Florentine triumvirate are now praised for their more than human geniuses which allowed them to overcome the limitations of their age – they stand out as exceptional geniuses in the same way that Niccoli had singled out Salutati in the first dialogue [. . .]

Where does the author Bruni stand behind the words of his characters? The dialogue form prevents the reader from assigning him a fixed position – although this has not stopped virtually all of the *Dialogues'* critics from wishing to see Bruni coming down on the side of the Niccoli of the second dialogue, the oestensible vindicator of Dante and Petrarch [. . .] Yet, as I have argued above, that praise is deeply qualified by Niccoli's other remarks which continue, rather than counter, his attack upon the *trecento* writers in the first dialogue. In that first dialogue, the character Bruni explicitly aligns himself with Niccoli against Salutati: his cause, he says, no less than Niccoli's is being pleaded in the discussion [. . .] In the second, Salutati's attack on the treatment of Caesar in the *Laudatio* again seems to put Bruni and Niccoli in the same camp: the younger humanist generation pitted against the fatherly elder statesman.

[. . .]

[T]he evidence of the *Dialogues* suggests a younger Bruni fascinated by a Niccoli who, from his position of privilege, inveighs against not only past humanist tradition but the very idea of a humanist Renaissance. Simply by virtue of the fact that he does the bulk of the talking in the *Dialogues*, Niccoli becomes their central character and "hero," and it is his violent, eccentric position which accounts for the real and enduring interest of Bruni's work. Niccoli's dissenting voice, the self-critical byproduct of humanism which the humanist community does its best to domesticate and contain, even to coerce into an apparent recantation, is the voice of a peculiarly modern consciousness, of the division of that consciousness against its own condition of modernity. In Bruni's *Dialogues*, perhaps for the first time, this new voice, troubling but insistent, becomes fully articulate.

Editor's Notes

1   young men
2   But I heard many things from him; I learned many things; many things too about
     which I was doubtful were confirmed for me by the authority of that man.
3   He very often professed not only their opinions and maxims but also their words
     in such a way that he seemed not to be quoting but expressing himself.
4   Do we not see how our times have been deprived of the ample and exquisite
     patrimony [of antiquity]?
5   bard

Chapter 12

Nicolai Rubinstein

■   from **FLORENTINE CONSTITUTIONALISM
AND MEDICI ASCENDANCY IN THE FIFTEENTH
CENTURY**, in *Florentine Studies. Politics and Society in
Renaissance Florence*, ed. N. Rubinstein, London, 1968,
pp. 442–462

W HEN, AT THE BEGINNING OF the fifteenth century, Leonardo
Bruni analysed, in his *Laudatio Florentinae urbis*, the basic principles of the
Florentine constitution, he introduced a new concept into the political literature
of Florence [. . .]

The value of this analysis for us depends largely on the extent to which it can
be considered a faithful expression of contemporary political thinking.

Dr Baron, in his detailed discussion of the *Laudatio*, has rightly rejected the
view that Bruni was "ready . . . to sacrifice the substance of things to eloquence."
The question remains to what extent Bruni's accounts were affected by the rhetorical topos of *amplificatio*; in a letter to Francesco Pizolpasso he explicitly justifies
his panegyric on Florence by pointing out that, unlike history, "laudatio . . . multa
supra veritatem extollit."[1] Moreover, in his analysis of the Florentine constitution,
Bruni is influenced by Aristotle and Cicero. The use of classical political philosophy could help him to arrive at a sharpened awareness of contemporary conditions
and problems, but it could also have the effect of forcing these into a schematic
theoretical framework. Before taking Bruni's judgements on the Florentine constitution at their face value as expressions of contemporary political thought, it is
therefore advisable to corroborate them by additional evidence.

Bruni's earliest attempt to analyse the Florentine constitution occurs, as we
have seen, in his *Laudatio*. About ten years later, he sent Sigismund, king of the
Romans, a brief description of the political institutions of Florence; and he returned
to this subject in his Greek treatise *On the Florentine Polity*, which he appears to
have written at the time of the Council of Florence in 1439. There are some
important differences between these three works. While in the *Laudatio* classical
influence is still limited to Roman authors, the "letter to the Emperor" and the
treatise *On the Florentine Polity* show Bruni's attempt to apply Aristotle's classification of constitutions to Florence. The Greek treatise is the fullest and
best-informed of the three accounts, which may largely be due to Bruni's having

been for many years Florentine chancellor when he wrote it. It also contains some subtle changes that may reflect political developments after Cosimo de' Medici's return from exile in 1434. But despite such differences, Bruni's interpretation of the nature of Florentine government remains basically the same throughout these three works. Its two basic principles, according to the *Laudatio*, are *ius*[2] and *libertas*; "towards these two joined together all institutions and laws of the republic are directed as towards a constellation and port." In his *History of the Florentine People*, he makes Giano della Bella say that *libertas populi*[3] is contained in two things, *legibus atque iudiciis*;[4] whenever these are more powerful than single citizens, liberty is preserved. Justice, he says in the *Laudatio*, is equal for all, rich as well as poor, and it is this "justice and equality" which produces *humanitas* among the citizens. Also in the "letter to the Emperor" he stresses equality, *paritas et equalitas*, towards which all Florentine laws are directed; in it, he says, consists true liberty. But here he gives equality an additional political meaning. In order to prevent the oppression of one class by another, the Magnate families are excluded from government and placed under specially severe legislation: for the Florentine laws aim at reducing the pre-eminence (*supereminentiam*) of individual citizens to the level of equality and the mean (*paritatem mediocritatemque*). The supreme authority in the State is vested not in one citizen, but in a magistracy of nine, the Signoria, whose term of office is limited to two months: in this way, the government is prevented from becoming tyrannical and from being used as an instrument of private ambition. Its power is further limited by the need to seek the consent of the Colleges (i.e. the Twelve Good Men and the Sixteen Gonfaloniers of Companies) and of the legislative councils for all the more important decisions; for, as Bruni says in the *Laudatio*, what concerns the many must be decided by the many. "In this way, freedom reigns and justice is preserved most scrupulously, as nothing can be achieved by the covetousness of single citizens against the will of so many men."

These safeguards against autocratic power are no longer mentioned in Bruni's last political treatise. By 1439, Cosimo de' Medici's ascendancy had been established for over four years, and although by no means as yet fully consolidated – in January 1441 the electoral controls introduced in 1434 were in fact abolished – there was clearly a case for the chancellor of the Florentine republic and protégé of Cosimo's not to harp too much on the suppression of autocratic tendencies. At the same time, there is no indication whatsoever in Bruni's last treatise on politics that the letter and spirit of the Florentine constitution had been changed by the rise to power of Cosimo; it is probable that in 1439 Bruni did not consider the Medicean electoral controls a lasting innovation. If anything, his last political treatise gives a more faithful analysis than his previous writings of the oligarchical régime which had prevailed before 1434, and which was in fact to survive to a large extent under Cosimo.

Political equality, according to Bruni, is, however, not only ensured, in a negative manner, by checking excessive power. In a positive way, equality means that the citizens are able to participate on equal terms in the government of the republic. He stresses this positive aspect of the concept of equality in his funeral oration on Nanni Strozzi of 1428: "Liberty is equal for all, subject only to law . . . The hope of attaining public office and of rising to higher status is equal for all . . ." This equality of opportunity serves as a powerful stimulus for intellectual and economic advance: "It is wonderful how this opportunity to attain office, as enjoyed by a free people . . . helps its citizens to awaken their natural abilities. . ."

In the "letter to the Emperor," Bruni uses Aristotle's constitutional classification to describe the Florentine constitution as *popularis* or democratic. Regard for the feelings of his addressee must have prevented him from affirming, as he does in the funeral oration on Nanni Strozzi, that of the three "legitimate" forms of government, this was the only one in which there was true liberty and equality before the law. In his Greek treatise, on the other hand, he describes the Florentine constitution no longer as a democracy, but as a mixture of democratic and aristocratic elements; in brief, as a mixed constitution on the Aristotelian pattern. The short terms of offices of the highest Florentine magistracies, as well as their appointment by lot, were, according to Bruni, democratic; that new laws had first to be approved by a small body of citizens before being presented to the councils, and that these had neither the right to initiate or to amend legislation, he considered, on the contrary, to be an aristocratic feature. Again, the exclusion of some of the greatest Florentine families from government was in his view democratic; but that men of the lowest social rank shared their fate was aristocratic: "shunning extremes," he adds in the vein of his earlier treatises, "this city prefers men of the middle condition." However, while mixed of democratic and aristocratic elements, the latter prevail over the former: on balance, the Florentine constitution has an aristocratic or oligarchical rather than a democratic slant. Yet just as *mediocritas* remains a basic principle of that constitution, so do liberty and equality: the short terms of office of the government and its Colleges aim at equality and liberty, "which we worship and guard as the end and goal of the entire constitution." Once more, then, we find these two notions singled out as cornerstones of the Florentine form of government.

Bruni was not alone in defining them in legal as well as political terms. The same interaction of freedom and equality in the Florentine constitution is also affirmed by Poggio, in a letter of 1438 to the Duke of Milan, with whom Florence was then at war: "neither individual citizens nor the aristocrats rule the city, but the entire people are admitted with equal right (*aequo iure*) to public offices; as a result of which high and low, noble and non-noble, rich and poor alike are united in the service of liberty, for whose preservation they do not shun any expenses, or fear any labours. . ."

As Dr Baron has pointed out, Bruni was the first to attempt an analysis of the Florentine institutions that showed their interaction and unity. He was also the first to use Aristotle's *Politics* for an enquiry into the nature of the Florentine constitution. It was hardly by accident that he probably wrote his treatise on the Florentine Polity shortly after completing, in 1438, his translation of the *Politics*.

But Aristotle was not the only source of his interpretation of Florentine political institutions; Cicero and the Roman historians provided him, as well as Salutati and Poggio, with ample evidence for the Roman concepts of *libertas*, *aequalitas* and *ius*. Thus when we read in Bruni's panegyric on Florence that *libertas* and *ius*, "simul coniuncta,"[5] represent the ultimate goal of all her institutions, we may remember that for the Romans, "the very existence of *libertas* depended on the rule of law." In his "letter to the Emperor," Bruni describes that goal as *paritas* and equality, "in which true liberty consists"; for the Roman republicans *libertas*, *ius* and *aequalitas* were closely connected concepts, and Cicero identified *aequa libertas* with *aequum ius*. Moreover, the different shades of meaning which were present in the Roman notions of *aequa libertas* and *aequum ius* are present also in the humanist adaptations of these notions to make them fit Florentine institutions: while in the *Laudatio* Bruni stresses equality before the law as an outstanding characteristic of Florentine freedom, in his later writings he discusses *aequalitas*, *libertas* and *aequum ius* in terms of fundamental political rights, as well as of law that was equally binding on all classes, and so does Poggio. At the same time, Bruni's analysis of the Florentine government as a mixed constitution, in which conflicting interests balance each other, but with the balance tilted towards the upper class, although derived from Aristotle, may also reflect his knowledge of the "contentio libertatis dignitatisque," the conflict between freedom and social status, under the Roman Republic, and of the attempts to find a solution for it. Similarly, if Bruni considers collegiate government and short terms of office guarantees of republican liberty against autocracy, so did Livy.

But while drawing on his knowledge of classical history and philosophy, Bruni also echoes Florentine political ideas that we can trace back to the fourteenth century and beyond. Above all else, the idea of liberty was deeply rooted in the political traditions of the Florentine republic. An ambivalent concept, for it was used by the Florentines, often simultaneously, with the meaning of republican freedom at home and of independence from foreign rule, its republican connotation was thrown into fresh relief by the two episodes of despotic rule which Florence experienced during the fourteenth century. Both the rule of Charles of Calabria from 1325 to 1328 and that of Walter of Brienne from 1342 to 1343 were followed by sharp republican reactions. In July 1329, the councils passed a law to the effect that the city must never submit to the autocratic rule of one man, "since liberty is called a celestial good which surpasses all the wealth of this world." After the expulsion of the Duke of Athens in 1343 the Florentine Signoria informed the Pope that although the Duke had sworn to preserve Florence *in libertate*, that is "in solito et consueto officiorum regimine,"[6] he had in fact usurped tyrannical power. Moreover, the conviction that their city owed her greatness to her republican liberty came to the Florentines easily enough. Thus Cino Rinuccini affirms, in about 1400, that in Italy republics are greater than despotic states. In the same vein, a speaker in a *pratica* of 1424 could say that "liberty makes cities and citizens great."

In innumerable State letters, written during the wars Florence fought first with the Papacy (1375–78) and then with Giangaleazzo Visconti of Milan (1390–1402), as well as in his *Invectiva* against the Milanese Chancellor Antonio Loschi, the first humanist head of the Florentine Chancery, Coluccio Salutati, used the vocabulary of the New Learning to praise Florentine liberty, but did not make any substantial addition to its definition in terms of political philosophy or constitutional analysis. This was left to his disciple Bruni, who was also the first to see the political implications of the new theory on the Roman origins of Florence, according to which the city had been founded not, as was the traditional belief, by Caesar, but before Rome had become subject to the power of one man.

Just as Bruni's concept of Florentine liberty owes much to Florentine political traditions, so does his concept of equality. His view that equality is secured by curbing the pre-eminence of single great families, while specifically referring to the legislation against the Magnates, also reflects one of the basic themes of Florentine politics during the fourteenth century. Bruni follows traditional lines of thought in ignoring the contradiction between political and legal equality inherent in the special penal legislation against the Magnates; for if the Ordinances of Justice were designed to reduce the political power of that class in favour of greater political equality, they also deprived it of equality before the law. Such equality existed, at least in theory, within the new popular régime as created by the Ordinances of Justice; but political equality remained an ideal in a régime which was, apart from the period of more democratic government between 1343–82, dominated by the Greater Gilds. The short terms of office of the highest magistracies were devised to prevent the seizure of power by single families, but also helped to spread the distribution of offices more widely. They were supplemented, during the fourteenth century, by the introduction of elections by lot for the Signoria and other magistracies, and by the *divieto* legislation which temporarily disqualified citizens from offices which they or their relatives had held recently, as well as barring members of the same family from simultaneous membership of magistracies. *Divieto* laws stated explicitly as their purpose equality in the participation in government and administration; at the same time their application effectively prevented the great families from monopolizing power. The law introducing elections by lot in 1328 opens with the solemn declaration that public offices should be accessible to all those who by their way of life have been shown fit to hold them. Such citizens should be able "gradually to ascend to and to attain public office"; while "those whose life does not render them worthy of it, should not climb up to government posts." We are reminded of Bruni's praise of Florentine equality: "the hope of attaining public office and of rising to higher status is equal for all. . ."

However, Bruni omits an important aspect of the Florentine concept of equality, which was often combined with its political aspect, namely fiscal equality. "Aequalitas in honoribus et oneribus"[7] was a pious wish at a time when, in fact, crass inequalities in taxation existed. Bruni's omission is the more striking as the *Catasto* of 1427 was widely considered an important progress in this direction. "The usual cause of [civic] discord is the uncertain distribution of either offices or taxes," says a speaker in a *practica* in 1431; "now the taxes are well distributed there remain the defects in the distribution of offices." Perhaps Bruni did not believe that, despite of the *Catasto*, fiscal equality deserved to be praised, together with legal and political equality, as the characteristic of the Florentine constitution. He may have shared Matteo Palmieri's pessimistic view that in matters of taxation "true justice is impossible," but that, since civic unity so much depends on it, the least imperfect system, which treats the citizens in equal fashion, ought to be adopted.

Nor is this Bruni's only omission of this kind. He discusses the place of the councils in the Florentine constitution, but not the freedom of speech in them; and he does not mention the restriction of government affairs to the Palace of the Signoria. Republicans regarded both as basic principles of the city's constitution. A law of 1375 declares that nothing is more important for the preservation of liberty than freedom in debates; and the Statutes of 1415 guarantee freedom of speech in the councils: every councillor had the right "dicendi libere velle suum."[8]

Palmieri demands that "all counsel be free, true, and open," at a time when the nascent Medici régime was beginning to clamp down on that freedom. Giovanni Cavalcanti, writing in about 1440, states that he had prophesied as early as 1420 that a tyrannical government would replace the constitutional one, because the government of the republic was being carried on outside the Palace of the Signoria.

There is certainly no mention of such dangers in Bruni's treatise on the Florentine Polity, which in all probability was written about the same time. But to what extent was Bruni altogether describing existing political conditions, rather than political ideals? This is a question which may fairly be asked, although it is somewhat marginal to our present enquiry into the nature and sources of Florentine constitutionalism. We have discussed the influence of classical authors and of local traditions on Bruni's attempts to analyse the Florentine constitution; to what extent does he give a faithful picture of contemporary political realities? Equality, one of the key notions of this analysis, is a case in point.

Bruni was, of course, perfectly aware of its ambivalent nature and used it both in its political as well as in its legal meaning. While in the *Laudatio* he stresses the latter, in his subsequent writings he is primarily concerned with the former. "Liberty is equal for all . . . the hope of attaining public office . . . is equal for all, provided they possess industry and natural gifts. . ." In 1428, this was certainly wishful thinking.

For one thing, after the collapse of the Ciompi Revolt of 1378, the political inferiority of the Lesser Gilds had found its institutional expression in the fact that members of those gilds became eligible for only a quarter of the vacancies in nearly all magistracies. In the highest of all, the Signoria, two members only were artisans, the Gonfalonier of Justice being always a member of the greater gilds. But also for the citizens belonging to the predominant greater gilds, there was more than one way in which the ideal of political equality could be deprived of some of its practical meaning. The system of appointment by lot necessitated periodical scrutinies carried out by special commissions, which qualified citizens for specific categories of offices. After the scrutinies, *accoppiatori* filled the purses of the three highest offices with the name tickets of those citizens who had been successful in the scrutiny. These officials, whose functions were primarily of a technical nature, had considerable discretionary powers enabling them to give some citizens greater opportunities than others of having their name actually drawn. For the *polizza*, or name ticket, a citizen had acquired for the Signoria could either be placed in a purse for the Priorate, or in that of the Gonfalonier of Justice, that is of the highest official in the State. Moreover, ever since 1387, there were two kinds of purses for the eight Priors, the so-called general purse and the little purse, the *borsellino*, which contained less names than the former, and the *accoppiatori*, in providing a citizen with a name-ticket for the Priorate, could choose between these two purses. Since the names of three of the eight Priors had to be drawn from the *borsellino*, such discrimination could have significant results in giving some citizens greater opportunities of being actually appointed to office.

Furthermore, while the scrutinies for the three highest offices formed the basis for the appointment to government, they could also be used for other purposes. Thus, the membership of the Council of 200, which was created in 1411, was recruited from the citizens who had either been appointed to those offices, i.e.

the Signoria and its Colleges, or whose names had been drawn for them, but who had been temporarily barred from accepting the office in question by having such disqualifications as having held it recently (*seduti o veduti*). In this way a distinction emerged among the theoretically equal citizens, between those who had been qualified for the highest magistracies and those who had not; a distinction which, in view of its evident political implications, was to become increasingly important under the Medici.

These practical limitations of the fundamental *aequalitas* of Florentine constitutionalist theory have their counterpart in the *de facto* prominence of the patriciate before 1434. This prominence was not limited to the greater opportunities the *ottimati* in fact enjoyed in being appointed to offices and councils. It was a Florentine custom for the government to ask the advice of specially summoned meetings (*pratiche*) of influential citizens before taking important decisions; and since it could summon any citizens it wished, patricians were heavily represented in these meetings. The same applies to the special councils with full powers which were created in revolutionary situations. One such *Balìa* recalled Cosimo de' Medici from exile in 1434; if we go through its membership list, we find that of the 86 households which had been assessed in the *Catasto* of 1427 for a capital of over 10,000 fl., 43 were represented in that council either by the taxpayers or by a brother or son.

In these circumstances, Bruni's claim that there existed in Florence a basic equality in attaining high public office can hardly be taken at its face value; as we have seen, he himself felt the need to modify it in his last treatise on the Florentine constitution, which consequently gives a more faithful picture of the political régime that prevailed in Florence before, as well as after, 1434. Yet whatever the historical veracity of Bruni's descriptions, and whatever the influence on them of rhetoric and classical learning, there can be no doubt that they also reflected traditional Florentine ideals. If these ideals were far from being realized before 1434, they were to stand an even more serious test under the Medici régime.

The humanist writings we have reviewed so far belong to the first four decades of the fifteenth century, when the traditional republican régime was either still intact, or was only just beginning to be transformed by the growing ascendancy of the Medici and their party. Our next comprehensive evidence on Florentine constitutionalist thought comes from the years 1464 and 1466, when that ascendancy was being successfully, though as it turned out only temporarily, challenged, after having been greatly consolidated in 1458. That this should be so, is perhaps not surprising: constitutionalist ideas are often formulated in opposition to prevailing trends [. . .]

The oath which about 400 citizens swore on 27 May 1466 contains the political programme of the opposition to Medici rule: "the city is to be ruled in the customary way by a just and popular government, the Signoria is to be elected by lot in future, as it is nowadays, and in no other way, and the citizens should not suffer any violence, so that they may be free to debate and judge public affairs . . ." Florentine constitutionalism in 1465–66, by linking the traditional principles of liberty and equality with elections by lot, and by emphasizing the importance of freedom of speech and of government by constitutional agencies, reflects the impact of the Medici régime on Florentine political attitudes. The views expressed by the members of the *pratiche* are accordingly more pragmatic than Bruni's theory of the Florentine constitution; however, they show the continued importance of classical constitutional theory on Florentine political thinking. Thus Agnolo Acciaiuoli pointed out that of the three forms of government, government by one, by a few, and by many, the last provides States with the greatest stability, "quia amore et benevolentia gubernantur."[9] When Niccolò Soderini proposed a reform that was bound to make Florentine government more oligarchical, one speaker argued that Florence had prospered under a democratic régime, a *popularis admin-istratio*, while another countered this by pointing out that according to Aristotle a *popularis administratio* was the lowest in rank of the constitutions. But it was a far cry from such occasional remarks to Bruni's attempt to analyse the Florentine constitution in Aristotelian terms. Florentine constitutionalism of 1465–66 has its roots in communal political traditions rather than in humanist writings. It is significant that speakers in the *pratiche* could look back to the good old days around 1418, when "Florence was at the height of her power and reputation," as an example of ideal Florentine government: in those days, civic virtues flourished and the Florentines preferred the common good to private interest, and thus increased and defended the Florentine empire. But if Florentine republicans were longing for the system of government which had prevailed before the Medici came to power, for many of them its oligarchical aspects were, no doubt, despite all the egalitarianism professed in the *Pratiche*, an additional attraction. This was clearly the deeper meaning of Niccolò Soderini's outburst, in a *practica* of July 1466, that "who has not governed before 1433, does not know how to govern."

The republican revival of 1465 was followed, in September 1466, by a Medicean reaction which not only restored the political controls of the régime that had been recently abolished, but further strengthened them; elections *a mano*[10] of the Signoria were now decreed for no less than twenty years. In 1478, the Pazzi conspiracy created yet another serious threat to the régime, but the unsuccessful attempt on Lorenzo's life was not followed, as the conspirators had hoped, by a popular rising, and there was no organized republican opposition as in 1465–66. However, the conspiracy had given rise to a situation in which at least one Florentine citizen was led to voice, once more, some of the principles of Florentine constitutionalism.

In his dialogue *De libertate* of 1479, Alamanno Rinuccini proceeds from a philosophical definition of liberty to a violent attack on Medici tyranny, which he contrasts with the good old times when republican freedom reigned in Florence longer and more splendidly than anywhere in Italy. Like Bruni, he considers freedom and equality the twin principles of good government: "who does not know," he says, "that the equality of the citizens is the chief foundation of liberty?" In emphasizing the legal aspects of equality, he follows the arguments of the *Laudatio* rather than of Bruni's later writings: observance of her laws had made Florence great and prosperous; now they are valued little, and Florentine justice, which was once sought from the furthest places, is a thing of the past. Yet Rinuccini does not altogether omit the political aspects of equality: in republics, he says, elections by lot make it possible for all those citizens who help the community by paying taxes to participate in government; such elections are accordingly most appropriate to liberty and justice. But now the highest magistracies are filled by simple election, with the result that instead of men distinguished by wisdom or

nobility, clients of the Medici are appointed. Rinuccini similarly contrasts the traditional freedom of speech with the present silence in the councils, as "our Catos
take the advice of a few men only"; yet that freedom "is of the greatest advantage
to free cities, where the citizens freely state what they consider best for the
commonwealth." We seem to hear the echoes of the debates of 1465–66; but their
optimism contrasts with Rinuccini's pessimistic belief that under Lorenzo de'
Medici things were going from bad to worse, their readiness for action with his
professed belief that withdrawal from public life was the only solution left to honest
citizens. For the last time under the Medici régime, Rinuccini states some of the
basic beliefs of Florentine constitutionalism: equality before the law, elections by
lot providing equal opportunities for all citizens, and freedom of speech. That his
concept of equality should have an oligarchical slant reflects a characteristic trend
in Florentine constitutionalist thought. And like Manno Temperani in 1466, he
looks back, nostalgically, to the good old days before the rise of the Medici, when
the citizens cared so much for the preservation of liberty and equality, and when
Florence excelled all other cities in Tuscany not only because of her power but
also as an exemplar of good life, "bene vivendi exemplar."

Fifteen years later, the Medici were expelled from Florence. On 2 December
1494, a *Parlamento* restored the republican constitution in the form which had
prevailed before 1434. But while republican liberty could thus be considered
revived, political equality became, almost immediately, a central problem of constitutional legislation. As we have seen, the concept of equality had been subject to
democratic as well as oligarchical interpretations. Under the influence and leadership of Savonarola, it assumed a decidedly democratic slant. The reaction against
the conservative reform of 2 December led, three weeks later, to the creation of
the Great Council, which placed the government of Florence on a broader foundation than it had ever possessed. The official reform scheme which had proposed
a Great Council, and which was finally adopted, pleads for a fundamental change
on the grounds that "tyranny is now defunct and that every one desires liberty and
equality and stability." It thus voices, once more, although with a fresh meaning,
constitutionalist principles that had survived the Medici régime.

Editor's Notes

1   panegyric greatly exceeds truth
2   justice
3   the freedom of the people
4   laws and judgements
5   joined together
6   in the usual and customary rule of magistracies
7   Equality in offices and taxes
8   of freely declaring his wishes
9   since they are governed by love and goodwill
10   by hand, that is, by direct intervention of the *accoppiatori*, who were political
     figures entrusted with pre-selecting a shortlist of suitable candidates for public
     office from a large number of formally qualified potential office-holders.

Chapter 13

Alison Brown

■   from **THE HUMANIST PORTRAIT OF COSIMO DE' MEDICI, PATER PATRIAE**, *Journal of the Warburg and Courtauld Institutes*, 24 (1961), pp. 186–214

HONOURED BY HIS FELLOW-CITIZENS as Pater Patriae of Florence and condemned by Pius II as her paramour, the figure of Cosimo de' Medici still remains enigmatic. For although he was eulogized by the humanists as *princeps* of the republic and given the title of Pater Patriae on his death, Florentine chronicles are strangely silent about his political role in the city and rarely mention his name after his return from exile in 1434 until his death thirty years later.

No serious attempt was made to appraise his political position in the city until the following century. The histories which were then written, however, in many ways differed little from the panegyrics of the humanists, and Machiavelli, whose description of Cosimo was the source of so much that was later written about him, actually cautioned his readers not to be surprised if in describing Cosimo's life he had "imitated those who write the lives of princes instead of those who write universal histories." Despite Leonardo Bruni's dictum *aliud est historia, aliud laudatio*,[1] it is difficult to draw a clear dividing line between humanist eulogies and histories, and for this reason the writings in which Cosimo was praised during his lifetime, although they made no claim to be histories, are nevertheless important as contemporary evidence of how the Florentines idealized Cosimo and interpreted his role in the republic.

These writings fall into four fairly well defined categories: prefaces to translations dedicated to Cosimo; letters of consolation; orations written for public delivery; and poetic elegies and epigrams. Each one of these types of writing is to be found in the *Collectiones Cosmianae*, a codex of writings in praise of Cosimo in the Biblioteca Laurenziana in Florence upon which this study of the humanist portrait of Cosimo is largely based. It was compiled by Bartolommeo Scala, who lived in the Medici house until Cosimo's death and later became Chancellor of Florence, and was sent to Lorenzo de' Medici some time after the death of Cosimo with the following prefatory note: "I have collected, dearest Lorenzo, many writings and almost all of those I came across in which the name of Cosimo, your grandfather, father of this city, may be read. I have gathered them together in the book which I am now sending to you." The collection contains prefaces and letters of famous humanists which are already well known and other less well-known and mainly unpublished letters, eulogies and poems, all of which, although important in themselves, are given increased importance by being brought together into a memorial volume to serve, like a history, as evidence of Cosimo's greatness.

The close relationship of these writings with the fifteenth-century revival of classical literature needs no emphasis, for at this time the Italian humanists were recovering and translating not only models of each of the four types of writing mentioned above, but also classical handbooks on rhetoric, teaching the concept of an epideictic literature whose sole purpose was to please, which made possible the development of eulogistic writing in Italy. Cosimo was first described in this epideictic type of literature closely influenced by classical models, and emerged not surprisingly in classical guise, as a statesman of ancient Greece or Rome. What is far more surprising is that although the humanists possessed models of classical panegyrics to imitate (Pliny's *Panegyricon*, for instance, was discovered by Aurispa in 1433), it was not until after the middle of the fifteenth century that any Florentine addressed an open panegyric to Cosimo.

Just as remarkable as their restraint was the consistency with which they praised him, for in his lifetime Cosimo was praised first as a Roman republican statesman whose greatest virtues were practical and patriotic; later as an Aristotelian philosopher-ruler who "governing the Republic attained to philosophy and philosophizing governed the Republic"; and at the same time, though by a different class of men, as a generous Maecenas and Augustan ruler. These three traditions of praise were never confused or merged in Cosimo's lifetime, but were developed independently with notable consistency and, I think, sincerity. So while insisting on its classical and rhetorical origins, it is also necessary to stress the restraint and consistency of the humanists' portrait of Cosimo which make it possible to describe it as it developed in three different, coherent literary traditions.

Cosimo was first praised as a practical republican statesman by famous humanists like Leonardo Bruni and Poggio Bracciolini, *littérateurs* rather than politicians, whose praise of Cosimo was intimately connected with their work of recovering and translating classical texts. The earliest writing in his praise was the preface to a translation, which as a form of writing was inevitably limited both in scope and style. In Bruni's preface to his translation of ps [eudo]-Aristotle's *Economics* dealing with the administration of family affairs, which he sent to Cosimo in 1420, Cosimo is described in terms of his wealth, as head of a prosperous merchant family. But by the time of his next preface to Cosimo (in 1427, accompanying his translation of Plato's *Letters*) the emphasis has changed; riches are no longer praised as "both an ornament to those who possess them and a means of practising virtue" but are dismissed as "nec animi neque corporis bona,"[2] and Bruni extols instead the virtues of the mind, advising Cosimo to remember Plato's words, "especially those concerning the republic."

Bruni's terms of praise were, of course, largely imposed on him by the subject of the translation he was sending to Cosimo, but one may well wonder whether his change of emphasis from private family virtues to public political virtues does not reflect Cosimo's increasing authority in the city. By the time of the next writings to be addressed to Cosimo some six or more years later, during and after his return from exile, his role as a leading republican statesman in Florence is unambiguously stated. The most important of these are Poggio Bracciolini's letters of consolation and congratulation to Cosimo on his exile and return and the prefaces of Lapo da Castiglionchio and Antonio Pacini to their translations of Plutarch's *Lives of Themistocles* and *Timoleon*, in which the events of 1433–34 in Florence are translated into terms of Greek and Roman history.

In his letter of consolation to Cosimo on his exile in 1433 Poggio likened Cosimo's fate to that of famous Romans like Furius Camillus, Scipio Africanus, Publius Rutilius and Cicero, all of whom had been exiled from their native city, and when Cosimo returned to Florence a year later Poggio sent him a letter of congratulation in which he praised him as unequalled in past or present times for being recalled to his country without any initiative on his own part and, unlike Cicero, for being rewarded on his return with increased dignities: in order to recall him, he said, the supreme magistracy was of one accord; the state took up arms; the people were summoned to a meeting and came; and a plebiscite was formed "de summo imperio creando"[3] (an event which happened only in very important and difficult times), Cosimo and his brother being recalled to Florence on the Roman cry of "pax et otium."[4]

Following closely this interpretation of Cosimo's exile and return, Lapo da Castilionchio and Antonio Pacini also described Cosimo in a classical role in prefaces to their translations from Plutarch's *Lives*, a work engaging the attention of nearly all the leading humanists of the time, upon whom its influence must have been considerable. Obvious precedents for Cosimo's return were offered by Aristides and Furius Camillus who also survived exile to return in glory to their native cities, and Lapo in his preface to the *Life of Themistocles* praised Cosimo for accepting exile as they had done and like them being recalled by his citizens as a reward for the constancy and wisdom he had shown in exile. Antonio Pacini of Todi, too, praised Cosimo in his preface to the *Life of Timoleon* "as if he had been born at Rome or Athens" and described how he returned from exile with the favour of all good citizens and incredible popular support, all those who had acted against him being exiled and the names of those believed to be hostile to him destroyed by the senate and the magistrates.

In all these writings Cosimo was praised for defending the liberty of Florence and suffering exile in the interests of his country, for which he was rewarded by recall and honours greater than any he had previously enjoyed, a portrait of selfless patriotism which recurs in all the other writings addressed to Cosimo in this period. In the year of Poggio's Consolation to Cosimo on his exile, Carlo Marsuppini sent him and his brother Lorenzo a letter of consolation on the death of their mother, Piccarda Bueri. Like the writings already discussed, this letter was also strongly influenced by classical models to which it adhered too closely to have much original literary value, but it provides further evidence of the consistency with which Cosimo was being idealized in the role of a Roman republican statesman, praising him for his "gravity, skill and prudence" in governing the republic and for his patriotism in always acting in its best interests. Ambrogio Traversari, another and very important member of this early circle of Florentine humanists, also praised Cosimo for the same virtues, and in a letter to Niccolò Niccoli after Cosimo had ceased to serve on the magistracy of the Dieci mourned Cosimo's departure as a great public loss to the city, for while he had served them, he had brought nothing but good to Florence: he was generous and helped the fallen, was vigilant and industrious. "Would we had more such citizens," he concluded, "for never was a republic more happy and prosperous."

At the beginning of the next decade, in 1440, Antonio Pacini's funeral oration on the death of Lorenzo de' Medici praised Cosimo and his brother again as famous Roman statesmen who always acted to defend the liberty of their country. There is little new in Pacini's comparison of Lorenzo's humanity or liberality with that of Scipio or Caesar, but what is novel is his suggestion that if Camillus or Cicero deserved to be called Patres Patriae by the Romans, then why not Lorenzo, who like them had expelled the enemy from the gates of his city at a time of extreme danger. In the very same year a similar idea was expressed by Francesco Filelfo in a letter appealing to Cosimo to recall the exiles to Florence, in which he promised Cosimo that "if you prefer to restore the exiled citizens to their *patria* instead of awaiting with such determination for them to restore their *patria* to its ancient liberty and dignity, then you will most certainly, with no opposition, be called *princeps* of the republic and Pater Patriae, then all will honour you, all admire you." Cosimo did not recall him and so laid himself open to being vilified by Filelfo as a tyrant, upstart and evil-liver, but Filelfo's letter is important because, together with Pacini's oration, it provides evidence that in rhetorical humanist writings Cosimo and his brother were being discussed as Patres Patriae twenty-four years before this title was formally bestowed on Cosimo.

The early humanists' idealization of Cosimo as a Roman statesman is closely related to the first humanist histories of Florence, for they were both inspired by the same patriotism and republican pride. Bruni said his intention in writing his *History of Florence* was to rescue present times from the obscurity in which they lay, and it was with the same cry of "let us celebrate our famous citizens like the Ancients to restore glory to our age" that Benedetto Accolti and Vespasiano da Bisticci later wrote their *Lives* of famous Italians. This is the context in which Cosimo was first praised, and long before he was eulogized in his own right he was being called "another Aristides" or "another Cato" by patriotic Florentines and described as her Pater Patriae at the same time as Bruni was given the role of the Florentine Livy in the literary battle for prestige with the Ancients.

The patriotism of the early humanists was inherited by their successors in Florence[5] [. . .] and with it their tradition of eulogizing Cosimo; for in this later period Cosimo was praised like Poggio and Bruni as an exemplar of the greatness of Florence. Before Argyropoulos arrived in Florence, Alamanno Rinuccini had written to him in praise of the city to which he was coming as "inferior to none in Italy in beauty and charm," and seven years after his arrival there Donato Acciaiuoli wrote a glowing eulogy of his city to Alonso da Palencia on behalf of Vespasiano da Bisticci. In this letter he told Alonso that at no time would Florence give more pleasure than at present, for the study of letters was flourishing under the teaching of Argyropoulos; her young citizens were most learned; and the city was daily made more beautiful by buildings constructed by her citizens. He continued: "Cosimo himself, a most famous man, builds now private homes, now sacred buildings, now monasteries, inside and outside the city, at such expense that they seem to equal the magnificence of ancient kings or emperors." Note that Donato praises Cosimo not in his own right but for his contribution towards embellishing his *patria*, and some years later Alamanno Rinuccini when writing to Federigo of Urbino in praise of Florence included Cosimo in his list of exemplars of men who in his time were "so excellent in the different kinds of arts and disciplines that they can be compared with the ancients."

It was in exactly the same context that Benedetto Accolti praised Cosimo in his *Dialogus de praestantia virorum sui aevi*, written probably about 1460. For although Cosimo was given a place of undoubted supremacy among the protagonists of the *Dialogus* (which was dedicated to him) and praised more extravagantly than in any of the writings so far discussed, yet the context of the praise remains the same and Accolti, who as we have already seen wrote his book in order to defend the glory of present times, bestowed his highest praise on Cosimo by calling him "inter praeclaros veteres togatos cives pari gradu esse annumerandum, et illis forsitan merito antepondendum."[6]

The title of Pater Patriae which was awarded to Cosimo when he died, in accordance, we are told, with the custom of the ancients who similarly rewarded citizens deserving well of their country, is part of exactly the same republican tradition which for the past thirty years had been praising Cosimo as though he were a statesman of Greece or Rome. The orations of Donato Acciaiuoli and Alamanno Rinuccini conferring this title on Cosimo were inspired by the same republicanism as their earlier writings, for in them they praised him for his outstanding services to his *patria* and expressed the hope that in honouring him in this way they would create an exemplar to stimulate future generations to a ready defence of the liberty of Florence.

In form these orations differ little from the oration of Antonio Pacini of Todi written in 1440 on the death of Cosimo's brother, which also praised Cosimo and Lorenzo for their liberality and compared their help to Florence with that for which Cicero and Camillus had been called Patres Patriae; similar, too, to Andrea Alamanni's oration of the previous year, which he wrote to be delivered before the "patres conscripti" of the senate on the death of Cosimo's son Giovanni. Nor was there anything unusual in the custom of honouring Florentine citizens when they died: the deaths of both Bruni and Marsuppini were celebrated publicly by the Commune and both were awarded laurel wreaths "secondo l'antica consuetudine,"[7] and other private citizens seem to have been mourned with little less ceremony when they died. Cosimo himself left strict instructions that his death was to be celebrated with no pomp, and in the previous year he had not allowed his son's death to be celebrated in public, so the decision to confer on him the title of Pater Patriae was made after long discussion in despite of Cosimo's wishes and perhaps in recompense for them. Although this honour is unique in Florentine history as a reward to a private citizen for political greatness, too much importance need not be attributed to it, since it is closely paralleled by the literary honours bestowed on Bruni and Poggio when they died and owes as much as they did to the classical enthusiasm of the humanists; to their tradition of praising Cosimo as a leading republican statesman of ancient Greece or Rome the bestowal of this decree provided a natural and fitting climax.

In idealizing Cosimo as a Pater Patriae, these young *ottimati* were following the literary tradition of the earlier generation of humanists in Florence which was inspired by an ardent republican patriotism. In 1456 an event of considerable importance took place, namely the appointment of Johannes Argyropoulos to the Chair of Greek in Florence. From his lectures on Aristotle stemmed new ways of thought in Florence, and with them a new tradition of praising Cosimo; beside the old tradition of Roman republicanism grew up a new philosophic tradition which praised Cosimo in terms of his learning and wisdom.[8]

[. . .]

Evidence of this new interpretation is contained in Argyropoulos's prefaces to his translations of Aristotle (made at Cosimo's behest and dedicated to him), in which Cosimo is for the first time praised consistently as a learned and virtuous Aristotelian ruler whose task of ruling has a moral rather than a practical purpose. Hitherto Cosimo had been praised for his practical virtues as a statesman and for the outward and visible signs of his political and financial power in the city, but by Argyropoulos he was praised first for his wisdom and his moral responsibility to his citizens, and only secondly for his more material achievements. The traditional ideal of the perfect ruler as a man of arms and letters was somewhat difficult to apply to a merchant banker like Cosimo, but Argyropoulos resolved this difficulty in using Aristotelian terminology to say that material possessions were necessary to achieve ideal ends, that virtues of the body and mind were both necessary although one was subordinate to the other, in this way praising the material aspects of Cosimo's prosperity within a strictly moral framework. He never forgot to teach, however, that material possessions are no more than means to achieve a moral and intellectual end which is the discovery of truth and enjoyment of happiness.

In these prefaces Cosimo was described for the first time as the undisputed head of Florence and his authority in the city sanctioned by metaphysical arguments. Whereas he had been described as one of the principal citizens of the republic or even its *de facto* leader, he had never been praised in such absolute terms as those used by Argyropoulos, as the philosopher-ruler whom "that divine Plato wished to govern cities and public affairs" and as "the very man in real form whom Aristotle described as perfectly blessed." It is important, perhaps, to recall that Argyropoulos was not a Florentine nor even an Italian by birth, so that his writings do not reflect the same degree of political responsibility as those of the Florentine *ottimati* whom he taught. Although the *ottimati* later idealized Cosimo's learning, they never at this time described his political power in this form.

The only other man to do so, Niccolò Tignosi, was not a Florentine either by birth but came to Florence from Foligno as a doctor. In the eulogy he sent Giovanni de' Medici "De laudibus Cosme Parentis Eius Opusculum"[9] he described Cosimo's position in Florence in natural Aristotelian terminology as Argyropoulos had done, justifying Cosimo's magnificence because it provided "potentiam ad agendum"[10] and defending his authority in Florence on the analogy of the superiority of mind to matter, since states need to be directed by rulers just as workmen need direction from architects. He praised Cosimo's wisdom and learning and described his intelligence and mental pre-eminence as equally natural to him "as flying is to a bird, leaping to panthers, racing to horses and savageness to lions." Such was Cosimo's extraordinary authority in Florence that he directed and decided everything, "quasi gubernator omnium";[11] he was consulted before marriages were arranged, before buildings were constructed, before any decision of importance was taken, and was revered and respected not only by his fellow-citizens but by kings, princes and popes.

Tignosi's eulogy is important for its description of the extent of Cosimo's authority in Florence, but even more for its justification of the limited republicanism which this entailed, for although he never described Cosimo as more than leader of the republic ("qui civis solum fuerit, non rex, non divinus, nec imperator"),[12] Tignosi nevertheless justified his extraordinary position there as essential for the well-being and prosperity of the state, and after attributing the fall of the Greek and Roman republics to the want of such leadership, declared that a happy republic is one in which " . . . the greatest and most respected citizen is he who alone (for several can rarely agree) can devote himself sedulously to considering how to increase the state and care for its interests in such a way that the whole republic will benefit by it."

His description of Cosimo as the man "who rules and regulates all your inclinations as God moves the heavens" was not, however, endorsed by Florentine *ottimati*, who although no less influenced by Argyropoulos's teaching, praised Cosimo merely in terms of his learning, attributing to him the wisdom of Plato's philosopher-ruler without his political power. So Donato Acciaiuoli in the preface to his *Exposition* of Argyropoulos's commentaries on the *Ethics* praised Cosimo and his son Piero for their help in bringing Argyropoulos to Florence to resolve the crisis caused by the deaths of all the older generation of Greek scholars. Later, in the preface to his translation of Plutarch's *Life of Hannibal* addressed to Piero de' Medici, he again paid tribute to Cosimo's wisdom and learning, praising his study of letters and calling him the father of learned men, their patron and constant friend and helper. Alamanno Rinuccini, too, largely attributed Argyropoulos's appointment in Florence to the influence of Cosimo, whose desire to encourage ability and "incredible love of letters" moved him to support the project of the young *ottimati*. Yet apart from these prefaces, there seems to be little evidence of Cosimo's responsibility for inviting Argyropoulos to Florence. Certainly, Piero as an Official of the Studio at the time was partly responsible for his ultimate appointment, but the delay in making this appointment (more than a year after the decree of the Commune, three years after Marsuppini's death) and the fact that the Medici possibly supported another candidate, Landino, suggest that Cosimo's initial enthusiasm for Argyropoulos was not as great as his promoters imply.

A more vivid picture of Cosimo's learning is contained in Rinuccini's preface to his translation of Plutarch's *Consolation to Apollonius* which he sent to Cosimo after the death of his son in 1463. This preface, which at first appears to contain little original material, leaves the customary form of such writings to describe the occasion when Argyropoulos visited Cosimo and was told of his decision to read Aristotle's *Ethics*; Cosimo, who had been defending the merits of republics with great dexterity against Nicodemo Tranchedini, "quoting from Cicero from memory as if from a book," suddenly recalled the study of philosophy after the example of that wise man Cato, and said he had decided to read Aristotle's *Ethics*. We are told by Vespasiano that in the year before he died Cosimo asked for the *Ethics* and

Donato Acciaiuoli's *Commentary* on them to be read to him by Bartolommeo Scala, and it is to Scala that we must turn for a fuller and more detailed description of the picture of Cosimo's learning suggested by Alamanno Rinuccini.

At the beginning of the year following the death of Giovanni de' Medici, Scala sent a letter of consolation to Lorenzo de' Medici describing a long conversation he had with Cosimo shortly after Giovanni's death. Scala lived in the Medici house up to the time of Cosimo's death and as we have seen read to Cosimo at his request, so it is likely that the conversation he describes actually took place. If so, it provides a fascinating account of Cosimo's conversation and learning which corroborates Vespasiano's description of him as "tanto universale in ogni cosa che con tutti quelli che parlava aveva materia"[13] and reveals him as a man with a wide knowledge of classical, especially Roman, literature and *exempla*,[14] well versed in the arguments of Roman philosophies, yet at heart deeply Christian. Scala said he reported his conversation with Cosimo in order to hand down to posterity this incredible exemplar of "divine fortitude and wisdom," and after Cosimo's death he did all he could to impress his example upon his descendants, particularly Lorenzo as future "princeps"[15] of the republic, and when he quoted to Lorenzo Plato's words, "beatas republicas futuras cum aut illas philosophi administrunt aut ii a quibus administrantur philosophari ceperint,"[16] and urged on him the importance of study, there is little doubt he had in mind the image of Cosimo whom he had begun to idealize even during his lifetime in terms of his wisdom and learning.

The difference between this ideal of the learned ruler and the ideal of the practical republican politician praised by the earlier generation is the measure to a large extent of the influence of Argyropoulos's teaching in Florence. It was he who first idealized Cosimo as the divinely inspired philosopher-ruler of Florence and from his writing and teaching developed the tradition which praised Cosimo rather as a philosopher than as a politician, a tradition summarized by Benedetto Coluccio when he described how Cosimo on his death-bed "spoke of divine matters so divinely that those who were present thought of him not as a politician but much rather as a most fertile metaphysician." It did not attain its most exalted form until some years later, in the writings of Ficino, but even during his lifetime Cosimo was being praised in a third tradition which was less restrained than either of the two earlier ones.

This tradition originated in the new school of lyric poetry founded in Florence by Carlo Marsuppini and Cristoforo Landino and praised Cosimo as a Maecenas and imperial Augustus. It was inevitable that Landino's lectures on Vergil and Horace in the Studio should have led to the development of a more extravagant form of praise, for Vergil had been the eulogist of imperial Augustus, not of republican Rome, and gradually all the themes of Augustan verse praising the return of a Golden Age, the imperial greatness of a Caesar and the generous patronage of a Maecenas were absorbed into this poetic tradition until Cosimo was praised with less restraint than before. The moment when he emerged in the role of Augustus and Maecenas and was praised for his "imperialism" was of great significance, for it implied a transition from one ideal of political rule to another.

At first Cosimo was praised in verse as in prose for his patriotism and republicanism: Marsuppini's long poem on the death of Bruni described Cosimo in terms of his patriotism for making his city famous, and Landino in his two poems "De primordiis urbis Florentiae" and "Ad urbem Florentinam" praised him as "another

Cato" and "another Aristides" for making Florence as great as Greece and Rome. But it was not long before Landino wrote to the Medici as patrons of learning and announced the arrival of another Maecenas in Tyrrhenian shores whom he encouraged the poets to praise. Not surprisingly they showed little hesitation in doing so, for, as Ugolino Verino told the Medici, Landino had become famous in Florence through the favour shown to him by the Medici, and it was natural for other poets to hope for similar success. Gradually all the themes used by Landino to praise the Medici were imitated by his disciples; his praise of Cosimo's "benigna manus"[17] recurs in poems by Ugolino Verino, Gentile Becchi and Alberto Advogadri; his celebration of the return of a Golden Age under the Medici in poems of Ugolino Verino, Gentile Becchi ("Gratie pro anno Aureo")[18] and Naldo Naldi.

At first Cosimo was represented as the *civis togatus* who had helped his country as a private citizen, but soon Naldo Naldi compared his glory to that of Augustus, and his role became increasingly exalted until after his death he was deified and given a divine mission more in keeping with the epic tradition of Dante or Vergil than with the lyrical tradition of pastoral verse.

But the theme underlying all these poems was the search for patronage. Landino eulogized Piero de' Medici as a "Maecenas Tyrrhenis alter in oris/Claris qui favet ingeniis,"[19] Naldo Naldi praised him as the Maecenas celebrated by all the ancient poets of Rome; and other aspiring poets like Francesco da Castiglione or Angelo Lapo of Faenza referred to Cosimo's patronage and openly expressed their hope of being rewarded for their verse. Antonio Benevieni's *Enkomion Cosmi*,[20] written after Cosimo's death in 1464, also adheres closely to the literary tradition of Landino's school, praising Cosimo for bringing glory, peace and quiet to his city as a *civis togatus*, and describing his help to learned men as that of a Maecenas. In order to illustrate Cosimo's patronage, Benevieni cites examples of Florentines who had received help from him, among whom the names of Ficino, Scala and Landino are conspicuous. Until then only famous humanists like Poggio, Bruni or Marsuppini had been cited to illustrate Cosimo's patronage of the arts, all of whom brought credit to their patron in the field of letters; the names of Ficino or Scala, on the contrary, can in these early years have brought no glory to Cosimo and are interesting as evidence of the development of patronage of a new class of men, which was most praised by those who benefited from it most.

One of these men, Marsilio Ficino, as poor and dependent on the support of a Maecenas as any of the poets, described his relationship with Cosimo as that of philosopher and prince and later praised Cosimo in his most exalted form. In its origins, Ficino's idealization of Cosimo's cultural mission in Florence owed much to the ideal of the learned ruler praised by Argyropoulos and his disciples, and in a preface to Piero de' Medici in 1465 he interpreted his work of translation as the continuation of the work which Cosimo had entrusted to Argyropoulos. Twenty-five years after this, however, he re-interpreted this same work as a divine mission with which he had been personally entrusted by Cosimo. In the intervening years he developed his idealized account of Cosimo's patronage to him.

Cosimo's gift to Ficino in 1462 was a generous one consisting of a house in S. Egidio in Florence, a *poderetto*[21] near Careggi and codices of Plato and Plotinus from which he was to make his translations, and before Cosimo died Ficino was able to send him translations of the *Pimander* of Mercurius Trismegistus and ten

Dialogues of Plato. After Cosimo's death Ficino continued to dedicate his work to the Medici, first to Piero and then to Lorenzo, whom he praised as "the cultivator of religion and patron of philosophy" by whose help and favour he had been recalled to the great Platonic mission for which Cosimo had destined him. Gradually, however, the Valori family were assuming the place of the Medici as Ficino's patrons and from this time Ficino began consistently to idealize the image of Cosimo as a moral exemplar. It is evident from Ficino's letters that Lorenzo's interest in him was beginning to wane and it was natural he should want to urge Lorenzo to imitate the example of the man from whom he had received so much generous help: as a Platonist believing in the potency of the visual image, he attempted to do this by recreating the image of Cosimo with all the force of a moral exemplar. Writing to thank Amerigo Benci for his gift of Plato's *Dialogues* he said, "I think you wanted to imitate the great Cosimo in this as in many other things," and went on to explain how "the deeds of heroes inflame men to virtue more ardently and form them more exactly than the words of ancient philosophers disputing about ethics." He told Niccolò Michelozzi that he recognized in Cosimo as an old man "not human, but heroic virtue," and in a letter to Giovanni Calvalcanti said he had experienced in actual fact that philosophers are reborn from the love of heroes.

To Lorenzo, Ficino used Cosimo's image to caution him against wasting time and to encourage him to celebrate the Festival of SS. Cosmas and Damianus in Careggi. But his most impassioned appeal to Lorenzo to imitate Cosimo is contained in a letter extolling the value of moral exemplars: as the example of Christ teaches more than the words of orators and philosophers and the example of Socrates more than the words of Aristotle, he wrote, so Lorenzo should learn from the example of "the great Cosimo, his grandfather." He broke into a glowing eulogy of Cosimo, to whom he confessed he owed as much as to Plato, for Cosimo practised every day that ideal of virtue which Plato once showed him. And emphasizing the amount of time Cosimo used to devote to the study of philosophy and how he died while reading Plato's *De summo bono*, he concluded: "Farewell, and just as God formed Cosimo [Cosmas] in the image of the world, so you should model yourself, as you have begun, on the image of Cosimo."

Although Ficino's idealization of Cosimo in this letter owes much both to the optimate ideal of the learned ruler and to the poets' ideal of the generous patron, it alone praises him in the philosophical image of a Platonic Idea and it is in this image that Cosimo's portrait attains its most exalted form.

These were the three traditions in which Cosimo was praised during his lifetime and shortly after his death. One thing that emerges clearly from them is [. . .][22] their restraint and consistency. It is remarkable that Cosimo was praised by three generations in three different literary traditions. The earliest generation of writers were humanists of international repute, more interested in literature than politics, and all well acquainted with the whole field of classical writing. If because of this their praise of Cosimo tended to be rhetorical, they never sent him an open panegyric or wrote his Life as they might well have done. Non-Florentine humanists like Filelfo or Panormita who had once sought Cosimo's patronage (as early as 1426 Panormita had praised Cosimo as a Maecenas of poets) settled in the courts of Milan and Naples where they wrote epic praises and Lives of their patrons, but in Florence the humanists praised Cosimo with restraint and never as more than the leading citizen of a free republic.

The second generation of writers were socially a more coherent group, for they all belonged to the great optimate families of Florence who played a pre-eminent part in the political and economic life of the city. The restraint of their praise of Cosimo is perhaps even more remarkable, for at a time when Cosimo's power in the city was undoubtedly greater than it had been in earlier years they praised him still only in terms of his selfless patriotism and republicanism, and although they could, like Argyropoulos and Niccolò Tignosi, have exalted him as the Aristotelian ruler whose power was sanctioned by metaphysical arguments, they never did so and only commanded his encouragement of learning in Florence.

The third tradition which eulogized him extravagantly as a Maecenas and Augustus was not developed at all until after 1454, and then not by the *ottimati* but by a different social class of poverty-stricken poets in whose interest it was to extol the political power of the Medici, since it was from them that they received what wealth and position they enjoyed.

This is the second striking feature of the portrait, that far from being detached it was directly affected and influenced by the humanists' own political and social preoccupations in the city – in a word, it was *engagé*. Of the three generations the first was the least involved politically or socially in the Florentine scene and their praise of Cosimo is correspondingly the more detached. Bruni and Poggio were both papal secretaries before settling in Florence and enjoyed fame and standing throughout Europe in the field of letters. Bruni, who became Chancellor of Florence in 1427, addressed only two of his writings to the Medici, for which it is unlikely that he received any special help or protection; most of his early works he sent to Niccolò Niccoli, his later ones to such patrons as Pope Eugenius IV, Alfonso of Aragon, or the Duke of Gloucester. Only to one family did he express devoted service,[23] and as a Papal Secretary and Chancellor of Florence he was in any case able to exercise some small patronage himself in the form of recommendations to offices. Poggio, whose complaints of poverty were constant and who appealed openly for the patronage of men like Alfonso of Aragon, the Marquis of Mantua or Cardinal Beaufort, nevertheless died a rich man and although in debt to the Medici for small sums in 1430–33 appears by 1457 to be in their credit for as much as 2,600 florins. Both Ambrogio Traversari (in 1431 General of the Camaldulensian Order) and Niccolò Niccoli were helped by Cosimo's money, but this probably implied supplying them with ready money to buy books, and although Cosimo was owed 344 florins by Niccolò in 1433 and undertook to pay all his debts on his death, he did so in return for Niccolò's library which was to be placed in S. Marco with a plaque to commemorate the generosity of Cosimo as well as that of its original owner. Probably only Carlo Marsuppini of this generation benefited directly from Medici patronage, and when he died the Medici were privately responsible for having his epitaph written. The help Cosimo was able to give these humanists was that of laying open to them the facilities of his bank with its supplies of ready money, its courier-system between Florence and Rome, and its agents scattered throughout Europe who could help to recover newly discovered manuscripts; his relationship with them was probably that of a friend who shared common literary interests rather than that of a patron.

Their writings were nevertheless involved in Florentine politics to the extent that as Chancellors of Florence, Bruni and Poggio, at least, had to act as her official apologists: from this point of view their praise of Cosimo as an exemplar of the present glory of Florence was entirely consistent with the patriotism their office required of them. Moreover, their praise of Cosimo had more immediate political importance as evidence of their support of the Medici faction during the years of political change from 1433 to 1434. Poggio, before sending Cosimo his letter of consolation on his exile in 1433, wrote to Niccolò Niccoli for his approval, and having received it wrote another letter to Niccolò in which he referred to what must surely be the political situation in Florence in 1433: "You already know," he wrote, "what state our affairs are in, but they could not be worse than they are. Unless you look ahead as quickly as possible, this storm will break upon you, or rather bear you away, for these counsels are the work of him who has always hated peace."

Even before these years it was evident, at least to Filelfo, that Bruni, Poggio and Marsuppini were supporters of the Medici and he attributed his displacement in the Studio by Marsuppini in 1431 to their influence. Marsuppini retreated from Florence with the Medici in 1433 and when he returned in the following year, Filelfo was once more displaced from his Chair and left Florence for good. The fact that he appealed simultaneously to the Signoria of Florence and to Cosimo to be allowed to return from exile in 1440 suggests that there was no doubt in his own mind who was responsible for preventing his return to Florence. In a situation such as this, praise of the prosperous state of Florence and the greatness of Cosimo as a republican statesman indicated approval of the Medici régime as clearly as criticism of Cosimo as a libertine and tyrant suggested opposition to it.

The political significance of the writings of the second generation is undoubtedly much greater, for their authors were all members of the prosperous, politically responsible optimate class which was closely involved in the political and economic life of Florence and whose attitude to Cosimo would be all-important in determining whether the Medici régime would be established there or not. In 1448 Donato Acciaiuoli had written to a friend in bitter criticism of the government by whom, he said, the citizens were being beguiled and misled, and even twenty years later Lorenzo was apparently still uncertain of his attitude to the régime. Alamanno Rinuccini, like Donato a member of one of the leading optimate families of Florence, in his *Dialogus de libertate* (composed in 1479) wrote a trenchant criticism of Lorenzo, "who exercises the tyranny *which he inherited from his grandfather* much more savagely and insolently than either his father or grandfather had done" (the italics are mine). So the fact that in the middle years of this period between 1454 and 1464 Cosimo was praised by them as a republican statesman and protector of learning is of considerable importance. Although this evidence is too limited to be considered representative of all the *ottimati*, its consistency and the absence of other evidence to the contrary at least suggests that it was to some extent typical of them and throws interesting light on their attitude to Cosimo in this period of changing power.

Of all the writings in praise of Cosimo the most prejudiced were those of the poets. The practical purpose of their praise of Cosimo's patronage is made all too apparent by the fact that every poet to praise him in this way did in fact seek patronage from the Medici family, and although they were far less involved in

Florentine politics than the *ottimati* discussed above, it is surely no coincidence that Cosimo was first praised as an imperial Augustus and Maecenas by men of humble social origin who were entirely dependent on the Medici for wealth and honours.

[. . .][24]

The poets' praise of Cosimo, therefore, was undeniably self-interested, for in glorifying the return of the Golden Age of peace and plenty in which the Muses would flourish under the patronage of the Medici they were attempting to stimulate the Medici to play an imperial role in Florence, a role which they were in any case only too soon to adopt.

In conclusion, the study of the literary origins of the humanist portrait of Cosimo and its possible political significance help to emphasize the danger of exaggerating Cosimo's power in Florence. A letter written by Angelo Acciaiuoli to his son Jacopo in the year of Cosimo's death in fact suggests that far from being too great, it was that time insufficient to do what was necessary for the city. Cosimo himself, when asked personally by the Pope in 1463 to use his public and private authority in Florence to grant him a subsidy, replied that he could only do what was possible for a private citizen in a free republic, while to Piero his son he wrote that "I replied to him [Otto Niccolini, Florentine envoy at the Papal Court] that what belongs to my *specialtà* determines and obliges me to do what I have directed him to say, and that I care nothing for his other arguments, nor for them would I spend ten ducats. But what I have said I will do, I do first for the honour of God, next for the honour of his Beatitude, and lastly in respect of my soul."

Yet such was the power of the humanists' pens that the eulogies they wrote of Cosimo during his lifetime to some extent helped to mould all later portraits of him. Machiavelli, as we have already seen, actually confessed how closely his description of Cosimo resembles a panegyric and his praise of Cosimo's virtues of liberality, magnificence, prudence and modesty conforms quite closely to the classical pattern. Less restrained than Guicciardini, who although praising Cosimo for similar virtues described how he was buried at his own request without ceremony and given all those honours which "a free republic could give to one of its citizens," Machiavelli praised all Cosimo's actions as regal, called him alone "principe" in Florence, a lover and patron of learned men ("condusse in Firenze lo Argiropolo . . . Nutrì nelle sue case Marsilio Ficino"),[25] who was accompanied to his grave by all his citizens with the greatest pomp and honoured with the title of Father of his Country. More than a century later the orations delivered in S. Lorenzo on the Feast of SS. Cosmas and Damianus in praise of Cosimo reiterate the same praises. In his oration of 1693, Salvino Salvini, like Poggio, compared Cosimo's exile and return with those of Aristides and Publius Rutilius, his title of Pater Patriae with that given to Cicero; he described his love of letters (fostering Ficino and restoring to light books which had long lain in squalor), and praised especially Cosimo's piety and immortal wisdom which he had attained through the study of philosophy. And scarcely less panegyrical is Angelo Fabroni's *Magni Cosmi Medicei vita* published in 1789, the first and only fully documented biography of Cosimo to be written, which praised Cosimo with uncritical admiration for the same virtues, as a moral exemplar worthy of imitation.

Compare this with Angelo Gaddi's summary but no less impressive description of Cosimo on his death as "il principale cittadino di Firenze, huomo di grandissima fama e virtu e ricchezza"[26] and one has some idea of how far the humanists were responsible for the traditional portrait of Cosimo as Pater Patriae, Maecenas and divine philosopher of Florence.

Editor's Notes

1. history is one thing, praise another
2. good things neither of the spirit nor of the body
3. about instituting the highest authority
4. peace and leisure
5. The author here gives as examples Donato Acciaiuoli and Alamanno Rinuccini.
6. to be numbered as equal to many distinguished ancient Roman citizens, and perhaps justifiably to be considered superior
7. according to ancient custom
8. The author here gives details of Argyropoulos' lectures in Florence.
9. *A work Regarding the Praises of Cosimo, his Parent*
10. the potential for action
11. as if governor of everything
12. who was only a citizen, not a king, not a prelate, nor a commander
13. so well versed in all things that he could speak weightily with everyone
14. examples
15. leader
16. blessed are those republics which are governed by philosophers or whose governors begin to philosophize
17. benign hand
18. "Thanks for a golden year"
19. another Maecenas on Tyrrhenian shores who favours distinguished talents
20. praise of Cosimo
21. small farm
22. The author points out here that these praises were not mere rhetorical extravagances.
23. the Malatesta
24. The author here cites the examples of Cristoforo Landino, Ugolino Verino, Naldo Naldi, Peregrino Aglio, Bartolommeo Scala, Niccolò Tignosi, Lorenzo Lippi, Francesco da Castiglione, Antonio Aglio and Gentile Becchi.
25. he brought Argyropulous to Florence . . . He looked after Marsilio Ficino in his own houses
26. the principal citizen of Florence, a man of great fame, virtue and riches

PART FOUR

Renaissance Philosophy

Chapter 14

P. O. Kristeller

■   from **FLORENTINE PLATONISM AND
ITS RELATIONS WITH HUMANISM AND
SCHOLASTICISM**, *Church History*, 8 (1939),
pp. 201–211

T HE EARLY HUMANISM IN ITALY from the second half of the fourteenth to the middle of the fifteenth century, characterized by the discovery
and revival of classical antiquity, was at the same time the first expression of
modern ideals and feelings. Although it was in several points closely connected
with the preceding age, it produced a lively reaction against the medieval civilization and its form of philosophical and scientific thought, scholasticism. Petrarch,
the father of humanism, began the polemics against scholasticism which have
remained since then a commonplace in the writings of his followers: according to
him the scholastics wasted their time in subtle and useless disputations without
resolving the basic questions of human life; their unpolished Latin style was a
consequence of their barbarous thought; they could not be compared with the
great writers and thinkers of classical antiquity whom they were not able to read
or imitate; and even their chief authority, Aristotle, in many respects must be
considered inferior to his greater master, Plato.

This attack failed to have that effect which one might expect. Scholastic teaching
and tradition were continued not only in the European countries where the new
humanistic movement arrived much later, but in Italy itself there was a strong
scholastic and Aristotelian tradition throughout the fifteenth and sixteenth centuries
which had its centre in the University of Padua. This fact means not only that new
periods always possess traces of the old ones, and that with the rising of new ideas
the old continue to survive for a certain time, but also that the scholastic tradition persisted because early humanism did not provide a substitute in the form of
a real philosophy. Humanism was a general movement of great force which had
indirect philosophical importance because it was preparing new concepts and problems; it contained religious feelings, political views, moral opinions, and above all
a general ideal of education, but no metaphysical ideas or speculative systems. The
humanists made translations of Plato, Aristotle, and other ancient philosophers,
but the discussions of the contemporary Greek scholars brought forth no response

among their Italian fellows. The humanists produced mere literature, not philosophy; they wanted to remove the authority of Aristotle, but they put in his place not Plato, but Cicero.

Only in the second half of the fifteenth century there appeared a truly philosophical school in Italian humanism, namely the Florentine Academy, represented by its leader, Marsilio Ficino, and his younger friend, Giovanni Pico della Mirandola. A new speculative thought was rising, not only a program of general education and literary style, and Plato was really taking the place of Aristotle.

That Ficino and Pico were humanists can not be denied. They lived in the same social and cultural atmosphere as the earlier humanists. Their Latin style reveals the formal education of the humanistic school and the imitation of the classical writers. They cultivated their correspondence and collected for publication, as did their predecessors, letters, in which we can see, aside from the rhetorical form, the immediate expression of personal life and feeling. Pico composed Latin and Italian poems and commented in Italian on a *canzone* of his friend Benivieni, as Lorenzo de' Medici commented on his own sonnets. Ficino was interested in the old Tuscan poets and translated Dante's *De monarchia* and some of his own tracts into Italian, in this respect illustrating the particular tendency of Florentine humanism of his time. His translations of Plato, Plotinus, and other ancient philosophers, and his commentaries on them, may be compared with what the other humanists did for ancient Greek rhetors, poets, and historians. His revival of Platonism may be considered as a realization of Petrarch's vague dream. And many of Ficino's and Pico's philosophical problems were closely connected with modern tendencies of humanistic thought; we may mention the theory of love, the doctrine of the *dignitas hominis*,[1] and above all the whole anthropocentrism of their speculation opposed to the medieval theocentrism. So the intellectual movement of humanism found in Ficino and Pico at last its philosophical expression. And certainly Ficino himself felt that his Platonism was in perfect harmony with the renaissance of classical antiquity in other regions of art and science. "This century," so he writes to Paulus Middelbergensis, "like a golden one has brought to light the liberal arts formerly nearly extinguished: that is grammar, poetry, rhetoric, painting, sculpture, architecture, music . . . At Florence it has also brought the Platonic doctrine into light from darkness."

But if after that we expect from the Platonists a continuation of the preceding humanistic polemic against scholasticism, we shall be much disappointed; we find that the opposite has happened. As for Pico, the fact is much simpler and generally admitted by his interpreters. He studied at Padua and at Paris, the most important centres of scholastic tradition. The disputation he proposed to hold in Rome was conceived after the model of the frequent scholastic disputations in Paris. The *Conclusiones* and the *Apologia* have an obviously scholastic character in quotations, problems, and method. But his whole position was clearly expressed in his correspondence with his friend Ermolao Barbaro. Ermolao, a noble Venetian humanist, accused Pico of wasting his time with the reading of barbarian scholastic writers. Only the ancient philosophers deserve our interest, because their eloquent style reveals clear thought, while the bad Latin of the medieval authors is the reflex of their useless subtlety. Pico answered with a long letter, defending the medieval philosophers against Ermolao's accusations. Certainly we must first of all follow the model of the ancient authors, but the scholastics are also full of precious doctrines and thought. We must not care for the bad style, because for a philosopher the content is more important. Mere eloquence without intellectual content has less interest for the philosopher than a serious concept formulated without elegance of style. This correspondence between Pico and Ermolao, which had its posthumous epilogue in a fictitious letter to Pico written in the name of Ermolao by Melanchthon to defend the value of rhetoric, is extremely significant. Ermolao calls himself a modern Aristotelian who tries to oppose the original Aristotle to his later interpreters, but he made no positive philosophical contribution, but only perpetuated the position of early humanism against scholasticism. Pico, although himself a humanist, defended the scholastics against humanism, philosophy against rhetoric, content against form. The old contrast of humanism and scholasticism had thus passed into the humanistic movement itself so that Pico, not Ermolao, represented the more progressive position. For when humanism became philosophical, scholasticism had to be absorbed as an element of philosophical tradition.

Quite different is the common opinion about Ficino. Giuseppe Saitta, in his monograph, described him as a pure representative of modern thinking in contrast with the tradition of scholastic theology. Guiseppe Toffanin formulated the paradoxical statement that humanism was a reaction of Christian feeling against the heretical tendencies of scholasticism and based his thesis especially upon Ficino's concept of *docta pietas*. Those modern interpreters of Pico, like Anagnine and Garin, who had clearly recognized the scholastic element in his writings, asserted that he was just for that reason not a mere representative of Platonism and the Florentine Academy; and they drew a distinction between Pico, the scholastic thinker, and Ficino, the Christian humanist and writer.

I cannot accept this judgment as to Ficino. Certainly there are many differences between Pico and Ficino; but Ficino is not a mere humanistic writer or free from all scholastic influences. He never launched a general polemic against scholasticism, and when he attacked Averroism in the fifteenth book of his *Theologia Platonica*, he represented not only humanistic but also scholastic tradition. He frequently quoted Aristotle, and sometimes the scholastics, especially Thomas Aquinas, with great respect. There is a tradition that he accurately studied in his youth Thomas' *Summa contra gentiles*, and he really knew this author very well. The whole *Theologia Platonica*, his principal work, is in the form of a *Summa de immortalitate animarum*, and is composed in all its parts after the scholastic scheme of demonstration, enumerating a great number of single arguments for (or sometimes against) a given statement. Important concepts and propositions are directly derived from the scholastics, like those of *essentia* and *esse*, *perfectio*, hierarchy of being, and natural order. Other important theories of Ficino contain clearly scholastic elements like those of the *primum in aliquo genere* or the *appetitus naturalis*. Whoever reads some pages of the *Theologia* cannot but notice this scholastic element. And the reason for it is the same as in the case of Pico. Early humanism did not furnish any philosophical concept, method or system, but only general tendencies and orientations. Whoever wanted to study philosophy was driven to return to the only philosophical tradition then existing, i.e. scholasticism. The germ of this attitude is already contained in an early tract of Ficino which has an exclusively humanistic character, but concludes with the following words: "The studies of humanity made you eloquent . . . those of philosophy will make you become God." This distinction between *humanitatis studia* and *philosophia* hardly could exist in the mind of the early humanists. Here we find already the same motive developed as by Pico in his letter to Ermolao.

These statements are clearly confirmed by some newly discovered texts of Ficino which indeed prompted the thesis just set forth. While engaged in searching for humanistic materials in a small and nearly unknown collection, I found a manuscript described in the catalogue as containing some philosophical works of Ficino. [. . .]

As to the contents and character of the texts, the most remarkable fact, as I said, is the strongly scholastic element we find in them. The name of Aristotle occurs on nearly every page, entire passages are mere quotations taken from his various works which the author demonstrates he knows very well. Aristotelian influences may be observed also in another sense. In the *Summa philosophiae*, the consideration about dialectic is a simple survey of Aristotle's logical works. The definition of the soul in the tract *de anima* is taken from Aristotle's work *de anima*. The discussion about the elements and the introduction of *materia forma* and *privatio* as principles are derived from Aristotle's *Metaphysics*. The whole group of questions refers to the second book of his *de anima*. And the young Ficino not only shows a direct knowledge of Aristotle's works, but also a truly scholastic tradition and education. The most quoted author after Aristotle is Averroes, the Arabic commentator. Once Ficino quotes Avicenna and opposes to him the opinion of Averroes and of the *Philosophi moderni*. Once he quotes Porphyry, and once Ghilbertus, i.e., Porphyry's *Isogoge* and Gilbertus Porretanus' *de sex principiis*, the two writings which formed, together with some Aristotelian works, the *ars vetus*, the logical schoolbook of the Middle Ages. Scholastic is the definition of God as *actus purissimus*, the Peripatetic description of the intellect as *tabula rasa*, the distinction between *intellectus agens* and *intellectus possibilis*, and many other particulars. The whole form of the *quaestiones*, referred to an Aristotelian text, founded on Aristotle's authority, beginning with fixed formulas, and executed in a static form of argumentation, is closely connected with scholastic tradition. Besides these scholastic features, we have also other elements witnessing to Ficino's further development. Plato is quoted much less than Aristotle, but nearly as often as Averroes, and the young Ficino seems to know only three of his works, i.e. *Timaeus*, *Phaedo* and *Phaedrus*, all of which were translated. Once he quoted Proclus' *elementatio theologica*, also translated by William of Moerbeke, and in the *divisio philosophiae* he revealed Cicero's influence by listing *De finibus* and *De officiis* as parts of moral philosophy. But his admiration for Plato was greater than his direct knowledge. Already in the dedication he spoke of *Plato noster*, and elsewhere he asserted that his authority was the greatest. And in the *divisio philosophiae*, he emphasized the fact that the Platonists believed in celestial souls. As for Petrarch, as we said, Plato's name is for the young Ficino a symbol, before he knew him intimately. On the other hand, his admiration for Plato did not diminish that for Aristotle, and Ficino insisted twice on the essential identity of their opinions. It is also characteristic of young Ficino that he tried to reconcile Aristotelian and Platonic tradition in two points where he later espoused a clear Platonic position. Accordingly, adopting Aristotle's definition of the soul as *forma corporis*, he insisted

at the same time that it was a non-corporeal substance. And admitting that percep-
tion is passivity, he asserted at once it is not properly passivity. Important for him
was the theory of God and matter as extremes of all existent things, probably of
Neoplatonic derivation, which was not openly repeated in his later works, although
it left some traces in them. Important was also the analogy between God and the
artist developed in the *Theologia Platonica*, or the statement that language in general
is a natural and common quality of man, but that a given language depends on
particular, artificial factors.

    [. . .]

Considering all that, it would be easy and interesting to assert that Ficino was
not the first speculative thinker of the Italian Renaissance as he was hitherto believed
to be, but was only one of the last scholastics. One could likewise assert that
young Ficino was a mere scholastic, and that he passed through a profound crisis
which brought him to Platonism and modern feeling. Both assertions would be
sensational, but not exact. We merely conclude that besides the influence of Plato
and the Neoplatonists, and besides the modern motives suggested to Ficino by his
century and by his own personality, there was a third element in his thought, i.e.,
the medieval, scholastic tradition. This fact could also be derived from his other
works, but it is seen more clearly from his newly discovered early tracts. His own
feeling suggested to Ficino the general tendency of his speculation, the starting
points, the preference for certain problems; to Plato and the Neoplatonists he
owed many propositions, formulas, speculative solutions; but from the scholastic
tradition he took many of the forms of his thinking, especially the metaphysical
terminology and the logical method or procedure of his argumentation. This fact
is wholly in accordance with the laws of historical process. Humanism began as a
non-philosophical reaction against scholasticism, and in order to become philosophical speculation, it had to absorb the scholastic tradition of the Middle Ages.

Editor's Note

1   dignity of man

Chapter 15

Brian Copenhaver

■   from **HERMES TRISMEGISTUS, PROCLUS, AND THE QUESTION OF A PHILOSOPHY OF MAGIC IN THE RENAISSANCE**, in I. Merkel and A. G. Debus, eds, *Hermeticism and the Renaissance*, Washington, DC, London and Toronto, 1988, pp. 79–93

A N IMPORTANT CHANGE in the writing of European intellectual history in our lifetimes can be dated from the publication of D. P. Walker's *Spiritual and Demonic Magic* in 1958, Frances Yates's *Giordano Bruno* in 1964, and Keith Thomas's *Religion and the Decline in Magic* in 1971, for such works finally established the study of occultism in the early modern period as a serious and autonomous topic of historical discourse. No longer, for example, would historians of science see magical thought as a continuing embarrassment in the story of genuine science or as a primitive survival in otherwise modern currents of ideas, though such attitudes were not unusual as long as the chief guideposts to the occultist tradition were the invaluable volumes of Lynn Thorndike. Magic had been an object of critical, if not disinterested historical scholarship at least since Thorndike defended his dissertation at Columbia in 1905; but the more recent and remarkable reversal of opinion in the academic study of Western occultism demanded and still demands that such scholarship shed some of the burden of its ancestry – a triple burden. First, the anthropology of the generations around the turn of the century, represented by such figures as Robertson Smith, Frazer, and Lévy-Bruhl, taught the twentieth century to think of magic as something distinctly primitive. At roughly the same time, New Testament and classical scholars had begun to penetrate the secrets of Hellenistic magic, especially as they were revealed in the Greek Magical Papyri, but some of the best of this scholarship betrayed an anxiety to distinguish the magical from the religious as fixed and opposing categories and to find the exemplar of the religious in Christianity. Most important, the amazing success of post-Newtonian science had long since relegated magic to the boneyard of "unscientific" and "anti-progressive" species of human thought. And so a naive scientism, learned piety, and an antiquated anthropology continue up to our own day to propagate a view of magic that makes little sense for the age of Marsilio Ficino. Far from being opposed to religion, Ficino's magic grew out of an impulse to reform Christianity; it was also part of his science, by no means something intrinsically unscientific; and above all it was erudite, as unlike anything that could be called primitive as one can imagine.

For all students of Renaissance magic, Marsilio Ficino's *De triplici vita* (1489) is a cardinal text. Having seen more than thirty editions by the middle of the seventeenth century, it was by far the most popular of Ficino's original works, and its third book, *De vita coelitus comparanda*, was arguably the most significant statement on magic written in the Renaissance. Twenty-six years before the appearance of *De triplici vita*, Ficino had completed his translation of the first fourteen *logoi* of the Hermetic *Corpus*, which was published in 1471. In 1484 his translation of Plato appeared. Ficino's commentaries on and translations of Plotinus, Proclus, Iamblichus, and other Neoplatonists saw the light only in the 1490s, but he had read this body of Hellenistic philosophy by the time he wrote his major work on medical and astrological magic. Given what he knew by 1489, it is not surprising that Ficino made good use of his philosophical learning in preparing *De vita coelitus comparanda*, as any page of that work will show. In Plato he found the doctrine of *anima mundi*, and he deduced from him the belief that number is the basis of magical harmony. Iamblichus showed him the effects of stellar influence on earthly matter, and Porphyry explained how images could be made to receive aerial demons through the magical use of smoke. A text of Plotinus on magic was the starting point for the work as a whole. These and other, obscurer names from Ficino's pages make up a full roster of antique testimony on behalf of magic. At first glance, then, it may seem remarkable that the famous name of Hermes Trismegistus occurs in only two chapters of *De vita coelitus comparanda*.

The first passage that names the Hermes of Ficino's Hermetica is a single sentence from a list of ancient and modern authorities who explained how an astrological talisman could be made more efficacious if it were engraved under the influence of the celestial body whose image it was to bear. One of these witnesses, writes Ficino, was "Trismegistus [who] says that the Egyptians used to make such [moving images] from special terrestrial materials and then at the right moment implant the souls of demons and the soul of their ancestor Mercury into them." This first reference to the famous god-making passages of the Hermetic *Asclepius* is repeated and extended throughout the ambiguous concluding chapter of *De vita coelitus comparanda*. I call it ambiguous because the reader leaves the work with less than a clear sense of Ficino's position on the role of decorated talismans in medicine. On the one hand, Ficino links Hermetic statue magic with the Plotinian metaphysics and cosmology that he so much admired; on the other hand, he associates the statues with a religious deception worked upon the Egyptian people by their priests, and he shows how Iamblichus preferred the purer religion of the *Chaldaean Oracles* to the demonolatry of the Egyptians. Despite the appearance of Hermes in the concluding chapter of *De vita* and despite the relevance of the *Asclepius* to Ficino's interest in talismans, Ficino's treatment of Hermes is not consistently positive nor is his presence indispensable for Ficino's overall argument.

Readers of the Hermetica will understand why Ficino treated Hermes as he did in *De vita*. It is because the Hermetica say rather little about magic, Ficino's topic. Ficino's analysis of magic in *De vita* consists primarily of what we would call philosophical and physical and even scientific arguments. *Natural philosophy*, however, is really a better term than *science* for Ficino's views on what we now call cosmology, physics, matter theory, geology, and biology, for in his day these were all within the province of *philosophia*, not yet autonomous sciences. As a humanist, Ficino naturally hunted out such materials in the remains of ancient wisdom, but it was difficult for him to find them in the Hermetica, where magic is only a matter of incidental comment, where most physical questions get even skimpier and more banal treatment, and where philosophy emerges at best eclectically, at worst incoherently. The intellectual disorder of the Hermetic tradition was known even to its original exponents: Asclepius opens *Logos* 16 by confessing to King Ammon that in his discourse "contradiction even of some of my own teachings may be apparent to you."

No one familiar with the more systematic and extensive treatments of magic in ancient Neoplatonism or the Greek Magical Papyri or in the later works of Ficino and his followers will have trouble identifying allusions to ingredients of the magical world view scattered throughout the Hermetica: the cosmos is an organic unity whose parts affect one another as participants in the same life; the unity of the cosmos is ascribed sometimes to the physical agency of πνεῦμα[1] or δύναμις,[2] referred at other times to the ability of immaterial νοῦς[3] to penetrate all that exists; the geography of the Hermetic universe corresponds loosely to the familiar post-Aristotelian conception, where things above are the causes of things below; more specifically, physical causality begins in the stars and is transmitted through the spheres to the earth; the agency of the stars is as much personal as physical, so it is fitting that man's whole identity, not just his body, is the receptor at the nether end of this system of magical and celestial influences.

Nothing from this catalog of magical and astrological commonplaces is a principal topic in any of the *logoi* translated by Ficino, whose leading themes are: *cosmogony*, the origin of the world and the question of a divine creation; *cosmology*, especially the nature of matter and place; *theology*, the existence, attributes, and names of God; *ethics*, the moral properties of God, cosmos, and man; *anthropogony* and *anthropology*, man's origin, nature, and position in the universe; *psychology*, the activities of mind and soul in man and elsewhere; *soteriology* and *eschatology*, the return of man's soul to God, presupposing its fall and depending on revelation and contemplation as relations between man and the various hierarchies of being. Ficino's great interest in these texts is explained not only by his mistaken and well-known views on their antiquity, provenance, and influence but also by the possibility of finding in some of them what has been called an "optimist gnosis" roughly compatible with Christianity. That is to say, one can read in the Hermetica the message that the human soul is immortal and a part of divine creation. Through sin and the allurements of matter, man has fallen, but man's fall can be redeemed because his evil is not absolute. The discovery of such a revelation in works thought to be Mosaic in age and context likewise redeemed not only Hermes, Asclepius, and other pagan sages in the tradition of *prisca theologia* but also Ficino and other humanists for whom erudition was a primary means to the perfection of Christendom.

As part of the venerable heritage of antiquity, magic was also to be salvaged by this humanist undertaking, but insofar as the saving of magic required physical and philosophical arguments, it was not to be accomplished on the basis of the Hermetica. Ficino and others formulated theories of magical action that were altogether credible and respectable in terms of their physical and philosophical under-pinnings, but the ingredients of such formulations were rarely to be found in what Hermes said to his disciples. There are only a few extensive passages in Ficino's Hermetica where such evidence might be discovered. Twenty lines of the compen-dious tenth treatise, called "The Key," speak of a community of actions among the hierarchies whose "operations are like rays of God, whose properties are like rays of the cosmos . . . and the operations work through the world and work upon man through the physical rays of the cosmos, while properties work through the elements." This text, which emphasizes the astrological unity of the cosmos, is also a possible basis for distinguishing occult properties based on celestial influence from manifest properties based on the elements. In a passage near the beginning of the *Asclepius*, Hermes alludes to the kindred notion of ἐπιτηδειότης ("fitness"), which explains how two natural objects can be related in an occult manner without the intervention of a personal agent, and he also hints at something like the Neoplatonic idea of astrological σειραί or "chains":

> Heaven, the sensible god, is the minister of all bodies . . ., but heaven and soul itself and all things in the world are governed by the God who made them. From all these things I have mentioned,. . . influence passes continuously through the world. . . But the world has been prepared by God as a receptacle for species of all forms, and Nature, using the four elements to make an image of the world through species, leads up to heaven all things made to be pleasing in the sight of God.

Festugière has shown how the larger context of this passage is a distinct section of the *Asclepius* (2–7), which depicts the cosmos as a continuous hierarchy. He has also connected *Asclepius* 19 with this "opening theme of *nexus*" and with the σειραί of the *Oracula chaldaica* and the Neoplatonists. We can only guess how Renaissance readers, laboring without the benefit of Festugière's erudition, might have under-stood many of these allusions, but there is no doubt that they appreciated the magical import of the god-making texts of the *Asclepius*, where Hermes explains that the *qualitas* or magical power of the earthly gods that move the statues results from "plants, stones and spices that have in them a natural power of divinity" attuned to the heavens and sensitive to celestial prayer and music. None of these passages, however, gives us clear instruction on the philosophical or physical grounds for belief in magic. From the Hermetica one cannot really learn *why* belief in magic is justified by philosophical reasoning or in terms of physical under-standing, though one can discover in these and other passages *that* magic was part of what Hermes taught and so must be very old and hallowed by association with his name.

But the use of that name, especially in its adjectival and derived forms (*Hermetic, Hermetism*, and the inelegant *Hermeticism*), bears its own, ancient load of ambiguity. Writing about Hermetic astrological literature in the eighth book of *De mysteriis*, Iamblichus claimed that writings

> circulating under the name Hermes contain Hermetic (ἑρμαικὰς) notions, though these are frequently expressed in the language of the

philosophers because they were translated from the Egyptian language
by men who were not altogether ignorant of philosophy.

By the time Iamblichus (who died *c.* AD 325) wrote these words, the origins of
Hermetic astrology in genethlialogical manuals composed by Egyptian priests six
centuries earlier had become so obscure that a Syrian writing in Greek could
embrace with the word *philosophy* a body of practical, religious literature that bore
little trace of the rational analysis still implied by φιλοσοφία, even after its long
utilitarian career in the Hellenistic schools. Iamblichus addressed an audience whose
understanding of words such as *Egypt, Hermes,* and *philosophy* was colored as much
by the special conditions of literary culture in late antiquity as by any consciousness that we might call historical. Likewise, our own use of expressions like *Hermetic
magic* will have been conditioned by the modern cultural circumstances described
above. "Hermetic magic," "the magic of the Hermetica," and "the magical world
picture of the Hermetic writings" all occur in an article by J. E. McGuire, which
I cite not to debate its main arguments (as I have done elsewhere) but chiefly
because it is a recent and well-known piece that illustrates problems arising from
the use of such expressions. McGuire argues that these "traditions of magic . . .
[have not] been an essential part of . . . Neoplatonism." Since the Cambridge
Platonists and hence Newton were influenced by Neoplatonism, McGuire's aim is
to exculpate Neoplatonic philosophy of interest in anything so dubious as magic,
leaving the blame for magical influences with the mythical Hermes and removing
it from Plotinus and his successors. This argument fails on two counts. First, as I
have already said, magic is not a central issue in the Hermetica. Second, the ancient
Neoplatonists did in fact supply important physical and metaphysical support for
belief in magic.

Frances Yates recognized how the term "Renaissance Neo-Platonism may
dissolve into a rather vague eclecticism," and to clarify the situation she argued
"that the core of [this] . . . movement was Hermetic, involving a view of the
cosmos as a network of magical forces with which man can operate." While the
idea of a *prisca theologia* certainly inspired Ficino and others to read Plotinus or
even Plato as heirs of Hermes, there was also independent interest in the texts of
the *Platonici*, without reference to any Hermetic "core." This autonomous reading
of the Neoplatonists is evident in *De vita*, for example, where the *Platonici* are
cited more often than Hermes and to greater effect as theoreticians of magic. But
in an article widely read by historians of science, Dame Frances emphasized "the
Hermetic core of Ficinian Neoplatonism" and "the Hermetic attitude toward the
cosmos . . . [as] the chief stimulus of that new turning toward the world and operating on the world which, appearing first as Renaissance magic, was to turn into
seventeenth-century science." She mentioned three texts from the Hermetica in
her account of the Hermetic magus as operator-scientist. Her conclusion that it
was "upon the magical passages in the *Asclepius* that Ficino based the magical practices which he described in *De vita*" in my view exaggerates the influence of those
admittedly important passages at the expense of other sources, and her claim that
"the 'Pimander' describes the creation, fall and redemption not of a man but of a
magus" seems to me related to the cosmogonical, anthropological, and eschato-
logical vision of *Corpus Hermeticum* 1, not textually but imaginatively. And if

Giordano Bruno's reading of a passage in *Corpus Hermeticum* 12 on a living and moving earth moved him to associate "Copernicanism with the animist philosophy of an extreme type of magus," then we must recognize the Hermetic component of any such magical philosophy to have been textually meager. If one wishes to find the philosophical and scientific roots of Renaissance magical theory – as distinguished from the genealogy of the magus – one looks not to the eclectic pieties of Hermes Trismegistus but to the Neoplatonists.

In roughly the same sense that Platonic, Peripatetic, and Stoic teachings on substance, form, quality, matter, and motion provided theoretical frameworks for science in late antiquity, there also emerged by the time of Bolos Democritus (*c.* 200 BC) what we can loosely call physico-philosophical theories of magic. The evidence for them is thin and scattered, though Plotinus in *Ennead* 4.4, Iamblichus in *De mysteriis*, Apuleius in his *Apology*, and various texts from Pliny, Galen, and others have been analyzed to show what they were like. Some of this material was known to Ficino. In fact, until the work of Joseph Bidez in this century, Ficino seems to have been the only reader of the Greek original of perhaps the most important surviving statement of ancient magical theory, the work of Proclus that Ficino called *De sacrificio*. Titled Περὶ τῆς καθ᾽ Ἕλληνας ἱερατικῆς τέχνης in Bidez's edition, this little tract of 105 lines is probably a précis made by Michael Psellus from a larger work of Proclus on magic. The art (τέχνη) described here by Proclus is called priestly (ἱερατική) because it derives from his deep interest in the theurgic magic of the *Chaldean Oracles*. The intent of this magic was religious – man's immortalization and union with the god – but its prerequisites were scientific and philosophical in as much as its procedures were based on distinct and coherent views of the nature of the cosmos. Having made his copy of the Greek text of *De sacrificio* sometime after 1461, Ficino completed his Latin translation by 1489, around the time when he wrote *De vita*, but it was not published until 1497 along with Proclus's commentary on *Alcibiades 1*, Iamblichus's *De mysteriis*, and other, mostly Neoplatonic, works [. . .]

Without ever precisely identifying it, Ficino uses Proclus's *De sacrificio* some half-dozen times in *De vita coelitus comparanda*, most importantly in Chapters 13 through 15 to show how celestial influence can be manipulated by the proper understanding and disposition of common terrestrial objects. In these chapters Ficino amplifies essentially the same point made in the *Asclepius* about the magical power of "plants and stones and spices" used in the theurgic ritual of the statues, but in Proclus he finds a coherent physical and philosophical setting for what stands as a simple, isolated assertion in the Hermetic text. Ficino explains that the principle in question is "that most Platonic maxim,. . . that heavenly things exist on earth in an earthly condition, while earthly things in turn attain a heavenly dignity in heaven." This closely resembles the end of Proclus's first sentence [. . .], and the philosophical context for this principle [. . .] must be read in terms of Proclus's longer writings, especially the *Elements of Theology*. In that work, which does not concern itself directly with magic, Proclus sets forth a double hierarchical structure for all entities, described sometimes as σειραί or "chains," sometimes as "orders" or τάξεις. Both aspects of the hierarchy begin with higher entities called monads and henads, the latter identified with the various Olympian gods. In both parts of the structure, divine power from above is transmitted even to the lowest members of an order or chain. As Proclus puts it in proposition 145 of the *Elements*, "the distinctive character of any divine order (τάξεως) travels through all the derivative existents and bestows itself upon all inferior kinds." This is what Ficino has in mind when he says at the beginning of Chapter 14 that

> from each and every star there depends a series of things proper to it, even to the very lowest. Under the heart of Scorpio, after its demons and its men and the animal scorpion, we can also locate the plant aster, . . . which the physicians say had . . . wondrous power against genital diseases. . . Under Sirius, a solar star, come first the sun, then Phoebean demons as well, which sometimes appeared to men in the form of lions or cocks, as Proclus testifies. . . And there is no reason why the lion fears the cock except that in the Phoebean order the cock is higher than the lion. For the same reason, says Proclus, the Apollonian demon, which sometimes appeared in the shape of a lion, immediately disappeared when a cock was displayed.

Lines 46 through 64 of *De sacrificio*, read once again in terms of the *Elements*, clarify Ficino's point. The lion and the cock are in the same solar series whose henad is Apollo or Phoebus – the lion probably because of the solar associations of the constellation Leo in astrology, the cock because he crows at sunrise. Since the cock is a creature of the air, he stands higher in the series, and his proximity and receptivity to the sun are reflected in his behavior. Other members of the solar series enumerated here by Ficino – laurel, lotus, sunstone, sun's eye – also turn up in Proclus (lines 33–45, 65–67), and Ficino includes a long list of such heliotropia in the first chapter of *De vita*, thus again emphasizing the centrality of this solar series in his magic.

It cannot be said too emphatically that this idea of chains or orders linking terrestrial to celestial entities and thereby providing a basis for astrological magic was a leading feature of a philosophy that was above all else systematic and rigorous. Proclus was no fatuous theosophist. Besides his original philosophy and his commentaries on Plato, he made important contributions in mathematics, physics, and astronomy. Unlike the Hermetica, his work cannot be dismissed as eclectic, inconsistent, or superficial. He shared with Porphyry and Iamblichus a stronger interest in magic than what is implied in the *Enneads*, but he was faithful to Plotinus in his desire to ground these interests firmly in theory. Thus, Proclus's high regard for theurgy, which Plotinus never mentions, is of a piece with his own ontology and psychology, the latter developed in conscious opposition to what Plotinus taught. This disposition to theorize is evident throughout *De sacrificio*. His claim in line 20 that "likeness is sufficient to join beings to one another" depends on his philosophical rule that there can be no causality without similarity between cause and effect. In Proclus's universe, moreover, the likelihood of discovering similarities is magnified by his belief "that all things are in all," the subject of lines 2 through 7 of *De sacrificio* and of proposition 103 of the *Elements*. The intricate metaphor of lines 20 through 32 gives support to the possibility of a natural, nondemonic magic depending only on dispositions naturally present in objects. Another philosophical rule – that unity is ontologically and causally prior to multiplicity – lies behind the advice to the magician in lines 69 through 80 that magic is a process of concentration, unification, and blending. The signs or symbols (συνθήματα σύμβολα) of lines 56 and 62, as we learn from Plotinus and Iamblichus, work *ex opere operato* and thus provide another alternative to the demonic magic implied by any specifically noetic act of the magician. Surprisingly, throughout *De sacrificio* [. . .] Proclus also shows how empirical observation can serve the magician, not so much in saving the phenomena as in justifying magical theory in terms of phenomena alleged by tradition.

But the most important philosophical context for Proclus's theory of magic is established by allusions at the beginning and end of *De sacrificio* to Diotima's conversation with Socrates in the *Symposium*. Diotima begins [. . .] by calling Love one of the spirits who mediate between heaven and earth and "form the medium of the prophetic arts, of the priestly rites of sacrifice [. . .], initiation, and incantation, of divination and of sorcery [. . .]" Love, she explains, is "an adept in sorcery, enchantment [. . .] and seduction." Diotima ends her discourse [. . .] with an account of Love's progress from sensible to abstract to authentic beauty. This makes sense of Proclus's comparing lovers and priests [. . .] and also of his concluding [. . .] with an account of ascent to the ideal. The magic described in *De sacrificio* depends on the manipulation of sensible objects, but in this context natural magic becomes an erotic embrace of the insensible divine. Ficino also identified love with magic and saw the operations of magic in terms which, if we hesitate to call them scientific, we should surely call cosmological. Because God's love had created and vitalized the world, knowledge of the world was a means of knowing God. Cosmology was propaedeutic to natural theology and justified by it. Let Ficino explain how magic, far from being unscientific or antireligious, was a central feature of such a cosmology. "Why," he asks in his *Commentary* on the *Symposium*,

> do we think that Love is a magician? Because all the power of magic consists in love. An act of magic is the attraction of one thing by another in accordance with a certain natural kinship. The parts of this world, members of one living being, all originating from the same maker, are joined together in the communion of one nature. Therefore, just as our brain, lungs, heart, liver, and other organs act on one another, assist each other to some extent, and suffer together when any one of them suffers, in just this way the organs of this enormous living being, all the bodies of the world joined together in like manner, borrow and lend each other's natures. Common love grows out of common kinship, and common attraction is born of love. This is true magic. Thus, out of an agreement of nature, fire is drawn upward by the hollow of the lunar sphere, air by the hollow of fire; earth is drawn to the depths by the center of the world, and water likewise is pulled by its place. The magnet does the same with iron, amber with chaff, and sulfur with fire. . . Acts of magic, therefore, are acts of nature, and art is her handmaid. . . Out of natural love all nature gets the name "magician."

In the concluding chapter of *De vita*, Ficino treats the same question in a strikingly similar fashion, but this time he is commenting on the latter sections of *Ennead* 4.4, one of the primary inspirations of the whole treatise:

> Everywhere . . . nature is a magician, as Plotinus and Synesius say, everywhere baiting traps with particular foods for particular objects; this is no different from her attracting heavy things with the center of the earth, light things with the sphere of the moon. . . Wise men in India claim that this is the attraction whereby the world binds itself together, and they say that the world is an animal throughout male and female alike, and that it joins with itself everywhere in the mutual love of its members. . . Taking careful note of such things, the farmer prepares his field and seeds for gifts from heaven and uses various grafts to prolong life in his plant and change it to a new and better species. The physician, the scientist, and the surgeon bring about similar effects in our bodies, both to take care of our ills and to make a more fruitful disposition of the nature of the cosmos. The philosopher, who is learned in natural science and astronomy and whom we are wont rightly to call a magician, likewise implants heavenly things in earthly objects by means of certain alluring charms used at the right moment, doing no more than the farmer diligent in grafting, who binds the fresh sprout to the old stump. . . The magician sets earthly things under heaven, subjects all things below to those above, so that everywhere feminine entities are fertilized by male entities suited to them.

To the modern ear, talk about the physical world seems a strange context for a word like *love*, and Ficino's language sounds all the more bizarre when he makes *love* and *magic* near synonyms for the forces of kinship and attraction that grow out of the divine creative act and sustain the organic sympathies that bind the cosmos together. But the historian will listen more patiently to Ficino. Both his love and his magic are forces: They drive the motions of the heavenly bodies, cause the changes of elements, humors, and compounds, and support the mutual attractions of all these organs of the living cosmos. There is a real, if imperfect, analogy among the function of love in Ficino's physics, the function of πνεῦμα in Stoic physics, and the function of force in Newton's physics. Though Ficino's love lacked both the explanatory power of Newton's force and the systematic coherence of the Stoic πνεῦμα, all three were terms of scientific intention in that they *aimed* to explain important features of the physical world. Ficino's ideas about the role of erotic magic in the physical universe were not personal aberrations or idiosyncrasies peculiar to his historical moment. They were consistent developments of his commitment to the sources of Neoplatonic philosophy. "Love is given in Nature," Plotinus argued, and "the qualities inducing love induce mutual approach: hence there has arisen an art of magic . . . [that] knit[s] soul to soul." In his most immanentist, anti-Gnostic moments, Plotinus insists on the organic unity of the world and on the erotic forces binding it together, just as Proclus does by specific assertion in *De sacrificio* and by that treatise's allusions to the *Symposium*. Attention to the philosophical, cosmological, and theological contexts of such thinking about magic will be a healthy antidote to the impulse to view any interest in occultism as a deviation from religious probity or scientific rigor or philosophical depth. Such contexts are clearly evoked in *De sacrificio*, and, though their resonance has weakened in our own time, they rang loud for Ficino and his contemporaries.

[. . .]

Let me know draw five general and unequally significant conclusions about Proclus and Hermes in the Renaissance magical texts I have examined:

1   Ficino's Hermetica say little of theoretical interest about magic. Modern scholars should not use *Hermetic* and related terms as if they were vaguely synonymous with *magical* and its cognates.

2   The works of Plotinus, Porphyry, Iamblichus, Synesius, and Proclus are the most important ancient philosophical sources for the theory of magic in the Renaissance. Research on magic in the Renaissance should shift its attention to these texts and to their interpretation in the early modern period.

3   Magic cannot justly be made the victim of an indictment of Hermetism. Critics who believe that magic is not an important issue in early modern thought should not dismiss it for the same reasons used to belittle the Hermetica: eclecticism, incoherence, banality, the dating issue, and so on. New and better reasons for ignoring magic must be found. Moreover, the general reputation of Neoplatonic philosophy as an important foundation for magic must come to the fore in such debates along with the reputations of other ancient and medieval sources also important for Ficino's magic but not discussed here – Plato, Aristotle, Galen, Aquinas, and Albertus Magnus, to name some of the most important. Any critique of Renaissance belief in magic must confront the weight of Ficino's learning in these sources, for his magic was part and parcel of his philosophical, theological, and medical erudition, not a throwback to some "primitive" way of thinking.

4   The Hermetica provided more genealogical or historical than theoretical justification for belief in magic. Association with the ancient theology may have made magic more admirable, but the "older" ancient theologians – Hermes, Zoroaster, Orpheus – were of little help in analyzing magic physically or philosophically. Hermetic allusions to magical ideas were frequent enough to associate magic with the *prisca theologia* but insufficiently rich in the relevant physical and philosophical arguments to provide the elements of a convincing, substantive theory of magic.

5   The popular Hermetica as transmitted through the Middle Ages were more important as a source of magical data than Ficino's Hermetica, but since they were mainly collections of recipes and curiosities unattached to any coherent philosophy, their theoretical value was not much greater. Their influence on Renaissance texts is evident in such writers as Agrippa and Symphorien Champier, and it should be investigated elsewhere.

Editor's Notes

1   air
2   power
3   mind

Chapter 16

Charles Schmitt

■ from **TOWARDS A REASSESSMENT OF RENAISSANCE ARISTOTELIANISM**, *History of Science*, 11 (1973), pp. 159–193

[. . .]

ESPECIALLY DURING THE PAST dozen or so years a number of serious and detailed investigations have been initiated, which tend to show that the Peripatetic tradition during the period 1350–1650 is worthy of further consideration and must be seen as one of the dominant streams of thought of the Renaissance period. Alongside the renewed interest in classical literature, the visual arts, the development of humanism, and printing, not to mention the emergence of new social patterns, which characterize the period, we also find the continued development and vitality of the scholastic Aristotelian philosophy, which is usually considered to be typically medieval. Here I propose to present some arguments why I think [. . .] that this tradition is more important in the general intellectual and cultural context of the Renaissance than has usually been realized [. . .]

Before beginning this, however, it would be well to clarify what is here meant by "Renaissance Aristotelianism," if we decide to use this term. In many ways it is highly inappropriate, for a closer investigation reveals to us that there were, in fact, many Renaissance "Aristotelianisms." This is perhaps a key to understanding the whole subject. Though the university teaching of philosophy (which included what we would call biology, physics, certain medical sciences, astronomy, and much more) was based to a very large degree on the writings of the Stagirite, as time went on there developed significant differences in interpretation and many different schools. We are all familiar with the medieval divisions such as Averroism, Thomism, Scotism, Albertism, and Ockhamism. Each of these continued into the Renaissance and became even more fragmented. There was still a core of allegiance to Aristotle, to be sure, but often there was also disagreement on very fundamental issues indeed. Moreover, the diversities of approach to the understanding of Aristotle's philosophy which were produced by time or imposed by geographical distance were not insignificant. To take but one example, the difference in the approach to the study of natural philosophy followed by Paul of Venice (d. 1429) and by Jacopo Zabarella (1533–89), both members of the same "School of Padua," was indeed great. The former brought back to Italy, from his Oxford studies, a strong interest in the "English physics" of the fourteenth century, but this "Oxford influence" had all but disappeared from Padua by the time of Zabarella. What is more, with Zabarella we find constant recourse, not only to the Greek text of Aristotle, but to the sixth-century Greek commentaries of Simplicius and Philoponus as well, and all of this was beyond Paul's knowledge.

Consequently, the Aristotelians of the Renaissance do not form a single compact school, in any but the vaguest of senses [. . .]

A further point to be borne in mind is that Aristotelianism, as it developed in Western culture from the Middle Ages onward, was closely tied to a scholastic and textbook tradition. It seems to me to be vital, at some stage, to attempt a clear-cut distinction between "Aristotelianism" and "Scholasticism," as the terms have been used – and continue to be used – to refer to philosophy, science, and theology during the Middle Ages and early modern period. As this crucial and very complex problem of terminology is one which requires a specific and detailed treatment of its own, I think it best to avoid it for the most part in the present paper. But one point can profitably be made. Scholasticism, as I understand it and shall use it in this paper, is predominantly a method of study and of teaching developed and used within the framework of institutional instruction and pedagogy; Aristotelianism, besides having a specific and quite clearly definable method of its own, is much broader and encompasses a more or less comprehensive system of philosophy and science. Though Aristotelianiam developed largely within the specific pedagogical framework of scholasticism (more through an historical accident than for any other reason), this was not necessarily nor was it uniformly the case. It could just as easily have developed as did the Platonic tradition in the Renaissance, i.e. *outside* the normal formalized and institutional pedagogical structure. In fact, this is what happened with certain sections of the Aristotelian *corpus*. The *Poetics*, for example, played little role in the normal scholastic curriculum (i.e. it became generally known in the West only in the sixteenth century by which time the fundamental structure of the scholastic curriculum was already well established), but it came to have an influential and important position in the non-scholastic culture of the sixteenth and seventeenth centuries. Consequently, while Aristotelianism and scholasticism are to some degree co-extensive, there are important differences and these should not be lost sight of. A further point [. . .] is that the scholastic textbook tradition of the period absorbed doctrines, of both major and minor import, deriving from various scientific and philosophical traditions other than the Aristotelian. Therefore, even though scholasticism (i.e. the tradition of school and university textbooks) was predominantly Aristotelian in orientation – the majority of the specific doctrines which it propounded could ultimately be traced back to the *corpus Aristotelicum* – many other teachings were drawn from a variety of different sources. By the seventeenth century we can see that the range of these sources is quite far reaching: other ancient philosophical traditions; developments, distinctions, and new clarifications which emerged in the scholastic-Aristotelian tradition itself; and both empirical and theoretical contributions made by the newer philosophical and scientific systems which were then emerging. Thus scholasticism encompassed more than Aristotelianism did, while the range and influence of Aristotelianism were not wholly confined to scholasticism.

[. . .]

According to the popularly received view, Aristotelian philosophy and science were the dominant intellectual forces from the time of Aristotle himself down to Copernicus and Galileo, when a "new philosophy" emerged and the old Peripatetic one was discarded. Though such an interpretation is enticing and has much to recommend it, it fails to stand up to historical analysis for at least two reasons. First, there was hardly a time, even in the High Middle Ages, when there was not a strong opposition to the Aristotelian direction of thought. Secondly, the casting aside of the Aristotelian world view was a highly complicated and prolonged process, which required several centuries to complete.

From the time of Antiquity onward there was a current of opposition to Aristotle and this lasted until Aristotelianism really did decline as a major cultural force, which was apparently sometime toward the end of the seventeenth century. In fact, we already find a rejection of certain Aristotelian doctrines among his earliest followers: Theophrastus questioned several central metaphysical doctrines, including that of the unmoved mover, and Strato rejected the characteristic teaching of *horror vacui*. Such criticisms continued until the end of Antiquity – both within the Aristotelian School itself and by members of other philosophical schools. In the Middle Ages thinkers such as Al-Ghazzali (1059–1111), Bonaventura (1221–74) and Crescas (1340–1410) rejected Peripatetic philosophy in no uncertain terms. The tradition of criticism in the West continued with Nicolaus of Autrecourt (*fl.* 1347), who rejected the principle of causality among other central Aristotelian doctrines, down to the humanists such as Petrarch (1304–74), Bruni (1369–1444), Valla (1407–57), to Thomas More (1478–1535) and Erasmus (1466–1536). The better known anti-Aristotelian outbursts of late sixteenth- and seventeenth-century thinkers, which we shall discuss shortly, are, in part at least, merely a continuation of this already well-developed opposition.

Aristotelianism did not end with Copernicus, nor even with Galileo and Bacon. In fact, it thrived throughout the sixteenth century, as it never had before, and was still in full bloom for most of the seventeenth century. Only gradually was Aristotelian-based scholasticism eased out of the universities. When Gassendi (1592–1655) taught a non-Aristotelian course at Aix-en-Provence in the early seventeenth century it was still considered to be most unusual indeed. Though Patrizi (1529–97) taught Platonism at Ferrara and later at Rome at the end of the sixteenth century and there was a course in Platonic philosophy taught at Pisa from the 1570s onward, these were novel innovations and represented one optional Platonic course among many Peripatetic ones. Moreover, Sassen's careful researches on philosophy teaching in seventeenth-century Holland – among the most progressive and liberal regions of Europe – indicates that Aristotelianism lost out to Cartesianism only at the very end of the seventeenth and beginning of the eighteenth century. That is to say: Aristotelianism did not end as the dominant university philosophy with the onset of humanism, nor with the Copernican Revolution, nor with the seventeenth-century Scientific Revolution.

Another fact which becomes increasingly apparent as one investigates the situation in a variety of universities in different localities during the period 1550–1650 is that reforms were made and new materials were accepted into the curriculum at the same time as more traditional elements were retained. Let us take the case of Oxford as an example. Though revised statutes were drawn up, new chairs established, and various reforms brought about, a remarkable number of the older elements – even those which may strike us today as "Romish" or "medieval" – persisted and, apparently, without undue opposition. One can look through the reformed statutes of 1549, of 1564, as well as the more completely rewritten Laudian Statutes of 1636, and what one discovers is that the basic structure of Aristotelian instruction underwent few changes. In fact, the same works of Aristotle – the *Organon*, *Physics*, *De caelo*, *De anima*, *Metaphysics*, *Ethics* and *Politics* – were maintained at the core of the curriculum. This was at a time when new chairs in various subjects, including fields which had never been taught in the university before, were being introduced with some frequency. In fact the basic Aristotelian structure of the university during that period seems to occasion more alarm and indignation – as well as more invective – on the part of recent interpreters than it provoked in the sixteenth and seventeenth centuries.

These facts, however, should not lead us to go to another extreme in our interpretation. In retrospect we can see that by the seventeenth century, although the traditional scholastic Aristotelian approach to philosophy was still in the fore – at least in the official instruction of most universities – it was beginning to lose ground. The criticisms of Telesio (1509–88), Bruno (1548–1600), Campanella (1568–1639), and Galileo in Italy; of Ramus (1515–72), Gassendi, and Descartes in France; of Bacon and Hobbes in England, all began to tell. Indeed, a radical change took place during the century 1550–1650 and, if Aristotelianism had not lost its institutional hold, it was certainly undergoing more attacks than it could answer. This is not to say that it was yet dead, for there were still many highly intelligent Aristotelians around, whose philosophical sophistication has largely been lost sight of by posterity merely because their side lost the battle, so to speak. This is the period of Zabarella, whose writings on methodology were read with profit all over Europe; of the Coimbra Commentators, whose impact on Descartes is well known, but whose true significance is yet but little realized; of Hermann Conring (1606–81), whose counterattack on Bacon is enlightened Aristotelianism at its best.

What did happen during the period 1550–1650, however, is that the criticisms of school philosophy – those of Galileo, Bacon, Descartes, and others – became prominent and they have coloured later historiography in a radically one-sided way. Already in his early *De motu* Galileo exhibited a strong antipathy for the peripatetic philosophy of nature which he had learned as a student a few years before. This aversion continued throughout his life and can be documented nearly year by year. By the time of his mature dialogues, the character of Simplicio is drawn with a subtlety and biting wit, which betrays a radical mistrust of things Aristotelian, coupled with the incisive sarcasm of the seventeenth-century Italian satirical tradition.

Bacon, in a series of cleverly written and memorable works, severely criticized the Aristotelian approach to nature and sought to replace it with his own *novum organum*. Not only did he accuse Aristotle of being an out-and-out sophist, but he charged the Stagirite's modern followers with completely abandoning experience as a philosophical method.

Descartes's rejection of the tradition which preceded him was perhaps even more far-reaching than that of Galileo and Bacon. Though scholastic philosophy was only one among many which he eschewed, several times his dislike for the peripatetic tradition comes to the fore in his writings. Though having a certain respect for Aristotle himself, Descartes bemoaned the fact that young minds have been so indoctrinated by the Aristotelianism of the schools that they have become incapable of grasping "true principles."

For a variety of reasons the judgements of these three men have exerted an overwhelming influence on posterity. Not only are many of their ideas brilliant and challenging, but they are presented in a pleasing and polished style. The vernacular writings of all three are still regarded as models of clarity and eloquence, to be emulated by the young. Consequently, they have been read for centuries, whereas their scholastic opponents, who nearly always wrote in less than elegant Latin, have been passed by and forgotten. For whatever the reason, the judgements of these three men have coloured the historical evaluations of nearly all subsequent interpreters.

[. . .]

In fact, there have always been certain undercurrents of interpretation and criticism which have given some attention to early modern scholastic thought. If we look at the seventeenth century itself we see that the university scholastic tradition was taken much more seriously by participants in the "century of genius" than by recent historians. Aside from the well known passages where Galileo, Bacon, and Descartes were critical of the Peripatetics, we can see through a closer investigation of their writings – and especially their correspondence – just how seriously they took their scholastic contemporaries. The same is evident in Mersenne's *Correspondence* or in Bayle's *Dictionnaire*, where the article on Aristotle is still more informative on the history of Aristotelianism during the Renaissance than more recent large scale co-operative ventures such as the *Encyclopedia of Philosophy* or the *Dictionary of Scientific Biography*. The tendency to give serious consideration to the peripatetic thinkers continued with Leibnitz, who of course seemed to grasp and draw from all earlier traditions. Scholars like Brucker and Tiraboschi in the eighteenth century treated the late Peripatetics as respectable thinkers in their own right and attempted to give them their due. Such, however, have been in the minority down to the present day.

Perhaps we should here call to mind the fact that the history of Aristotelianism in the West reached its apogee (if for a moment we consider it merely from a quantitative point of view) during the period 1150–1650. During those five centuries we find an enormous number of translations, commentaries, epitomes, textbooks, and editions based upon the *corpus Aristotelicum*. Most of this material was then forgotten for several centuries, finding little place in the standard syntheses of intellectual history, when that discipline began to rise in the nineteenth century [. . .]

The continuity of the scholastic tradition has been but little studied, though Aristotelian-based scholasticism demonstrably remained important until the end of the seventeenth century [. . .]

By its very nature "Aristotelianism" is conservative, given that its adherents must constantly hark back to the writings of the Stagirite himself, some eighteen centuries removed from the Renaissance. On the other hand, the tradition showed a remarkable flexibility, a characteristic which certainly must explain to some extent the school's longevity. With these things in mind let us now turn to several areas in which Peripatetic philosophy continued to develop or to remain influential during the early modern period.

One way in which this flexibility was shown is in how the Aristotelian tradition was able to absorb various new materials, thus developing through its interaction with outside influences. We shall consider one instance of this in some detail, namely the interaction of the humanist movement with Aristotelianism. Humanism, as it evolved in the fourteenth and fifteenth centuries, developed new philological methods, new approaches to the study of classical texts, new criteria for the evaluation of literature. Already with Petrarch we find a rejection of Aristotelian writings in the Latin garb they had taken on during the Middle Ages and a recommendation to return to the Greek original. With Valla the philological methods worked out by three generations of humanists have reached the stage where ancient texts could be critically evaluated, and reliable judgement passed upon their authenticity. This aspect was quite soon applied to the *corpus Aristotelicum* and works such as the *De signis* and a metaphysical fragment, which had been assigned to Aristotle in the Middle Ages, were attributed to Theophrastus. The fineness of distinction became increasingly well honed, so that the *Mechanica*, though included in the *editio princeps* of 1495–98, was removed from the list of legitimate works by the early seventeenth century. In short, from 1400 to 1600 and even later the *corpus Aristotelicum* was subjected to a careful examination; consequently, many *dubia* and *spuria* had been weeded out by 1600 and all serious scholars had a clearer understanding of precisely which texts contained the authentic writings of Aristotle. Though much detailed work remains to be done on the textual criticisms and translations of the *corpus* during the Renaissance, the basic pattern of the development is becoming increasingly clear.

This more accurate philological approach developed by the humanists led to an improved understanding of the Greek text of Aristotle. By the time of Bessarion (1403–72) and Gaza (1400–76) in the middle of the fifteenth century the process of both understanding and translating Aristotle was on a much sounder footing than it had been in the Middle Ages. Even a severe critic of the barbarous medieval translations of Aristotle such as Gianfrancesco Pico (1469–1533) was forced to express his admiration for these new humanist translations commissioned by Pope Nicolas V (1447–55). Moreover, this new approach rapidly spread beyond the bounds of Italy with the work of Lefèvre d'Étaples and others.

Even more important was the work on the Greek text, which was accompanied by an interest in studying Aristotle in the original language and teaching him from Greek editions. Petrarch had already advocated a return to the study of Greek authors in the original language, but it was during the fifteenth century that we find humanistically oriented Aristotelians such as Ermolao Barbaro (1454–93) teaching moral philosophy essentially from the Greek text. The practice of teaching Aristotle's writings from the Greek text by professors of humanities (i.e. of Greek and Latin) seems to have become quite common by the end of the fifteenth century.

Just before the turn of the sixteenth century a special Chair of Greek Philosophy was established at Padua and Niccolò Leonico Tomeo (1456–1531) began teaching other writings of Aristotle from the Greek text. This is significant, for the basis of philosophical instruction at that time in Italy was in the field of natural philosophy rather than moral philosophy and the latter subject had only a peripheral position in the curriculum. A continuing interest in the Greek text was shown at Padua a short time later by Agostino Nifo (1470–1538), who exhibited a remarkable ability to adapt to new situations, to make use of the new materials then being introduced. Jacques Lefèvre d'Étaples (c. 1450–1536) also began about the same time to utilize the Greek text in teaching Aristotle at Paris. This tradition was continued there with the establishment of a chair in 1542 specifically devoted to the teaching of Greek philosophy. Incumbants in this position, which include Francesco Vimercato and Petrus Ramus, and in the next century Guillaume duVal, the great seventeenth-century editor of Aristotle, were expected to teach from the Greek text. By the end of the century, Zabarella was acutely aware of the importance of studying Aristotle in Greek and his writings on logic and natural philosophy are sprinkled through with Greek phrases, which he felt compelled to introduce to clarify numerous points obscured by translation. A few years later the enormously influential commentaries on the major works of Aristotle appeared at Coimbra under the auspices of the Jesuit fathers of that university. These remarkably useful volumes are probably the best example of a fusion of the humanist approach to Aristotle with that of the long-established scholastic approach. Each text is presented in the Greek original, accompanied by a parallel Latin translation and followed first by a series of explanatory notes and then by a series of *quaestiones*, somewhat along the lines of the medieval model, though fully up-to-date and cognizant of recent philosophical and scientific developments. At the same time there also appeared the more philologically oriented editions of Giulio Pace (1550–1635). All three of these late sixteenth-century approaches to Aristotle – the philosophical one of Zabarella, the philological one of Pace, and the fusion of the two in that of the Jesuits of Coimbra – can be still consulted with profit. What is more, all three are quite different from what one finds in the medieval approaches to Aristotle, each having been influenced to a greater or lesser degree by the humanist revolution.

Though innovation, progress, and changes of the sort we have noted did take place, a more conservative strand of Aristotelianism also continued. While Nifo was introducing a more humanistic and more broadly based approach to Aristotle, his conservative contemporaries such as Achillini (1463–1512) and Pomponazzi (1462–1525) continued to rely on medieval translations and, in fact, never learned Greek. Even much later, in the second half of the century, a teacher such as Girolamo Borro (1512–92), whom Galileo heard at Pisa, gives little evidence of having studied the Greek text of Aristotle, but apparently relied wholly on translations. The same somewhat old-fashioned approach is also evident in the frequently reprinted editions of the works of Averroes and Aristotle, which were continually produced until the end of the sixteenth century. These were very medieval in form – for example, the Greek text is not printed and generally little note is taken to new approaches to the text. Even here, however, there are changes, not perhaps obvious at first glance. Not only are many of the translations contained in these editions the ones made by humanists such as Bessarion, but there are included a significant number of translations of writings of Averroes which were not available in the Middle Ages. Thus the study of Averroes and interest in his writings as well as knowledge of them increased in the Renaissance rather than decreased, though Averroism is generally thought to be a predominantly medieval phenomenon.

Nevertheless, the basic movement of the Aristotelianism of the fifteenth, sixteenth, and seventeenth centuries was toward a more broadly based interpretation, utilizing not only the Latin version of Aristotle and the medieval commentaries, but the Greek text and the commentaries of the ancient followers of Aristotle as well. Far from being as intransigent as many interpreters hold, Renaissance Aristotelians moved gradually toward a more critical interpretation of their master, based not only on a fuller comprehension of the context of the Stagirite's thought but on a deeper understanding of the text itself. The dead wood of *spuria* was cleared away, as well as the shadow cast over the genuine text by translation. The result was a better understanding of Aristotle's philosophy, both in its strengths and in its weaknesses. Perhaps this more critical approach to the text, as much as anything [. . .] led to its eventual downfall as the dominant philosophy of Europe.

In view even of this sketchy evidence it should be apparent that Aristotelianism developed, changed, and became more critical during the Renaissance through the external stimulus of the humanistic movement. Nor was that the only external influence which was felt. Here can be noted, for example, the fact that the new anatomical teachings of Vesalius and Falloppio were quickly absorbed by Aristotelians, as were a number of newly introduced Platonic, Neoplatonic, Stoic, and atomistic doctrines. There were also other developments, however, which were more or less internal to the system. Though there are a number of specific instances of this which could be mentioned, there is one in particular which I shall discuss, both because of its intrinsic importance and because it has drawn a good deal of attention on the part of scholars during the past thirty years, though serious research on the subject has barely begun. This is the problem of scientific methodology.

One of Aristotle's unstated, but assumed, premises seems to have been that there is a clear connection between a philosophical articulation of scientific methodology and the practice of scientific investigation itself. Not all modern philosophers would agree with this and those involved in the study of the history of science could cite many cases in which the most creative scientists apparently broke all – or, at least, most – of the rules for scientific method which, according to authorities on the subject, they should have been following. On the other hand, there are numerous instances in which eminent scientists of proven mettle have themselves outlined clear standardized rules of what procedure should be followed to "do good science." Regardless of whether discussions of scientific method have anything to do with the actual practice of good science, it has long been thought that the two are intimately connected. Aristotle, as we have mentioned, and his followers during the Renaissance were no exceptions to this. In fact, we find a blossoming forth of discussions on scientific methodology during the Renaissance, in part surely stimulated by the emphasis placed on the study of the *Posterior analytics* in the statutes of university after university of the time. Though it cannot be denied that even here Aristotelianism was deeply influenced by outside traditions – especially the medical tradition through Galen and the method of mathematical analysis as it developed in the Greek world – much of the discussion on this issue, the content as well as the form, was within the closed framework of university Aristotelian philosophy.

Professor Randall was the first to call our attention unequivocally to this aspect of Renaissance Aristotelianism [see p. 289 below]. Since the time of his provocative and stimulating article of thirty years ago, a number of other scholars have taken up some of his suggestions, expanding, clarifying, correcting, and deepening his original work. Though perhaps his central thesis – that there was a direct influence of the Aristotelian methodological discussions on Galileo's scientific method – can no longer be sustained, his work has called attention to this important aspect of Renaissance intellectual history.

Though there was certainly an interest during the Middle Ages in the question of scientific methodology, attention for the subject seems to have been considerably heightened from the fifteenth century onward. The origins of this interest are obscure and will remain so, at least until we have a full-scale study of the logical and methodological works of Paul of Venice, whose dominance in his field lasted for well over a century. We can now trace the development of the discussions on these matters through most of the sixteenth century down to the towering figure of Zabarella, whose authority in logic continued for many years, especially in Germany. What we find is that certain concepts such as "demonstration" and "synthetic" and "analytic" method became increasingly clarified and refined in their application. The notion of *regressus* (the use of a twofold "method," in which both analytic and synthetic procedures were included), for example, evolved from being for Pomponazzi a more or less purely logical concept to being a practical procedure recommended by Zabarella for the investigation of natural physical science. In fact, Zabarella devoted an entire *opusculum* to the notion and was able to clarify certain aspects of scientific investigation. Without here going into the technical details involved, let us say that this *regressus* was considered by him to be a useful procedure in science, and one in which it was hoped to join logical theory to scientific practice. What is more, and perhaps this is of even greater importance, the very thought process involved in making such distinctions was carefully analysed – in a way somewhat similar to that later used by Descartes – thus making it possible to distinguish several stages and aspects involved in scientific investigation. The last word has not been said regarding Galileo's relation to this tradition, nor will it be until his unpublished *Logical Questions* are finally published and studied with the care they deserve.

In the case of the *regressus*, as in several others regarding the methodological developments of Aristotelianism, we see the evolution of various techniques and concepts which are not to be found in the writings of Aristotle himself, but indicate a very real development within the tradition. Though I personally find doubtful the assertion that such things influenced Galileo, it seems to me obvious that analyses such as Zabarella's imposed a certain clarity and structure on scientific investigation, which had a permanent value as the vocabulary of the philosophy of science became stabilized. All of this, however, requires much further investigation.

If the connection of Aristotelian methodology to Galileo is on somewhat shaky ground, there can be little doubt of a strong Aristotelian methodological component in the thought of William Harvey. Perhaps nowhere does such a debt become more explicit than in the methodological introduction to his *De generatione* (1651). Here not only does he repeatedly praise Aristotle, saying that he follows him before any of the other ancients, but time and again he puts forward principles of scientific investigation to be used in his work which are derived directly from the *Posterior analytics*. In fact, the "Introduction" to Harvey's work is in large measure a paraphrase of certain key ideas found in Aristotle's work, supported by several lengthy direct quotations. Recent research has indicated with increasing clarity that the Aristotelian writings furnished an important influence on Harvey throughout his life. It can no longer be held that the strongly Aristotelian cast of certain passages represents merely the deterioration of senility. It is perhaps not insignificant that Herman Conring, the chief supporter in Germany of Harvey's doctrine of circulation, was one of the most prominent Aristotelians of his time.

Further, not all of the *corpus Aristotelicum* was known in the Middle Ages and new relevant works were introduced into Europe during the course of the Renaissance. Several of these had a great impact, indeed, changing the character of Aristotelianism in a radical way.

Largely through the painstaking studies of Bernard Weinberg we now know that the influence of Aristotle's *Poetics* and *Rhetoric* was enormous, especially in sixteenth-century Italy. Not only were these works taught by the *humanisti*, who held university chairs, but they influenced a wide range of *litterati* as well. If Aristotelian natural philosophy or logic was often looked on as old-fashioned and out-of-date, the case with the *Poetics* was much different. As the careful researches of Tigerstedt have shown, this work was little known in the West before 1500, and was still fresh enough – as well as being instructive enough – to maintain its place as *the* dominant work of literary theory throughout the sixteenth century.

A similar freshness and importance was also found in the *Mechanica* attributed to Aristotle by the sixteenth century, but later found to be by an early member of the Peripatetic School. Though not all problems have been solved, not all avenues of exploration covered, we can now see that this "new" Aristotelian work gave considerable impetus to the study of theoretical mechanics in the sixteenth century. Thanks to the work of Drake and Rose, among others, we now see the importance of this work not only on a variety of mid-sixteenth-century mathematicians and scientists, but on Galileo himself.

Along with the recovery of a few new Aristotelian texts, the Renaissance also saw the recovery of a far greater number of writings of the ancient Peripatetic school. Works such as Theophrastus's botanical works, the *De anima* commentaries by Alexander and Simplicius, and the *Physica* commentaries of Simplicius and Philoponus had a profound influence on philosophical and scientific thought of the period, which has yet to be fully evaluated. This is an aspect of Renaissance Aristotelianism often lost sight of. The ancient Peripatetic tradition was very rich indeed, and it was one of the accomplishments of the Renaissance to recover much of the material unknown in the Middle Ages, thus allowing sixteenth-century thinkers to have a much fuller view of the wide-ranging variety of the Greek Aristotelian tradition.

It is perhaps worth elaborating further on at least one of the above instances. By far the most important botanical writings surviving from Antiquity were the two extensive treatises of Theophrastus of Eresos, the successor to Aristotle as head of the Peripatetic school and one of the most important continuators of the Aristotelian tradition. Though some of the doctrines of Theophrastus's *De causis plantarum* and *De historia plantarum* were known in a very diminished form to the Western Middle Ages through Pliny and other compilers, the very titles of the works themselves were lost sight of by all Western thinkers before the fifteenth century. About 1405 the first manuscripts of these works were brought to Italy from Constantinople by Giovanni Aurispa. Further manuscript copies were made, Latin translations prepared by Theodorus Gaza at the behest of Pope Nicolas V about 1450 circulated freely during the second half of the century, and the *editio princeps* appeared in 1497 as part of the great five-volume Aldine edition of Aristotle. During the sixteenth century the works were widely studied, reprinted often, and commented on, and, later in the century, important progress was made in botanical studies with these ancient works serving as the foundation.

Leaving aside many other significant contributions of Aristotelianism to the development of early modern thought, I should now like to turn to a consideration of a somewhat different aspect of the question. In addition to numerous easily documentable instances in which Aristotelianism contributed to the general cultural complex of the Renaissance, there is also evidence of a more subtle form of the interpenetration of Aristotelian ideas into the picture. What I refer to is the unconscious acceptance of many Aristotelian ideas and doctrines on the part of early modern thinkers who made every attempt to be anti-Aristotelian. It is my contention that certain doctrines which were transmitted through the Aristotelian stream eventually became so deeply ingrained in the European consciousness as to be accepted unquestioningly and their original source lost sight of. This particularly applies to the fields of logic and natural philosophy. The reasons for this are not difficult to find. By late Antiquity, Aristotelian logic and natural philosophy had been taken over by most of the rival schools who disagreed with the Peripatetics on key issues of moral or political philosophy or metaphysics. Therefore, rival logical systems, such as that of the Stoics, largely fell into oblivion from late Antiquity to very recent times. Moreover, Aristotelian natural philosophy gradually became absorbed into the neoplatonic synthesis and many characteristic aspects of Plotinus's thought on such matters, for example, are Aristotelian. By the time of the Renaissance, such things were so deeply imbedded in the whole educational structure that it was very difficult, even for such "anti-Aristotelian" writers as Gianfrancesco Pico, Nicolaus Copernicus, Petrus Ramus, and Bernardino Telesio, to escape from certain Aristotelian influences, try as they would. In my terminology I refer to this as the problem of "the escape from the Aristotelian predicament." By this I mean that, though dissatisfaction with various aspects of the Peripatetic system began to emerge during the late Middle Ages, it took several centuries for thinkers to escape the domination of the system. This was in part due to the fact that viable alternatives were lacking for a large number of specific Aristotelian doctrines. It is also in part because, even in cases where there were viable alternatives (e.g. the problem of the void), they could not be readily absorbed into the existing Aristotelian world structure. All too often to reject one Aristotelian doctrine meant only to place undue emphasis on other equally Aristotelian conceptions. Perhaps several examples will help clarify what I mean.

Among the two most devastating and original critics of the Aristotelian systems were Copernicus and Galileo. Both, however, much as they would have liked to, had difficulty "escaping from the Aristotelian predicament." In Copernicus's revolutionary work he advocated replacing the Aristotelian earth-centred cosmos by a heliocentric system. In doing so he certainly went against traditional Aristotelian ideas. On the other hand, many aspects of his natural philosophy remained quite Aristotelian and, as Koyré and others have so clearly shown us, he was quite bound to the tradition in many ways, not least of all in accepting a basically Aristotelian "closed universe."

With regard to Galileo we see much the same thing. In fact, since we have writings from all periods of his life, we can see in a pellucid fashion just how he clearly moved away from Aristotle as he matured. For example, in his earliest writings he still held to the Aristotelian duality of levity and gravity, but later abolished the former notion in favour of a single concept of heaviness. Moreover, though he came close to formulating the crucial principle of inertia, he was prevented from doing so, largely because of his continued acceptance of the Aristotelian idea of the eternity of circular motion. In fact, the emphasis on the perfection of the circle (which indeed is Platonic, as well as Aristotelian) played a significant role not only in the thought of Copernicus and Galileo, but in that of Harvey as well.

If two of the most original and iconoclastic thinkers of the Renaissance never escaped certain aspects of Aristotelianism, it is not surprising that lesser men were unsuccessful. Bernardino Telesio, one of the most vehement of sixteenth century critics of Aristotle, wished to replace the whole structure of Aristotelian natural philosophy by a new one, but ended with a system with striking resemblances in structure, if not in content, to that of the Aristotelians. Though Petrus Ramus and his school were intensely critical of Aristotelian logic, bringing many incisive and valid criticisms against it, they never succeeded in getting rid of Aristotle's basic logical unit, the syllogism. Moreover, a reading of Galileo or even Newton reveals a Latin vocabulary remarkably Aristotelian and Scholastic in character. Although little attention has been given to this matter, the connection is clear to anyone familiar with the vocabulary of the medieval Aristotelian tradition.

[. . .]

Behind the somewhat weak intellects and personalities caricatured by Galileo, Bacon and Descartes, we find something of substance, not in all cases to be sure, but often enough to cause serious historical concern. If Cremonini would not look through the telescope, some of his ideas on biology, logic and psychology were more in tune with contemporary developments. If Liceto was a somewhat fanatic anti-Harveian, he maintained an amiable and fruitful correspondence with Galileo and others. If Honoré Fabri continued to write text books in the Jesuit Aristotelian mould, it did not prevent him from becoming a mathematician of some originality and of high repute. In short, alongside the banal, intransigent, and slavish Aristotelianism of those rejected by certain of the more forward looking thinkers, we find also an intelligent, progressive philosophy continuing in the tradition. For example, in retrospect Conring's Aristotelian attack upon Bacon seems quite as valid as his support of the same Harvey, whom Bacon, that great spokesman for "modern scientific method," had rejected.

In fact, Harvey represents, as well as anyone, a pivotal point in the whole development. It requires little imagination to realize that it would not be difficult to see him and the development in the biological sciences as the key moment in the so-called Scientific Revolution. Hitherto perhaps undue emphasis has been put upon the physical sciences and mathematics – Copernicus, Galileo, Descartes, Newton – and little attempt has been made to fit the revolutionary changes in the biological sciences into the schemata. In fact, it is now becoming increasingly realized that the adoption of a model of scientific change largely based on those branches of science to which mathematical and quantitative methods could be easily applied has led to distortion. Not only is it difficult to explain the contemporaneous rise in interest in occultism and pseudo-science (and this did demonstrably increase during the period when the roots of "modern science" were being set down) in terms of the model which the generally accepted Scientific Revolution historiography has given us, but it is also difficult to fit the evolution of the biological sciences into this scheme. Were we to look with unjaundiced eyes at the bio-medical developments of the sixteenth and seventeenth centuries, with Harvey as the obvious focal point, the role of Aristotle in the emergence of modern science would undoubtedly undergo significant modification.

I am not here suggesting that the application of mathematics and the development of quantitative methods were unimportant for the far-reaching changes which took place in scientific methodology and outlook during the sixteenth and seventeenth centuries. But I think that too much emphasis has been put upon this aspect of the matter in the past and it is time that we began to take a more considered view, utilizing a wider range of examples and source materials.

Such a full scale revaluation, regardless of whether it would bear substantial fruit or not, lies in the future. For the present, let us recapitulate by summarizing a few of the important positive contributions of the Aristotelian tradition during the course of the sixteenth and seventeenth centuries.

First, the fundamental logical methodology and emphasis on rational and valid modes of argument came from the Aristotelian tradition. Consequently, the writings of a philosopher such as Zabarella on logic and methodology were accepted by a wide range of thinkers, even those who were most inimical to Aristotelian metaphysics or natural philosophy. This fact, which has often been lost sight of, shows unequivocally the continuing potency of the *Organon* for which no viable ancient substitute has survived. Even the Platonic tradition does not offer a real replacement, though the mathematics of Euclid and Archimedes, among others, did offer partial alternatives. All things considered, however, Aristotelian logic did remain the foundation-stone of rational discourse until very recent times.

Secondly, the basically scholastic core structure of the Aristotelian pedagogical method, which grew from medieval university instruction, continued to dominate. The organization of the Aristotelian scholastic textbook, which began to emerge as a viable teaching tool in the late Middle Ages and was progressively improved and perfected during the sixteenth and early seventeenth centuries, remained a useful vehicle for expounding knowledge and instructing students. One excellent example of the tenacity of this approach is afforded by the very influential Wolffian synthesis, which might be termed Leibnizian wine in scholastic bottles. The doctrine was largely from Leibniz – though material from many other sources, including Aristotelian ones, was included in the synthesis – but the form into which it was cast was that of the scholastic textbook.

My third point is closely related to the preceding. One major reason for the longevity of the Aristotelian dominance and a continued reliance on that system lies in its ability to adapt itself and to absorb within itself many novel elements. This process of assimilation and adaptation had already begun in Antiquity with Aristotle's early followers who did not hesitate to disagree with the master and to introduce arguments culled from many sources which ran counter to Aristotle's own doctrines. This process continued through the Middle Ages and into the Renaissance and the seventeenth century. The details of how this came about are perhaps most apparent in late sixteenth and early seventeenth-century scholastic textbooks. Thus the structure of this systematic philosophy provided a schematization of knowledge both useful as a pedagogical tool and at the same time not unchanging or unchangeable. In short, Aristotelianism, in its more progressive form at least, provided both a link with the past (and this was certainly still important for many people in the seventeenth century) and an openness towards the present.

Fourthly, even after that section of Aristotle's natural philosophy dealing with the inanimate world had been called irredeemably into question, the part concerning the realm of living organisms continued to be an acceptable framework for some of the most original and creative thinkers. Though the debt of Harvey and other major figures in the field of biological science to this tradition has been known for some time, most historians of science have found this fact uncongenial and this has prevented them from exploring its implications with due attention. Nevertheless, perhaps as well as anything else, this debt illustrates the continued viability of the Aristotelian synthesis.

In the present paper I have tried to indicate reasons why more attention should be devoted to broad and deep explorations of early modern Aristotelianism, if we are to arrive at a more balanced and historically accurate understanding of the intellectual history of the period. In particular I have tried to demonstrate – albeit often basing myself upon the study of a limited selection of the many relevant source materials – that Aristotelianism retained importance and vitality a good deal longer than is usually realized. The question then arises, when and why did Aristotelian-based scholasticism cease to dominate the university system and to maintain itself as a viable vehicle for general higher education? Though I believe this matter has yet to be investigated in any detail, it seems that scholasticism generally lost its hold on the more progressive and up-to-date universities during the fifty years around 1700.

As to why confidence was lost in the Aristotelian system at that stage, it seems to me that two factors are especially important: the increasing experimental (as well as just plain experiential) evidence against certain central Aristotelian doctrines, and the increasing realization that mathematics and quantitative methods had a role to play in natural philosophy which was far beyond the knowledge of Aristotle. In short, the two primary methods which were being so fruitfully conjoined by men like Galileo, Pascal, and Newton found little support in the *corpus Aristotelicum*.

The efficacy of experimentalism was dramatically made evident in the baro-metric and vacuum pump experiments of the 1640s and 1650s, which, despite Aristotelian attempts at refutation, demonstrated once and for all the untenability of the doctrine of *horror vacui*. The application of mathematical and quantitative methods to problems of mechanics by Galileo and others demonstrated the effec-tiveness of this approach as compared to the traditional one to be found in the Aristotelian tradition. Though the logic, ethics, politics, and, in large measure, the biological side of natural philosophy had been little touched by these developments, the blow to the physics was substantial enough to lead to a full scale revamping of the educational system. Natural philosophy became increasingly taught from experimentally and mathematically oriented textbooks, and the traditional Aristo-telian manuals which still continued to dominate for much of the seventeenth century were gradually discarded. The fully demonstrated power of the New Science in matters of physics seems to have occasioned the dropping of Aristotle as a basis for scientific and philosophical education in general. Fuller details of the effects of this abandonment of Aristotle, which even then was not complete, must be given elsewhere. Here I can merely say that I think that the twin-edged sword of experimentalism and the fruitful application of mathematical methods gave the *coup de grâce* to Aristotelianism as a comprehensive and viable philosophical system. There finally happened what fourteenth century nominalism, fifteenth-century Platonism and humanism, and sixteenth-century Copernicanism, reformed religion, and scepticism could not accomplish.

Fragments of the old system certainly did remain, but the heart of it, as it were, had been cut out. While many Aristotelian doctrines could still be – and, in fact, were – adhered to, the unifying principle had been lost. The teaching of philosophy and science in schools and universities entered a new era, a post-Aristotelian one.

Chapter 17

John Monfasani

■   from **LORENZO VALLA AND RUDOLPH
AGRICOLA**, *Journal of the History of Philosophy*,
28 (1990), pp. 181–200

1.   A discontinuity in humanist logic

A KIND OF "APOSTOLIC SUCCESSION" has frequently been
claimed by historical personages in order to legitimize their authority or ideas.
Historians, too, are sometimes given to discovering it, or presuming it, in order
to impose some sort of order on the flow of events and opinions. In Renaissance
studies, the relationship between Lorenzo Valla and Rudolph Agricola is a prime
example of such an "apostolic succession" in humanist logic created not by Agricola,
but rather by scholars seeking to place either or both men within a historical
context.

Valla first wrote the *Dialectica* at the court of Naples in the late 1430s. In
scope and content, his *Dialectica* had no predecessor as a frontal assault on scholastic
logic and philosophy. Rudolph Agricola's *De inventione dialectica*, on the other hand,
was the first humanist work in logic to become a best seller. It enjoyed a pheno-
menal press run for about sixty years after 1515, and unquestionably played a
major role in the humanist victory over scholasticism in the schools of Northern
Europe. So it is only natural to suppose that when the Dutch humanist Rudolph
Agricola came to write his *De inventione dialectica* while in Ferrara in the late 1470s,
he did so under the influence of Valla's *Dialectica*. Indeed, it has even been asserted
that "the three books of Agricola's work consolidate Valla's innovatory emphases
into something like textbook form." Such a thesis makes possible a neat linear
scheme in the development of humanist rhetoric and logic. But in this instance
the notion of an apostolic succession is, I propose to show, a distortion of what
actually happened.

Direct contact between the Italian humanist and the Dutch scholar is, of course,
out of the question. Valla died in 1457 and Agricola first took up residence in
Italy in 1469. Furthermore, Agricola did not cite Valla in the *De inventione*, and,
as far as I have been able to discover, the only work of Valla explicitly mentioned

by Agricola is the *De vero bono*. Valla's *Dialectica* experienced only a modest manuscript diffusion, and it is very unlikely that any of the extant manuscripts would have been available to Agricola. The *Dialectica* was first printed in 1496–1500, some ten years after Agricola himself had died. Consequently, one may legitimately wonder if Agricola ever had access to Valla's *Dialectica*.

I happen to think that Agricola did read Valla's *Dialectica*, from a manuscript no longer extant, but only because I have come across a passage in Agricola which, I believe, is virtually a quotation of Valla's *Dialectica* and which, up to the present time, has been ignored in the scholarly literature. Unfortunately for the believers in the apostolic succession from Valla to Agricola, if one concedes that this passage is a quotation, then it proves that Agricola deliberately rejected Valla's understanding of the relationship between rhetoric and logic. Furthermore, it proves that Agricola did so with the malicious intent of throwing that understanding right back into Valla's face.

At the start of Book 2 of the *Dialectica*, Valla made three points. The first was that [. . .] not only was logic basically child's play, a *res brevis prorsus et facilis*, but also nothing more than one of the parts of invention; furthermore, invention, in turn, was one of the five parts of rhetoric. Short of eliminating logic as a valid discipline, it is difficult to think of a more drastic reduction of the status and range of what the medievals called the "art of arts" and "science of sciences." Valla had made logic merely part of the argumentative section of rhetorical invention.

His second point was that [. . .] the argumentative repertoire of rhetoric is far larger and more complex than logic's. In a famous dictum (quoted by Cicero and Quintilian), Zeno, the founder of Stoicism, had compared the relationship of logic and rhetoric to that between a fist and an open hand. Zeno meant that rhetoric said in a looser and more attractive way what had been strictly and economically demonstrated by logic. Rhetoric was mere cosmetics, prettying up for popular consumption conclusions and propositions which logic arrived at in a far more scientifically satisfying manner. Quintilian, Valla's great authority in all matters rhetorical and linguistic, had quoted Zeno's saying approvingly. Nonetheless, without acknowledging either his divergence from Quintilian or his reworking of Zeno's dictum, which he does not mention, Valla stood the dictum on its head: rhetoric was not a mere elaboration of logic, but rather a superior, broader discipline, which encompassed logic.

The third point brings us to the *officia oratoris* [. . .] [O]f the three responsibilities of an orator, to teach, to please, and to move, the logician had as his task only the first, to teach. As far as I have been able to determine, Valla was the first person to make this identification of logic with one of the *officia oratoris*. Moreover, in Valla's eyes, all of logic supplied only a segment of the inferential techniques used by the orator.

Cicero is the first extant author to lay out in a clear scheme the three *officia oratoris*. His best known discussion of the *officia oratoris* is *Orator* 69, where he listed them as *probare, delectare*, and *flectere*. But in the *De oratore*, the *Brutus*, and *De optimo genere oratorum*, he replaced *probare* with *docere*. No less importantly, at least for Valla, Quintilian also preferred *docere* to *probare*. Finally, St. Augustine, in Book 4, Chapter 12 ff. of his *De doctrina Christiana*, quoted Cicero's discussion of the *officia oratoris* as found in the *Orator*, but still substituted *docere* for *probare*.

In none of these classical discussions was *docere* ever identified with logic, nor were the *officia oratoris* ever treated as having a specific relationship with logic.

The situation changed in the Middle Ages as logic became the "art of arts" and "science of sciences." We can find a faint echo of the classical *officia oratoris* in St Bonaventure's *De reductione artium ad theologiam*, where he divided the *philosophia sermocinalis* into "grammaticam, logicam et rhetoricam, quarum prima est ad exprimendum, *secunda ad docendum*, tertia ad movendum" (my emphasis).[1] Far more radically, Valla combined the medieval tradition of *logica docens* and the classical *offica oratoris* into a new synthesis in which logic as teaching became a mere segment of invention and therefore a distinctly minor part of the discipline of rhetoric. Valla had transformed the classical and medieval conception of logic. Rightly, therefore, could he say: "erat enim dialectica res brevis prorsus et facilis."[2]

Rudolph Agricola agreed that logic was teaching, but envisaged its relationship to rhetoric differently than Valla. In the opening lines of the *De inventione dialectica*, he laid down the axiom that the primary task (*officium*) of speech is to teach the listener the things thought by the speaker. Speech is "the sign of those things which the speaker understands in his soul." From this he drew a rather extended corollary to the *officia oratoris*:

> I know that the greatest authorities would have the perfect oration consist in three things: that it teach, that it move, and that it please; I also know that teaching is supposed to be indeed an easy business [*et docere quidem rem facilem esse*] at which anyone who is not utterly stupid can excel. To stir the listener emotionally, however, and to bring him to the mood you desire, or, again, to attract the listener and by his desire to hear you hold him in suspense: this is supposed to be the lot of only the greatest talents, incited by a certain exceptional inspiration of the Muses . . . Concerning these theories I shall speak at greater length later on. For now let me just say that a discourse can teach without moving or pleasing, but it cannot move or please without also teaching.

Since teaching was the fundamental function of speech, teaching was also the fundamental function of the speaker. The other two traditional *officia oratoris* (moving and pleasing) were therefore secondary to the *officium* of teaching. We can summarize the remainder of Agricola's position as follows. Teaching either conveys information or produces belief (*fidem facere*). The former is exposition, the latter argumentation (cf. Quint., *Inst. orat.* 8, praef. 7). Argumentation brings about persuasion through probable arguments. Agricola does not even refer to scientific demonstration through apodictic proof. For him probabilistic *dialectica* is synonymous with *logica* in the strict sense. Probable argumentation rests upon the theory of commonplaces (*ratio locurum*, the theory of the dialectical *topoi*). But in arguing from commonplaces we arrive from our starting point to a conclusion by means of a middle term. Finding the middle term is invention, one of the two parts of dialectics. The other part of dialectics is judgment, which is primarily concerned with the syllogism. In his own book, Agricola ignored judgment and concentrated on topical invention, the *ratio locorum*, which constituted the basis of probable argumentation. Modern books, he explained, were all filled with the *ratio iudicandi*, but this part of dialectic was less important, and could be achieved with many fewer and less difficult rules than were presently being taught. The more fundamental *ratio inveniendi*, on the other hand, had been ignored since Boethius. Furthermore, inasmuch as Agricola had assigned argumentation exclusively to dialectic, rhetoric was left with only *elocutio*, style, a prettying up of what dialectics had discovered in order to please the listener, and not always to the good of the argument or of the listener. The dialectician dealt with substance, the orator with superficial appearances.

Agricola repeated Zeno's fist/open hand simile and interpreted it in a way that was more reductive of rhetoric than Zeno had ever intended. According to Agricola, the simile merely contrasted the tight, technical *alternantia certamina* of philosophical debate (*oratio concisa*) and the continuous discourse of public speech (*oratio continens:* "quales sunt oratorum actiones, laudationes, hortationes"). Both kinds of *oratio* belonged to the dialectician since he was responsible for the *ratio probabiliter disserendi*. The only contribution of the rhetor was to see that the speech was given *ornate*. In Agricola's eyes, the logician created and shaped the substance of a speech. The dialectician persuaded the minds of the auditors. The rhetorician only spruced up and expanded upon the words in order to appeal to the sensibilities of the auditors. This last task was useful, but clearly not essential.

In sum, by identifying teaching with logic, and logic, in turn, with topical invention, Agricola had rhetoricized logic and devalued rhetoric. Paradoxically, he had created a humanist conception of logic which reduced rhetoric to its medieval role of mere verbal ornament, and returned logic in this new form, in his own words, to the status of *dux directrixque omnium artium*. The logician, not the rhetorician, was the master of persuasive speech. Agricola had given the back of his hand to those who considered teaching (= dialectic) a *res quidem facilis*.

I find it very probable that Agricola was alluding here to Valla's provocative assertion that "erat enim dialectica res brevis prorsus et facilis." Further on in the *De inventione dialectica*, Agricola rebuked those who would reject the word *quiditas* on grammatical grounds. Valla did precisely this in a celebrated section of the *Dialectica*, where he banned *quiditas, haecceitas*, and other such "barbarisms." Agricola even more explicitly declared his opposition to Valla in a letter to a fellow Northern humanist, Alexander Hegius: "Ego et Socratitas et Platonitas et entitas forte dixerim, quamvis repugnet Vallensis noster."[3] In this quotation, Agricola cited *entitas* as an example. In the *De inventione dialectica* he insisted on using the word *ens* as a substantive (e.g., "in omni ente"), which is another usage banned by Valla.

To be sure, Agricola's *De inventione dialectica* is a humanist logic. Agricola rhetoricized logic. He reduced logic to the demands and values of rhetoric. But he did so in a way which was totally incompatible with Valla's *Dialectica*. In terms of their conception of logic, general philosophical orientation, and even vocabulary, the two works are incompatible. Indeed, the *De inventione dialectica* could be considered a corrective to the *Dialectica*. Agricola categorically rejected the position of those who, like Valla, wished to subordinate the logician to the rhetorician. Agricola reduced rhetoric to the discipline of mere verbal ornament, whereas Valla had made it a comprehensive intellectual discipline. Furthermore, Agricola formulated a two-part logic in which invention played the predominant role, while Valla conceived his *Dialectica* as corresponding to the Aristotelian *Organon*, covering words, sentences, and arguments, a scheme in which topical invention played a relatively small role. In the *Dialectica*, topical invention is nothing more than a verbatim quotation of Book 5, Chapter 10 of Quintilian's *Institutio oratoria*, which takes up less than 22 of the 356 pages of the final recension.

Valla was not especially interested in topical invention, nor did he feel he had anything of his own worth saying on the subject. Rather, he saw his main task to be the reformation of logic by criticizing and correcting Aristotle and Boethius. Agricola generously praised Aristotle and Boethius, and made much use of the system of dialectical *topoi* in Boethius's *De topicis differentiis*. Indeed, when Agricola says that he takes ill any criticism of the *optime de studiis meritus* Aristotle, he seems virtually to be reproving Valla for his attacks on the Philosopher. Moreover, whereas Valla vigorously maintained a nominalist position concerning universals, Agricola staunchly defended the extramental existence of the universals. Indeed [. . .] Agricola praised the most sophisticated proponent of philosophical realism of the later Middle Ages, John Duns Scotus, and resorted to the Scotist principle of individuation (though not using the word *haecceitas*) in explaining how one individual is distinguished from another.

Bibliography can be a dull business, but in the case of humanist logic it holds the key to understanding an important development. As I have pointed out elsewhere [see pp. 290–1 below], the humanist logics of the Italian Quattrocento hardly made a dent in the scholastic curriculum of Italy. The situation changed dramatically in Northern Europe about 1515 with the printing of Agricola's *De inventione dialectica*. In the next sixty years, it was reprinted in the original text, in epitome, or in translation about fifty times and almost exclusively in Northern Europe. In the same period, the new handbooks in logic of Philip Melanchthon and John Caesarius gained popularity. But neither of these surpassed the success of the little *Isagoge dialectica* of George of Trebizond, Valla's Quattrocento contemporary and an admirer of Aristotle. George's *Isagoge* was printed more than fifty times in the same sixty-year period, frequently by the same editors who put out the *De inventione dialectica*, and even received the benefit of explication by some of the same scholars who commented upon or epitomized the *De inventione dialectica*. In the growing vogue for Agricola's two-part logic, Northern schoolmasters chose George of Trebizond's compendium of scholastic logic as the mate to Agricola's *De inventione dialectica*. The latter taught invention, the former judgment. George had written his *Isagoge dialectica* in the late 1430s without knowledge of Lorenzo Valla's *Dialectica*. He had intended it as a companion to the sections on rhetorical invention in his monumental *Rhetoricorum libri V*. But since Agricola had transferred rhetorical invention to dialectic, sixteenth-century northern humanists seized upon George's *Isagoge* as a ready-made companion to instruction in dialectical invention.

In the same period that Agricola's and George's works were conquering the classrooms of Northern Europe, Valla's *Dialectica* was printed separately four times, and twice more as part of Valla's *opera omnia*. The *Dialectica* provoked interest because of its criticism of Aristotelian philosophy and logic, but had no real successor until Mario Nizolio's *De veris principiis* of 1553, whose general approach, including a tendency towards nominalism, quite consciously reflected a Vallan inspiration.

Renaissance humanism was hardly monolithic. The humanists shared certain forms of learning, cultural predilections, and professional aptitudes. But their intellectual differences could be as real and profound as those between Thomas Aquinas and William of Ockham. If it is simplistic to make ideological soulmates out of Thomas and William because culturally they were both medieval scholastics, it is no less wrong to assume that on a given issue we can somehow bring the totality of humanists under some ideological umbrella. More often than not, such apparent unanimity is based on a selective reading of the texts. In the case of Valla and Agricola, modern scholarship has mistakenly created a succession which Agricola himself had patently and correctly repudiated.

2.   The "scepticism" of Valla and Agricola

Of all the arguments for Valla's influence upon Agricola, none has been more forcibly put forward in recent years than that which would have us view Valla and his "codifier" Agricola as true Academic sceptics. My purpose here is to show that this thesis is wrong concerning Valla and marginally plausible, though not very consequential, in regard to Agricola.

According to this thesis, Valla and Agricola drew their inspiration from Cicero, and were Academic rather than "Pyrrhonian" sceptics. This means that they denied the possibility of certain knowledge, but admitted probability into what we apprehend and act upon. So what is crucial for the issue at hand is whether or not Valla and his supposed follower Agricola denied that we can attain certain truth, and if not, why not.

No text has ever been adduced where Valla actually denied certainty of knowledge or advocated the sceptical suspension of judgment or laid out a theory of probabilism as the basis of his epistemology. Hence, in arguing for Valla's scepticism, one is reduced to arguing that he revealed his true position by his overriding interest in argumentative techniques such as *sorites* and dilemma, which destroyed certainty of knowledge. Valla was also supposed to be virtually obsessed with arguments that relied on verisimilitude, which is the goal of topical invention, rather than on necessity, which is the goal of the syllogism.

We already know one problem with the thesis. The discussion of topical invention really formed quite a minor part of the *Dialectica* and was *in toto* a quotation from Quintilian. Moreover, the argument for Valla's scepticism does not account for Valla's lengthy and controversial discussion of the transcendentals, abstract terms, categories, the figures and moods of the syllogism, etc. One wonders why Valla bothered to write so much and so assertively on these subjects, and why it was these other parts of the *Dialectica* that provoked comment in the Renaissance.
[. . .]
Another text used to argue for Valla's scepticism is the opening passage of the *Dialectica*, where Valla praises Pythagoras for modestly refusing to be called wise (*sophus*), but only a lover of wisdom (*philosophus*), where he points out how the rival philosophical sects each thought they had a monopoly on truth, and where he rejects the notion that Aristotle is the supreme authority whose *ipse-dixit* suffices to settle an issue. In the first recension he also had called attention to Socrates'

modesty as exemplified in the dictum: "Hoc tantum scio, quod nescio!"[4] According to [Lisa] Jardine, Valla thus "denies that there can be any certainty in human knowledge" and is asking us "to endorse Lactantius's argument for adopting the Academic position in philosophy." This is a difficult conclusion given that Valla then proceeds to tell us quite vigorously in the rest of the book exactly what he thinks the truth is. In fact, nowhere in the *Dialectica* or any other work did Valla ever deny that there can be certainty in human knowledge. In the *Dialectica* he argued forcibly that we attain truth by correct judgments and we fall into error by wrong judgments. Indeed, he even suggested that we reach truth through direct enlightenment from God, the *fons veritatis*. Furthermore, in the *De libero arbitrio* he directly confronted sceptical doubt and refuted it by retorsion, neatly pointing out that sceptics cannot doubt that they doubt. And in the *Dialectica* he even bragged that his earlier *De libero arbitrio* solved a *quaestio insolubilis* proposed by the philosophers. The preface of the *Dialectica* is a proclamation not of philosophical doubt, but of philosophical liberty. Valla was asserting his right to assert the truth against the authority of Aristotle, Boethius, and the scholastic tradition.

[. . .]

When we turn to Agricola, we immediately have the problem that if his *De inventione dialectica* is an anti-Vallan work, then, ironically, this means that we cannot presume that Agricola shared Valla's antisceptical bias. So in debunking the supposed scepticism of Lorenzo Valla, we have left open the possibility that Agricola himself was a sceptic. However, since the expressed purpose of Rudolph Agricola's *De inventione dialectica* was to teach the reader how to establish belief (*fidem facere*), at first blush Agricola also would not seem to have been a sceptic. Consequently, before accepting Agricola's scepticism, we have to have clear evidence of his sceptical intentions.

[. . .]

A more plausible case for Agricola's supposed scepticism can be made from another text. As the start of the *De inventione dialectica*, Agricola asserts that the *locorum ratio* was useful because the greater part of human studies partake of ambiguities and engender divergent opinions. "For only an exiguous portion of what we learn is certain and stable; and indeed, if we are to trust the Academy, we only know this: that we know nothing." Twice elsewhere in the *De inventione dialectica*, Agricola repeated this comment on the scepticism of the Academy. Since Agricola insists that the task of dialectic is to argue from probabilities (*probabiliter dicere*), we seem finally to have encountered in the person of Agricola the matrix of Academic scepticism/topical argumentation/probabilism which could not be found in Valla. However, that dialectic's task is *probabiliter dicere* had been standard doctrine since Aristotle's *Topica*. Moreover, Agricola himself never endorsed the sceptical view of the Academy, and in the context of the *De inventione dialectica* he seems to have been using this sceptical dictum merely rhetorically to emphasize the great range of dialectical argumentation. Lastly, as far as I can discover, in his other writings Agricola showed no sympathy towards scepticism. For instance, in his oration *In laudem philosophiae et reliquarum artium*[5] he praised the certitude and necessity found in geometry, arithmetic, and astronomy. So we have reason to be sceptical of the supposed sceptical inspiration of the *De inventione dialectica*.

The novelty of the *De inventione dialectica* was to identify probable argumentation with logic *tout court*. But despite the enormous popularity of Agricola's work, this particular aspect of the book had only limited appeal. Of the three most popular humanist rhetoric manuals of the first half of the sixteenth century, only that of John Caesarius taught this definition of logic. Philip Melanchthon ignored it, and George of Trebizond, writing forty years earlier than Agricola, of course knew nothing of such a notion. No less importantly, John Sturm, who helped popularize Agricola and was himself a major force in Protestant education, specifically divided logic into apodictic, which arrived at necessary conclusions from necessary proofs, and dialectic, which argued *probabiliter*. In the second half of the century, the Jesuit colleges had little to do with Agricolan logic, and the dominant humanist authority in logic in Protestant lands, Peter Ramus, was hostile to the idea of logic as probabilism. Hence, even if for the sake of argument we grant that Agricola's supposed tenderness towards Academic scepticism led him to equate logic with probable argumentation, this attitude had a limited effect on humanist logic and cannot be taken as representative of humanist logicians as a whole.

Editor's Notes

1   grammar, logic and rhetoric, of which the first expresses, the second teaches, the third moves
2   for dialectic was certainly something quick and facile
3   I should perhaps say *Socratitis* and *Platonitas* and *entitas*, although our Valla objects.
4   The only thing I know is that I don't know!
5   *In Praise of Philosophy and Other Disciplines*

PART FIVE

The Spread of Humanism

PART THREE

The Spread of Humanism

Chapter 18

Felix Gilbert

■ from **HUMANISM IN VENICE**, in S. Bertelli *et al.*,
Florence and Venice: comparisons and relations, Florence,
1979, I, pp. 13–26

"**MAJESTIC VENICE, THE ONE HOME** today of liberty, peace, and
justice, the one refuge of honorable men, the one port to which can repair
the storm-tossed, tyrant-hounded craft of men who seek the good life."

These are the words with which Petrarch began his famous praise of Venice,
and they reflect the feelings which inspired him to make San Marco his heir and to
leave his books to Venice so that "they would be preserved, protected from fire and
water and give permanent pleasure to the wise and noble citizens of Venice." Almost
one hundred years later the bond which Petrarch had established between Venice
and the *studia humanitatis* was confirmed and strengthened by another great humanist. "Since my childhood," Bessarion wrote to the Venetian government, "my one
great passion was to collect books. Among all the cities of Italy I don't know of any
to which I could entrust more safely my beloved books than to your city whose government is honest, just, and wise and to which visitors come from East and West."
And finally, the rich material which Bessarion's collection contained inspired
Aldus Manutius to establish in Venice a printing shop which, through its publication
of reliable and inexpensive Greek and Latin texts, initiated a new epoch in the quest
for an understanding of the classical world. Venice has a definite place in the history
of the development of the *studia humanitatis*.

Yet, despite these events which tie Venice to the history of humanism, the
intellectual climate in Renaissance Venice is considered not to have been propitious to the development of humanistic studies. Paolo de Bernardo, a Venetian
disciple of Petrarch, wrote a few years after the master's death: "In my own city
– I say it unwillingly – nothing is less appreciated than the study of literature";
and the same complaints were uttered by other humanists throughout the
Quattrocento. Modern scholars think along very much the same lines. Burckhardt
wrote that in Venice the literary impulse was wanting, "especially that enthusiasm
for classical antiquity which prevailed elsewhere in the Italian cities," and that
"humanist culture for a city of such importance was most scantily represented."

With this remark Burckhardt states views which had been expressed before him and which have been held to the present time. Indeed, we have treatments of Florentine humanism and Neapolitan humanism, and of the humanism of the papal court. Venetian humanism, however, is a much less clearly defined, less identifiable term to which neither particular humanists nor particular ideas or aims can be assigned. Moreover, we frequently encounter the statement that humanism came to Venice astonishingly late. And, indeed, only in the middle of the fifteenth century did humanism obtain some official recognition in Venice.

Certainly this is a paradoxical situation. The prerequisites for a fruitful development of the *studia humanitatis* were in existence in Venice from the thirteenth century on, but – at least until late in the fourteenth century – these opportunities were hardly used. One cannot discuss Venetian humanism without confronting this question squarely and trying to answer it.

I

Examination of this problem, I think, demands a sociological approach. A distinction must be made between professionals and amateurs, between those who lived from pursuit of the *studia humanitatis* and those for whom the *studia humanitatis* – to use a category of *Who's Who* – were "recreation." I believe that in a general analysis of Italian humanism it would be helpful if more attention were given to this distinction; for an understanding of the fortune of the *studia humanitatis* in Venice it is essential. Burckhardt, in justification of his less than flattering evaluation of Venetian humanistic endeavours, wrote that "[Francesco] Filelfo, summoned to Venice not by the state but by private individuals, soon found his expectations deceived; . . . and George of Trebisond soon left the city in dissatisfaction." The list of professional humanists, drawn to Venice by promises of members of the Venetian ruling group but departing in disappointment after a brief residence, can be easily augmented: Giovanni da Ravenna, Guarino Guarini, Cristoforo da Parma, Giovanni Filelfo, Giorgio Merula, Giorgio Valla – they all acted that way.

Even if due weight is given to the restlessness, quarrelsomeness and over-sensitivity of the humanists, the number of professional humanists who were but birds of passage in Venice is striking. Indeed, Venice lacked the center of humanist studies which Florence, Rome, Naples and other Italian cities possessed: chancelleries, usually headed by a humanist whose intellectual prominence, and eminent and secure position, gave him the possibility of employing and attracting others and of guaranteeing continuity in the pursuit of the *studia humanitatis*; it is enough to refer to the succession of great Florentine chancellor-humanists – from Salutati, Bruni, Marsuppini, Poggio, and Scala to Virgilio Adriani. Of course, Venice too, had a chancellery, and it was there that the cultivation of the *studia humanitatis* began in Venice in the late Trecento, with Benintendi dei Ravagnani, the friend of Petrarch, as Grand Chancellor from 1352 to 1365, and with the chancellor of Crete, Lorenzo de Monacis, an admiring imitator of Bruni. At that time the Venetian chancellery seems to assume a leading role in the promotion of the *studia humanitatis*, but in the fifteenth century, in connection with the political experiences of Venice, the Venetian chancellery expanded and consequently its character changed. The Grand Chancellor became head of a large bureaucratic guild, the members of which had to be citizens; that meant belonging to a small, legally defined stratum of the Venetian population. The chancellery bureaucracy comprised the secretaries of the Doge and the secretaries of the principal councils and executive committees, the Pregadi, the Ten, the Savi, as well as a number of auxiliary secretaries available for emergency tasks. A contemporary source counts fifty secretaries and fifty extraordinary secretaries. The Grand Chancellor himself, in addition to performing the administrative duties involved in organizing this secretarial bureaucracy, had to attend the meetings of the Great Council for which he established the agenda, in which he read to the Great Council the documents and laws bearing on the agenda, and in which he was responsible for observance of the rules and for supervision of the balloting. Moreover, he was obligated to take a prominent place in all official processions and functions. This was hardly a position which allowed much time for scholarly pursuits; with the exception of a brief mentioning of Febo Cappella in a humanistic context, the Venetian Grand Chancellors took no part in the humanist movement.

With work in the Venetian chancellery outside the reach of the professional humanists, teaching became their only resource for earning a living. There was no university in Venice. The School at the Rialto, which was established in the early years of the fifteenth century, was intended to teach logic and philosophy. Briefly, it was strictly Aristotelian, and the Venetian government then and until the end of the republic refused permission to add to the existing Venetian schools a *studium generale* because the government did not want any institution to encroach upon the fields of instruction offered at Venice's state university, Padua. The task that remained to the professional humanists was private tutoring of the sons of the Venetian nobles. The most influential and most admired tutor was Guarino Veronese, who kept school in Venice from 1415 to 1419 and among whose pupils were the two young Venetian nobles who played a crucial role in the introduction of the *studia humanitatis* in Venice: Francesco Barbaro and Leonardo Giustiniani. But despite many attempts to bring Guarino back to Venice after he had left it in 1419, he could not be persuaded. The stays of other humanists who taught the classical languages in Venice in the first quarter of the Quattrocento – Christoforo da Parma, Francesco Filefo, George of Trebisond – were equally short. Because their pupils, when they were grown up, were soon absorbed by government business inside and outside Venice, there was much uncertainty in teaching activities and it is comprehensible that these tutors left Venice when prospects for a more permanent position opened up somewhere else.

Probably it was this situation which impelled those interested in the promotion of humanism to urge the government to establish a new school for the teaching of the *studia humanitatis*. But the School of San Marco, which began to function in 1450, was also unable to keep the services of a prominent humanist for any length of time. The lectureship at the School of San Marco was anything but a sinecure, and although the usual humanist rivalries and intrigues will have played a role, the most likely explanation for the inability of the School of San Marco to keep Giovan Maria Filelfo, George of Trebisond and Merula, or to attract Biondo, was the great amount of work this lectureship required. The School of San Marco had a particular official purpose. In order to be provided with a sufficient number of candidates for the many jobs in the chancellery, government scholarships were granted to sons of citizens who wanted to follow such a career so that they would acquire the skills needed for service in the chancellery, mostly of course, a good mastery of classical Latin. The training of these young chancellery candidates was the chief duty of the lecturer at the School of San Marco and language teaching, therefore, his main activity. Only for two or three hours in the afternoons was he expected to offer public lectures on classical subjects.

Some good description of the work at the School of San Marco can be found in the letters of Sabellico, who taught there for twenty years – from 1486 to 1506, longer than any other humanist. However, a remark in one of these letters suggests that not only the heavy burden of work, but also another reason might have limited the attractiveness of the School of San Marco: the low, or at least uncertain, position of a professional humanist in the Venetian social structure. Sabellico mentioned with pride that not only the sons of citizens but also sons of members of the Venetian nobility attended his language classes; he added that although they were frequently held at his house he never heard from his pupils anything about Venetian politics. The intention of this remark was to praise Venice, to provide a concrete example of the much-admired ability of the Venetian ruling group to maintain secrecy about political affairs. Sabellico, who came to Venice from Udine, had probably learned in this Venetian dependency to look with veneration upon Venetian institutions and the Venetian ruling group, and this attitude probably made it easy for him to feel at home in Venice. Evidently he found nothing objectionable in being excluded from participation in or knowledge of government affairs. But others might have regarded the lack of social mobility in Venice as frustrating and humiliating. There was no possibility of any kind of political participation or activity such as Salutati, or Bruni, or Scala could exercise in Florence. The political monopoly of the Venetian nobility, and the reservation of service in the chancellery for citizens, were various aspects of the rigid social structure of Venice; professional humanists came to Venice as clients of an individual member of the nobility, and throughout the Quattrocento the favor or friendship of a member of the ruling group remained decisive for the career of a humanist in Venice. How little the humanists counted in the official world is indicated by the fact that the lecturers at the School of San Marco were less well paid than the members of the chancellery.

The difficulties which the development of the *studia humanitatis* met in Venice have been frequently explained as originating in a mental attitude dominated by business interests. Nobody seems to me to have shown satisfactorily that such material interests played a more important role in the minds of the citizens of Venice than in those of other city republics. Explanations assuming the existence of a particular national or regional psychology are always very dubious and, if nothing else, the sociological and institutional features which I have adduced seem to be a better explanation, or serve to implement theories of a more psychological character. Nevertheless, we must ask whether every effort was made to remove the obstacles which social and institutional traditions placed in the way of the *studia humanitatis*, or whether these obstacles were not – consciously or unconsciously – used to prevent or delay the penetration of this novel intellectual movement into Venice. Did the Venetian ruling group, or at least important elements of the

Venetian ruling group, regard humanism as antagonistic to the traditional intellectual outlook and dangerous for it? Did they consider the *studia humanitatis* as incompatible with their religious faith?

Burckhardt believed that there was a conflict between humanism and Christianity. Since Burckhardt many scholars have been zealous in refuting the view of the anti-religious and anti-Christian character of the *studia humanitatis*. They represented – and I quote Trinkaus – "an effort to devise new methods with which to deal with the spiritual, moral, cultural and intellectual problems." This may be right, but there is still another aspect to the problem of the compatibility of humanism and Christianity. Did the Church, or the great majority of the clergy, accept the view of the Christian nature of the *studia humanitatis*? The question is not only that of the existence of a Christian element in humanist thought but of its relation to organized Christianity, to the Church as an institution. Although certainly the *studia humanitatis* enjoyed the favor of various popes, cardinals and high Church dignitaries, there was also the opposite trend running from Giovanni Dominici, the adversary of Salutati, through St Bernardino's bonfire of worldly pleasures, foreshadowing Savonarola's burning of the vanities, to the condemnation of classical studies by the Fifth Lateran Council. In Venice a tendency to doubt the usefulness of the enthusiasm for the classical world certainly existed. At the end of the fourteenth century, in years crucial for the development of humanism, Giovanni Dominici worked in Venice restoring strict discipline in the Dominican order. St Lorenzo Giustiniani, despite the strong humanistic inclinations of his family, kept away from classical learning, and two Venetians, Tommaso Giustiniani and Vincenzo Quirino, were responsible for the warning against classical literature which the Fifth Lateran Council issued and the Synod of Florence reinforced. These tendencies had steady support in the Aristotelianism of the University of Padua which represented the bulwark against the extension of classical studies into the broader fields of moral philosophy.

[. . .]

Whether the professional humanists felt that the intellectual climate in Venice was inimical to them is hardly possible to say; they must have been aware that their views ran up against strongly held traditions, that there were limits for their discussion of philosophical and religious questions, that their work could not freely develop in whatever direction they wanted to go. Such experience will not have helped them to feel safe and at home in Venice.

II

Our analysis of the position of the professional humanists in Venice explains why in a study of work done in the area of the *studia humanitatis* in Venice in the Quattrocento, our interest must focus less on the professional humanists than on the group of Venetian patricians who were responsible for bringing professional humanists to Venice and were themselves authors of humanistic works. Considering the situation which existed in Venice, why were men like Francesco Barbaro or Ludovico Foscarini or Bernardo Giustiniani interested in the humanist approach, and why did they want to make Venice a center of the *studia humanitatis*?

First of all it must be stated that the circle of humanist patricians, although it comprised very prominent names, was small. Interest in humanism was particularly strong in two families: Barbaro and Giustiniani. In addition, a Foscarini, a Morosini and a Bembo appear as promoters of the *studia humanitatis* and actively involved in their pursuit. They all were statesmen; none of them would have been satisfied with using his wealth for a *vita contemplativa*. Their intellectual interests were highly diversified. They wrote poems, like Leonardo Giustiniani; they explained psalms; they composed treatises about the vices of the Jews; and they wrote lives of the saints: Bernardo Giustiniani about St Mark, and Domenico Morosini about St Lorenzo Giustiniani. The religious subjects with which several of them dealt indicate that they accepted and lived within the traditional ideas of Venetian church–state relationships. They were enjoying the opportunities of their position as members of the Venetian ruling class.

If we turn to those of their writings which show them to be convinced adherents of the *studia humanitatis*, they demonstrate their interest in the classical languages by translating Greek classical writers into Latin. Francesco Barbaro and Leonardo Giustiniani translated Plutarch: Bernardo Giustiniani, Isocrates. They embarked on typical humanist pursuits; they wrote letters meant for posterity rather than for the person to whom they were addressed, and they collected this correspondence. The letters of Francesco Barbaro, Bernardo Giustiniani and Ermolao Barbaro, of course, are well known. But an equally important *Epistolario*, that of Ludovico Foscarini, which is both typical in its indulgence in a rhetorical style and revealing in its wide contacts among the humanist world, has never been published. The Venetian statesmen-humanists also cultivated another literary form popular with all humanists as combining instruction and persuasion – the oration. Orations were rhetorical showpieces, spoken, or sometimes only pretended to have been spoken, at the reception of a Venetian diplomat at a foreign court, on a mission of congratulation to a newly elected pope, in praise of a victorious general, or at the funeral of a famous man. Such orations, divulged in manuscript or printed, gave occasion to strengthen the reputation of Venice. Another literary genre – a favorite with these Venetian statesmen because it turned the *studia humanitatis* to political use – consisted of treatises on the nature of the Venetian institutions. This topic was also taken up by some professional humanists like Francesco Negri or Sabellico, eager to increase their reputation in Venice. But the important treatments of the topic are those by humanist statesmen. The series begins with Paolo Morosini's explanation of the Venetian constitution to Gregory of Heimburg. It was transformed into a general discussion of an ideal republic by Domenico Morosini, and normative and descriptive elements are combined in the most famous of this series, Gasparo Contarini's book on the institutions and administration of the Venetian republic. Almost all the treatises contain historical data; the authors use the old annals, and adopt them to humanist aims. History was in the center of their minds and what they all wanted to have was a Venetian history according to humanist prescripts. Complaints about the lack of such a humanist history of Venice can already be found early in the fifteenth century. In the middle of that century there were many attempts to engage professional humanists in such tasks; as Foscarini's letters show, Sabellico's *Venetian History* was not regarded as a fully satisfactory solution of this problem. Thus, in the end, a Venetian humanist statesman, Bernardo Giustiniani himself, undertook the task and produced a work which in my opinion is the best humanist history of the Quattrocento – pointing back to Bruni in the method and clarity with which the foundation of Venice is treated, and pointing forward to Machiavelli in the realism and maturity of political judgment.

The concerns which we find in the humanist activities of the Venetian humanist-statesmen have a practical ingredient: languages and politics. These Venetian humanists were not concerned with problems of a fundamental philosophical and theological character. This is not astonishing, considering the close connection of Venetian social and institutional life with traditional religious attitudes and organization. However, the unwillingness to view humanism as a new philosophy appropriate to changed times gives increased significance to the question why these Venetians were attracted by humanism at all and why they wanted the *studia humanitatis* introduced into Venice.

One influence in this direction is evident: that of Florence. For Francesco Barbaro the friendship with the Medici family, particularly with Cosimo's brother Lorenzo, to whom Barbaro dedicated his *De re uxoria*, was a decisive factor in his intellectual development. Ludovico Foscarini conducted important diplomatic negotiations in Florence. Likewise, Bernardo Bembo resided in Florence on a lengthy diplomatic mission during which he became an intimate of Lorenzo Magnifico and his circle. In the relation between Venice and Florence, however, there was not only admiration but also rivalry. Paolo Morosini, in his letter to Gregory of Heimburg, emphasized that Venice took up the struggle for the *libertas Italiae* when Florence was succumbing to Visconti's aggression, and Bernardo Giustiniani stated that Florence was unable and unwilling to play the role which Venice filled, that of the protection of Christianity against the Turks.

But competition with Florence was probably only one aspect of the political motives for the promotion of the *studia humanitatis*. The Venetians, who in the first half of the fifteenth century worked for promotion of the *studia humanitatis* and were actively engaged in humanist pursuits themselves, formed a small, closely connected circle. The oldest among them were Francesco Barbaro and Leonardo Giustiniani. They were almost contemporaries, both born in the Trecento, in 1390 and 1389 respectively. Their efforts were continued by Ludovico Foscarini, Bernardo Giustiniani and Paolo Morosini, relatives of the two older humanist-statesmen and close friends of each other. All of them had leading roles – as diplomats and military commanders – in the expansion of Venice on the *terra firma*, and ended as Procurators of San Marco. It has been said that until the middle of the 'twenties of the Quattrocento the Venetian expansion on the *terra firma* was primarily intended to prevent loss of control over the trade routes to the North, but that from the 'twenties to the 'sixties the Venetian rulers became convinced that security could be achieved only by further expansion which would weaken Milan, that is, by Venice becoming a great Italian power. The transition from a locally limited policy to an Italian policy took place under the leadership of Doge Francesco Foscari, and the Venetian humanist-statesmen whom I have mentioned gave him full-hearted support and were his close collaborators. Francesco Barbaro defended Foscari's war policy as necessary for maintenance of the *libertas Italiae* and, in a warm personal letter in the time of an epidemic, admonished Foscari to spare himself because the well-being of so many depended on his life. Leonardo Giustiniani was one of Foscari's most trusted advisers. Paolo Morosini gave, in his letter to Gregory of Heimburg, a passionate and detailed defense of Venetian policy on the *terra firma*. Bernardo Giustiniani held the funeral oration for Foscari. In his discussion of Foscari's policy he emphasized that neither Foscari nor Venice was inspired by ambition or lust for fame; it was necessary to halt the Visconti expansion, and such action made further advance into the *terra firma* and entanglement in Italian politics inevitable. There are two brief allusions in this funeral oration which are particularly interesting in our context. Bernardo Giustiniani praised the inclusion of young men in the Venetian government "so that the gravity of the old which by nature was frigid might, when the need arose, be warmed by some vigor of spirit." It is difficult not to conclude that he was thinking of his role and the role of his friends under Foscari, because they were still rather young when they became actively involved in the decisive events of the war against Milan. Bernardo also praises Foscari's lively intellectual interests. When he was tired from the affairs of state his favorite relaxation was participation in learned discussions. Francesco Foscari does not seem to have been averse to the literary interests of some of his close collaborators.

Whatever people thought about the reasons for the expansion on the *terra firma* and the anti-Milanese policy of the Venetian government, Venetian foreign policy was regarded as having entered a new stage. The promotion and cultivation of a new intellectual outlook, particularly the establishment of the School of San Marco, is coincidental with these events. It is comprehensible that the increased contacts with the Italian scene stimulated interest in acquaintance with humanism as a movement dominating Italian intellectual life and some adjustment to this trend may have seemed to be advantageous. The political situation certainly facilitated the acceptance of the new *studia humanitatis* in a society in which institutional and intellectual traditions had a strong hold. On the other hand, the political context played its part in emphasizing those aspects of the *studia humanitatis* that could be of practical political use: classical languages, above all Greek, which helped to emphasize Venice's position as bridge to the East and as protagonist against the Turks, and those literary genres which could confirm Venice's claim as Italy's principal republic. This does not mean that those Venetian humanist-statesmen who strove to make Venice a humanist center lacked genuine humanist enthusiasm, but it seems evident that the political events helped to overcome obstacles and to determine which directions these efforts took.

But after the School of San Marco had been established and the humanist efforts had taken root, did they develop their own impetus or did they remain within the limits which had originally been set? The answer to this question can be found in the fate of the two Venetian nobles who undoubtedly were the greatest humanists the Venetian ruling group produced: Ermolao Barbaro and Pietro Bembo. Vittore Branca has observed that the Barbaro family was distinguished by a strong humanist tradition, that Ermolao admired Francesco Barbaro and tried to imitate him. But if Ermolao's youthful treatise *De coelibatu* was meant to be a complementary piece to his uncle's *De re uxoria* – also written at a youthful age – the difference in subject-matter is immense. Whereas the elder Barbaro tried to show the importance of the family for meaningful social life and action, Ermolao's treatise tried to demonstrate the happiness of a solitary *vita contemplativa*. And the *vita contemplativa*, an existence devoted to scholarship and literature, remained Ermolao's ideal. That is shown in the famous letter to Pico della Mirandola and it is reflected in the statement that he recognized only two rulers, "Christum et litteras"; and we should not overlook that this confession follows a declaration that he never intended to take on the functions of a priest and that he was convinced that a scholar and writer, an observer of God, of the stars and of nature, must be free and unhampered by any bonds. Whatever the actual missteps and misunderstandings were, it was no accident that he had to live in exile from Venice in the last years of his life. Pietro Bembo's genius also led beyond the political and intellectual limits of Venice into a world which had rules and values quite outside the control of a particular social body. It was no wonder, therefore, that he did not advance in the political career for which his father had prepared him and had to live and find occupation outside Venice. In Bembo's case the Venetian government was willing to make use of him after decades had passed and he had become a man famous all over Italy.

But if studies of a purely literary or philosophical character and an attitude which placed the pursuit of intellectual aims above the fulfillment of social duties continued to be considered a threat to the existence of Venetian society, there was approval of those humanistic activities which had proven to be in the interest of society. Of course, it was the genius of Aldus Manutius that recognized how the interests of the humanistically inclined Venetian nobles in the classical languages could be systematically used and organized. Thus, the establishment of the *studia humanitatis* in Venice had the result that a new industry, book publishing, became an important factor in Venetian economic life, and the further result that the concern with classical languages became transformed into a special scholarly discipline, that of classical philology.

The concern with the reputation and prestige of the republic also had far-reaching consequences. Contarini's book, the most brilliant product of this interest, was read all over Europe. If Machiavelli and the Florentine political thinkers discussed the qualities which an individual must possess for successful political action, Contarini and the Venetian political writers focused on the functioning of institutions and thereby made their mark in the development of another fundamental problem of political theory.

[. . .]

The particular question which I think needs some further comment is the Venetian concern with the Greek language; I have stated that the study of the classical languages was regarded as a principal task of the *studia humanitatis*. It needs emphasis that the chief interest of the Venetian humanists was not Latin but Greek. For this there were obvious reasons: the Greek language formed the bond of common interest between the Venetian humanists and the Aristotelianism of the University of Padua. The career of Marcus Musurus is a good indication of this connection. He was first teacher of Greek at the University of Padua and then at the School of San Marco; even before he went to Padua in 1503, he was Aldus Manutius' assistant and became one of the most important members of the Aldine Academy. Knowledge of Greek was the area in which the interests of the government and of scholarship most closely coincided. It was to the credit of Venice that

Francesco Barbaro and Leonardo Giustiniani could welcome the Byzantine emperor in the Greek tongue when he passed through Venice on his way to the Council of Ferrara-Florence. Musurus served as official translator. There was good reason to give the Aldine Academy official support. For the Venetians Greek was not only an instrument for learning about the wisdom of the ancients but a living language.

But the Venetian concern with Greek had deeper roots. In the first centuries of its existence Venice had been part of the Eastern empire, and it had remained in close contact with Byzantium. A good part of Greece and some of the Greek islands had been and were Venetian possessions, and although we might find little in common between the writers of the classical world and the intellectuals of Byzantium, the latter believed themselves to be the guardians, the heirs and the continuators of the great writers and thinkers of classical times.

[. . .]

Chapter 19

Charles Nauert, Jr.

■ from **THE HUMANIST CHALLENGE TO MEDIEVAL GERMAN CULTURE**, *Daphnis Zeitschrift für mittlere deutsche Literatur*, 15 (1986), pp. 277–306

T**HE RECENT PUBLICATION OF** James Overfield's book, *Humanism and Scholasticism in Late Medieval Germany* (1984), represents a landmark in the study of the reception of Renaissance humanism among the learned classes of the German Empire. Overfield sweeps aside many untenable myths concerning the relationship between humanism and scholasticism. He documents fully what earlier scholars from at least the time of Paul Joachimsen, Gerhard Ritter, and Hajo Holborn had already suggested: that by 1500 humanism was present to a substantial degree in all German universities. He also demonstrates that humanists, at first so modest and respectful in their behavior toward traditional scholastic learning, became more aggressive and even more openly hostile during the two decades that followed 1500. He concludes, nevertheless, that our conventional picture of open war between humanists and scholastics is a gross exaggeration; and after shrewdly analyzing several well-advertised instances of conflict between the two groups, he observes that virtually all the contemporary accounts of these conflicts are polemics against scholasticism by humanists, while there is virtually no anti-humanistic polemic from the pens of scholastic authors. Indeed, the only two anti-humanist polemical treatises were the work not of tradition-bound scholastics but of humanists (albeit conservative ones), Jacob Wimfeling of Strasbourg and Ortwin Gratius of Cologne. He shows that the true issue in the infamous Reuchlin affair was not hatred of humanism but rather hatred of Jews. Finally, after outlining the demands of the humanists for academic reform and documenting the resistance of the university faculties to most of these proposals, he makes a comparative study of the fate of humanistic reforms at various universities and draws the rather surprising conclusion that "medieval scholasticism lost its hold on Germany's universities in the two decades between 1515 and 1535." He is not maintaining that all traces of scholasticism were obliterated or that the educational ideals of the humanists were everywhere (or anywhere) realized in full. But he does demonstrate that significant academic reforms were achieved everywhere – more in some places (such as Wittenberg) and less in others (such as Cologne) – but still, everywhere.

One may not agree with all of Professor Overfield's judgments, but his book encompasses the whole story of humanist–scholastic relations in pre-Reformation Germany with such comprehensive erudition and such penetrating insight that it seems high time to step back and reflect on the history of humanism's entry into German cultural life.

The main outlines of this history are now clear. From about the 1450s until the end of the century, itinerant humanistic scholars – the "Wanderpoeten" – lectured at various German universities, giving instruction on various humanistic topics, chiefly oratory or rhetoric, letter-writing, and poetry. Some of them were Italian scholars of secondary rank. More of them were Germans who had lived and studied in Italy. None of them held an official – still less, salaried – position, and their lecturers were not an integral part of the academic program. Nevertheless, though all of them seem to have experienced poverty and insecurity and to have been painfully aware of how marginal their position was, there clearly was a demand for their services. They did earn enough to live, even if not to live well. As individuals, most of them were of mediocre talent; and while their surviving works certainly show them touting the importance of their own subjects in the formation of a well educated man, rarely did they even hint at any direct challenge to the traditional curriculum of the faculties of arts to which most of them were loosely attached. The only significant exception was Rudolf Agricola (1444–1485), who had far deeper learning and a far more penetrating intelligence than the ruck of wandering humanists. He was sharply critical of the German universities, especially on account of what he regarded as the pervasive and destructive dominance of a narrowly conceived, sophistical logic over all other academic subjects. Yet though he had the ability to produce a revolutionary new work of logic, *De dialectica inventione*, which became a university textbook widely adopted by humanist academic reformers of the sixteenth century, he was far too sophisticated to have much influence on his own generation; and his famous book was not even printed until 1515, long after his death. One final point about the "Wanderpoeten" is that much of the limited success that they had was due to the support they received from powerful people outside the academic world. During the last three years of his life, when he lectured at the University of Heidelberg, Agricola enjoyed the patronage of the Elector Philipp, Count Palatine, and resided in the home of his close friend Johannes von Dalberg, Bishop of Worms. An even better example comes from the life of the ablest poet among the "Wanderpoeten", Conrad Celtis, who despite an incredibly irregular career at several German universities where his performance was marked chiefly by absenteeism and lack of diligence in teaching, was appointed lecturer in poetry in 1497 by authority of the Emperor Maximilian I and with the support of Bernhard Perger, whom the Emperor had put in charge of reform and reorganization of the University of Vienna.

Although the "Wanderpoeten" may indeed have been the pioneers, Overfield argues that the occasional teaching of classical texts by regular masters in the faculties of arts was probably more lastingly important, even though those masters also taught more traditional subjects. The most prominent early figures of this sort were Georg Peurbach and Johannes Regiomontanus, both at Vienna, and both noted astronomers who also lectured on Vergil, Cicero, and other ancient authors. Since the early twentieth century, historical scholarship has usually called such teachers scholastic humanists, because their lectures were presented as supplemental to the academic subjects required for traditional bachelor of arts and master of arts degrees. Unlike a number of the "Wanderpoeten", they themselves pursued and received conventional academic degrees and taught traditional arts subjects. Sometimes they proposed modest changes in degree requirements or methods of instruction, but they proposed no sweeping alterations in scholastic education. In general, they accepted their role as junior and marginal figures in their university and were in turn accepted as junior colleagues whose humanistic courses – usually private courses – had some utility.

The past two decades of scholarship have shown that there is a certain generational difference within German humanism and that what Lewis Spitz defines as the second and third generations of German humanists became increasingly critical of the established academic system. Whereas the earliest humanists rarely voiced any fundamental disagreements with the traditional program of studies, younger humanists who became active after about 1500 were openly critical. Their criticism aimed at the textbook used for teaching arts subjects, such as the *Doctrinale* of Alexander of Villedieu, the most widely used textbook for study of Latin grammar. They also criticized the accuracy and literary quality of the medieval translations of Aristotle's works, and the great attention paid to logic at the expense of grammar, rhetoric, and other liberal arts. They wanted to cut back the time devoted to logic, to increase the number of courses devoted to the study of poetry and other works of classical literature, and to introduce the use of new translations of Aristotle made by Italian humanists. They also wanted to teach from new humanistic textbooks of grammar. In time, some of them also wanted to introduce regular instruction, at least private and perhaps public (that is, official and formal), in Greek and Hebrew. And an increasing number of them began urging that the new humanistic courses must be made compulsory for degrees in arts and must be included in the examinations for degrees.

A complication in this generational pattern of increasing radicalism is the emergence of the Lutheran Reformation. Lewis Spitz and Bernd Moeller have both noted that while most humanists who were mature, established leaders before 1517 gave Luther some support in the early years, they drew back when they realized that the agenda of the Lutheran reformers went far beyond anything they had proposed and might even threaten the further progress of humanistic studies. But, according to Spitz and Moeller, the younger humanists, the "third generation", who were not yet mature and established figures in 1517, were more permanently attracted to Lutheranism. Although men like Melanchthon or Lang or Capito remained in many respects humanists, they had also become something more than humanists. Their primary goal now became the reform of religion, and humanistic studies were valued only as a means to achieve that goal. Thus we now have a credible account not only of the origins of humanism but also of its maturation and increasing radicalism, and finally of its further transformation into a different and still more radical entity, early Protestantism. Of course there were also many humanists, including even young ones, who remained Catholic. But humanism, both Catholic and Protestant, existed under new conditions and inevitably became something different from what it had been before 1517.

One of the great issues in interpreting the origins of German humanism has been to define its relationship to the humanism of Italy. While the decline of classical nineteenth-century liberalism and the growth of German nationalism in the early twentieth century produced some tendency to minimize the Italian influence on German culture, research has shown in case after case that Italian influence was decisive, though of course the demonstration of an Italian source does not prove that German humanism remained an identical twin of its Italian predecessor. The biographies of the key figures in the introduction and early diffusion of humanism offer clear evidence. Every one of the crucial early figures, Peter Luder, Rudolf Agricola, Georg Peurbach, Johannes Regiomontanus, Conrad Celtis, Mutianus Rufus, Willibald Pirckheimer, and even Ulrich von Hutten, had travelled, lived, and studied in Italy for some period in his youth. Erasmus did get to Italy, but not until he was already a mature man, when he probably had little to learn from the Italians [. . .]

This evidence from the biographies of major humanists is only the shadow of a much broader reality. Study of the increasing number of Germans who flocked to Italian universities, especially to Italian faculties of law, explains not just how German humanists assimilated the new learning but also why there were well-placed and wealthy patrons to assist them after they returned to Germany. A recent study provides some suggestive examples of Italian-educated German jurists who became advisers to princes and city councils, university professors, canons of cathedrals and collegiate churches, and even bishops and cardinals. Such persons could provide not only encouragement but also salaries, gifts, permission to lecture, and even ecclesiastical benefices and positions in secular administration. Bernhard Perger at Vienna is an excellent example of an Italian-trained scholar who brought back an interest in humanism and subsequently used his position as an adviser to the Emperor Maximilian I to promote humanism at the University of Vienna. The humanistic interests of many Italian-educated prelates and princely councillors can be documented in good part from the books they collected in Italy and brought back to Germany. What all this means is that the upper reaches of German society were increasingly filled by men whose study of law (or medicine) in Italy had also made them well disposed to the new learning. The high positions they attained made them able to foster the growth of humanism in Germany.

Scholarship of the early twentieth century also raised another issue about early German humanism: where did it find its main centers for diffusion into German society? In one sense, this emergence of an Italian-educated elite is an answer. In addition, Elizabeth Eisenstein has demonstrated the decisive role of the printing press in diffusing humanistic culture throughout Europe; and she shows specifically that both Erasmus and Reuchlin depended heavily on books published by Aldus Manutius of Venice for their pioneering work in advancing humanism north of the Alps.

But how were young Germans of the fifteenth century made ready to feel the attraction of the new Italian culture? They went to Italy to study the practical and lucrative profession of law, not languages and literature. What were the native educational foundations of their interest in humanism? The traditional answer has pointed to certain popular religious movements in the Netherlands and north-western Germany, notably the "Devotio Moderna", sometimes emphasizing an affinity between humanists and Devotionalists based on the Devotionalists' antipathy for scholastic intellectualism, and sometimes emphasizing rather the association of the Brethren of the Common Life with the Latin grammar schools where boys were prepared for the university. This explanation was established largely through the works of Paul Mestwerdt on Erasmus and of Albert Hyma on the "Devotio Moderna"; and it is more recently reflected in the influential works of Myron Gilmore and Lewis Spitz. But whatever one may say in criticism of the polemical style and awkward structure of his book *The Modern Devotion*, R. R. Post has demonstrated beyond question that the foundation for regarding the Brethren of the Common Life as a major force in preparing the way for humanism in the German Empire is weak. The Brethren as a matter of policy avoided the university education that alone would have prepared them to teach in Latin grammar schools. Only in a few cases did they conduct schools of their own, and rarely were their members employed (or qualified to be employed) as teachers in schools owned by ecclesiastical corporations or by city governments. Their primary connection with such schools was that they conducted hostels in which students lived and ministered to the spiritual needs of the students. In some places they seem to have conducted repetitions, or review sessions, for students who resided in their hostels.

What this deflation of claims for the "Devotio Moderna" means is that we are left with the universities as the main centers through which humanism was diffused among the educated classes of pre-Reformation Germany. Despite their reluctance to change their official courses of instruction, their traditional textbooks, and their requirements for degrees, the universities were the most important places where young Germans acquired humanistic interests and learning. Most of the relevant teaching occurred in private classes taught by masters of arts who sought part of their living from fees paid by those who attended. They lectured on popular Latin authors, on letter-writing, and occasionally on such rare subjects as Greek and Hebrew grammar. Such subjects formed no part of the curriculum required for degrees, but their availability from private teaching meant that those who were interested in the newer studies often had opportunities to investigate them many decades before there were official courses in them. Availability of private courses in humanistic subjects gradually increased; and complaints from faculties that humanist teachers were unlawfully offering private lessons at hours reserved for mandatory subjects suggest that interest in the new learning spread readily among German university students.

The universities, therefore, were the principal points where the new culture of humanism came into close contact with the old culture of scholasticism; and if for a long time the humanistic subjects were peripheral to the formal program of study, they were nevertheless present in or around the universities. If there was sometimes friction between humanists and defenders of traditional studies, the reason was that the two groups lived together within the same institutions but held different views of the goals and also the methods that should be adopted. Since masters in the arts faculties lived chiefly from student fees, there was also a financial reason for traditional masters' resentment of the new learning. Nevertheless, the eventual success of the humanists in winning some concessions for their own educational program was almost inevitable. Young masters of arts and students still studying for their BA and MA degrees were those most likely to be attracted to humanism. Older professors were those most likely to feel loyalty to the traditional subjects which they had studied in their youth. But young masters (then as now) eventually become old professors. As those youths who were attracted to humanism but had quietly conformed to the old degree system gradually acquired seniority and influence within the universities, they were in a position to adopt humanistic reform proposals which earlier generations of professors would never have considered.

[. . .]

By the beginning of the sixteenth century, while the traditional scholastic curriculum of studies was intact and the domination of the universities by conservative senior professors not only was intact but even was tending to become more pronounced, humanism was also everywhere present, though in a subordinate role. Even Cologne, notorious as it became for hostility to humanism, educated men who later became important humanists, including Rudolf Agricola, Conrad Celtis, Petrus Mosellanus, and Heinrich Glareanus. Although there was no official course in Greek until the middle of the sixteenth century, both Greek and Hebrew were occasionally available through private lessons, first documented with the arrival of the Spanish "converso" Flavius Wilhelmus Raimundus in 1484. About 1510–1511, both Georg Libanius of Leignitz and the far more noted humanist Johannes Caesarius of Jülich were giving private lessons in Greek. So although many Cologne humanists (Celtis and Caesarius, for example) complained about indifference and even hostility to humanism on the part of the university, and although study of library records and Cologne imprints suggests that local libraries held mostly scholastic books and were poor in the works of classical authors and recent Italian humanists, the picture even in Germany's most tradition-bound university was mixed. Study at Cologne certainly did not guarantee a humanistic education; but it was possible to lay the foundations of humanistic learning there, especially after about 1500, when Cologne presses became more active in publishing classical texts and when humanists of considerable reputation, such as Hermann von dem Busche, Johannes Caesarius, and Johannes Aesticampianus, as well as the Italian jurist Peter of Ravenna, taught there. If this was true at Cologne, humanistic influence on students must have been far more available at universities like Erfurt or Wittenberg, where a far stronger humanist presence is demonstrable.

Humanism was ubiquitous in German universities by the early sixteenth century, but until about 1500 its claims were modest. Its early spokesmen made no direct attack on traditional scholastic learning but merely argued that their subjects, grammar, rhetoric, and poetry, were also a worthy part of a good education. Such "scholastic humanists" conformed to the imperatives of institutional tradition; and even the best-received of them held marginal positions in the universities. They rarely held salaried positions; and when they did, the salary was often paid by a prince or some other external patron. Only with the passage of time, as young humanists acquired seniority and became heads of "bursae" or doctors in the higher faculties, did humanists have any voice on faculty councils or other agencies which were used to keep control of universities safely in the hands of senior professors and out of the hands of the numerous and impoverished young masters of arts. But of course the humanists or humanist sympathizers who eventually rose to power within the academic institutions were moderate, cautious, compromise-minded figures, not leaders and agitators; and Kleineidam shows that although the humanists were becoming influential on the faculty council of Erfurt by the second decade of the sixteenth century, those known to be closely linked to the radical group around Mutianus Rufus were systematically kept out of positions of power.

This willingness to tolerate humanism but determination to keep extremists out of power is a prime example of a trait little noted by historians of the pre-Reformation universities, their emphasis on solidarity. The medieval university was organized as an autonomous corporation (the word *unversitas* itself implies as much) and was keenly aware of its claim to autonomy. Of course universities were authorized, and their liberties confirmed, by charters granted by the pope and the emperor. As ecclesiastical institutions they were subject to church supervision, and their authority to grant degrees always depended on the co-operation of an external ecclesiastical officer, the chancellor. Also, many senior professors, chiefly in the higher faculties, were supported by ecclesiastical benefices over which prelates or secular rulers had some control. All German universities were more dependent than they admitted on the authority of the territorial prince or the local city council. Indeed, all of them had been originally founded by some such territorial power. Already in the fifteenth century, princely intervention in the collation of benefices, in the rivalry between "antiqui" and "moderni", and in compelling acceptance of humanist lecturers showed signs of the future. In the sixteenth century, princes or city governments repeatedly intervened in the struggles over humanistic reform of universities. And of course in the Reformation, princes ruthlessly pushed aside claims of autonomy and imposed their own decisions for or against adoption of the Reformation.

Nevertheless, the principle of corporate liberties did impede attempts by princes and city councils to break through the governing structures of the universities and dictate academic or ecclesiastical reform. But it also worked against changes proposed from within the academic world. The use of benefices and of salaried positions within "bursae" to support university teachers created great rigidity when universities were considering reform, for incumbent older faculty possessed property rights in their sources of income and so tied up benefices that might otherwise have been used to finance new humanistic instructors. The rigidity of institutional structures also meant that when reformers did manage to finance the appointment of a humanist professor, his position within the academy was isolated and indeterminate. Laetitia Boehm has noted that because of this rigidity, universities where humanism did find external patronage experimented with awkward new structural forms that left humanists relatively isolated and powerless. The humanist institute at Louvain, the Collegium Trilingue, was organized as a separate college; and its courses did not qualify students for degrees. At Vienna, the Poets' College organized under Celtis was within the university (subject to the rector) but not within the faculty of arts (hence not subject to the dean). Hence it also was unable to confer degrees in the liberal arts. At Paris, Francis I created an ill-defined group of public lecturers who were completely external to the university. Sometimes part or all of the humanistic institution was organized as a "Paedagogium" or pre-university preparatory school, as at Ingolstadt and Wittenberg.

To introduce a new humanistic program of studies on a basis not dependent on student fees or on temporary grants by princes or city councils was a difficult and costly business. Of the first two German universities to undertake far-reaching humanistic reform, Erfurt was able to enact the necessary statutory changes (a remarkable achievement in a university that did not have a prince to dictate reform); but though the reform was undertaken with great good will and enthusiasm by a group of younger masters who had gained dominance gradually between 1510 and 1519, its final result was failure. The city government was too impoverished to finance the new professorships required, and the social and religious tensions produced by the Reformation tore the university apart and left it depopulated. Matriculations (and the resultant income from fees) declined precipitately; and most of the younger masters, the men who had pushed for the reform, departed forever. What remained was the older men, holders of endowed prebends and salaried collegiate positions in the "bursae". Though some of these were still well disposed to humanism, they were firmly opposed to the Protestant religious movement. A Catholic university in a largely Protestant town had no future; and its well-intentioned humanistic reforms of 1519 thus failed in the long run. Erfurt never recovered either the enrollments or the educational reputation which had made it one of the leading German universities in the fifteenth century. The other university to undertake really significant humanistic reforms in the early period was Wittenberg. Its reform program was perhaps even more comprehensive, and in Martin Luther the reform had a leader so dynamic that at least some of the senior faculty members volunteered to abandon their statutory courses and to begin teaching the new subjects. But the other key to Wittenberg's success was that the Elector of Saxony was both willing and able to incur the substantial additional expenses involved in creating the new professorships of Greek and Hebrew that were the centerpiece of the whole reform. Given the inability (and unwillingness) of other university faculties to terminate existing lectures and to seize control of resources in the possession of doctors who taught either the old courses or nothing at all, far-reaching reform was impossible unless the state intervened vigorously.

One further result of the autonomous nature of the medieval university was the sense of group solidarity which university life fostered. Every matriculant at his matriculation swore an oath to obey the rector and to respect the statutes. Furthermore, university students normally began their studies at an early age, about thirteen or fourteen. Hence they quite literally grew up, emotionally and intellectually, within their "alma mater". The pressure to conform, to keep all disagreements private, and to go along with decisions of the rector, the dean, or the faculty was great. To dissent openly and persistently from decisions of the corporation seemed a sign of serious disloyalty. The humanist who pressed too hard to change existing degree requirements or to substitute new textbooks for traditional ones was likely to be regarded as a troublemaker. He might expect to be overlooked when salaried positions in a "bursa" were available. If he should be so foolish as to continue the argument outside the university by appealing to political authorities or publishing books critical of university decisions, he could expect to be summoned before the faculty, to be ordered to apologize, to be fined, or even to be expelled. This was true not only of a young humanist master but even of a senior and highly respected doctor of laws such as Peter of Ravenna. The sin for which Peter was forced to leave Cologne in 1508 was not just his criticism of the denial of the sacraments to condemned felons but rather his rashness, once the theological faculty had condemned his views, in publishing books that criticized the theologians and continued to defend his own opinions.

Scholarship on German humanism has been so captivated by the cases of conflict that there has been much confusion and misunderstanding about its relationship with scholasticism. Overfield has performed a real service by pointing out this confusion and reminding us that open conflicts were few and that most of the literary polemics were conducted by only one side, the humanists, with little response from the defenders of tradition. Neither irrepressible conflict nor peaceful coexistence is an accurate term to describe the relation between humanists and scholastics. Erich Kleineidam has shrewdly observed that because humanism was not a philosophical system, it could, up to a point, insinuate itself into the universities without generating immediate conflict. On the philosophical and theological issues that might exercise scholastic thinkers, humanism had absolutely nothing to say; and in its early decades in Germany, its representatives were usually prudent enough not to insist too openly that they regarded those issues as insignificant. Overfield looks carefully at the famous controversy between Johann Reuchlin and the Cologne theological faculty, and also at two interesting but less famous conflicts that broke out at Leipzig (Martin Polich von Mellerstadt vs. Konrad Wimpina) and at Ingolstadt (Jakob Locher Philomusus vs. Georg Zingel and others). He finds that while they were indeed bitter quarrels conducted both within university channels and through the press, they are not evidence of a clear confrontation between humanism and scholasticism. He also shows that when conflicts did break out, the humanists did indeed allege persecution and publish works expressing contempt for scholastic learning, but that the scholastics rarely expressed any general opposition to humanism (as distinguished from opposition to a specific humanist).

As noted above, it has recently become fashionable to explain the controversies (or at least the instances in which humanists alleged mistreatment and hatred of good learning) in terms of generational differences. The first generation of humanists, trying merely to establish a toehold for themselves and their subjects within the universities, were meek. They accepted without too much complaint their own subordinate position. The second generation, whose greatest figures were Erasmus, Reuchlin, and Mutianus Rufus, was much more openly critical of scholasticism and much more insistent on the need for drastic educational reforms which would put the literary and linguistic subjects, rather than the dialectical and philosophical ones, at the center of the curriculum in the liberal arts. But few people have remarked on the singular fact that while many – perhaps most – of this second generation lived from university teaching, none of the three great leaders of that generation had a very extensive teaching career. They made their living outside the academic world, and perhaps that is why they could dare to be openly critical of it. Then the third generation of German humanists, those who were still young in 1517, were strongly drawn toward the early Reformation. Unlike the generation of Erasmus, many of them remained permanently on the side of the Evangelical reformers. Indeed, though they retained many humanist interests and aspirations, they ceased being merely humanists. They were, next to Luther himself, the most important early leaders of the Protestant Reformation.

The same line of evolution can be defined in terms of years rather than generations. Up to about 1500, the German humanists were cautious and generally willing to work within the established scholastic culture, which they merely proposed to enrich. From about 1500 to 1518, humanists in many places began pushing harder for humanistic curricular reforms, though with only limited success. Then from late 1517 or early 1518 the humanists became involved in the events of the early Protestant Reformation, with which most of them warmly sympathized. From about 1524 or 1525, as the likelihood of a permanent religious schism began to become obvious, and as social and political unrest emerged as a possible by-product of the Reformation, humanism split. Some (mostly the older ones, led by Erasmus) broke openly with Luther, while others (chiefly young men under thirty) committed themselves fully to the Evangelical cause.

[. . .]

The conservatives had the advantage of being in power and having the statutes require the old subjects, old textbooks, and old methods of teaching. Control of universities rested securely with the heads of "bursae" and senior doctors from the three higher faculties. Thus any reform of importance, even so simple a one as authorizing use of new translations of Aristotle or replacing the *Doctrinale* or the logical textbooks of Petrus Hispanus with new humanistic books, was sure to be opposed and was likely to be blocked. Yet the situation in each university was confused precisely because humanists and scholastics were not two clearly distinct groups, but rather each faculty member had some affinities to both traditions. As time passed, more and more of the dominant doctors in the higher faculties were men who had been exposed to some degree of humanist teaching in their youth. Overfield shows that between about 1500 and 1515, as humanists increasingly voiced open criticism of traditional learning and pushed for adoption of new textbooks and other changes, senior faculty members realized that humanism was not just a harmless ornament but posed a threat to tradition. Hence at several universities, faculty authorities took steps to tighten discipline by forbidding lectures on unauthorized texts and restricting the teaching of poetry. But at most universities, even in this period of reaction, some changes favorable to humanism were introduced. And after 1515, as younger men educated as humanists began to succeed to positions of power, significant reforms became widespread though not universal. Even ultra-conservative Cologne, shocked out of its complacency by a catastrophic drop in matriculations (and hence in faculty income from fees) flirted with humanistic reform, especially between 1523 and 1526.

Yet one should not leave the question of university reform on such an optimistic note. The success of conservative doctors in either blocking reform or frustrating the execution of reforms that had been formally adopted shows that then, as now, universities were irreformable. Reform eventually came in some degree to all universities, but only because it was shoved in firmly from outside. Erfurt, where the younger faculty members gained control in 1518 and the following year enacted sweeping reforms, is the principal exception; and there the reform was abortive in the long run. At Wittenberg, the earliest and most outstanding case of successful and fundamental academic reform, there was dynamic leadership from Martin

Luther. Even so, the reform there was essentially the work of the Electoral Saxon government, which initiated the investigation of educational conditions, authorized the preparation of reform proposals, and approved their adoption. At least the Saxon government also proved remarkably generous in providing funds to make the reforms financially possible. Everywhere else, when reform came, the princely government took the leading role. Humanists within the universities had learned already in the fifteenth century that what the faculty would not give, might be obtained by appealing over the faculty's head to the political authorities. Such agitation outside normal channels of university governance, involving private appeals to friends at court and even use of printed propaganda, was a serious violation of academic etiquette. It compromised the university's claim to be an autonomous corporation exempt from intervention by external authorities. But such going out of channels worked, and we have already seen that princes had already intervened and overruled faculty preferences in the fifteenth century. Humanistic reform thus came by princely fiat, and it involved close collaboration between the regime and those persons within the faculty who favored humanism. In the great majority of cases – but not in all – princely action to support humanistic reform came as part of a broader decision to support the Lutheran Reformation. Whether the religious preference of the ruler was Protestant or Catholic, however, the successful adoption of humanistic reform required both the active intervention and the financial support of a princely government. At Erfurt and Cologne, where the territorial authority was a city council rather than a prince, successful reform was singularly difficult. Erfurt's problem has been discussed already. At Cologne, although there were sympathizers with humanism in the city council, among the higher clergy, and in the faculty itself, there was not the kind of insistent pressure that a princely government could exert; and so Cologne achieved only piecemeal reforms until after 1550.

Everywhere, however, the movement for abandonment of the old scholastic curriculum and adoption of new requirements that incorporated humanism proved irresistible. The final proof that humanistic culture had become dominant among educated Germans is in the subsequent history of the universities. All German universities, even Wittenberg, experienced a shocking decline in matriculations during the mid-1520s. But for some universities, the decline was permanent. These were the ones where humanistic reform failed: Erfurt, where reform was attempted but collapsed, and Cologne, where only small and inadequate reforms were adopted. Erfurt and Cologne had been two of Germany's three largest and most prosperous universities in the late fifteenth century (Leipzig was the largest of all). But now they sank into insignificance. Leadership fell to Wittenberg and the other Protestant centers, but those Catholic universities that underwent successful humanistic reform, such as Ingolstadt, eventually shared in the recovery of university life. The German universities, even Wittenberg, retained many characteristics of the medieval period, including a reliance on Aristotelian philosophy which survived the early attempts of Luther and Melanchthon to purge Aristotle from the schools. But they also offered a liberal arts education vastly enriched and broadened by the abolition of many scholastic practices and the incorporation of the linguistic-literary-philological method of humanism into the heart of their curriculum. To that extent, the new culture of humanism had triumphed among the educated classes of sixteenth-century Germany.

Further reading

Three short recent treatments of the Renaissance

C. Nauert Jr., *Humanism and the Culture of Renaissance Europe*, Cambridge, 1995
P. Burke, *The Renaissance*, 2nd edn, London, 1997
A. Brown, *The Renaissance*, 2nd edn, London, 1999

The definition of the Renaissance and of humanism

J. Burckhardt, *The Civilization of the Renaissance in Italy*, tr. S. Middlemore, intro. P. Burke, notes by P. Murray, London, 1990 [first published 1860]

A. Campana, "The origin of the word 'humanist'", *Journal of the Warburg and Courtauld Institutes*, 9 (1946), pp. 60–73

W. Ferguson, *The Renaissance in Historical Thought*, Boston, 1948

E. Panofsky, *Renaissance and Renascences in Western Art*, Stockholm, 1960

E. H. Gombrich, "From the revival of letters to the reform of the arts: Niccolò Niccoli and Filippo Brunelleschi", in *Essays in the History of Art Presented to Rudolf Wittkower*, ed. D. Fraser *et al.*, London, 1967, pp. 71–82 [reprinted in his *The Heritage of Apelles: studies in the art of the Renaissance*, London, 1976, pp. 93–110]

E. H. Gombrich, *In Search of Cultural History*, Oxford, 1969 [reprinted in his *Ideals and Idols: essays on values in history and in art*, London, 1979, pp. 24–59]

M. McLaughlin, "Humanist concepts of Renaissance and middle ages", *Renaissance Studies*, 2 (1988), pp. 131–142

B. Kohl, "The changing concept of the *studia humanitatis* in the early Renaissance", *Renaissance Studies*, 6 (1992), pp. 185–209

R. Black, "The Donation of Constantine: a new source for the concept of the Renaissance?", in *Language and Images of the Renaissance*, ed. A. Brown, Oxford, 1995, pp. 51–85

The Greek revival

D. Geanakoplos, *Byzantine East and Latin West: the two worlds of Christendom in middle ages and Renaissance; Studies in ecclesiastical and cultural history*, Oxford, 1966

J. Seigel, "The teaching of Argyropoulos and the rhetoric of the first humanists", in *Action and Conviction in Early Modern Europe*, ed. T. K. Rabb and J. E. Seigel, Princeton, 1969, pp. 237–260

D. Geanakoplos, *Interaction of the "Sibling" Byzantine and Western Cultures in the Middle Ages and Italian Renaissance (330–1600)*, New Haven, 1976

W. Berschin, *Greek Letters and the Latin Middle Ages: from Jerome to Nicholas of Cusa*, tr. Jerold Frakes, Washington, DC, 1988

D. Geanakoplos, "Italian humanism and Byzantine émigré scholars", in *Renaissance Humanism: foundations, forms, and legacy*, ed. A. Rabil Jr., Philadelphia, 1988, I, pp. 350–381

N. G. Wilson, *From Byzantium to Italy: Greek studies in the Italian Renaissance*, Baltimore, 1992

Classical scholarship

R. Weiss, *The Renaissance Discovery of Classical Antiquity*, Oxford, 1969

B. L. Ullman and P. A. Stadter, *The Public Library of the Renaissance: Niccolò Niccoli, Cosimo de' Medici and San Marco*, Padua, 1972

E. J. Kenney, *The Classical Text: aspects of editing in the age of the printed book*, Berkeley, 1974

R. Pfeiffer, *History of Classical Scholarship from 1300 to 1850*, Oxford, 1976

A. Grafton, *Joseph Scaliger: a study in the history of classical scholarship*, 2 vols, Oxford, 1983–1993

W. McCuaig, *Carlo Sigonio: the changing world of the late Renaissance*, Princeton, 1989

L. D. Reynolds and N. G. Wilson, *Scribes and Scholars: a guide to the transmission of Greek and Latin Literature*, 3rd edn, Oxford, 1991

M. D. Reeve, "Classical scholarship", in *The Cambridge Companion to Renaissance Humanism*, ed. J. Kraye, Cambridge, 1996, pp. 20–46

Printing

S. H. Steinberg, *Five Hundred Years of Printing*, 2nd edn, Harmondsworth, 1961

R. Hirsch, *Printing, Selling and Reading, 1450–1550*, 2nd edn, Wiesbaden, 1974

E. Eisenstein, *The Printing Press as an Agent of Change*, 2 vols, Cambridge, 1979

M. Lowry, *The World of Aldus Manutius: business and scholarship in Renaissance Venice*, Oxford, 1979

E. Eisenstein, *The Printing Revolution in Early Modern Europe*, Cambridge, 1983

L. Febvre and H.-J. Martin, *The Coming of the Book. The impact of printing 1450–1800*, tr. D. Gerard, ed. G. Nowell-Smith and D. Wootton, London, 1984

M. Lowry, *Nicholas Jenson and the Rise of Venetian Publishing in Renaissance Europe*, Oxford, 1991

M. Davies, "Humanism in script and print in the fifteenth century", in *The Cambridge Companion to Renaissance Humanism*, ed. J. Kraye, Cambridge, 1996, pp. 47–62

Humanist political thought and its medieval background

N. Rubinstein, "The beginnings of political thought in Florence", *Journal of the Warburg and Courtauld Institutes*, 5 (1942), pp. 198–227

N. Rubinstein, "Florence and the despots: some aspects of Florentine diplomacy in the fourteenth century", *Transactions of the Royal Historical Society*, 5 (1952), pp. 21–45

H. Baron, *The Crisis of the Early Italian Renaissance: civic humanism and republican liberty in an age of classicism and tyranny*, Princeton, 1966 [rev. edn in one volume; first published 1955 in two vols]

N. Rubinstein, "Political ideas in Sienese art. The frescoes by Ambrogio Lorenzetti and Taddeo di Bartolo in the Palazzo Pubblico", *Journal of the Warburg and Courtauld Institutes*, 21 (1958), pp. 179–207

N. Rubinstein, "Marsilius of Padua and Italian political thought of his time", in *Europe in the Late Middle Ages*, ed. J. Hale *et al.*, London, 1965, 44–75

J. Seigel, "'Civic humanism' or Ciceronian rhetoric?", *Past and Present*, 34 (1966), pp. 3–48

H. Baron, "Leonardo Bruni, 'professional rhetorician' or 'civic humanist'?", *Past and Present*, 36 (1967), pp. 21–37

R. Witt, *Coluccio Salutati and his Public Letters*, Geneva, 1976

Q. Skinner, *The Foundations of Modern Political Thought*, I: *The Renaissance*, Cambridge, 1978

J. Najemy, *Corporatism and Consensus in Florentine Electoral Politics, 1280–1400*, Chapel Hill, North Carolina, 1982, pp. 301–317

N. Rubinstein, "Political theories in the Renaissance", in *The Renaissance: essays in interpretation*, A. Chastel *et al.*, London, 1982, pp. 53–82

C. Davis, *Dante's Italy and Other Essays*, Philadelphia, 1984

R. Black, "The political thought of the Florentine chancellors", *The Historical Journal*, 29 (1986), pp. 991–1003

Q. Skinner, "Ambrogio Lorenzetti: the artist as political philosopher", *Proceedings of the British Academy*, 72 (1986), pp. 1–56

N. Rubinstein, "The history of the word *politicus* in early-modern Europe", in *The Languages of Political Theory in Early-Modern Europe*, ed. A. Pagden, Cambridge, 1987, pp. 41–56

Q. Skinner, "Machiavelli's *Discorsi* and the pre-humanist origins of republican ideas", in *Machiavelli and Republicanism*, G. Bock *et al.*, Cambridge, 1990, pp. 121–141 republished as "The vocabulary of Renaissance republicanism: a cultural *longue-durée*?", in *Language and Images of Renaissance Italy*, ed. A. Brown, Oxford, 1995, pp. 87–110

J. H. Burns, ed., *The Cambridge History of Political Thought 1450–1700*, Cambridge, 1991

M. Viroli, *From Politics to Reason of State: the acquisition and transformation of the language of politics 1250–1600*, Cambridge, 1992

P. Osmond, "*Princeps historiae romanae*: Sallust in Renaissance political thought", *Memoirs of the American Academy in Rome*, 40 (1995), pp. 101–143

J. Hankins, "Humanism and modern political thought", in *The Cambridge Companion to Renaissance Humanism*, ed. J. Kraye, Cambridge, 1996, pp. 118–141

J. Hankins, ed., *Renaissance Civic Humanism: reappraisals and reflections*, Cambridge, 2000

Renaissance philosophy

General

E. Garin, *Italian Humanism*, tr. P. Munz, Oxford, 1965 [first published 1947]

Q. Breen, "Giovanni Pico della Mirandola on the conflict of philosophy and rhetoric", and "Melanchthon's reply to G. Pico della Mirandola", *Journal of the History of Ideas*, 13 (1952), pp. 384–426

P. O. Kristeller, *Studies in Renaissance Thought and Letters*, I–IV, Rome, 1956–1996

P. O. Kristeller, *Renaissance Thought I: the classic, scholastic and humanistic strains*, New York, 1961

P. O. Kristeller, *Eight Philosophers of the Italian Renaissance*, Stanford, 1964

P. O. Kristeller, *Renaissance Thought II: papers on humanism and the arts*, New York, 1965 (reprinted as *Renaissance Thought and the Arts: collected essays*, Princeton, 1990)

C. Trinkaus, *In Our Image and Likeness: humanity and divinity in Italian Humanist Thought*, 2 vols, London, 1970

P. O. Kristeller, *Renaissance Thought and its Sources*, ed. M. Mooney, New York, 1979

Kretzmann N. *et al.* (eds.), *The Cambridge History of Later Medieval Philosophy*, Cambridge, 1982

Schmitt C. B., E. Kessler and Q. Skinner, *The Cambridge History of Renaissance Philosophy*, Cambridge, 1988

B. P. Copenhaver and C. B. Schmitt, *Renaissance Philosophy*, Oxford, 1992

J. Kraye, "The philosophy of the Italian Renaissance", in *The Renaissance and Seventeenth-Century Rationalism* (*Routledge History of Philosophy*, IV), ed. G. H. R. Parkinson, London, 1993, pp. 16–69

Moral philosophy

E. Rice Jr., *The Renaissance Idea of Wisdom*, Cambridge, Mass., 1958

P. O. Kristeller, "Moral philosophy", in *Renaissance Humanism: Foundations, Forms, and Legacy*, ed. A. Rabil Jr., Philadelphia, 1988, III, pp. 271–309 [a modified and updated version of "The moral thought of Renaissance humanism", in his *Renaissance Thought II: papers on humanism and the arts*, New York, 1965, pp. 20–68, itself reprinted in his *Renaissance Thought and the Arts. Collected essays*, Princeton, 1990]

J. E. Seigel, *Rhetoric and Philosophy in Renaissance Humanism: the union of eloquence and wisdom, Petrarch to Valla*, Princeton, 1968

P. O. Kristeller, "The active and the contemplative life in Renaissance humanism", in *Arbeit Musse Meditation: Betrachtungen zur Vita Activa und Vita Contemplativa*, ed. B. Vickers, Zurich, 1985, pp. 133–152

J. Kraye, "Moral philosophy", in *The Cambridge History of Renaissance Philosophy*, ed. C. Schmitt *et al.*, Cambridge, 1988, pp. 303–386

Scholasticism and Aristotle

J. H. Randall Jr., *The School of Padua and the Emergence of Modern Science*, Padua, 1961

C. B. Schmitt, *Aristotle and the Renaissance*, Cambridge, Mass., 1983

C. B. Schmitt, *The Aristotelian Tradition and Renaissance Universities*, London, 1984

M. L. Pine, *Pietro Pomponazzi: radical philosopher of the Renaissance*, Padua, 1986

H. Mikkeli, *An Aristotelian Response to Renaissance Humanism: Jacopo Zabarella on the nature of arts and sciences*, Helsinki, 1992

Logic

W. J. Ong, *Ramus, Method and the Decay of Dialogue*, Cambridge, Mass., 1958

N. Gilbert, *Renaissance Concepts of Method*, New York, 1960

E. J. Ashworth, *Language and Logic in the Post-Medieval Period*, Dordrecht and Boston, 1974, pp. 1–22

J. Monfasani, *George of Trebizond: a biography and a study of his rhetoric and logic*, Leiden, 1976

P. Mack, *Renaissance Argument: Valla and Agricola in the traditions of rhetoric and dialectic*, Leiden, 1993

Platonism, magic, hermeticism

A. Dulles, *Princeps concordiae: Pico della Mirandola and the scholastic tradition*, Cambridge, Mass., 1941

D. P. Walker, *Spiritual and Demonic Magic from Ficino to Campanella*, London, 1958

F. Yates, *Giordano Bruno and the Hermetic Tradition*, London, 1964

P. O. Kristeller, "Giovanni Pico della Mirandola and his sources", in *L'opera e il pensiero di Giovanni Pico della Mirandola nella storia dell'umanesimo: convegno internazionale (Mirandola: 15–18 settembre 1963)*, Florence, 1965, I, pp. 35–84

F. Yates, "Giovanni Pico della Mirandola and magic", in *L'opera e il pensiero di Giovanni Pico della Mirandola nella storia dell'umanesimo: convegno internazionale (Mirandola: 15–18 settembre 1963)*, Florence, 1965, I, pp. 159–196

W. Shumaker, *The Occult Sciences in the Renaissance: a study in intellectual patterns*, Berkeley, 1972

D. P. Walker, *The Ancient Theology: studies in Christian Platonism from the fifteenth to the eighteenth century*, London, 1972

W. G. Craven, *Giovanni Pico della Mirandola, Symbol of his Age: modern interpretations of a Renaissance philosopher*, Geneva, 1981

A. Brown, "Platonism in fifteenth-century Florence and its contribution to early modern political thought", *Journal of Modern History*, 58 (1986), pp. 383–413

A. Field, *The Origins of the Platonic Academy of Florence*, Princeton, 1988

A. G. Debus and I. Merkel, eds, *Hermeticism and the Renaissance: intellectual history and the occult in early modern Europe*, Washington, DC, 1988

J. Hankins, *Plato in the Renaissance*, 2nd edn, 2 vols, Leiden, 1991

S. A. Farmer, *Syncretism in the West: Pico's 900 Theses (1486). The evolution of traditional religious and philosophical systems, with text, translation, and commentary*, Tempe, Arizona, 1998

Other philosophical schools

D. C. Allen, "The rehabilitation of Epicurus and his theory of pleasure in the early Renaissance", *Studies in Philology*, 41 (1944), pp. 1–15

J. Saunders, *Justus Lipsius: the philosophy of Renaissance Stoicism*, New York, 1955

C. Nauert Jr., *Agrippa and the Crisis of Renaissance Thought*, Urbana, 1965

C. B. Schmitt, "Perennial philosophy from Agostino Steuco to Leibnitz", *Journal of the History of Ideas*, 27 (1966), pp. 505–532

C. B. Schmitt, *Gianfrancesco Pico della Mirandola (1469–1533) and his Critique of Aristotle*, The Hague, 1967

R. Popkin, *The History of Scepticism from Erasmus to Spinoza*, Berkeley, 1979

C. B. Schmitt, "The rediscovery of ancient skepticism in modern times", in *The Skeptical Tradition*, ed. M. Burnyeat, Berkeley, Los Angeles and London, 1983, pp. 225–251

H. Jones, *The Epicurean Tradition*, London, 1989, pp. 142–165

Origins of the Renaissance and of humanism

R. Weiss, "The dawn of humanism in Italy", *Bulletin of the Institute of Historical Research*, 42 (1969), pp. 1–16 [first published 1947]

B. L. Ullman, "Some aspects of the origin of Italian humanism" and "The Sorbonne library and the Italian Renaissance", in his *Studies in the Italian Renaissance*, Rome, 1955, pp. 27–53 [2nd edn, Rome, 1973]

P. O. Kristeller, "The medieval antecedents of Renaissance humanism", in his *Eight Philosophers of the Italian Renaissance*, Stanford, 1964, pp. 147–165

J. Hyde, *Padua in the Age of Dante*, Manchester, 1966, pp. 282–310

J. Monfasani, "Humanism and rhetoric", in *Renaissance Humanism: foundations, forms, and legacy*, ed. A. Rabil Jr., Philadelphia, 1988, III, pp. 171–235

N. Mann, "The origins of humanism", in *The Cambridge Companion to Renaissance Humanism*, ed. J. Kraye, Cambridge, 1996, pp. 1–19

R. G. Witt, *In the Footsteps of the Ancients: the origins of humanism from Lovato to Bruni*, Leiden, 2000

The establishment of the Renaissance

Petrarch

T. E. Mommsen, "Petrarch and the Dark Ages", *Speculum*, 17 (1942), pp. 226–242 [reprinted in his *Medieval and Renaissance Studies*, ed. E. Rice Jr., Ithaca, 1959, pp. 106–129]

P. O. Kristeller, "Augustine and the early Renaissance", in his *Studies in the Italian Renaissance*, I, Rome, 1956, pp. 355–372

R. Weiss, "Petrarch the antiquarian", in *Classical, Mediaeval, and Renaissance Studies in Honor of Berthold Louis Ullman*, ed. C. Henderson Jr., Rome, 1964, II, pp. 199–209

A. Mazzocco, "The antiquarianism of Petrarch", *Journal of Mediaeval and Renaissance Studies*, 7 (1977), pp. 203–224

K. Foster, *Petrarch, Poet and Humanist*, Edinburgh, 1984

N. Mann, *Petrarch*, Oxford, 1984

The establishment of humanism in Florence

B. L. Ullman, *The Humanism of Coluccio Salutati*, Padua, 1963

G. Holmes, *The Florentine Enlightenment*, London, 1969

R. Witt, *Hercules at the Crossroads: the life, works, and thought of Coluccio Salutati*, Durham, North Carolina, 1983

C. Stinger, "Humanism in Florence", in *Renaissance Humanism: foundations, forms, and legacy*, ed. A. Rabil Jr., Philadelphia, 1988, I, pp. 175–208

R. Black, "Florence", in *The Renaissance in National Context*, ed. R. Porter and M. Teich, Cambridge, 1992, pp. 21–41

The spread of the Renaissance

General

R. Weiss, "Italian humanism in Western Europe: 1460–1520", in *Italian Renaissance Studies*, ed. E. F. Jacob, London, 1960, pp. 69–93

R. Weiss, *The Spread of Italian Humanism*, London, 1964

H. A. Oberman, ed., with T. A. Brady Jr., *Itinerarium Italicum: the profile of the Italian Renaissance in the mirror of its European transformations*, Leiden, 1975

A. Goodman and A. MacKay, eds, *The Impact of Humanism on Western Europe*, New York, 1990

R. Porter and M. Teich, eds, *The Renaissance in National Context*, Cambridge, 1992

In Italy

V. Branca, "Ermolao Barbaro and late Quattrocento Venetian humanism", in *Renaissance Venice*, ed. J. Hale London, 1973, pp. 218–243

J. O'Malley, *Praise and Blame in Renaissance Rome: rhetoric, doctrine and reform in the sacred orators of the papal court, c. 1450–1521*, Durham, North Carolina, 1979

J. d'Amico, *Renaissance Humanism in Papal Rome: humanists and churchmen on the eve of the Reformation*, Baltimore, 1983

C. Stinger, *The Renaissance in Rome*, Bloomington, Indiana, 1985

M. King, *Venetian Humanism in an Age of Patrician Dominance*, Princeton, 1986

J. Bentley, *Politics and Culture in Renaissance Naples*, Princeton, 1987

G. Ianziti, *Humanist Historiography under the Sforzas. Politics and propaganda in fifteenth-century Milan*, Oxford, 1988

A. Rabil Jr., ed., *Renaissance Humanism: foundations, forms, and legacy*, Philadelphia, 1988, I, pp. 209–331

D. Robin, *Filelfo in Milan*, Princeton, 1991

In the rest of Europe

L. W. Spitz, *Conrad Celtis, the German Arch-Humanist*, Cambridge, Mass., 1957

R. Weiss, *Humanism in England during the Fifteenth Century*, 2nd edn, Oxford, 1957

L. W. Spitz, *The Religious Renaissance of the German Humanists*, Cambridge, Mass., 1963

R. R. Post, *The Modern Devotion: Confrontation with Reformation and Humanism*, Leiden, 1968

W. L. Gundersheimer, ed., *French Humanism, 1470–1600*, London, 1969

F. Simone, *The French Renaissance: medieval tradition and Italian influence in shaping the Renaissance in France*, tr. H. Gaston Hall, London, 1969

A. H. T. Levi, ed., *Humanism in France at the End of the Middle Ages and in the Early Renaissance*, Manchester, 1970

T. Heath, "Logical grammar, grammatical logic, and humanism in three German universities", *Studies in the Renaissance,* 18 (1971), pp. 9–64

C. Nauert Jr., "The clash of humanists and scholastics: an approach to pre-Reformation controversies", *Sixteenth Century Journal*, 4 (1973), pp. 1–18

G. Hoffmeister, ed., *The Renaissance and Reformation in Germany: an introduction*, New York, 1977

J. M. Fletcher, "Change and resistance to change: a consideration of the development of English and German universities during the sixteenth century", *History of Universities*, 1 (1981), pp. 1–36

E. Bernstein, *German Humanism*, Boston, 1983

J. H. Overfield, *Humanism and Scholasticism in Late Medieval Germany*, Princeton, 1984

A. Rabil Jr., ed., *Renaissance Humanism: foundations, forms, and legacy*, Philadelphia, 1988, II

L. W. Spitz, "Humanism and the Protestant Reformation", in *Renaissance Humanism: Foundations, Forms, and Legacy*, ed. A. Rabil Jr., Philadelphia, 1988, III, pp. 380–411

J. B. Gleason, *John Colet*, Berkeley, 1989

S. Karant-Nunn, "Alas, a lack: trends in the historiography of pre-university education in early modern Germany", *Renaissance Quarterly*, 43 (1990), pp. 788–798

C. Nauert Jr., "Humanist infiltration into the academic world: some studies of northern universities", *Renaissance Quarterly,* 43 (1990), pp. 799–812

More comprehensive recent bibliographies can be found in A. Rabil, ed., *Renaissance Humanism: Foundations, Forms, and Legacy*, Philadelphia, 1988, vol. III, pp. 531–656, which is especially useful for indications of sources in English translation; and *The Cambridge History of Renaissance Philosophy*, ed. C. B. Schmitt *et al.*, Cambridge, 1988, pp. 842–930. There is also a useful bibliographical essay, particularly for the Northern Renaissance, in Charles Nauert Jr., *Humanism and the Culture of Renaissance Europe*, Cambridge, 1995, pp. 216–228.

Biographical Index